# IN SEARCH OF THE NEVER-NEVER

MICKEY DEWAR: CHAMPION OF HISTORY
ACROSS MANY GENRES

**Aboriginal History Incorporated**
Aboriginal History Inc. is a part of the Australian Centre for Indigenous History, Research School of Social Sciences, The Australian National University, and gratefully acknowledges the support of the School of History and the National Centre for Indigenous Studies, The Australian National University. Aboriginal History Inc. is administered by an Editorial Board which is responsible for all unsigned material. Views and opinions expressed by the author are not necessarily shared by Board members.

**Contacting Aboriginal History**
All correspondence should be addressed to the Editors, Aboriginal History Inc., ACIH, School of History, RSSS, 9 Fellows Road (Coombs Building), ANU, Acton, ACT, 2601, or aboriginalhistoryinc@gmail.com.

**WARNING:** Readers are notified that this publication may contain names or images of deceased persons.

# IN SEARCH OF THE NEVER-NEVER

MICKEY DEWAR: CHAMPION OF HISTORY
ACROSS MANY GENRES

EDITED BY ANN MCGRATH

Published by ANU Press and Aboriginal History Inc.
The Australian National University
Acton ACT 2601, Australia
Email: anupress@anu.edu.au

Available to download for free at press.anu.edu.au

ISBN (print): 9781760462680
ISBN (online): 9781760462697

WorldCat (print): 1091598232
WorldCat (online): 1091598371

DOI: 10.22459/ISNN.2019

This title is published under a Creative Commons Attribution-NonCommercial-NoDerivatives 4.0 International (CC BY-NC-ND 4.0).

The full licence terms are available at
creativecommons.org/licenses/by-nc-nd/4.0/legalcode

Cover design and layout by ANU Press.
Cover photograph by Ed Dunens, flic.kr/p/oQCZwB.

This edition © 2019 ANU Press and Aboriginal History Inc.

# Contents

'Museums are terrific, especially for historians!' The many legacies
of Mickey Dewar (1 January 1956 – 23 April 2017)     1
Ann McGrath

Re-reading the Never-Never     19
Chris O'Brien

In Search of the Never-Never     45
Mickey Dewar

Mickey Dewar: Memories, books and museums     267
David Carment

Appendix 1: Resumé     299

Appendix 2: Selected publications     303

Contributors     309

# 'Museums are terrific, especially for historians!' The many legacies of Mickey Dewar (1 January 1956 – 23 April 2017)

Ann McGrath

It took a sense of an ending. But I realised belatedly that Mickey Dewar's contribution to Northern Territory history had not been adequately acknowledged. In March 2017, at age 61, Mickey had accepted that she did not have long to live, though friends and colleagues like myself were less willing to do so. She was in the midst of organising a conference to honour of our elderly mutual colleague Emeritus Professor Alan Powell, to which I'd been invited. I told her that I wanted to nominate her for some overdue recognition; I was certain that it would attract support. She responded that she was 'not that good a historian'. With characteristic self-deprecating humour, she followed up with a text message:

> Thank you… for your flattering and totally undeserved offer to nominate [me] for an AO. Ann – they only give them to live people!!! [Though] I'm sure your argued case would have me coming out a feminist cross between Herodotus, Mark [sic] Bloch, Simon Schama and Geoffrey Blainey!

Her light-hearted romp through her history heroes summed up her brazen wit, love of classical scholarship, interdisciplinarity, landscape history and eclectic politics. Admittedly, she gave them a 'feminist cross'; we were of a generation that heartily embraced feminism, with Germaine Greer being one of our celebrity heroines.[1] The list also encapsulated Mickey's belief in history's potential to reach popular audiences and to function as a catalyst

---

1   McGrath, 'The Female Eunuch in the Suburbs'.

for social change. It is easy to find ample evidence to refute her assertion that she was 'not that good a historian'. Michelle Dewar – called 'Mickey' by her family all her life and so known to her friends and colleagues – was a champion of history across many genres. Her contribution to the study of the north was rigorous, broad ranging and prolific. Her body of work is often highly entertaining, iconoclastic and always meticulously researched. Fiercely intelligent and articulate, with an enviable vocabulary, she had a strong command of literature from the Greek classics to the present. When I complimented her on this, she said 'I only read trash!'. She won major history prizes, including the Northern Territory's top history book award in 2011 for *Darwin – No Place Like Home,* a social history of Territory housing.[2] Although she grew up in Melbourne's south-east, for Mickey, Darwin had indeed become home.

Figure 1: Mickey Dewar and her lifetime hero Germaine Greer, 2010.
Source: Dewar Ritchie Photo Collection.

She excelled as a talented communicator across multiple forms of media, sharing historical research with diverse local and national audiences. In her enduring engagement with Northern Territory history, Mickey Dewar's interests ranged far and wide. The topics, the genres, the institutions in which she worked were remarkably varied. Professionally, she did not

---

2   Dewar, *Darwin – No Place Like Home.*

fit into any one group or conference circuit. She recognised how much research was needed on multiple interesting subjects and got on with it with energy and panache. But although she persevered long enough in each sector to make a difference, she moved on, gradually taking on the whole gamut.

She did not seek to climb the narrow and slippery academic ladder, but branched out, eventually taking her historical training and knowledge into the political arena, when she worked as senior adviser to the first female chief minister of the Northern Territory, Clare Martin, between 2002 and 2005. Yet, throughout her career, Mickey continued to develop her craft as a public historian, publishing not only heritage and other public policy reports, but regularly contributing to academic journals and book collections.[3]

Figure 2: Clare Martin and Mickey Dewar at the launch of their book *Speak for Yourself* on chief ministers of the Northern Territory, 2012.
Source: Dewar Ritchie Photo Collection.

---

3   See Dewar's selected publications in Appendix 2 of this volume.

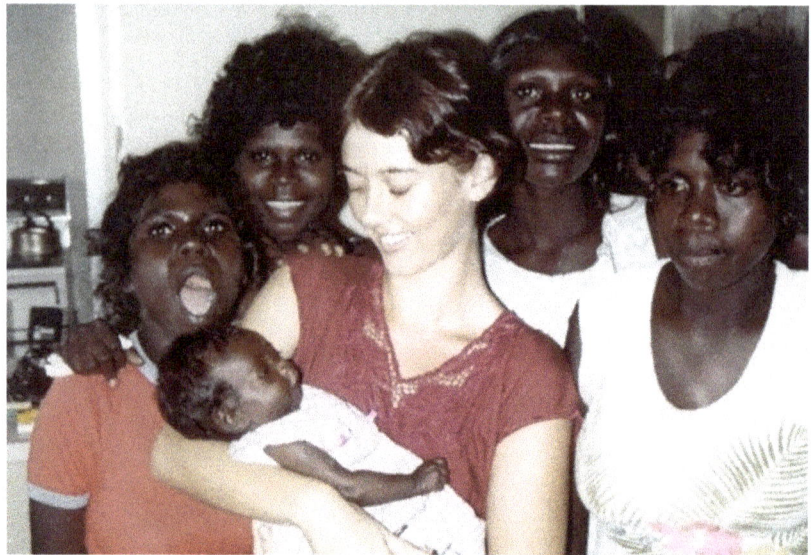

Figure 3: Mickey Dewar with her students and a baby in Milingimbi community, c. 1983.
Source: Dewar Ritchie Photo Collection.

Always serious about her scholarship, Mickey also saw history as great fun. She thought of her life, and her career, as 'a party'. As a young woman she had studied for her Bachelor of Arts (Honours) at the University of Melbourne, where she combined reading voraciously with having a wild time. At Ormond College, she made lifelong friends, and met her future husband. She enjoyed Greg Dening's classes, where she undertook a project on the notorious Captain Bligh, whom she was delighted to defend. She first went to the Northern Territory in 1981 to study for a Graduate Diploma in Education at the Darwin Community College, then took up a remote teaching post with an Aboriginal community, in Milingimbi.

She married David Ritchie and had two children, Sam and Susannah. When they were still young, she undertook a Master of Arts at the University of New England, winning the Louise T. Daley Prize for Australian History in 1989. She then commenced another postgraduate degree, completing it in an impressively short time, in 1994, becoming the first graduate to a Doctor of Philosophy at Charles Darwin University. Mickey worked as research assistant to Dr H. C. (Nugget) Coombs, for his book *Aboriginal Autonomy* (Cambridge University Press, 1994) and subsequently was appointed senior curator of history at the Museum and Art Gallery of the Northern Territory, a position she held for the next decade.

After her role as a political adviser and several years as principal of 'Mickey Dewar Historical Research & Consulting', Mickey decided on a new career as a librarian, undertaking a Diploma and then Masters of Library and Information Management from the University of South Australia, and completing it in 2015. For the last three years of her life, Mickey held the position in charge of the Special Collection in the Northern Territory Library, which is the reference collection on Territory history. In this role Mickey curated several exhibitions and organised public history programs.

Mickey Dewar was, then, a leading Territory historian, a museum developer, curator and manager, heritage specialist, consultant historian, teacher, political adviser, librarian, archivist and a highly effective board member, contributing to Territory-wide and national committees. In many ways, this diversified career trajectory makes Mickey Dewar an ideal role model for young historians. Yet, when one early career scholar asked her for advice on developing a successful career like her own, she dismissed her accomplishments as if accidental. There was wisdom, however, in the advice given, which I paraphrase: 'Just do the next fun project, and in 20 years' time you'll look back and you will have had a wonderful career'. But there was a deeper message: a history career was meant to be enjoyed – to be fun. That became her rule and her mantra.

Though if I may say so, not every party is all fun. Of course, there were the usual ups and downs – the tough times when facing institutional obstacles, being worn down by work stresses, the demands of motherhood, nasty party politics and, at times, personal insecurities. She was not to be defeated, however, moving onto new challenges, gaining new skills and undertaking additional degrees to ensure she was fully qualified in fresh fields of endeavour.

This collection aims to bring the historical works of Dr Mickey Dewar to the attention of the wider national and international audience. Although our present medium is text, we do not lose sight of the fact that Mickey became not only a champion of history in many venues, but also across many mediums. This book emerges from a special panel that was held at the Australian Historical Association Conference in Newcastle. Suggested by its then president Lynette Russell, this book builds upon the papers at that conference. Additionally, it takes up Lynette's suggestion to republish one of Mickey's most ambitious, significant and yet still little-known works, *In Search of the Never-Never*. First published in 1997 by the now defunct Northern Territory University (now Charles Darwin University) Press, it was well produced but not well distributed.[4] It is held in few libraries. In this publication, we are pleased to include the full text of this opus on Northern Territory writing, which was joint winner of the Jessie Litchfield Award for Literature.

To complement its timely republication, environmental historian Chris O'Brien provides a detailed discussion and thematic overview, which will assist in enriching readers' appreciation of it and enhance its value as a teaching tool. Chris outlines the book's many strengths, exploring its potential to inform and guide research directions and to thus provide a kind of road map for future scholarship. Also in this collection, leading Territory historian and Emeritus Professor David Carment, who was a colleague of Mickey's in the NT for decades, presents a first-hand overview of her work in museums, in the historical society and in heritage. He discusses her publications, which ranged over topics from Aboriginal history, massacres, outlaws, the frontier, telegraph stations, jails and urban heritage. His informative chapter provides us with a clear, often moving, picture of her lively and significant contribution to the Northern Territory. Although David and Mickey disagreed about some scholarly matters, and had one rather public spat, they remained firm and trusted friends.[5]

At the Newcastle conference, Acting Director of the National Archives of Australia Anne Lyons outlined some of the crucial work Mickey played as an advocate for regional archival collections. As a long-serving board member of the National Archives, Mickey not only used the archives to undertake quality research on Northern Territory housing for her prize-winning book, but she also played a vital role in saving the NT Archives from closure. To a somewhat bureaucratically oriented committee, she brought thoughtful intellectual concepts, stressing the significance of the archives for future education and future historical knowledge. Anne Lyons has attested that, as a board member, Mickey Dewar was often reserved, but that she would chip in at just the right time – with contributions that revealed conscientious preparation, well-made arguments and a wisdom drawn from wide experience. In honour of her contribution,

---

4   The press did an excellent job of producing her work, which is graced by a cover design based upon the painting *Akiletye atwerreme* by Rod Moss, an appropriate combination of ancient landscape and text that mirrors Mickey's interest in words and landscapes.
5   Dewar, 'If I Was Writing My Own History I'd Be a Hero'.

the National Archives Council has established an annual 'Mickey Dewar Oration' to further Mickey's belief that those of us with the capability to read the stories that emerge from the archival record have an obligation to tell them.[6]

Figure 4: Flyer for Dr Mickey Dewar Oration, Charles Darwin University, 29 August 2018.
Source: Dewar Ritchie Photo Collection.

---

6  'Northern Territory Historian Is Commemorated by the National Archives', National Archives of Australia, 14 June 2018, accessed 8 September 2018, www.naa.gov.au/about-us/media/media-releases/2018/nt-historian-commemorated.aspx.

Earlier in her career, Mickey was reluctant to serve on boards and committees, but in order to support Territory collections, she overcame this disinclination. She also served and played key roles on the NT Place Names Committee, Heritage Committee and the Historical Society, amongst others.

Although she had a big impact on my life as a friend and colleague, I was certainly not the only one to enjoy her sparkling company. Many people had an equally memorable time working with her, remembering her as erudite, extremely well read, a great conversationalist, warm, enthusiastic, funny, witty and often outrageous. Her passion for Territory history was contagious. Those who knew her recall her many talents, her efficiency and reliability, and her generosity towards colleagues and younger historians. One fondly recalled her aplomb in wearing stylish hats.

I want to add some of my own comments about *In Search of the Never-Never*, which was so comprehensive a survey of Territory writing that it could only have been tackled by an avid reader. This fast-moving analysis demonstrates an astonishing command of the entire published literature on the Northern Territory. In ways unconventional, it brings the disciplines of literature and history into the same conversation. Dewar does not select specific genres or pick one or two periods. Rather, she tackles the lot. And she has read the lot. In its lucid introduction, she writes:

> I began this study of Northern Territory writing and its relationship to Australian identity primarily because I enjoyed reading Northern Territory writing. What could be more pleasant than to sit down for three years with Ion Idriess or Jeannie Gunn and read exciting adventure stories of the Territory's past? After ploughing through some thousand or so novels and reference books, I began to feel as if I never cared if I read another Northern Territory novel in my life.[7]

Mickey does not categorise the books into popular and highbrow, into fiction and non-fiction, memoir or 'histories'. The results of her survey are seen through a historian's eyes; she contextualises these publications in their times, unearthing contrasting representations and unexpected emphases. Themes of landscape, class, colonialism, race, the atomic age, sexual relations on the frontier, ideas of 'wilderness' and Aboriginality are scrutinised, with conclusions well ahead of other writers. This is all complemented by a highly readable style and an excellent bibliography.

---

7   Dewar, *In Search of the Never-Never*, ix.

From the late nineteenth through the twentieth century, hundreds of books were published on the Territory – most replete with drama. It was Australia's wild west, its never-ending frontier zone – a land of often cruel and murderous 'colonisers', though most passed through temporarily rather than ever colonised or settled. It became an imagined space for adventure fantasy, crime mysteries, of larger-than-life sagas. A place of wild country and wild people, a threatening zone of colonial encounter and, later, of romanticised wilderness. Such visions were both central and apposite to the Australian dream of successful colonisation leading to a comfortable lifestyle and home.

*In Search of the Never-Never* presents critical insights into national and international imaginings of not only the Northern Territory but, in my opinion, fresh perspectives on northern Australia as a whole. The study of the north still needs many more scholars and far more detailed attention. How it has been encapsulated in literature reveals so much about the Australian national psyche and identity. Writers on the north inscribed peculiar imaginings of these spaces distant from urban centres – variously thought of as a dangerous or 'hostile land', an 'empty land', a far away 'Never Never' and a romantic 'wilderness', these were landscapes that both repelled and allured the 'white man'. In a matter-of-fact, illuminating writing style, Dewar discusses the blind spots, the tough violence and the euphemistic dismissal of colonising violence and the negation of women's presence. Only a 'little Missus' – a small and innocuous white woman – might occasionally be acceptable. Compellingly, she finds that male fears of both white and Aboriginal women morphed into the misogynist idea of the north as a 'white man's space'.

Mickey was swept up in the challenge to fill great gaps in historical knowledge of the Northern Territory – including in the development of key resources, analyses and communication. The appointments of Alan Powell and later David Carment made a big difference to the study of Northern Territory history, building upon the work of earlier researchers and the Northern Territory historical society. However, this loyalty to the local mission affected Mickey's profile amongst the wider Australian history community. Rather than going for more mainstream publishers, Mickey tended to choose small local publishing houses and regional collections. Mickey wrote regular articles on a range of topics for the *Journal of Northern Territory History*. Although she also published elsewhere, mostly she relied upon local outlets, which had an inevitably limited readership. Another reason for her work being less known is simply that it was undertaken and published far from the main centres of academe and of mainstream publishing and distribution. Charles Darwin University (previously the Northern Territory University and before that the Darwin Community College) was a latecomer on the Australian university scene. With the oldest, largest and most prestigious history departments based in the south-east, Australian history still suffers from its Melbourne–Sydney axis. Despite the best efforts of many historians, other cities and states receive less attention. Not being a state at all, and certainly not fitting into the well-worn narratives of Australian history that feature economic and legislative progress, Northern Territory history suffers a Cinderella status. Fortunately, the prestigious New South Wales Premier's History Prize, with its regional history category, provided Mickey with some important national recognition when her books were shortlisted.

As the museum curator of Northern Territory history, Mickey Dewar soon became better known in museum circles than in history circles. Serving as curator at the NT Museum and Art Gallery between 1994 and 2007, she left lasting legacies, having pioneered the development of significant Northern Territory history collections. She collected material culture concerning white Territory 'pioneers' in the cattle industry, diverse industries and missions, and materials associated with notable Aboriginal Australians. She recorded oral histories, sometimes forming enduring friendships with participants. Significantly, she led development of the Cyclone Tracy Gallery, which she curated between 1997 and 2007. It provides an immersive experience of the cyclone that hit Darwin on Christmas Eve 1974. She was keen to convey the look of the houses, the sounds and feel of the cyclone as it took place and the memories of those who lived through it, as well as its aftermath. It became a kind of unifying historical encounter that defined a common Darwinian identity – irrespective of whether people were even residents before or during the cyclone. Immersive and multi-sensory, it demonstrated her talent for combining visual evidence, oral history, material culture and archival research to bring social and urban history to life. The temporary exhibition was so successful that it became a permanent exhibition in the NT Museum and Art Gallery. It continues to be promoted as an international destination on such sites as TripAdvisor.

Also outstanding was Dewar's work in historical interpretation and development of displays for the Fannie Bay Gaol, now a popular destination for heritage tourists. Her creative flair enabled her to convey well-researched history in entertaining ways for all ages and interests.

She helped present an important site of Darwin's carceral history in ways that conveyed its complex social, cultural and colonial past. This was followed by her book *Inside-Out: A Social History of Fannie Bay Gaol* (1999),[8] one of the books shortlisted for the NSW Premier's History Award for Community and Regional History.

Mickey had the energy to explore and champion historical research via multimedia communication and commemoration events. She shared living history stories through publishing, curating memorial events, developing museum and library collections and exhibitions. Producer Kate O'Toole from ABC Radio Darwin and Radio National often called upon her, considering her a talented storyteller.[9] ABC Radio Darwin gave her a regular timeslot, which she took up with relish. She was also a valued contributor to the *Australian Dictionary of Biography* (*ADB*), a resource used in so many schools and by the general public. For the *ADB*, she wrote several biographies, on Indigenous and non-Indigenous Territorians, including on journalist Douglas Lockwood and Dhakiyarr Wirrpanda, who was punished for his role in the Caledon Bay massacres and who mysteriously disappeared after being released.[10] She was involved in both curating memorial events and publishing on them, such as in the case of Borella's War. Although not taking any credit for it, in one of her biographical entries she made mention of a documentary film and memorial event *Wukidi*,[11] which she played a key role in organising in 2003 when working for the chief minister: 'a ceremony of reconciliation [was] held at the Supreme Court, Darwin, where a memorial was dedicated to him and to McColl'.[12]

Mickey delighted in giving advice, which often verged on the dogmatic. I used to seek her counsel about all kinds of things, including what kind of hairstyle or outfit should be worn to important academic occasions. Sometimes I also sought her career advice. In 2000, I was considering switching from a secure tenured job at the University of New South Wales to a management position at the National Museum of Australia, then still

---

8   Dewar, *Inside-Out*.
9   Kate O'Toole, conversation with Ann McGrath, 26 April 2017. An ABC program marking Mickey's death was compiled and broadcast on 26 April.
10  Dewar and Lockwood, 'Lockwood, Douglas Wright (1918–1980)'.
11  Joan McColl, 'Wukidi! The Reconciliation of McColl and Wirrpanda', Independent Australia, 22 July 2015, accessed 8 September 2018, independentaustralia.net/australia/australia-display/wukidi-the-reconciliation-of-mccoll-and-wirrpanda,7975.
12  Dewar, 'Dhakiyarr Wirrpanda (1900–1934)'.

under construction. Although I shared Mickey's desire to communicate in multimedia and to wider audiences, it was a difficult decision. I headed my email plea: 'URGENT ADVICE ANSWER NOW!'. In a typically quirky email, Mickey promptly responded, combining her serious work commitment with lashings of irreverent humour.

> Dearest Ann
>
> Working in a museum is terrific. You really have a great time with fun openings, interesting visitors, work with lots of great people (not just academics) and communicate with meaning to all Australians!! You'd love all the glitterati stuff…And if you even publish one article a year people think it's really great and talk about your terrific publishing track record. (You never give a lecture again without slides because museum audiences get bored unless there's something to look at; ideas are not enough just on their own!)
>
> Legitimately you can worry about dressing up and spending money on your hair and stuff because everyone has to look reasonably good in a museum. … (I can never get used to how democratic universities are compared to museums…Museums are all smoked salmon and bottled wine and universities are all cafes and casks. Now this does have a down side of course but I can live with that!)
>
> By the way, I bet you think I'm joking about all this but in fact I'm deadly serious. Museums are terrific, especially for historians! Go for it. You'll have a great time and you'll never have to drink instant coffee at a meeting again!
>
> Love
> Mickey.

Mickey was an avid reader and a wordsmith. She wrote press releases, briefings and helped prepare speeches for the chief minister of the Northern Territory. Her own presentations had everyone riveted. At conferences, when she presented a paper, the only listening position to adopt was on the edge of your chair. She had a great sense of suspense, timing and drama. Listening to her once giving an after-dinner speech outdoors at the museum at sunset was akin to going to a ticketed performance. Clever, incisive, broad ranging, refreshing. So well prepared, rehearsed even. Yet she had warned me not to bother attending; it was going to be terribly boring. Little did I know she'd actively participated in the University of Melbourne student theatre group. Although she described herself as 'bookish', being a very fast reader who was always running out of material, she was physically assured and highly theatrical. Mickey was an artist of the visual, the aural, the three-dimensional and the experiential. Influenced by the likes of Greg Dening, Mickey was a very animated performer of history.

Gracious in recognising scholars who influenced her thinking, she was kind in her humour – at least to everyone but herself. Despite frequent displays of uber-confidence, she was both fiercely competitive and relentlessly self-effacing. She was fearful of the ways others would judge her and fearful of other things too. Although she could afford overseas adventures, and was fascinated by ancient Mediterranean and European history, she avoided long-distance travel and shunned planes as much as possible. It was only when she worked for the chief minister that she had no choice but to overcome her aviation fears. I was amazed to see her travelling frequently all over the Territory in tiny planes. Just a year before her death, she and her husband David travelled to Europe for the very first time.

Figure 5: Left to right: Anita Angel, Mickey Dewar and David Ritchie at the opening night of 'The Nature of Things' exhibition at the Charles Darwin University Art Gallery, 2011.
Source: Dewar Ritchie Photo Collection.

Being a good historian, she contextualised her life in terms of the *longue durée*, concluding: '[We] were lucky enough to live in very good times'.[13] Indeed, for the privileged amongst our generation, these were exciting, relatively peaceful times; the Vietnam War was over, university education had become accessible, Aboriginal Land Rights had been introduced in the Northern Territory, women's liberation was enabling, and our generation believed that we could make a difference for the better.

Once diagnosed with an aggressive form of motor neurone disease, Mickey accepted that there was no cure. She eschewed life-prolonging intervention, stating that she had enjoyed a full life, with her every dream fulfilled. Despite the disease quickly robbing her of all speech, in her text messages, she was as witty as ever. For her life narrative, she repeated that life was a big party. She wanted to enjoy memories of all the good times. She remembered – far better than I had – that the two of us had originally met at a party in Darwin. Born four days apart, both of us in our early 20s, all excited about just about everything, engaged in jolly repartee, being 'outrageous' – as she put it – and much dancing. More recently, she liked to say we were still 'partying on – albeit in a different way' – herself enjoying her newborn grandchild. Here is a slightly fuller excerpt from one of her cherished messages: 'We had such a good time, and were lucky enough to live in very good times. Can't get much better than that Ann – although I took a while to learn this when I was younger – I now do know when to leave the party!'

Although she looked back on her life and career as great fun, we know that she achieved as much as she did only through much hard yakka. Applying her sharp mind across a stunning array of genres, she brought northern history to both present and future publics with all the passion it deserved. These legacies live on in so many ways, including, for example, in her oral history recordings, voice recordings of her ABC radio segments, and in many historical collections. It will endure in the legacies of her policy work for the NT chief minister, where she applied herself to contemporary policy challenges. And as a board member of the archives, where she played a crucial role in ensuring that the Northern Territory did not lose its archive office.

---

13   Mickey Dewar, text message to Ann McGrath, 21 March 2017.

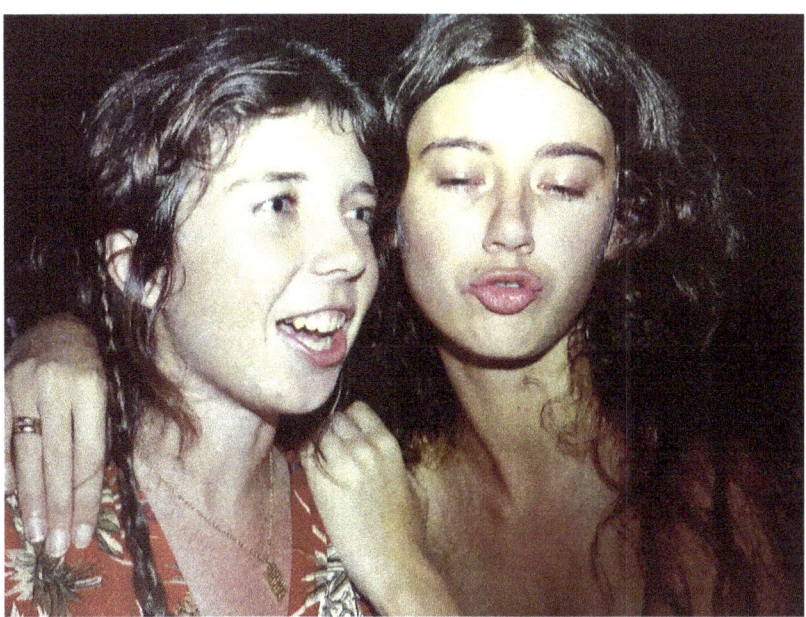

Figure 6: Ann McGrath and Mickey Dewar c. 1980. Partying mode. It looks like Mickey knew how to do duckface before anyone else had discovered it.
Source: Dewar Ritchie Photo Collection.

Like many people, I was shocked to hear of Mickey's illness and before long I would grieve her passing. While writing this introductory chapter reminded me anew of our immense loss, it has enabled me to better appreciate the quality and breadth of her work. Hopefully this book will bring her remarkable achievements to a larger national and international audience. Thanks to the Aboriginal History monograph series, we are pleased to share this collection in freely available and downloadable electronic format and in print.

As Lynette Russell, the President of the Australian Historical Association (who suggested this book in the first place), stated in *History Australia*, 'Mickey was in many ways an environmental historian before the label was used …'. Summing up: 'Over the course of her career she made an outstanding contribution to Northern Territory history … She worked as a teacher, a lecturer, a museum curator and an archivist'.[14] And as we know, so much more. However, although Mickey was an innovator and

---

14   Russell, 'From the President', 324.

a mentor, once she quickly fobbed off the 'flattery' contained in this book, she would have followed it with hyperbolic praise for contributors Chris O'Brien and David Carment.

Mickey was posthumously awarded a Medal of the Order of Australia in the 2018 Australia Day Honours, for 'service to the community of the Northern Territory'. A fitting description, as her *oeuvre* reached beyond history to enrich the people of the Territory as a whole. The award was presented by the Territory Administrator Vicki O'Halloran, only the second woman to occupy this position. It was accepted by Mickey's great love, husband David Ritchie. The setting was the Territory's historic Administrator's residence and its lush tropical garden. This fine heritage building, with its white latticed, colonial-style verandahs, had survived both the bombing of Darwin in the Second World War and Cyclone Tracy. Mickey would have loved the ceremony and the party. I can see her there, on that beautiful site abutting the Arafura Sea. She is dressed up in a gorgeous frock and hat, wolfing down salmon and caviar canapes, drinking champagne and talking history.

## Bibliography

Dewar, Mickey. *Darwin – No Place Like Home: Australia's northern capital in the 1950s through a social history of housing*. Darwin: Historical Society of the Northern Territory, 2010.

Dewar, Mickey. 'Dhakiyarr Wirrpanda (1900–1934)'. *Australian Dictionary of Biography*, National Centre of Biography, The Australian National University, adb.anu.edu.au/biography/dhakiyarr-wirrpanda-12885/text23275, published first in hardcopy 2005, accessed online 29 May 2018.

Dewar, Mickey. 'If I Was Writing My Own History I'd Be a Hero … A Response to Professor David Carment on Making History at the Museum and Art Gallery of the Northern Territory'. *Australian Historical Studies* 33, no. 119 (April 2002): 172–78. doi.org/10.1080/10314610208596208.

Dewar, Mickey. *In Search of the Never-Never: Looking for Australia in Northern Territory Writing*. Darwin: Northern Territory University Press, 1998.

Dewar, Mickey. *Inside-Out: A Social History of Fannie Bay Gaol*. Darwin: Northern Territory University Press, 1999.

Dewar, Mickey, and Kim Lockwood. 'Lockwood, Douglas Wright (1918–1980)'. *Australian Dictionary of Biography*, National Centre of Biography, The Australian National University, Australian Dictionary of Biography, adb.anu.edu.au/biography/lockwood-douglas-wright-10847, published first in hardcopy 2000 (accessed online 27 August 2018).

McGrath, Ann. 'The Female Eunuch in the Suburbs: Reflections on Adolescence, Autobiography and History Writing'. *Journal of Popular Culture* 33, no. 1 (Summer 1999): 177–90. doi.org/10.1111/j.0022-3840.1999.3301_177.x.

Russell, Lynette. 'From the President'. *History Australia* 14, no. 3 (September 2017): 324. doi.org/10.1080/14490854.2017.1361785.

# Re-reading the Never-Never

Chris O'Brien

You've probably never thought of the Northern Territory as a republic of letters. For most of my life I didn't either. Other, often conflicting, associations abound for this remarkable place: adventure, danger, spirituality, Aboriginal people and culture, desert, rainforest, heat, monsoons, crocodiles, cyclones, emptiness … synecdoche NT. Some of these even lured me there. Then I stayed a while. And I saw books on the shelves of Darwin bookshops that I had never seen elsewhere. Then I read Mickey Dewar's *In Search of the Never-Never*.

Unfortunately this reissue has a sad genesis. Mickey Dewar died prematurely in April 2017. Mickey bequeaths a rich body of work about a part of Australia we should all know more about. To honour Mickey's substantial contributions to the discipline of history the Australian Historical Association (AHA) and Professor Ann McGrath of The Australian National University, a decades-long friend and colleague to Mickey, organised a special session at the 2017 AHA conference. Extended the privilege to speak about Mickey's scholarly legacy, I took the opportunity to reflect on *In Search of the Never-Never*. This essay is an expansion of that paper. It is a meditative re-reading of a grossly underrated work of cultural history. My aim here is to persuade you of its significance and, frankly, to entice you read the book, carefully.

The Northern Territory, its communities and distinctive locales have been the subject of some great historical scholarship. Perhaps the best known relate to war history and the bombing of Darwin during the Second World War. But a vast corpus focused on other topics coexists with these. Alan Powell's best known works *Far Country* (1982) and *Northern Voyagers* (2010) are expansive histories of the Territory in its larger physical and geographical contexts. David Carment has written extensively on the material history, cultural history, built environment and politics of particular Territory settlements, as well as of the Territory as a whole.[1] Ann McGrath, Peter Read and Tim Rowse have written about NT Indigenous histories and place in the NT.[2] Detailing the sojourns of the Macassans, Campbell Macknight showed that the region has long been connected to Asia.[3] More recently, Deborah Bird Rose and Darrell Lewis have produced important Indigenous and environmental histories.[4] Regina Ganter has elucidated the intricacies of race relations in polyglot Darwin.[5] Henry Reynolds placed them in an even broader, northern Australian context.[6] Most recently, NT histories have investigated Aboriginal public servants, cultural contact between Aboriginal communities and Christian missionaries, sport, culture and race, architecture, even weather and climate.[7] Many more deserve mention but space restrictions forbid. Even among such a rich textual mosaic, Mickey Dewar's works stand out. They include *The 'Black War' in Arnhem Land* (1992) and *Darwin – No Place Like Home* (2010), which cover crucial aspects of Indigenous, political and cultural history in the Territory. But *In Search of the Never-Never* stands apart even from them.

Initially published in 1997, *Never-Never* is a cultural history unlike any other published about the Territory. As an environmental historian, I am interested in what US environmental historian William Cronon called 'stories about stories about nature'.[8] *Never-Never* reflects on stories about stories about the Northern Territory. Its scope is breathtaking: the body of surviving book-length and long-form fiction and non-fiction published about any part of the NT from the mid-nineteenth century to the 1990s. Ordering this ocean of words into currents of thought is an achievement in itself. Mickey Dewar is explicit about her method: identify the repeated use of recognisable images. Trace the origins of these images, then the history of their use, noting changes in meaning over time.[9] We get to see the life

---

1  Two of many examples include *Territorianism: Politics and Identity in Australia's Northern Territory 1978–2001* and *Looking at Darwin's Past.*
2  Examples include, McGrath, *'Born in the Cattle'*; Read, *Long Time, Olden Time*; Rowse, *Indigenous and Other Australians since 1901.*
3  Macknight, *The Voyage to Marege.*
4  Rose, *Reports from a Wild Country*; Lewis, *A Wild History.*
5  Ganter, *Mixed Relations.*
6  Reynolds, *North of Capricorn.*
7  Examples include Ganter, *Reluctant Representatives*; Rademaker, *Found in Translation*; O'Brien, 'Rethinking Seasons'.
8  Cronon, 'A Place for Stories', 1375.
9  Dewar, *In Search of the Never-Never*, xi.

of prevailing attitudes and representations of land, wilderness, Aboriginal people, women, the outback, the coast, towns, race, development and federal government policy. We see how they stay the same. How they recur. How they mutate. How they recur in different forms.

To be sure: this book is a study of Territory writing. But it is also a study of ideas: how they are born, live, change, die and, sometimes, are reincarnated. It is a study of a place so rich as to spark many different and often competing images and stories. This cultural history is also a study of the interaction between place and stories. About how stories and ideas about place and environment can influence our experience of places and how, in turn, this moulds our ideas and stories about both the places and our experience of them. We learn all of this while encountering men who trade in human skeletons; immense spaces, close, lush forests, the sense of freedom and the vertigo that comes with them; the warmth of human camaraderie; bloodcurdling brutality, murder, genocide; the prickly itching of teeming, swarming insects; callous exploitation; literary fraud; uneasy consciences awakening to injustice; unquenchable spiritual longing, unrestrained greedy fantasy and the nihilism of vanquished idealism. All distilled with alacrity and told through judicious quoting that lets us hear so many voices that otherwise had been consigned to oblivion.

*Never-Never* also reveals profound silences. Aboriginal people do not speak till near the end. In NT writing they are overwhelmingly spoken for, about, over – and almost always to their detriment. Aboriginal people are dehumanised and defined by people whose interests conflict with theirs. Mickey Dewar states in the introduction that despite the vast number and array of voices in NT writing, these voices served the purpose of legitimising the colonising of Australia. They also attempted to define the non-Aboriginal occupation of Australia.[10] The rest of *Never-Never* shows this. Laying bare such grievous injustice, this cultural history sheds much light on the present both in the NT and in Australia.

Although Chinese people have lived in the NT since the 1870s, they are also largely absent from this literature. Where they appear, they are also spoken for and about, usually in stereotypes. As a study of predominantly white literature, *Never-Never* goes a long way to explaining why we think about the NT as we do and how this has come about.

---

10   Dewar, *In Search of the Never-Never*, ix.

For the rest of this essay, I will concentrate on three elements of *Never-Never* that give it enormous value. The first concerns sources – voices if you will – and the strenuous labours Mickey Dewar brought to finding, reading, re-reading, interrogating and interpreting them. These efforts are exemplary. They are a stimulus to reflect on the place of reading in the work of the historian. The second concerns the life cycle(s) of key ideas and images. The third concentrates on ideas of landscape, wilderness and place relating to the NT. In particular, how these elements relate to other dominant ideas of land and wilderness in western culture, and the manner in which they reveal attitudes specific to the NT. We also see that *Never-Never* is a work that converses with other books from other places that discuss land and place, thereby illustrating ideas of the remote that transcend Australia's shores. A vastly different north to the frigid norths of the northern hemisphere, the NT is nonetheless seen in similar ways.

## Reading and reviving forgotten voices

First appearances can be very deceptive. *Never-Never*'s slender bulk belies the sprawling range and profound depth of its content. Its slim proportions (151 pages excluding notes) obscure the exhaustive labours of locating, reading, thinking about, writing, re-reading, thinking again, writing, interpreting, revising, re-reading, reinterpreting, writing … that went into its creation. Converted from a PhD thesis, it is relatively brief because the thinking is clear and the prose is uncluttered. But one of its distinctions is the volume and range of its source material.

Casually, the author mentions that she read 'a thousand or so novels and reference books' in her investigations.[11] This alone is impressive enough. It is also worth noting that this research was undertaken long before relevant public internet content became accessible and the digitising of library collections took place. Mickey Dewar found voices that had long been forgotten. Not only had they faded from memory in broader Australian culture; most had scarcely left a trace that they had once existed. Moreover, many were long forgotten even in the NT. It is worth noting that decades of postmodern sensibility have not completely dislodged centre/periphery notions in Australian cultural life. As Regina Ganter explained, Australian history has long and commonly been constructed as

---

11   Dewar, *In Search of the Never-Never*, ix.

a narrative starting at Sydney Cove and emanating outwards.[12] Of course, Australian historiography increasingly comprises narratives informed by better fitting structures of space and time. But the NT remains peripheral in Australian history and Australian cultural life. That so many of these works have slipped from cultural memory in the NT speaks to the extent of the forgetting. It also signifies the importance of *Never-Never*'s enormous act of retrieval and revival.

To get a sense of this it is worth looking at the notes and bibliography. Names such as Jeannie Gunn, Xavier Herbert, Bill Harney and Ted Eagan will register with many. Some would know of explorers such as P.P. King and Ludwig Leichhardt. People with a more geographical bent would probably know the works of A.G. Price and W. Howchin. What about A. McDonald's *The Lost Explorers* from 1906? Or W.B. Wildey's *Australasia and the Oceanic Region* (1876)? W.C. Willshire's *Land of the Dawning* (1896)? G. Cossins's *The Wings of Silence* (1899)? K. Dahl's *In Savage Australia* (1927)? W. Hatfield's *Buffalo Jim* (1938)? What about more recent works such as C. Wood's *Dead Centre* (1980) or I. Moffitt's *Death Adder Dreaming* (1988)? At a time when information engulfs us and the glut of text accelerates, forgetting is almost ineluctable. Acts of retrieval become especially important. Here the manner is praiseworthy too. Mickey Dewar liberally quotes many of the sources she analyses. We hear the rhythm, metre and cadence of individual voices and the rhythm, metre and cadence of other times.

Reading is the historian's core business. Mickey Dewar's efforts here are worth dwelling on as a reflection of the historian's practice. Historians study and interpret documents, whether written, spoken, illustrated or performed. Through them we encounter the past in its rich alterity. Having confirmed the authenticity of these documents, we examine what they say and how they say it. Language conceals as well as reveals. So we must try to interpret the lacunae as well as the light. We try to account for both deliberate and unintended refraction in the text. Endeavour to identify and interrogate ambiguities. Walter Benjamin referred to it as reading against the grain. The reward: deeper meanings and hidden purposes come to light. In his systematic study of historical thinking, Sam Wineburg identifies three levels at which historians engage with texts. First is the literal text, the meaning and logic of the words. Second,

---

12  Ganter, 'Turning the Map Upside Down', 26–35.

the inferred text, what can be logically drawn from the words but is not explicitly stated. Subtext is the third and it distinguishes how historians read from the way other people read. It is the text of 'hidden and latent meanings'.[13] Two aspects of the text can be read from the subtext. There are rhetorical artefacts from which historians reconstruct the author's purposes and intentions. What Wineburg calls human artefacts are visible in the way a work or document is framed and this discloses the author's assumptions, world-views and fundamental beliefs. Reading to see human artefacts, historians can grasp what authors try to conceal and glimpse their deeper motivations.[14] Such layered reading enables historians to not only say what a document says but also what it does. Reading *Never-Never* you will see that Mickey Dewar was adroit at this. However, it is only when we consider the range of source material that she engages with here that we get a real sense of her accomplishment as a reader.

Sources here don't merely divide into fiction and non-fiction. The fiction includes literature, middle- and low-brow novels, adventure stories, childrens' books, fantasy, historical fiction and poetry. Among the non-fiction are serious anthropological and geographical studies, travel journals, biographies, often aggrandising and self-exculpating autobiographies and all manner of government studies. In the 1960s and 1970s, J.H. Hexter, Jacques Derrida and Hayden White showed us that fiction and non-fiction, while distinct, are not completely separate. Non-fiction, including history, contains fictive elements. To fragment form and content is to eviscerate a work. It often undermines understanding of ideas, images and arguments. As a cultural history resource, a novel cannot just be read for what its words state about a time or a place. Events in a novel may have deeper meanings that can only be discerned in relation to other events, or recurring images; the course of a narrative often signifies ideas about history or a place. Characters and their development usually stand for important ideas. Sometimes they don't and the reader must understand this too. Recently in *Slow Reading in a Hurried Age*, literature scholar and critic David Mikics identified a dozen or so tasks necessary to reading fiction. These include: 'be patient', or don't rush to meaning. 'Ask the right questions', questions that connect elements of the book together, is next. Then, 'identify the voice', who speaks and how? Do they speak to each other? Do voices compete or complement each other? Then

---

13  Wineburg, *Historical Thinking and Other Unnatural Acts*, 65.
14  For a detailed discussion, Wineburg, *Historical Thinking and Other Unnatural Acts*, 64–67.

'get a sense of style', and 'notice beginnings and endings'. Another two are closely related: 'identify signposts' (key images, words, sentences and passages) and 'track key words'. Another, 'find the author's basic thought', is what historians try to do with any document. 'Find the parts' is more explicitly literary, in focusing on structure and turning points.[15] James Wood's *How Fiction Works* also emphasises form and structure. Not only the form and structure of a work as a whole, but the form and structure of character's voices – what do they reveal about the character? How do they relate to the work as a whole? What effects does this create? To what end? To understand a work of fiction as a document of cultural history, historians must master all of this. Along with text and subtext we must be able to read form; at the level of narrative, the plot, the sentence, the word. And these must be understood in terms of the conventions and practices of each form and each genre. Characters are more important in novels than in short stories, where theme matters more. In poetry, meaning is found in imagery, connotation, tone, mood, pace, texture and ambiguity, as well as in rhyme and metre. Literature scholar Terry Eagleton even maintains that syntax and punctuation are means to meaning. There is a politics of form and form is a mode of access, even to history.[16] Documents born of fiction are both rich and difficult for the historian. To be able to read well, across the range of forms and varieties of genres through which the sources of *Never-Never* speak to us, is laudable.

Examples abound in *Never-Never* where sources are read for more than content. Content is placed in historical context but is analysed in terms of literary constructs of forms. Throughout, we encounter discussions of stories and characters in relation to heroic models or, say, Arcadian models.[17] Or references to literary constructions that emphasise, for example, the role of women as 'idealised homemakers'.[18] Reflecting on Harriet Daly's and Jeannie Gunn's autobiographical fiction from the late nineteenth and early twentieth centuries, Dewar notices that the various male characters in the bush are not fully rounded and lack human complexity. Instead, they are caricatures who create a bifurcated image of bushmen: gentle/kind or antisocial; teetotaller or alcoholic.[19] In time, the more benign images came to dominate. Rather than freshly drawn

---

15  Mikics, *Slow Reading in a Hurried Age*, 55–156.
16  Eagleton, *How to Read a Poem*, 8.
17  Dewar, *In Search of the Never-Never*, 6.
18  Dewar, *In Search of the Never-Never*, 141.
19  Dewar, *In Search of the Never-Never*, 21.

characters, they are composites of stock images, largely drawn from Henry Lawson. Instead of epitomising and working through more universal human dramas, they paint a picture of the outback as wild but in parts tamed; remote but ultimately benevolent. Their role is to help create a place – the 'Never-Never'.

'Never-Never' is how both the outback and often the Territory – there's usually a lot of slippage here – have been imagined. Implying a place 'out of time', this concept immediately places the Territory as an OTHER, a different place to the rest of Australia. This idea is arresting in its strangeness. On interrogation it is as incoherent as it is strange. How could a physical place be out of time? How could a physical place never be, ever? But, it is a wonderfully evocative, if distancing, name. Reading character, plot, location, absences, silences and form in Jeannie Gunn's *We of the Never-Never*, Mickey Dewar identifies a literary construct at the core of our idea of the Northern Territory. The idea of the 'Never-Never' then does not issue from common, unmediated experience or even from systematic, empirical examination. It comes from a literary construct that accepts the hardships of the land and has supplied the significant icons and myths that the NT in turn has drawn upon to describe itself and distinguish itself from the rest of Australia, from around 1910 onwards.[20] Perhaps the vividness of this concept is a clue to its discursive origins and fictive nature. But it was a reading of Jeannie Gunn's opus, attentive to form and literary conventions, which discerned the literary construction that is the 'Never-Never'. A study of NT literature, *In Search of the Never-Never* is largely an enquiry into the dominant idea about the NT and its echoes. The title, *In Search of the Never-Never*, tells us exactly what the book is about, the author's central thought if you will.

James Bradley has urged that fiction not be valued for its non-fiction. Even as a work of history, *Never-Never* values fiction as fiction. We see this in a brief discussion of the literary merits of *Capricornia* and *Buffalo Jim*. Reflecting on Xavier Herbert's and William Hatfield's political commitment to justice and representation for Aboriginal people (in both life and literature), Dewar explicitly judges that 'their novels suffer from the soap-box style of their protagonists'.[21] But stories and literary construction are also examined in terms of their veracity, as adduced by historical evidence. For example, an interrogation of Hugh Atkinson's

---

20   Dewar, *In Search of the Never-Never*, 38.
21   Dewar, *In Search of the Never-Never*, 65.

historical novel *The Longest Wire* reveals that writers generally believed that Europeans committed genocide in the 1870s, when the Overland Telegraph was built. This novel specifically includes scenes where the men building the line engaged in racial violence and rape. Yet, as Dewar says, despite the undoubted allegorical and general truth about colonial/invader violence and even genocide, there is no historical evidence to support the specifics of Atkinson's portrayal.[22] Indeed, this represents an inversion of what Mickey Dewar terms the construction of the relationship of Europeans to Aborigines. Earliest accounts refused to acknowledge violence against Aboriginal people, even when overwhelming historical evidence corroborated these atrocities. By the 1980s and '90s, however, writers assumed this violence even where historical evidence tells us otherwise.

Before the insights of the linguistic turn came to influence history in Australia, prominent historians saw the worth of fiction for history. Manning Clark speaks of his voluminous and laborious reading that helped him conceive of how to tell 'the story' in his History of Australia series. Authors he attentively read and re-read in preparing to both write and research this work include Job, Luke, Aristotle, Dostoyevsky, Tolstoy, Nietzsche, Hardy, Shakespeare, Dickens, Melville, Henry Lawson, Thomas Carlyle and Edward Gibbon.[23] Declaring that without imagination there can be no history, Keith Hancock insisted that historians must be good readers, not just of non-fiction but also of novels and drama.[24] History, according to Hancock, must combine span and precision and, to do this, historians need also to become playwrights, poets, painters, musicians, novelists… Even at a time when the opacity of the word was perhaps not as well understood as it is now, distinguished historians did grasp the need to understand how narrative and various kinds of literary form are made. The Herculean reading at the foundation of *In Search of the Never-Never* evinces this understanding. It embodies Ranke's exhaustive study of documents, with perhaps more of an emphasis on symbols and semiotics than on philology, Hancock's span, Clarke's concern for form, character and story and post-structural insights about emplotment, language and power. What stories, then, does it tell us about the NT?

---

22  Dewar, *In Search of the Never-Never*, 179.
23  Clark, *A Historian's Apprenticeship*, 21–31.
24  Hancock, *Professing History*, 20–21.

## Stories about stories about 'The Territory'

A core of vital themes emerges from the ocean of words written about the NT. The original word worlds were crafted by people who resided in or visited the NT. For some, home was elsewhere and ideas of home were ideas of other places. Others tried to make a new home through their words. *Never-Never* orders this discourse into clear ideas. Its chapters, arranged both thematically and chronologically, carve out particular periods and ideas that I will now outline. Chapters 1 and 2 deal with the early post-invasion period: circa 1870 to the First World War. Chapter 1, 'Writing the Landscape', tells of early newcomer preoccupation with landscape, flora and fauna. Driven by cultural needs for both distinctive subject matter and style, this manifested in contradictory ideas about the land. Before 1910 or thereabouts land was depicted as enemy or as holding great economic potential – yes, the latter is a very old idea, as yet unrealised. Later in this period, land was also depicted within Arcadian models. Chapter 2, 'The People', examines how people were drawn in the writing of the time. Most images, whether about Aboriginal or non-Aboriginal people, were recognisable caricatures. Depictions of Aboriginal people conveyed a pervasive, relentless and brutal racism. Renderings of non-Aboriginal men gave birth to archetypes of outback bushmen that endure in two ideas.: one, in the outback, mateship transcends usual class barriers; and two, that men seek solace in the bush after a broken romance.

'Looking for Gold', Chapter 3, takes us to after the First World War. At this time, Territory writing emphasises the culture of the frontier. This is the genesis of ideas still associated with the NT: a place of adventure, violence; wilfully unruly, casual, excessive. But the title points to another strong strand: pursuit of mineral and industrial wealth. Yet, as the bush lifestyle was celebrated, others advocated its displacement through industry. This was animated by the potent twentieth-century myth: that of fabulous mineral wealth under the rocks of the NT.

Chapter 4, 'Race Relations', is an unflinching look at racist depictions of Aboriginal peoples in the period leading up to the Second World War. Preoccupied with essentialist notions of race and concerns about 'mixing and degeneration', we see that much literature of the period propagates such dominant scientific ideas. However, Xavier Herbert debunked these ideas in *Capricornia*. Then there are the stories about white women rendered decadent in the tropical north.

In Chapter 5, 'The Atomic Territory', we are in the postwar period. When, as uranium was discovered in the NT, outback iconography becomes prominent. No longer a place for adventure, the Territory is now made as a place for inspiration drawn from its unique landscapes. Yet, at the same time, the urge to develop becomes part of a broader narrative about science and progress.

Covering the same period, 'Sex and the Dreamtime' (Chapter 6) shows that other writers constructed a different Territory of the 1950s and 1960s. They depicted a place populated with sexual tensions, with particular concern for exploitative relationships between European men and Aboriginal women. For the first time, non-Aboriginal people came to be seen, explicitly, as outsiders to the Territory. Here the land became dangerous and hostile again to who trespassed.

The recasting of the NT landscape in the 1970s to a role more familiar to us now is the subject of Chapter 7. 'Welcome to Wilderness' places this change in the context of broader movements of environmentalism, pluralism and feminism. The NT came to be deliberately defined in relation to the rest of Australia. It was the one place to access wilderness and the spiritual renewal it affords, as well as to witness the people who have long lived harmoniously with this environment. Wilderness was no longer the frontier. The frontier and its ordeals of initiation were where the visitor encountered non-urban Territorians; the final barrier to accessing wilderness.

Finally, in a nod to Xavier Herbert, 'Poor Bugger All of Us', examines how literature portrays Territorians relating to each other and to the landscape. The period is the 1980s and '90s. Aboriginal people are largely depicted as spiritual beings. Gender manifests in distinctions between Aboriginal women and European women. The former are drawn as strong and intelligent; the latter as superficial and even bitter. More broadly, Europeans are identified as environmental destroyers; Aborigines as conservers.

I have gone into such detail to give a sense of just how many ways the NT and aspects of its life and people have been imagined by writers over time. This by no means exhausts the stock. What Mickey Dewar called the literary model of the Northern Territory has undergone yet more transformations. In this history, as she presents it, we see many continuities too. But this model is worth understanding because it informs how so many people who have not personally experienced the NT understand it and its history. I suspect these stories help residents better apprehend life in the NT and other stories about the Territory too. Geographer Edward Relph notes that the identity of a place features three interrelated components: physical features and appearance, functions and activities, and meanings/symbols.[25] Meanings come from stories and beliefs about places and kinds of places. More fundamentally, environmental scientist and literature scholar George Seddon observed that how we perceive, imagine, conceptualise and relate to the physical world is partly a result of cultural conditioning.[26] Stories, including histories, shape our sense of place. They supply ideas and images, which help us form beliefs that then inform our subsequent perception of place, experientially and in text. Conceptually, it is easy to see that certain ideas of place can gain currency without a substantial basis in reality. Other images can undermine this. *Never-Never* identifies vivid yet conflicting and even duelling images about the NT in its writing.

What do these stories about stories about the NT tell us?

We learn that this land of the imagination was a place where many ideas coexisted. This happened within certain periods; it happened across periods. In each period, ideas contradicted or were in direct contest with each other. Notions and ideas of land, race, development, wilderness and gender inform the literary model throughout the period but were refracted through particular ideas, images and motifs. These mutated frequently. This happened in response to larger social and political movements – sometimes in reaction to earlier ideas or concurrent concepts. Many of these ideas have long lives or multiple reincarnations. By tracing the major themes of Aboriginal people, gender, development and ideas of land/wilderness, we get an even better sense of all of this.

## Tracing themes

Most depictions of Aboriginal people in the corpus of NT writing are offensive. Yet, confronting them is necessary and instructive. Coming to know these images, we gain a good sense of the key problems inherent in relationships been Aboriginal and non-Aboriginal peoples in Australia –

---

25   Relph, *Place and Placelessness*, 61.
26   Seddon, *Landprints*, 13.

now and in the past. On a broader point of cultural history, they also show that ideas do not have to be good, nor do they even need to reflect reality in order to live a long life. Ideas don't need to make sense. They only need to have a use or to fill a void. Images of Aboriginal people were by no means uniform but they were denigrating. Mickey Dewar shows us that in NT literature before 1905, there is no example of anything as humane as friendship between Europeans and Aborigines. Aboriginal people are generally depicted as aggressive and threatening or, in late nineteenth–century fantasy writing, as a degraded form of a once 'higher, ancient civilisation'.[27] At the same time, Aborigines in the outback were portrayed in more favourable terms than those in the towns. In the 1920s and 1930s, the depictions have a strongly ethnographic and anthropological flavour, being particularly preoccupied by biological notions of race and miscegenation. Aborigines were understood as a doomed people. Aboriginality was graded in fractions of race, calibrated by flawed understandings of genetic descent and its meaning.

In adventure stories, Aboriginal people were still depicted as menacing. In other genres such as journalism, biography and fiction more broadly, Aboriginal people were defined by biology and racialised in a manner that justified white attitudes of racial and cultural superiority. Amid this, mythologies of cannibalism emerged in both fiction and non-fiction. Yet, during the same period, the idea of Aborigines with occult powers, especially telepathy and in relation to land and nature, also emerged. Following the Second World War and the discrediting of race-based thinking and eugenics, the idea of the doomed Aborigine lost credence. Images of Aborigines accorded with white political and cultural aspirations for assimilation. It is worth stressing here that these images were not the product of a remote and isolated culture: they reflected dominant scientific and political consensus. NT writing tapped into both national and global thinking.

The image of the telepathic Aborigine has recurred since this time. The 1950s saw a new interest in both Aboriginal mythology and in sexual relations between white men and Aboriginal women. *Never-Never* also shows us that on this the writing is ambivalent – focusing on either the exploitative nature of these relationships or on the widespread acceptance of them. The 1970s saw the emergence of Aboriginal people as spiritual

---

27   Dewar, *In Search of the Never-Never*, 3–4.

beings in NT writing, especially in relation to wilderness or the outback. While far more humane than other manifold derogatory stereotypes, this is still something of a mutation of older ideas of Aborigines and telepathy. It is also a white projection on Aboriginal people, not an expression of Aboriginal voices. Moreover, after being burdened with being represented as degraded and inferior, and as obstacles to progress and development, Aboriginal people were then burdened with providing a homegrown spirituality for Australia's existentially lost souls. We see a similar dynamic in portrayals of Aboriginal characters in 1980s and '90s Territory writing – as protectors and preservers of the environment in contrast to European destroyers. The content has changed and, thankfully, it is more humane and positive. But even in the 1990s, Aboriginal people were still being defined and spoken for, and they were still being cast instrumentally – in relation to the needs of non-Aboriginal people.

Some writing did dissent from this. But *Never-Never* shows that this represents a small proportion of the overall mass of text. Xavier Herbert's *Capricornia* (1938) is the most outstanding example. Two pages of *Never-Never* discuss how characters in *Capricornia* debunk the notion of Aborigines as cannibals, the rectitude of forced child removals and any sense that government administration did actually work for the benefit of Aborigines.[28] Herbert was not alone. Other writers such as William Hatfield and Bill Harney demonstrated similar thinking in their writing. In *Desert Saga* (1933) Hatfield even tried to present the narrative from an Aboriginal perspective. But, as Mickey Dewar discerned in her readings, the protagonist's thinking was biblical rather than Aboriginal.[29] In other words, despite the structure of the narrative, this character was not thinking and acting from an Aboriginal perspective at all. Overwhelmingly, then, for its multitude of voices, variety of images and characterisations and plethora of ideas, this was not a literature that challenged prevailing ideas of race or government policies in relation to Aborigines. On these matters it was startlingly conformist, supporting the argument of *Never-Never* that NT literature served to legitimise European occupation of Australia.

Literary images relating to gender were both remarkably fluid and remarkably resilient. Through the course of *Never-Never,* we see striking differences between the portrayal of Aboriginal women and white women. Aboriginal women tended to be invisible in the earliest literature.

---

28 Dewar, *In Search of the Never-Never*, 68–69.
29 Dewar, *In Search of the Never-Never*, 70–71.

Aboriginal men are present, represented as a general and pervasive threat to the European project of developing and 'civilising' the north. As Dewar shows, this is an image that recurs for many decades. When Aboriginal women do appear in the early twentieth century, they are in white domestic space and are depicted as good workers. From about the 1930s, portrayals of sexual relations between white men and Aboriginal women feature openly. With some depicting exploitation, it seems reasonable to read sexual exploitation of Aboriginal women into earlier stories portraying domestic service. In much NT writing post 1960, Aboriginal women (and men) are guardians of the land, skilled and knowledgeable about the environment. *Never-Never* identifies a remarkable contrast in the depiction of Aboriginal women compared to white women in the more recent literature it studies. While Aboriginal women are presented as strong and loyal, white women are often victims of violence, depicted with little or no sympathy; or portrayed as shrill 'femmocrats'.[30] And not only by male authors. Referring to a passage discussing relations between white and Aboriginal women in Herbert's *Poor Fellow My Country* (1975), Mickey Dewar explains this hostility. White women were seen to be a crimp on white bushmen's sexual licentiousness. They had been represented in this manner in earlier writing too.[31] This idea of white women as social guardians was a strong and recurrent one in NT literature. It features in the writing of Jeannie Gunn at the turn of the century. It is resurrected in the 1950s, Dewar argues, to support strong cultural and political aspirations for social stability, bolstered by an idealised notion of the nuclear family. Another and very different idea of white women in the NT was also constructed. This was the 'plucky', strong, feisty, independent woman. She appeared in the early twentieth century, usually on a pastoral station. In later depictions, she was usually of the outback rather than the town or city.

Constructions of white men, however, have been more politically potent. In early times they were the brave, noble, loyal yet independent and rule-breaking bushmen. Although idealised, they were not presented as perfect but sometimes as drinking and brawling. In later times, white men are often characterised as destroyers: some are defeated, nihilistic and self-destructive, while others are complacent, uncaring, prosperous and tenaciously narrow-minded. Of these images, it is that of the bushman

---

30  Dewar, *In Search of the Never-Never*, 183–87.
31  Dewar, *In Search of the Never-Never*, 185–86.

that has proven the most enduring and politically powerful. It is hard not to notice the likeness between the image of the NT bushmen and the caricatures at the heart of Russell Ward's *Australian Legend*. In the 1950s, Ward, among other radical nationalist thinkers, reflected on Australian culture in the period leading to the birth of the Australian nation. The bushman was not simply a local character in the pastoral north, but emerged as emblematic of a distinctive ethos of egalitarianism, independence and anti-authoritarianism that has long been used to further political and cultural agendas. To an extent, the bushman became a sacred cow in Australian cultural and political life. Anthropologist Tess Lea has recently highlighted the serious consequences of this in the Territory. The image of the largely benevolent bushman has been acquired by pastoralism in general. The endurance of this benign iconography, Lea argues, has kept many local historians in the NT from engaging critically with stories – even propaganda – circulated with the intention of casting industries such as pastoralism and mining in a favourable light.[32] Lea relates that in the early twentieth century, cattle empires Bovril's and the Union Cold Storage Company (Vestey's) exploited labour, suppressed wages, avoided tax, degraded the land and drove traditional owners off their own land.[33] Few know of this today: the icons of the bushman and the stockman have created many erasures and occluded knowledge of exploitation of both Aborigines and (their) land. Anthropologist Deborah Bird Rose contends that this is not so unusual. Indeed, forgetting is an inherent aspect of industrialisation and even modernity, especially in non-urban places targeted for development and for a long time regarded as terra nullius.[34] So, the true nature of pastoralism, at least in earlier times, remains unknown to most Australians and even most residents of the NT to this day. Unmasking icons and motif-ridden stories is vital. There is no reason to believe that various industries do not exploit the very same play between iconography and forgetting today.

If current plans to develop Australia's north seem stale, *Never-Never* helps explain why. Historian Libby Robin gives a thorough history and explanation of how previous grand plans for northern development have failed in *How a Continent Created a Nation* (2007). The schemes were too crude, imposing an environmental homogeneity upon the north and so paid little or no attention to local ecological realities. And they forgot earlier

---

32  Lea, *Darwin*, 55–62.
33  Lea, *Darwin*, 55–62.
34  Rose, *Reports from a Wild Country*, 53–72.

failures.³⁵ Agricultural economist Bruce Davidson identified physical and economical constraints on the project of northern development in *The Northern Myth* back in 1965. Yet *In Search of the Never-Never* reminds us that the idea of the Northern Territory as a source of boundless abundance and wealth dates back to the first half of the nineteenth century. So, it predates the establishment of a permanent colony at Darwin and came in two forms. There was biographical journalism that asserted the economic potential of the region. There were also fantasy stories featuring heroes who travelled to the centre of Australia in search of gold. Until about 1910, numerous novels appeared, serving to instil the idea that central and northern Australia were lands of 'fantastic possibility'.³⁶ Fears of a northern invasion strengthened their power, bolstering the development imperative of the late nineteenth century. Japan's victory in the Russo-Japanese War in 1905 invigorated these sentiments. But the idea that underneath the rocks of the NT lay exceptional mineral wealth became, between the two world wars, the most dominant and consuming myth in NT writing. *Never-Never* cities a large number of works that propagate this idea.³⁷ The later discovery of uranium gave this idea even more potency in Territory literature. Though we also learn that critics had emerged by then, with heightened environmental awareness from the 1970s onwards, qualifying these ideas. Yet the development imperative still dominates politics in and relating to north Australia today. Its durability can to a large extent be accounted for by persistent profit seeking. But, with the endurance of these ideas in NT writing, they have also established deep cultural roots. It is hard not to think that the persistence of the idea that the NT has vast reserves of untapped mineral wealth and limitless potential for economic development enables the repeated proposing of schemes that in other places might more readily be recognised as unviable.

Land, wilderness and place are the last major theme. In discussing *Never-Never*'s treatment of these, we see that the NT has had very distinctive ideas of wilderness in particular. It will also become clear that *Never-Never* reveals important and as yet unrecognised similarities between the NT and other 'norths' around the world. In examining stories about land and wilderness, *In Search of the Never-Never* also stands as a cultural history that does some important environmental history.

---

35   Robin, *How a Continent Created a Nation*, 145–74.
36   Dewar, *In Search of the Never-Never*, 4.
37   Dewar, *In Search of the Never-Never*, 48–49.

## The peopled wilderness

In Territory writing, depictions of land yield vivid images. Yet ideas of land and landscape have long been fluid and riven with contradiction. Early on, land was hostile, dangerous, to be subdued. In this very danger, in the power of its threat, it was seen to be imbued with spiritual powers. At the same time, it housed great bounties. The process of exploiting these would not only provide wealth but also quell the land's dangerous forces. Soon after, it was also conceived as Arcadian: harmonious and sustaining. In its hostile guise, it was a testing ground for character and heroism. Later it became a theatre of adventure and for authenticating masculinity. The land has been seen as empty and also as populated. In the 1950s and '60s it came to be depicted as part of outback iconography and re-imagined as a place not of adventure but of inspiration. More recently, it has been seen as a place of renewal, filled with spirituality, with the Indigenous people who have lived on it for millennia imagined as part of it. Here it is seen by white Australian writers as a place to engage in spiritual replenishment, through contact with the land and its long-term owners and custodians. At the same time, some literature has imagined the land as hostile to those non-Indigenous people who don't 'belong': the hostile landscape has returned in a different form.

Ecologically, the NT is particularly diverse. It has locales that are always rainforest, others that are always desert. It features islands, grasslands, scrub and dry forests and much of the Territory transforms into various kinds of desert for a variable six- to eight-month period each year. *Never-Never* convincingly illustrates patterns that show how the influence of culture has been at least as strong in NT writing as the influence of nature.

Contradictory attitudes to nature have a long history in western letters. Kinds of environment and particular places also elicit contending attitudes and images. In *Wilderness and the American Mind*, United States cultural and environmental historian Roderick Nash shows that wilderness has been conceived as different kinds of environment, usually desert or 'untamed' forest. Using biblical texts, he also reveals that even when imagined as a particular kind of environment, say, desert, wilderness has been imbued with different and usually contradictory characteristics and values. This is to say that the same environment has long represented disparate things. The term 'wilderness' is used 245 times in the Old Testament and is mostly equated with desolation or wasteland. In numerous biblical stories, 'wilderness' is also explicitly desert. Its key contrast is with the Garden of Eden and the tamed cultivation that it symbolises. In early Judeo-Christian thinking, wilderness isn't amoral, but from Hebraic folk tales, it inherited a sense of being populated with malevolent and immoral forces.[38] The idea of a hostile, forbidding land gains enormous currency in the Old Testament and we see in *Never-Never* that it resonated with early writers about the NT. But other ideas of wilderness come with the totemic biblical story of the Israelites wandering in the desert for 40 years. Here wilderness appears as a place of sanctuary, purity, a spiritual place to come closer to god and as testing ground. Variously defined in NT writing as the outback or the lands beyond town limits that hadn't been converted to pastoralism, wilderness in NT writing also reverberated with these ideas of spiritual encounter, sanctuary and testing ground. This contradiction, this duality, persists through the whole period that *Never-Never* takes into account. Wilderness has long been a cultural place even more than a physical place.

NT writing has transposed the culture of other places and times onto the NT landscape and environment. However, in this literature, older ideas acquire a new flavour. Biblical notions of wilderness refer to desolate places devoid of humans. Notwithstanding the erroneous and now discredited legal fiction of terra nullius, people lived in the NT wilderness and had for a period that registers on the scale of deep time: about 60,000 years. Very early writings mostly depicted the NT as a wilderness to be subdued: empty and hostile.[39] But in W.C. Willshire's *Land of the Dawning* (1896) Aboriginal people come to be represented as yet another danger in this wilderness. After this, as Mickey Dewar shows, adventure stories construct Aboriginal people as a threat to Europeans that defines this dangerous environment.[40] Dewar also reveals that such depictions of Aboriginal people are a stock image copied from depictions of Aborigines in the journals of Matthew Flinders, Ludwig Leichhardt and David Lindsay. Only much later are Aboriginal people depicted as the land's protectors. As we have seen, *Never-Never* explains that in NT writing, the Territory wilderness is inhabited by people who appear in various guises: the telepathic Aborigine, the wise custodian, the keeper of Indigenous knowledge and, in the late twentieth century, mostly as a spiritual being deeply connected to the spiritual bounty of the wilderness. So whereas

---

38   See Nash, *Wilderness and the American Mind*, 13–17.
39   Dewar, *In Search of the Never-Never*, 2–4.
40   Dewar, *In Search of the Never-Never*, 23.

early on, Aboriginal people were depicted as part of the wild's menace, later they are represented as integral to the NT wilderness as a place for renewal, restoration and inspiration. Just as some white Australian writers came to project profound existential demands on to Aboriginal people, so too have they done the same in relation their lands.

*Never-Never* unveils a very distinctive incarnation of the wilderness idea. Even today, wilderness is predominantly understood as a place without people. Inherent in conservation battles in North America and southern Australia was the idea that wilderness is either untouched or lightly touched by humans and largely devoid of man-made structures and permanent human habitation. This is the conceptual basis of laws relating to wilderness. Influenced by the Bible, Henry David Thoreau, John Muir, Aldo Leopold, and others, this is an enduring and influential idea in western thinking. The Franklin Wilderness of Tasmania was depicted as a pristine environment and this conceptual framing helped animate the successful battle to save it. But *Never-Never* illustrates that NT literature – at the same time and afterwards – depicted a wilderness in which Aboriginal people lived in harmony with nature.[41] We should again note that much of this literature was written by people who came from or who lived in other parts of Australia. Accordingly, many would have held these different ideas of wilderness simultaneously. Portrayed as spiritual guardians of the land and its enigmatic truths, Aboriginal people, however, had become inseparable from the constructs of land and wilderness drawn by NT writing. Crucially, this was a peopled wilderness.

The idea of the wilderness as a place of trial has also endured. However, the nature of the trial has changed. In late twentieth–century writing about the NT, before the outsider gets to the character-building, self-revealing wilds, they must endure the trial of contact with the townsfolk who live on the frontier between the rest of Australia and the wilderness.[42] The land itself ceased to be the testing ground; accessing it had become the trial. This was just the latest idea of trial in the NT landscape. First, it was to overcome the hostile wilds to impose order and extract wealth. After the First World War it was a trial in terms of adventure, courage and individual strength and endurance, and these two incompatible notions were in direct conflict with each other. Then the land was seen as suffused with spiritually nourishing qualities. This idea conflicted with plans,

---

41  Dewar, *In Search of the Never-Never*, 150–53.
42  Dewar, *In Search of the Never-Never*, 151.

aspirations and narratives of development, geared at securing wealth and guiding 'progress': a tamed wilderness no longer offers spiritual sustenance. Over time, the development/conservation battles in the NT have been animated by vastly different values and aspirations. Wilderness has meant many things to different people, but it is not the only literary construction developed for imagining land and place in NT writing.

Circa 1900, the far north was depicted as Arcadian. Arcadian models of nature come from Roman literature, particularly works such as Virgil's *Georgics and Eclogues*. The Arcadian ideal is of land and nature that are tamed, harmonious and fruitful. It is a coloniser's idyll. In *Never-Never* we see that writers such as Harriet Daly use it in a manner that depicts the far north of the NT as having been subdued and as no longer wild.[43] At the time, some may have read this to suggest that in time the same would happen throughout the rest of the NT. But was it ever wild, except in the invader imagination? Using accounts of George Goyder and his team as they set about establishing the colony at Darwin in 1869, historian Bill Gammage indicates otherwise. Although Goyder did not recognise it himself, this was a land tended to by the Larrakia people who had long systematically burned the land in attentive mosaic patterns that varied depending on local ecological conditions.[44] This was not wilderness, but managed land. Indeed, as Gammage, as well as others including Rhys Jones in the late 1960s, tell us, this has long happened across Australia.

Indeed, for the Aboriginal peoples of the NT, 'wilderness' did not emerge until after invasion and the imposing of colonial land regimes on the Territory. For example, Aboriginal people from the Victoria River district believe that wilderness is man-made and cattle-made.[45] To quote anthropologist Deborah Bird Rose, a wild place is 'where the life of the country was falling down into the gullies and washing away with the rains'.[46] It is worth noting, too, that when Aboriginal voices finally appear in NT writing, they do not discuss landscape and wilderness. Instead their focus is on dispossession, inequality and institutionalised racism;[47] root causes of what some Aboriginal people term wilderness.

---

43  Dewar, *In Search of the Never-Never*, 6.
44  Gammage, *The Biggest Estate on Earth*, 271–75.
45  Rose, *Reports from a Wild Country*, 4.
46  Rose, *Reports from a Wild Country*, 4.
47  Dewar, *In Search of the Never-Never*, 182.

Wilderness is a European import. It is more a product of imagination than of the physical world. It is vivid, is applied to often spectacular and evocative physical environments and has been a worthwhile concept for people who reasonably are trying to curb industrialisation and unrelenting economic exploitation. But, as William Cronon highlights, it is an incoherent idea that can undermine its very goals. The core of the most dominant idea of wilderness in North America (and Australia) sets humans outside of nature and so flees history and its own cultural context.[48] Establishing this human/non-human dichotomy leads us to misunderstand and undervalue all manner of ecologies that might be worth preserving. It can render people blind to places of value or result in failures to grasp fully what is ecologically and culturally significant in places people already favour for conservation. Moreover, this dualism is morally dubious because it structurally denies that people have lived in places that they had long made their home. In *Never-Never* we see how the wilderness idea has served various needs in the NT. Writers constructed a distinctive wilderness in the NT, one usually linked to people – the traditional owners and custodians. People are present in this wilderness and in recent times are somewhat idealised. Before this idea emerged, wilderness in the NT was the same as elsewhere in Australia or North America: a place to be conquered, a place in which to test oneself, or a place where a visitor or new arrival might be renewed. The emergence of a new wilderness idea indicates particular cultural and spiritual needs among Australian writers in the late twentieth century for homegrown meaning and spiritual sustenance. With its distinctive landscapes and people, the NT was the one part of Australia onto which these needs and aspirations could be projected.

Re-reading *Never-Never* now also reveals the NT to be another kind of place: a north. In 1997 when it was first published this was harder to discern. Now, Mickey Dewar's opus can be read in dialogue with books such as Peter Davidson's *The Idea of North* (2016 [2005]). Davidson canvasses the way northern parts of various northern hemisphere countries are imagined by the larger populations that live in southern parts of Britain, Scandinavia, Canada, Japan and China. He identified that each had a place identified as 'north'. But north here does not designate a mere geographical bearing or physical placing. North is imbued with meaning and symbolism. The north is a kind of place. From manifold works of

---

48   Cronon, 'The Trouble With Wilderness', 80–90.

art and literature, Davidson has interpreted the north as a harder place, isolated, a place of dearth, desolation, 'intractable elements of climate, topography and humanity'.[49] It is also a powerful testing zone; a place of exile, of absence, of failed industries and of a lack of alternatives; and an Other.[50]

Notwithstanding that the dominant motifs of these norths are ice, snow and whiteness, the overlap with the ideas of place in NT literature is remarkable. At first blush this reinforces what we already know about how our understandings of the NT as a place are based on imported ideas and concepts. More reflection on this will reveal even more about how we have understood the NT in word and imagination: not just the content but also how we structure key concepts and the assumptions behind this structure.

# New knowing

A republic of letters we hardly knew existed has shaped how we see a vast, evocative part of this continent. Unveiling this, *In Search of the Never-Never* has shown not only how that entity has come about, but attests to its enduring force. This work allows us to better understand the Northern Territory and the role it has played in the Australian nation and beyond. This most attentive reading of countless sources, with deliberate regard for form, tone, voice, character, place, content, symbols, imagery, makes for a rich work of history. It is a history of ideas about the NT, and it is a history of constructing a place. It is also a history of ideas in themselves.

Ideas are born, they live, they change, they go dormant, they are born again; occasionally they even die. Ideas are historical; literature and culture are historical. *In Search of the Never-Never* demonstrates this; it discerns and details these multiple Territory histories. We see that the search for the 'Never-Never' is a search that never arrives at a stable, whole and unified locus called the NT. This is a place of the imagination – the physical place one of multiple, competing, even entangled histories, stories and imaginings.

---

49   Davidson, *The Idea of North*, 11.
50   Davidson, *The Idea of North*, 12–20.

'The most generous thing a scholar can do is read', Tom Griffiths tells us in *The Art of Time Travel*.[51] 'Read thoughtfully, widely and in context', Tom exhorts us.[52] Mickey Dewar, clearly, has been remarkably generous in labouring to produce *In Search of the Never-Never*. Read it carefully. Then, read it again. You may come to know the Northern Territory as you have never known it before. You may come to reflect on Australia, even your particular part of it, and come to know both as you never have before.

## Bibliography

Carment, David. *Looking at Darwin's Past: Material Evidence of European Settlement in Tropical Australia*. Darwin: North Australia Research Unit (NARU), ANU, 1992.

Carment, David. *Territorianism: Politics and Identity in Australia's Northern Territory 1978–2001*. Melbourne: Australian Scholarly Publishing, 2007.

Clark, Manning. *A Historian's Apprenticeship*. Melbourne: Melbourne University Press, 1992.

Cronon, William. 'A Place for Stories: Nature, History, Narrative'. *Journal of American History* 78 (1992): 1375. doi.org/10.2307/2079346.

Cronon, William. 'The Trouble With Wilderness'. In *Uncommon Ground*, edited by William Cronon, 80–90. New York: W.W. Norton, 1996.

Davidson, Peter. *The Idea of North*. 2nd ed. London: Reakton, 2016.

Dewar, Mickey. *In Search of the Never-Never, Looking for Australia in Northern Territory Writing*. Darwin: Northern Territory University Press, 1997.

Eagleton, Terry. *How to Read a Poem*. Oxford: Blackwell, 2007.

Gammage, Bill. *The Biggest Estate on Earth*. Sydney: Allen & Unwin, 2012.

Ganter, Elizabeth. *Reluctant Representatives: Blackfella Bureaucrats Speak in Australia's North*. Canberra: ANU Press, 2017. doi.org/10.22459/CAEPR37.11.2016.

---

51  Griffiths, *The Art of Time Travel*, 15.
52  Griffiths, *The Art of Time Travel*, 15.

Ganter, Regina. 'Turning the Map Upside Down', *History Compass* 4 (2006): 26–35. doi.org/10.1111/j.1478-0542.2006.00301.x.

Ganter, Regina. *Mixed Relations: Asian–Aboriginal Contact in North Australia*, with contributions from Julia Martinez and Gary Lee. Crawley: University of Western Australia Press, 2006.

Griffiths, Tom. *The Art of Time Travel*. Melbourne: Black Inc., 2016.

Hancock, Keith. *Professing History*. Sydney: Sydney University Press, 1976.

Lea, Tess. *Darwin*. Sydney: NewSouth Publishing, 2014.

Lewis, Darrell. *A Wild History*. Melbourne: Monash University Publishing, 2012.

Macknight, Campbell. *The Voyage to Marege*. Melbourne: Melbourne University Press, 1976.

McGrath, Ann. *'Born in the Cattle': Aborigines in the Cattle Country*. Sydney: Allen & Unwin, 1987 (republished 2012).

Mikics, David. *Slow Reading in a Hurried Age*. Boston: President and Fellows of Harvard College, 2013.

Nash, Roderick. *Wilderness and the American Mind*. 4th ed. New Haven: Yale University Press, 2001.

O'Brien, Chris. 'Rethinking Seasons: Changing Climate, Changing Time'. In *A Cultural History of Climate Change*, edited by Tom Bristow and Thomas H. Ford. Oxford: Routledge, 2016.

Rademaker, Laura. *Found in Translation: Many Meanings on a North Australian Mission*. Honolulu: University of Hawai'i Press, 2018.

Read, P. and Read, J. eds. *Long Time, Olden Time: Aboriginal Accounts of Northern Territory History*. Alice Springs: Institute for Aboriginal Development Publications, 1991.

Relph, Edward. *Place and Placelessness*. London: Pion, 1976.

Reynolds, Henry. *North of Capricorn*. Sydney: Allen & Unwin, 2003.

Robin, Libby. *How a Continent Created a Nation*. Sydney: UNSW Press, 2007.

Rose, Deborah Bird. *Reports from a Wild Country: Ethics for Decolonisation*. Sydney: UNSW Press, 2004.

Rowse, Tim. *Indigenous and Other Australians since 1901*. Sydney: UNSW Press, 2017.

Seddon, George. *Landprints: Reflections on Place and Landscape*. Cambridge: Cambridge University Press, 1997.

Wineburg, Sam. *Historical Thinking and Other Unnatural Acts*. Philidelphia: Temple University Press, 2001.

# IN SEARCH OF THE 'NEVER-NEVER'

*Mickey Dewar*

*For Geoff, Maureen, Adrienne and Carol*

# CONTENTS

| | | |
|---|---|---|
| Acknowledgments | | 51 |
| Introduction | | 53 |
| 1 | Writing the landscape | 59 |
| 2 | The people | 69 |
| 3 | Looking for gold | 97 |
| 4 | Race relations | 113 |
| 5 | The atomic Territory | 139 |
| 6 | Sex and the Dreamtime | 167 |
| 7 | Welcome to wilderness | 193 |
| 8 | Poor bugger all of us | 211 |
| Select Territory bibliography | | 235 |

# ACKNOWLEDGMENTS

A great many people assisted me in this project and I feel myself privileged that I had so much personal and professional support. In particular I am grateful to the Northern Territory University and the Museum and Art Gallery of the Northern Territory. Both institutions support and see as a priority, research and publications into Northern Territory history. My thanks also to the Australia Foundation for Culture and the Humanities. The Foundation's support of research and publications, such as this one, is greatly appreciated.

I would like to thank the following people for assistance with this research topic, in particular David Carment and Alan Powell, but also Lyn Riddett, Christine Doran, Mark Davies, Carmel Gaffney, Donald Campbell, Julie Wells, Val Hawkes, Suzanne Parry, Kerin Coulehan, Juan Federer, Bill Perrett, Jim Jose, Tim Rowse, Barbara James, Suzanne Spunner, John Avery, Trish Hoyne, Colleen Pyne, Yvonne Forrest, Elaine Glover, Annette Ford, Janet Chaloupka, Robbie Braithwaite, Sheila Forrest, Jenny Armour, Michael Loos, Terry Knight, staff of NTUniprint, Jacky Healy, Daena Murray, Ann Webb, and everyone else kind enough to let me bore them to death on this subject (but there would be too many to list!).

Without the loving support of my family—Sam, Susannah and especially David—this project could never even have begun.

# INTRODUCTION

I began this study of Northern Territory writing and its relationship to Australian identity primarily because I enjoyed reading Northern Territory writing. What could be more pleasant than to sit down for three years with Ion Idriess or Jeannie Gunn and read exciting adventure stories of the Territory's past? After ploughing through some thousand or so novels and reference books, I began to feel as if I never cared if I read another Northern Territory novel in my life. As David Headon was to note, it is easy to underestimate the extent of Territory writing.[1] But as I read, I discovered that people had come to the Territory because they believed it to be the place of legends and mythical Australian events. In a large measure, this construction has been generated by the wealth of writing on this subject.

Northern Territory writing explores a variety of themes based around settler attitudes to landscape, culture, Aborigines, gender, distance and frontier. After reading all I could about the Territory, I came to believe that the focus on the region in the writing was an attempt to locate and define the non-Aboriginal occupation of Australia from all aspects: physically, spatially, morally and temporally. Northern Territory writing offers an interpretation of the settlement of Australia which seeks to legitimise European settlement. Representations of the Northern Territory can be seen to have developed and modified in response to changing events in Australian society generally. The Northern Territory as metaphor in Australian writing is the microcosm where the European occupation of the continent is reconciled. As David Day noted, 'European Australians

---

1   D. Headon, *North of the Ten Commandments: A Collection of Northern Territory Literature* (Sydney: Hodder & Stoughton, 1991), 'Introduction'.

have tried in the space of 200 years to evolve a country out of a continent and establish a claim to its proprietorship that can rival that of the original inhabitants'.[2]

The majority of Australian writing which deals with the Northern Territory falls into the category of 'popular' writing rather than 'literature'. This meant that the ideas and dissemination of images about the Territory had a broad audience. David Headon considered Northern Territory writing as 'the most exciting expression of regional literature in the country for an assortment of cultural, geographical, environmental and social reasons'.[3] His argument for considering the Territory as regionally distinct went as follows: firstly, there was a sense of 'identity' both in the Territory and outside it, that Territorians existed as distinct from the rest of Australia; secondly, that the Northern Territory, with its defined state borders, was a measurable region in the political sense; thirdly, that in the writing there was a 'distinctive flavour to the region of the Northern Territory ... an embattled sense of Territory humour'.[4] Suzanne Falkiner concurred, finding 'the adventure tales and bush yarns' 'authentic European regional writing'.[5]

Other commentators agreed that the Territory should be regarded as distinct from the rest of Australia. Jon Stratton argued convincingly that 'the Northern Territory is the least "real" area of Australia ... the weakest moment in the articulation of the dominant discourse of "Australia"'[6] Trevor James wrote:

> For the Australian imagination the Northern Territory remained what Jeannie Gunn gave a name to—the 'Never-Never'. Even today there is no proper name, it is merely the 'Territory', a frontier separated from the 'real' Australian of popular imagination by a psychological Brisbane-line.[7]

---

2  D. Day, 'Alien in a Hostile Land: A Re-Appraisal of Australian History', *Journal of Australian Studies*, 1, 23 (November 1988), p. 4.
3  Headon, *North of the Ten Commandments*, p. xix.
4  D. Headon, 'The Most Beautiful Lies, the Ugliest Truths ... the compiling of *North of the Ten Commandments*', public lecture, Northern Territory University, 3 April 1991.
5  S. Falkiner, *The Writers' Landscape: Settlement*, vol. 2. (East Roseville, New South Wales: Simon & Schuster, 1992), p. 214.
6  J. Stratton, 'Reconstructing the Territory', *Cultural Studies* 3, 1 (1989), p. 38.
7  T. James, 'From Exploration to Celebration: Writers and the Landscape in Australia's Northern Territory', presented at a seminar on Australian literature, University of Stirling, 9–11 September 1983, p. 1.

In the writing, the Territory is seen as both a geographic and political entity distinct from the rest of Australia and as a place with its own cultural and mythic values.

Russel Ward in *The Australian Legend* commented that the archetypal Australian was an egalitarian bushman from the outback[8] and as Thomas Keneally once said, 'the region which in the imaginations of most Australians is outback *par excellence* is the Northern Territory'.[9] 'Outback' like 'Never-Never' has its existence in the imaginary rather than the corporeal world. The outback is the frontier of white Australian imagination and the Northern Territory (where car number plates read 'Outback Australia' in ochre-coloured lettering) is the geographical region where this image is regularly given literary form. For Frederick Jackson Turner, the frontier was the 'process' by which the behaviour of the frontier became codified and transformed as a celebration of American national cultural identity.[10] The Northern Territory represents a frontier to Australians, in the sense that it is seen as quintessential of a national experience. Robyn Davidson described her response to the film *Crocodile Dundee*:[11] 'There was Australia as it would like to be seen, as it would like to see itself ... under all that toughness and bravado the heart of a pussy cat and a spirit full of wilderness'.[12]

Commentators have also looked at the frontier tag for the Territory. Peter Loveday found the notion of frontier in north Australia unworkable[13] but other academics from a variety of disciplines have found the label appropriate. Alan Powell suggested that the Territory is promoted by Territorians as a frontier as a way of defining themselves as distinct in

---

8   R. Ward, *The Australian Legend* (Melbourne: Oxford University Press, 1977 (1958)), pp. 1–2.
9   T. Keneally, *Outback* (London: Hodder & Stoughton, 1984), p. 8.
10  F.J. Turner, *The Frontier in American History* (New York: Holt, Rinehart & Winston, 1962), p. 22.
11  As the discussion in *Meanjin* has demonstrated, Crocodile Dundee does not necessarily represent 'aggressive nationalism', as Davidson, 'Locating Crocodile Dundee', *Meanjin*, 46, 1 (1987), pp. 122–28; R. Abbey & J. Crawford, 'Crocodile Dundee or Davy Crockett?', *Meanjin*, 46, 2 (1987), pp. 145–52. In a neat inversion of national/regional mythology, a recently subdivided estate outside Darwin has been called 'Dundee Beach' clearly intending to evoke the Crocodile rather than Caledonian influence.
12  R. Davidson, 'The Mythological Crucible', T. Keneally, P. Adam-Smith, R. Davidson, *Australia Beyond the Dreamtime* (Richmond, Victoria: William Heinemann Australia, 1987), p. 240.
13  P. Loveday, 'Political History of the North', I. Moffat & A. Webb, eds, *North Australian Research: Some Past Themes and New Directions* (Darwin: North Australia Research Unit, The Australian National University 1991), pp. 148–49.

the Australian context.[14] Lyn Riddett regarded the Territory as a frontier as evidenced in the primitive, simple lifestyle experienced by the white settlers,[15] Russel Ward in the sense of freedom of the 'wide open spaces'.[16] Diane Bell regarded the Territory as frontier because of the perpetuation and tolerance of certain violent behaviour.[17]

Writing about the Northern Territory is characterised by the repeated use of images that are recognisable to the reader. It is possible to trace the history of the origin and the use of these images and, in some cases, the change in meaning of these images over time.

Suzanne Falkiner has noted a dichotomy inherent throughout Australian writing:

> Was Terra Australis a mythical land of invention and inversion, a paradise on earth, or a harsh terrain of death and exile? ... the last two projections of the landscape, though violently opposed, would recur frequently in Australian literature. Both ran concurrently with equally contradictory social theories in circulation at the time of settlement ... Australian writing today is still marked by a dichotomy as to whether the country represent a haven of liberty or an uncivilised place of evil.[18]

In Northern Territory writing, the boundaries between such oppositions may be fluid. Writers may assign relative worth to one side of such pairs depending on context. For instance, the bush is often a positive image associated with purity and innocence in contrast to a city with negative connotations of dirt and corruption.

Categories can be subjective and the images contradictory. For instance, a writer may contrast 'city' (negative) with 'bush' (positive) and then go on to use the images 'wilderness' (negative) and 'pioneer settlement'

---

14  Alan Powell stated: 'Heaven help us, we who live on it rather like the image, not just for the sake of tourist dollars, but because it causes us to stand out from the general mass of Australians'; A. Powell, 'In Search of a True Territorian', Inaugural Lecture by the Dean, Faculty of Arts, University College of the Northern Territory, 1988.
15  L. Riddett, *Growing Up in the Pastoral Frontier: Conception, Birth and Childhood on Cattle Stations in the NT 1920–1950 and Recreation and Entertainment on Northern Territory Pastoral Stations, 1910–1950* (Darwin: State Library of the Northern Territory, Occasional Papers, 23, 1991), p. 1.
16  Ward, *The Australian Legend*, p. 79.
17  D. Bell & T. Nelson, 'Speaking About Rape is Everyone's Business', *Women's Studies International Forum* 12, 4 (1989), p. 412.
18  S. Falkiner, *The Writers' Landscape: Wilderness*, vol. 1, (East Roseville, New South Wales: Simon & Schuster, 1992), p. 10.

(positive) yet both 'bush' and 'wilderness' signify the same physical landscape. In much of the writing about the Territory such contradiction are not overtly acknowledged although they betray an ambiguity.

I use the term 'Aborigine' for indigenous Territorians but I realise that this term, as a European construct, can be potentially offensive. Since I am dealing with the literary construction, primarily from a non-Aboriginal perspective, it has been unavoidable. Similarly, I have had to find an encompassing term for non-Aborigine. I have used the standby 'European' for white Anglo-Australian, as well as people from Britain, the United States or Europe, meaning people who broadly share the values inherent in the western tradition. 'European', while not altogether satisfactory, is less cumbersome than some other terms. Occasionally I have had to use 'white Australian' where the use of 'European' creates ambiguity. 'Non-Aboriginal' has been employed as a composite term to refer to all the persons in the Territory who are not Aborigines. The construction of the Northern Territory in literature contains these and other potentially insulting delineations of 'race' and 'colour'. I intend no offence to anyone by their use.

This publication is heavily based on my doctoral thesis but readers who would like further information may find the thesis more informative.[19] Books (unlike theses!) carry a requirement to be interesting as well as informative. To this end, some of the minutiae included in a thesis, particularly the theoretical perspectives and biographical details, have been discarded from the book. Similarly, the more obscure aspects of Northern Territory literature, which although fascinating for the aficionado, were eliminated in the editorial requirement to include mainly 'prime examples'. Readers who are interested in chasing the obscure are recommended to look at the thesis!

This study is concerned with the development of the Northern Territory as metaphor in Australian published writing. Analysis of the material suggested a broadly chronological progression of definitions. Throughout all the writing of the Northern Territory, in varying degrees, runs the common theme of the conflicting demands of European settlement against the rights of Aboriginal people. This preoccupation is fundamental to the identity and understanding of European settlement of Australia.

---

19 M. Dewar, 'In Search of the "Never-Never": The Northern Territory Metaphor in Australian Writing 1837–1992', PhD thesis, Northern Territory University, 1993.

By the twentieth century, the colonial experience of European occupation of Aboriginal land could be forgotten in the southern, more populated areas. Aborigines had been restricted to reserves or urban ghettoes, their numbers decimated by introduced disease, poverty and malnutrition. The Northern Territory, with its large, visible Aboriginal population, in contrast, provided the theatre in which a reassessment of the European settlement of Australia could be played out. The tension generated by the European occupation of the continent, the rights of its indigenous population, unacknowledged and unresolved, finds expression in the writing. Throughout the period of European settlement, the 'Northern Territory' in Australian literature has been of national cultural significance and continues to be so today.

# 1

# WRITING THE LANDSCAPE

In the nineteenth century, as a homegrown 'Australian' school of writing developed, writers looked for both subject matter and style which defined their experience as distinct from the British inheritance. Alongside the more enduring talents of Lawson, Paterson, Baynton and others, there flourished writing which focussed on the fantastic and the bizarre and featured as settings the remote parts of the continent. This writing, although unfamiliar today, would, at the time, have been instrumental in creating a mental picture of the area which was to become the Northern Territory. There was a primary preoccupation with the landscape, flora and fauna of the 'new' country. In the spirit of inquiry which pursued exploration and scientific expeditions, the newcomers to the continent explored more and more remote areas looking for new surprises and revelations. The area of land which was to become the Northern Territory was always (and some would argue remains so today) remote from the capitals of the eastern seaboard and those areas which most resembled the British villages and towns from which the settlers had come from. Perhaps because little was known about the place, the Territory was used as the location for some of the earliest period of Australian writing.

In all of the writing about the Territory, however, the landscape was a major preoccupation. Whether fantasy or anecdote, biography or reference, survival in the Territory, particularly in this early period, became firmly linked to character. The British grit of the colonial period gave way to a creed of colourful characters as the nation marched to federation. *A Mother's Offering to her Children*, published anonymously in 1838 (sometimes known as the first Australian children's book), was the first popular account to describe a recognisable location from the region that would eventually become known as the Northern Territory. In this early period most of the writing took the form of either biographical journalistic reporting on the economic potential of the landscape or fantasy adventure stories where heroes journeyed to the Centre of Australia in search of gold and lost civilisations. The landscape remained the preoccupation for the writers as the wilderness which needed to be conquered or subdued.

Little effort was made to distinguish the indigenous inhabitant of the region individually. The Aborigines, in this period, were located firmly within the landscape as another part of the assorted flora and fauna of the region, and the landscape did not always meet with the writers' approval. Mrs R Lee's 1850 novel, *Adventures in Australia*, for example, described the 'northern coast of Australia', its 'barbarous people' and 'slimy mangroves' with a kind of awed disgust. Louis Becke's description of the Northern Territory coastline in his collaborative historical novel *A First Fleet Family* (1896) was equally unequivocal:

> This part of New Holland is truly a dreadful country, for all the shores are muddy and full of crocodiles, and the woods infested with serpents; … we saw but few Indians here.[1]

But in this period, the writers were looking to describe the potential of the country from the point of potential settlement. The ability of the landscape to sustain life was considered critical. Perhaps influenced by explorer Ludwig Leichhardt's account of the Territory, writers spent considerable portions of the text on the edibility of the fauna. Mrs Lee praised the resources of the coastline and described Malay trepang and shark fin collection, and crocodile and ibis shooting—the latter tasting 'like excellent veal'.[2] Anne Bowman described an implausibly fecund Central Australia where the Mayburns killed and ate almost everything that moved—the wombat 'steaks were really excellent with sliced melon'.[3] Hope for mineral discoveries also ran high but through discovery rather than industry. Towards the end of the nineteenth century, the Territory (at least in the fictional writing) became a region of fantastic possibilities.

---

1   L. Becke & W. Jeffery, *A First Fleet Family: A Hitherto Unpublished Narrative of Certain Remarkable Adventures Compiled From the Papers of Sergeant William Dew of the Marines* (London: Fisher Unwin, 1896), pp. 234–35.
2   Mrs R. Lee, *Adventures in Australia; or, the Wanderings of Captain Spencer in the Bush and the Wilds* (London: Grant & Griffith, 1851), pp. 17–22.
3   A. Bowman, *The Kangaroo Hunters; or Adventures in the Bush* (Philadelphia: Porter & Coates, 1859), p. 313.

Commentators have noted that Carlton Dawe's *The Golden Lake* was inspired by Rider Haggard's *King Solomon's Mines*.[4] Dawe maintained that Central Australia was once the home of a sophisticated race of people whose customs included the worship of intricately constructed idols encrusted with precious stones, but that the technology and sophistication has been lost.[5] This construction was immensely popular in the late nineteenth century. James Francis Hogan's *The Lost Explorer: An Australian Story* (1890) described a party who travel to Central Australia in search of an explorer who has been lost for twenty years and discover that 'this isolated community in the heart of Australia was the sole surviving remnant of the superior, semi-civilised native race that once inhabited the interior of the great southern continent'.[6] Ernest Favenc's *The Secret of the Australian Desert* (1894) and *Marooned on Australia being the Narration by Diedrich Buys of his Discoveries and Exploits in Terra Australis Incognita* (1896) held that the Northern Territory Aborigines were degraded remnants of a great and ancient civilisation. George Cossins's *The Wing of Silence: An Australian Tale* (1899) was in much the same vein. In Alexander Macdonald's *The Lost Explorers* (1906) the party journeyed to a remote mountain range on the Western Australian, South Australian and Northern Territory borders in search of treasure and found Aborigines 'still infinitely superior in knowledge and intellect to any other aboriginal race ... but ... degenerating slowly these last many centuries'.[7] In a version of this theme, William Walker's *The Silver Queen: A Tale of the Northern Territory* (1909) described an entire race who dwelt underground, all descended from three long-ago shipwrecked mariners. Although these novels[8] were clearly fantasy and not really about the region of land which was to become the Northern Territory, they firmly planted in the mind of the British and Australian reading public that the central and northern

---

4   D. Headon, T. Scanlon, D. Carment & S. Saunders, 'Northern Territory', P. Pierce, gen. ed., *The Oxford Literary Guide to Australia* (Melbourne: Oxford University Press, 1987), p. 11.
5   W.C. Dawe, *The Golden Lake or The Marvellous History of a Journey Through the Great Lone Land of Australia* (Melbourne: Petherick, 1891), p. 123.
6   J.F. Hogan, *The Lost Explorer: An Australian Story* (London: Ward & Downey, 1890), p. 139.
7   A. Macdonald, *The Lost Explorers* (London: Blackie, n.d. [1906]), p. 360.
8   The idea that the indigenous population of the Australian continent had become degraded into a base remnant also was a convenient notion for those who supported the idea that occupation did not necessarily mean ownership. It could be argued that Aborigines did not have possession since they no longer appeared to utilise, build upon or work the land.

areas of the continent were lands of fantastic possibility.⁹ J.J. Healy argued that the novels were popular because they placed the Australian experience in the more ancient context of the western tradition.¹⁰

The early writing shared a preoccupation with the perceived emptiness and inhospitality of the landscape: 'Of the Northern Territory, it was only known that it was very big, very hot, very empty; a gap on the map, yawning for population, yet not at all a white man's land'.¹¹ Perhaps the insecurity with the subject mirrored the insecurity South Australia felt when faced with the development of its Northern Territory. The non-fictional writers were considerably less euphoric about the Territory. There was an almost immediate concern that South Australia's newest acquisition would prove a drain on the colony's resources. Charles Wentworth Dilke commented pessimistically:

> The immense northern territory, being supposed to be valueless, has generously been handed over to South Australia, which thus becomes the widest of all British colonies, and nearly as large as English Hindostan … The only important result that seems likely to follow from this annexation of the northern territory to South Australia is that schoolboys' geography will suffer.¹²

Writers in this period felt an obligation to portray an affinity with the bush landscape in order to legitimate the colonisers' right to ownership. Reality intruded occasionally in the work of those who had experienced the bush providing a glimpse of the chaotic world which defied and

---

9   These themes continued as a motif well into the writing of the twentieth century. In *The Treasure of the Tropics* 'Professor Andrews' found the remains of an ancient civilisation, B. Cronin, *The Treasure of the Tropics* (London: Ward Lock, 1928), p. 11; in *The Valley of a Thousand Deaths*, at a cave at God's Boundary Stone, the evil Sleat and Old Daftie find artwork and carvings of an incredible age. 'Old Daftie, the instincts of the scholar he once was … began to talk about the Lemurian race which peopled Australia and the Pacific, fabulous ages ago, and of which the present blacks were probably the degraded descendants', C. Sayce, (J. Bushman), *The Valley of a Thousand Deaths* (London: Blackie, n.d.), p. 163; E.V. Timms, *The Valley of Adventure: A Story for Boys* (Sydney: Angus & Robertson, 1948 (1926)), narrated the story of a trek into a hidden valley for fabulous riches only to find an extraordinary people different from Aboriginal society. The two villages in the valley are matriarchal, they worship snakes and have an island sanctuary with a huge elevated stone altar. Michael Terry's *War of the Warramullas* (1974) finished with the hypothesis that many of the carvings of Central Australia 'were executed by strangers superior in culture to our Aborigines', M. Terry, *War of the Warramullas* (Rigby: Adelaide, 1974), p. 166. The nineteenth century ideas appear to have retained considerable appeal.
10  J.J. Healy, 'The Lemurian Nineties', *Australian Literary Studies*, 8, 3 (May, 1978), p. 314.
11  C.H. Kirmess, *The Australian Crisis* (London: Walter Scott, 1909), p. 62.
12  C.W. Dilke, *Greater Britain: A Record of Travel in English-Speaking Countries During 1866 and 1867* vol. 2, (London: Macmillan, 1869), pp. 111–12.

mocked regulation by the colonists. Literary critic Trevor James found Jeannie Gunn was 'both estranged from' and 'bound to' the landscape of the Northern Territory.[13]

The Northern Territory landscape appeared as inhospitable to many of the writers who emphasised uncomfortable, strange or hostile aspects. Central Australia was seen as particularly harsh and infertile yet the protagonists frequently made mineral discoveries in this apparent barren landscape.[14] Alexander Macdonald wrote of the 'seemingly everlasting monotonous desert'.[15] James Hogan noted: 'The continuous glare from this hot and shining sand was a grievous oppression to our eyes, for there was nothing to relieve the monotony of this torrid waste save a few stunted box-trees'.[16] It was not so much the Aborigines who were the enemy, commentators noted, but the land itself.[17] The harshness imbued the land with spirituality because it threatened life.[18] The writers felt alternatively attracted to the potential, yet afraid of the extremes, of the landscape.

Surviving the harsh conditions and ability to maintain general health were the preoccupation of the writers in a time where it was felt that Europeans could not work in the tropics without suffering the consequences. J.A.G. Little, the Senior Officer at the telegraph station in Darwin noted:

> With regard to the suitability of the country for European labour, the writer of this article can affirm—after four years' experience—that a man cannot perform the amount of constant work that he is capable of accomplishing in a more moderate climate; but there is still nothing to prevent a moderate day's work being done …[19]

Much detail was included in the texts over a range of minutiae that were felt could affect the health and well-being of the prospective settlers. William Sowden described the monotony of the country and the unpleasantness

---

13  James, 'From Exploration to Celebration', p. 11.
14  G. Cossins, *The Wings of Silence: An Australian Tale* (London: Gay & Bird, 1899), p. 212; Hogan, *The Lost Explorer*, p. 84.
15  Macdonald, *The Lost Explorers*, p. 228.
16  Hogan, *The Lost Explorer*, p. 60.
17  B. Niall, *Australia Through the Looking-Glass: Children's Fiction 1830–1980* (Melbourne: Melbourne University Press, 1984), p. 183.
18  Dawe, *The Golden Lake*, p. 47.
19  J.A.G. Little, 'Climate', W. Harcus, ed., *South Australia: Its History, Resources, and Productions* (Adelaide: W.C. Cox Govt Printer, 1876), p. 98.

created by the extremes of temperature.[20] William Wildey praised the geography and climate but listed among the requirements of travel for the potential visitor to the Territory: a revolver, ammunition, suitable clothing, mosquito net, hammock, a 'large pot, with cover, of Holloway's ointment',[21] zinc powder, quinine, castor oil, two hats and a compass. He included descriptions of malaria,[22] and a host of biting pests which caused ulcers such as mosquitoes, sand flies, march flies, bung flies, tarantulas, snakes, centipedes and rats.[23] Sowden cautioned the reader against the 'ferocious horde' of mosquitoes and 'their allies' the sandflies.[24] 'Prickly heat,' Wildey noted, 'is terribly annoying to new comers, but is said to be healthy'.[25]

The writers were keen to assert their imperviousness to the hazards of the northern climate. J.G. Knight commented (mendaciously) that, 'The writer has had seven years' residence in the Territory, and never suffered an hour's sickness'.[26] In Macdonald's *The Lost Explorer*, Mackay told Bob and Jim that in Central Australia, 'The air o' this country is too dry and clear for any microbe to fancy'.[27] Health was emphasised at a time when it was paradoxically, unhealthy to live in the Northern Territory:

> 'I'm standing testimony against the lies that are told about the north. The tropics are as health as any zone upon the earth ...'
>
> 'But isn't the place full of alligators, crocodiles, pythons, bunyips, and fever and ague?'
>
> 'To be serious ... the climate is endurable, and with ordinary precaution one will suffer little from malaria. As for danger—well, that risk has to be encountered everywhere.'

---

20   W.J. Sowden, *The Northern Territory As It Is: A Narrative of the South Australian Parliamentary Party's Trip, and Full Descriptions of the Northern Territory; its Settlements and Industries*. (Darwin: History Unit, University Planning Authority. Facsimile edition, Adelaide: W.K. Thomas & Co, 1882), p. 24.
21   W.B. Wildey, *Australasia and the Oceanic Region* (Melbourne: George Robertson, 1876), p. 93.
22   Wildey, *Australasia*, p. 100.
23   Wildey, *Australasia*, pp. 125–26.
24   Sowden, *The Northern Territory*, p. 25.
25   Wildey, *Australasia*, p. 126.
26   J.G. Knight, *The Northern Territory of South Australia* (Adelaide: E. Spiller South Australian Government Printer, 1880). p. 55.
27   Macdonald, *The Lost Explorers*, p. 200.

'Ah, well, uncle, from this time forth I'll think of the Northern Territory as being as healthy as a sanatorium, as cool as an icecream, and as peaceful and safe as life in our own village.'[28]

As well as the salubrious nature of the environment, some writers emphasised the aesthetic charms. The landscape was sometimes presented in quite Arcadian terms, particularly the most northern region. Harriet Daly described Port Darwin with 'masses of rich green vegetation ... cliffs overspread with thickly growing palms ... a land of perpetual summer'.[29] Commentary about exploration and landscape generally emphasised the favourable, heroic model. Robert Caldwell's lengthy verse describing his travels through Central Australia is fairly typical in attitude if not medium:

> From the Goyder well of water clear,
> Where men and cattle drink,
> A ride of twenty miles will gain
> The valley of the Finke.
>
> This wondrous valley, fair and broad,
> South-eastward ever tends;
> It rises in the central range,
> We know not where it ends.[30]

But by the end of this period, certain accord had been reached by the writers in their attitude to the landscape. Although some nineteenth-century writers emphasised the hostile and threatening, by the early twentieth century, Bowes wrote,

> The honey blossoms of the ti-trees filled the air with a sweet fragrance, and at the same time furnished a morning meal to numerous birds and insects ... the parakeets, as they flew from tree to tree, were atoned for by the brilliant colouring they presented of turquoise blue, ruby red, sulphur yellow, rich scarlet, olive green, sea green, deep purple, together with intermediate tones and shadings. These brilliances were heightened by the sombre background of the scrub.[31]

---

28  J. Bowes, *Comrades: A Story of the Australian Bush* (London: Henry Frowde Hodder & Stoughton, 1912), pp. 23–24.
29  H.W. Daly, *Digging, Squatting and Pioneering Life in the Northern Territory of South Australia*, (Facsimile edition, Carlisle: Hesperian Press, 1984 (1887)), p. 43.
30  R. Caldwell, *In Our Great North-West or incidents and Impressions in Central Australia* (Adelaide: Bonython, 1894), p. 34.
31  Bowes, *Comrades*, p. 167.

For the most part, writers who spent any length of time in the Territory came to appreciate the landscape in a more favourable way than the journalists who came for only brief periods. Longer-term resident Alfred Searcy maintained a robust frontier enthusiasm for the exploitation of the resources of the wilderness.[32] Searcy described shooting buffalo[33] and cattle:[34] 'It always gave me intense satisfaction to know that I had rubbed out a snake, or a shark, or an alligator'.[35] Searcy's description of bird shooting indicates the settlers' exploitative attitude to the environment:

> At one time we used to get some splendid parrot-shooting on a small island known as Shell Island, on the other side of Darwin Harbour, which was a favourite camping place for a very large variety of them. We used to post ourselves just before sundown, under the trees near the mangroves, and wait the coming of the birds. As soon as they happened along, proceedings commenced, and continued until it was too dark to see them … The largest take I heard of was two hundred and fifty. Suddenly the birds ceased to turn up at the island.[36]

He described the hunting of goose, duck, wild pigs, kangaroo[37] and fishing for groper, rock-cod, schnapper, barramundi, stingray,[38] oyster, crab and dugong.[39]

Searcy rejoiced in the resources of a country that seemed unlimited:

> I have persuaded the niggers never to kill these turtle when up laying, and they have acted up to it splendidly; consequently one canoe will bring in a thousand eggs in one trip from Quail Island … We use thousands of turtle eggs annually, and I now prefer them to hen's eggs, especially when made into custard, sponge-cake, tapioca, rice or sago puddings.[40]

---

32   This attitude was shared by the explorers who frequently stressed the abundance of the landscape. For example, Francis Napier who accompanied Cadell in the search for a site for a northern capital wrote: 'we had evidently got to a breeding place of the white cockatoo; the trees on each bank were literally covered with them, like a mantle of snow. There must have been at least 50,000 of them all screeching, and making such a horrible noise that we could not hear each other speak.'; F. Napier, *Notes of a Voyage From New South Wales to the North Coast of Australia From the Journal of the Late Francis Napier* [Glasgow, 1876], p. 43.
33   A. Searcy, *In Australian Tropics*, (Facsimile edition, Carlisle: Hesperian Press, 1984 (1909)), p. 34.
34   Searcy, *In Australian Tropics*, p. 61.
35   Searcy, *In Australian Tropics*, p. 243.
36   Searcy, *In Australian Tropics*, p. 302.
37   Searcy, *In Australian Tropics*, pp. 291–97.
38   Searcy, *In Australian Tropics*, pp. 304–10.
39   Searcy does not actually catch these himself but relies upon Aboriginal labour, Searcy, *In Australian Tropics*, pp. 64–65.
40   Searcy, *In Australian Tropics*, p. 313.

Author and Customs officer Alfred Searcy; suitably attired for northern adventure.

In the early European settlement of Port Darwin, writers felt alternatively attracted by the wilderness at the same time that they were consumed by a desire to tame it. The Territory was frontier in its 'boundless' resources but the authors were conscious that 'civilisation' had come to the wilderness.

Source: Searcy A. *In Australian Tropics*, London: George Robertson & Co, 1909.
Photographer T.H. Harwood.

Nineteenth-century engraving, n.d., artist unknown, showing the 'Northern Territory—jungle near Port Darwin'.
Source: Reproduced with permission Museum and Art Gallery of the Northern Territory PR 00247.

The boundless resources of the untamed wilderness presented an abundance to sustain the incomer. But for the first writers, that wilderness was not yet populated. It would take a writer like Jeannie Gunn to move the protagonists from two-dimensional heroes to flesh and blood individuals who then inhabited and, indeed, became heirs to the Territory. This model proved so popular that it has yet to be finally extinguished from Territory writing.

2

# THE PEOPLE

In the literature, people were, and always have been, difficult to isolate from the Territory landscape, although initially the early white settlers tried very hard. In the earliest accounts of the settlement of Palmerston (as Darwin was originally known) considerable efforts appear to have been made to recreate the conditions and lifestyles that the settlers had come from. The few white women, particularly, maintain this perspective. Harriet Daly's descriptions of the primitive conditions of Palmerston camp cover musical evenings, picnics, 'admirers' and she noted that: 'the men dressed with most scrupulous neatness. They wore the whitest shirts and prettiest neckties imaginable'.[1] But other settlers evidently found relief in a lifestyle remote from the niceties of settled life. Paterson and Searcy both stressed that the Territory was a refuge for men and women who wished to live outside the law.[2] Bowes wrote, 'The Northern Territory ... was too remote to have any allurement save to the most adventurous ... the hiding-place of hardened criminals'.[3] This begins a kind of dichotomy about Territory writing that continues today. The writing is frequently critical of the dress standards and formality—which are considered essential, particularly for the towns—while at the same time there is a rejoicing in a sense of anarchy and lawlessness in the Territory bush.

Wildey gave a detailed description of the Palmerston and Southport shops and amenities which suggested some degree of civilisation. He noted that the best quarters in Palmerston were those of the employees of the British

---

1 Daly, *Digging, Squatting and Pioneering Life*, p. 6.
2 Searcy, *In Australian Tropics*, pp. 111, 163.
3 Bowes, *Comrades,* p. 49.

Australia Telegraph Company. 'Their rooms are lofty, and the walls of the office are thick. They have a fine billiard table, piano and some have wives.'[4] The construction of amenities and services served to denote the priorities of the settler. Although Wildey noted that the town had a chemist, tailor, cordial maker and restaurant at the time of his writing, the funds were still being raised for a church. Sowden noted a high alcohol consumption as part of the Territory lifestyle[5] as well as a marked informality: 'on the first morning I arrived I presented a letter of introduction to a high official who disguised his physical conformation by a bath-towel only'.[6]

Most writers of this period looked forward to a future where the Northern Territory ceased to represent a wilderness and had become civilised. Like Daly and Sowden there was a celebration in prose of the urban amenities of a comfortable life. The writers looked to a future where only a European society occupied the land. The first and last stanzas of Ernest Favenc's poem, 'An Ideal of the Future', summed up this nineteenth century optimism for a tamed landscape and also anticipated the attempts to minimise Aboriginal occupation:

> Shunned and dreaded; untrodden, drear;
> A realm of hunger, of thirst, of fear,
> The desert heart of Australia lies—
> An iron land-beneath brazen skies …
>
> The iron horse has bridged the space
> That only camel before dared face …
> And children play in the grassy glade
> Where the lost explorers' bones are laid.[7]

A popular theory of the period was that the hardships of European settlement in the north provided a way of sorting out the worth of a newcomer. C.H. Kirmess wrote, 'It has been said that the Northern Territory was not a white man's land … The truth is that it was, and is the land of the worker; only to the loafer is the climate enervating'.[8] Jeannie Gunn regarded those who responded favourably to the landscape with the proposal that the Territory could be seen as a testing ground for character and integrity:

---

4   Wildey, *Australasia*, p. 90.
5   Sowden, *The Northern Territory*, p. 141.
6   Sowden, *The Northern Territory*, p. 147.
7   E. Favenc, *Voices of the Desert* (London: Elliott Stock, 1905), pp. 20–22.
8   Kirmess, *The Australian Crisis*, p. 34.

whatever their rank or race, our travellers were men, not riff-raff; the long, formidable stages that wall in the Never-Never have seen to that, turning back the weaklings and worthless to the flesh-pots of Egypt, and proving the worth and mettle of the brave-hearted.[9]

Whatever the motivation and views of the settlers, they all shared a primary preoccupation with making money. At the same time, personal fortunes somehow became identified with the overall success of the Territory. Almost every writer paused in the narrative at least once to give an active promotion to the economic potential of the Territory. J.C. Knight praised the region's potential in the face of growing South Australian doubts:

> During his holiday in Adelaide he has met with some who deplore that the Territory was ever taken over by South Australia, and call it a 'White Elephant'! To such gloomy people he has said, 'Try to induce those in authority to sell the animal in question, as he has "a friend in the city" ready to pay a good price for the neglected creature, and to cultivate choice produce for its future nourishment'.[10]

Harriet Daly asserted confidently, 'South Australia's "white elephant" was really going to prove a valuable possession after all!'[11] Wildey believed that for, 'a comparatively small national outlay, ... the south would discover that the north is anything but a white elephant'.[12] In a familiar echo of sentiments, Sowden commented that the reader, 'will be convinced that that extreme northern country of ours, which we have called by courtesy the Northern Territory ... is a rich possession which other colonies well might envy us'.[13] Searcy concurred: 'This vast portion of our Territory has never been explored ... the possibilities are simply immense'.[14] In 1901 J. Langdon Parsons, South Australian Member of the Legislative Council and sometime Minister for the Northern Territory, advised that, 'The Northern Territory is intrinsically certainly worth a great deal more than its liabilities'.[15]

---

9   Mrs A. Gunn, *We of the Never-Never* (Richmond: Hutchinson, 1977 (1908), p. 57.
10  Knight, *The Northern Territory*, p. 55.
11  Daly, *Digging, Squatting and Pioneering Life*, p. 140.
12  Wildey, *Australasia*, p. 136.
13  Sowden, *The Northern Territory*, p. 3.
14  Searcy, *In Australian Tropics*, p. 198.
15  Admittedly this was not an unbiased account. Parsons wrote the pamphlet with a view to interest the Commonwealth in taking over from South Australia the responsibility for its Northern Territory administration. M.W. Holtze & Hon. J.L. Parsons M.L.C., *The Northern Territory of South Australia* (Adelaide: W.K. Thomas, 1901), p. 15.

There was consensus between the writers from this period that the north should be settled, if only to establish a territorial claim on behalf of white Australia. But paralleling this sentiment was an acknowledgment that not as much had been achieved under South Australian control as had been anticipated at the beginning of their administration. Kirmess was a firm exponent of the 'empty north' theory of settlement which demanded that European settlement take place to exclude the possibility of Asian settlement from the north: 'A great deal depends on successful white settlement in the North. So far little has been achieved'.[16] Herbert Parsons wrote that, 'South Australia has had its White Elephant. We have tended it to the best of our ability. We have made mistakes ... Meanwhile our north is empty, quite empty, and it is costing South Australia £130,000 a year to keep it empty'.[17] But Jessie Ackermann viewed the results of the Commonwealth administration with nearly as much pessimism:

> the white elephant of the Northern Territory recklessly thrusts its mighty trunk in to the common treasury of the people, gulping down bushels of gold coins of the realm; with the result that it merely waxes fat, and its enlarged proportions render it an increasing problem for the Commonwealth and a genuine curiosity to the world.[18]

Although a minority, some writers had to admit that during this period, the Territory had actually produced very little revenue for the administering agency, whether the New South Wales, South Australia or Federal Governments.

But this period encompassed the depression of the 1890s and understandably, as pastoral leases were abandoned throughout the Top End, the economic potential of the Northern Territory seemed bleak. Banjo Paterson's *An Outback Marriage* looked at some of the hardships of the pastoral industry and detailed the fate of many in the difficult economic conditions of the 1890s:

> And I slaved like a driven nigger, day in and day out, brandin' calves all day long in the dust, with the sun that hot, the brandin' iron 'ud mark without puttin' it in the fire at all. And then down comes the tick, and kills my cattle by the hundred, dyin' and perishin' all over the place. And what lived through it I couldn't sell anywhere, because they won't let tick-

---

16  Kirmess, *The Australian Crisis*, p. 335.
17  H.A. Parsons, *The Truth About the Northern Territory: An Enquiry* (Adelaide: Hussey & Gillingham, 1907), pp. 70, 72.
18  J. Ackermann, *Australia From a Woman's Point of View* (Melbourne: Cassell, 1981 (1913)), p. 26.

infested cattle go south, and the Dutch won't let us ship 'em north to Java, the wretches! And then Mr. Grant's debt was over everything; and at last I had to chuck it up. That's how I got broke, Mister. I hope you'll have better luck.[19]

Notwithstanding the economic downturn described so vividly by Paterson, pastoral leases were seen as the embodiment of the 'real' Territory. Even in the nineteenth century, the Northern Territory urban settlements, such as they were, were described prosaically. The theatre of myth-making was the outback, the Never-Never, where the men were all characters and mates. Police Constable William Willshire sharply differentiated between the 'practical bushmen ... brave pioneers who push out to the frontier'[20] and 'Nincompoops'[21] from the cities. There are the beginnings of the idea that the heroes of the Northern Territory are bigger, stronger, braver and more adventurous than heroes elsewhere: 'When Tom Noble had his grip on a man's arm there were few in the Northern Territory who could shake themselves free'.[22]

A part of the celebration of the bush ideal was in the relationship shared by the men of the Territory. Willshire, although uncharacteristically brief on the subject of male friendships, included a dedication to 'a practical bushman' in the preface to *Land of the Dawning*. Close friendship between males was an accepted part of the bush ethos. In *The Golden Lake* Dick Hardwicke and his cousin Archie are great friends, which not even the rivalry for the hand of the beautiful maiden, Ada ('Laughing Hair'), can threaten. The title of Joseph Bowes's *Comrades* is self-explanatory. In *An Outback Marriage*, such different characters as Charlie Gordon and the English 'new chum' Carew, Hugh and bushman Tommy Prince become friends. In *The Australian Crisis*, Thomas Burt and 'the Yorkshireman' are friends committed to stopping the Japanese invasion of the Northern Territory. Mateship was the topic of much discussion by Territory writers, and surprisingly female writers as well. This was despite it being presented as a completely masculine ritual, often involving individuals from different classes, from which women were strictly excluded. Harriet Daly commented of the custom,

---

19   A.B. Paterson, *An Outback Marriage* (Sydney, Angus & Robertson, 1906), p. 148.
20   W.C. Willshire, *The Land of the Dawning: Being Facts Gleaned from Cannibals in the Australian Stone Age* (Adelaide: W.K. Thomas & Co, 1896), p. 52.
21   Willshire, *The Land of the Dawning*, p. 90.
22   H. Strang, *The Air Scout: A Story of National Defence* (London: Henry Frowde Hodder & Stoughton, 1912), p. 323.

> A 'mate' was a 'mate'—share and share alike … some cases of devotion that were met with were quite touching; and very often to all appearances the pair were not always mated from the same class of society. Could one have known the past histories of some of the oddly-selected couples who shared everything in common, many a romance might have been written …[23]

Harriet Daly's attitudes are epitomised in the long story describing 'Gentleman George' and his death in the bush. Two interesting elements are contained in the narrative which will become paradigms in descriptions of the Territory: firstly, that mateship transcends the usual class barriers and that secondly, men take to the bush as solace for a broken romance.[24] Daly's account opens with both mates dressed in rough clothes and travelling steerage, but George displayed 'the little things that mark a man of refinement'. The loyal Bill was a 'smart, tall, well set-up old soldier, extremely devoted to his mate, and he waited upon him … as assiduously as the most perfectly trained London valet'. Their story has all the elements of Victorian melodrama: the come-down (and uppance) of a decent man, who was betrayed by a woman, Marion, when George's 'governor' 'poisoned the girl's mind' against George. George's governor is clearly a rotter paradoxically because 'he had a wonderful influence over women'. The tragedy continued with Marion unable to resist 'so grand a match … as Lord Angerford'. But Marion wears George's flower at her throat at the wedding and pleads that 'we shall always be friends, won't we?'. But George is off to 'Hindostan' where 'I played hard, I drank hard, I rode hard, and … If it hadn't been for my mother I would willingly have gone to the dog altogether'. George eventually dies of fever calling for his mother and forgiving Marion. Bill's 'tears flowed freely as he closed those beautiful eyes, into whose luminous depths no mortal would ever look again' and marvelling to the narrator how 'Mr George … was a real gentleman … it was share and share alike down to the last pipe o'baccy'. Harriet comments that the story has been included both because it was touching and because it was 'a somewhat typical incident in gold-digging

---

23   Daly, *Digging, Squatting and Pioneering Life*, p. 152.
24   Dino Hodge has argued convincingly of the strong homosexual element inherent in bush mateship using George and Bill's relationship as one example: D. Hodge, 'A History of Top End Sodomy 1840s–1970s', draft, 1992, pp. 3f; this theme was further developed in D. Hodge, *Did You Meet Any Malagas? A Homosexual History of Australia's Tropical Capital* (Darwin: Little Gem, 1993).

life'.²⁵ Mothers, like mates, were sacred to the bushmen. As Macdonald's bushman, Mackay, in *The Lost Explorers* points out to the lads, 'ye can never get a truer friend than yer mother, an' I hope ye'll no forget that'.²⁶

But mothers, if they are mentioned at all, are always very far away from the action of the texts. Mates on the other hand are by definition always there. Jeannie Gunn narrated a story comparable with Harriet Daly's. Also, like Daly, Gunn managed to imply that there was something more noble and higher spiritually in male friendship than in anything that could be experienced by a woman: 'Then a man rode into our lives who was to teach us the depth and breath of the meaning of the word mate'. A man rode in with news that his mate was sick with malaria. The hospitable Gunns offered to send the station buck-board out for him or ride out to bring him in. The man,

> flushed hotly and stammered: 'If you please, ma'am. If the boss'll excuse me, me mate's dead set against a woman doing things for him. If you wouldn't mind not coming. He'd rather have me. Me and him's been mates this seven years. The boss'll understand.'²⁷

The Maluka (Gunn) did understand. For three days the man lay out bush very ill, being assisted by his mate and men from Elsey, until he became so ill he had to be brought in to the homestead anyway. The Maluka thought he would pull through but unfortunately he died and had to be buried at Elsey. The mate only breaks down when the Maluka refused payment for services by saying: 'We give no charity here: only hospitality to our guests. Surely no man would refuse that.' Jeannie interprets this sensitivity as the superiority of males and notes that, 'daily the bushman put the woman to shame'.²⁸

Mateship, it can be assumed, was a part of the isolation and loneliness of the bush. In the light of this Jeannie Gunn presents a paradoxical view of the remoteness of pastoral life. Elsey Station received a regular mail service eight times a year and Gunn noted, 'Two hundred and fifty guest was the tally for that year'. Elsey Station was itself within an hour's ride of the Overland Telegraph Line.²⁹

---

25  Daly, *Digging, Squatting and Pioneering Life*, pp. 153–69.
26  Macdonald, *The Lost Explorers*, p. 27.
27  Gunn, *We of the Never-Never*, p. 146.
28  Gunn, *We of the Never-Never*, pp. 145–51.
29  Gunn, *We of the Never-Never*, pp. 58–60.

### Jeannie Gunn.

Author Jeannie Gunn provided a construction of Northern Territory life in her two autobiographical novels *The Little Black Princess and We of the Never Never* which endures to this day. Jeannie and the bush 'characters' she created were based upon real people who rapidly achieved a mythological status in their own lifetimes. Her writing gained enormous popularity and *The Little Black Princess* was a prescribed primary school textbook for decades.

Source: Reproduced with permission. Northern Territory Library, Bucknall Collection PH147/68.

The bush characters. V.C. Raymond (The Dandy), Tom Pearce (Mine Host), David Suttie (Quiet Stockman), John McCarthy (Irish Mac).

Source: Reproduced with permission, Northern Territory Library, Spillett Collection PH238/2090.

The contradiction that the 'outback', although covering vast distances, contained a good information network linking all people who travelled there was a problem for the true 'bush man'.[30] This misanthropic stance of retreating away from the company of fellow individuals was somehow seen as a virtue and part of the prerequisite of a good bushman. Bushmen are described by Gunn as 'characters' but it is probably more correct to say caricatures. These images of the lovable bushmen—'The Maluka', 'The Sanguine Scot', 'The Head Stockman', 'The Dandy', 'The Quiet Stockman', ' The Fizzer', 'Mine Host', 'The Wag', and so on—haunt the pages of *We of the Never-Never*. Following a Lawson-like tradition, Jeannie Gunn portrayed bushmen invariably[31] as gentle, kind, anti-social, abstainers or alcoholics.[32] This became a popular way of dealing with the laconic men of the Territory outback that was much used after Gunn.

A central theme of all Territory writers was the role played by Aboriginal people and their relationships to the European communities. There was very little in the Aboriginal population that the European writers found to praise, although they frequently went to great lengths to indiscriminately document aspects of Aboriginal language and culture.[33] This habit continued as a theme of the writing with Europeans interpreting and defining Aboriginal culture, as they saw it, right up to the contemporary period. As with the descriptions of lifestyle and environment, there was a sharp delineation between the urban and the bush experiences. Europeans uniformly throughout Territory writing preferred Aborigines living in the bush, away from urban centre of population. Although descriptions of Aborigines in the bush are hardly those of noble savages, they are considerably less negative than accounts of Aborigines living in

---

30  Gunn, *We of the Never-Never*, p. 37.
31  Not quite invariably but near enough. Jeannie Gunn mentions the one exception to the bush rule: a man who refuses to deliver mail to a neighbour he is on bad terms with thus contravening the bush code. Gunn, *We of the Never-Never*, p. 202.
32  Gunn, *We of the Never-Never*, pp. 90, 110, 130.
33  For example, Sowden, *The Northern Territory*, recorded language groups around Palmerston, p. 26; Daly, *Digging and Squatting* differentiated between tribal groups, e.g. pp. 70, 261; Wildey, *Australasia*, included language groups and country, health, tribal practices and relationship to the European community at Palmerston, pp. 114–20; Jeannie Gunn described many of the beliefs and customs practised by the Elsey people of corroborees, avoidance, sophisticated sign language, sacred sites, message sticks and smoke signals, respect for traditional law and clearly recognised the subordinate role white people play in Aboriginal society; Mrs A. Gunn, *The Little Black Princess of the Never-Never* (Sydney: Angus & Robertson, 1962 (1905)), pp. 14f, 24, 37–42, 55, 62, 67.

or near towns.³⁴ From the initial period of settlement, Europeans espoused contempt when Aborigines lived in situations of propinquity. Aboriginal camps were moved further away from Port Darwin in 1874 because of complaints about proximity.³⁵

Harriet Daly herself was surprised to note the presence of the Larrakia so close to European settlement. Harriet, while romanticising about the scenery, did not romanticise about the Larrakia whom she regarded as 'the least interesting specimens of at best an uninteresting race'.³⁶ Sowden too found the Larrakia were 'degraded specimens of humanity!—less manlike some than a grinning chattering monkey looking at them from the hotel door'.³⁷ Although Wildey considered the Aborigines 'warlike and treacherous' cannibals, he did not see them as a source of danger:

> The natives are but little feared, and seldom seen. They know everyone to be well-armed, and so are inspired with a wholesome fear of the white man. Moreover, they have been invariably carefully and kindly treated by the government. In fact, in the Territory it is a common saying that the killing of a native would be more quickly followed up and avenged by the Adelaide Government, than would be the killing of a white man by a native.³⁸

Daly also did not believe the Aborigines were any threat to European settlement at Port Darwin³⁹ but saw them as dangerous to European settlement elsewhere.⁴⁰

In Central Australia containment of the Aboriginal population was considered an issue. Although in *A Thrilling Tale* (1895) Willshire argued for the European man to stay out of Aboriginal country because

---

34  As Patrick Wolfe noted, 'the incorporation of blacks into white society split into two the ambivalent post-Enlightenment image of savagery, attaching its negative side to the acculturated, leaving the good savage (or "bush black") as a completely good residue but always somewhere else. The ideal was a formula for imposing liability upon its empirical counterparts. Thus the romantic ideal and the repugnant hybrid represent opposite sides of the single message that bad savages do not deserve the land and good savages do not use it.' P. Wolfe, 'On Being Woken Up: The Dreamtime in Anthropology and in Australian Settler Culture', *Comparative Studies in Society and History* 33, 2 (April 1991), p. 215.
35  H. Reynolds, *With the White People* (Ringwood: Penguin, 1990), p. 144.
36  Daly, *Digging, Squatting and Pioneering Life*, pp. 45, 67.
37  Sowden, *The Northern Territory*, p. 28.
38  Wildey, *Australasia*, p. 99.
39  Daly, *Digging, Squatting and Pioneering Life*, p. 182.
40  Daly, *Digging, Squatting and Pioneering Life*, pp. 261–63.

a European presence would ultimately result in Aboriginal destruction,[41] by the time he wrote *Land of the Dawning* (1896), Willshire believed that the Aborigine were savage cannibals[42] and that they should be controlled by the establishment of ration depots.[43] There was a sense that the Territory citizen felt themselves to be justified in taking the law into their own hands and not to be judged by the standards held elsewhere in Australia by, 'the far-away sympathisers … in the security of their own houses'.[44] Police Constable Willshire argued that people outside the Territory were not fit to comment upon Territory practices (in a sentiment still expressed in the Territory today): 'Many have the arguments and controversies about the aborigine of Australia, and those who live in large cities in luxury and know the least about them, are the ones who sympathise with them'.[45]

But the writers of the adventure stories revelled in the threat that the Aborigines posed to the brave Europeans. It is almost a necessary component of the adventure yarn that the natives are stronger and more fearless in the land of the writer's experience than elsewhere. The idea that the Aborigines of the north coast were different—that is, stronger, more aggressive, more intelligent, fearless—had been repeated to a lesser or greater extent by the Northern Territory explorers Flinders,[46] Leichhardt[47] and Lindsay.[48] Searcy commented that the Aborigines of the Northern Territory:

> were far and away superior, both in physique and intelligence, to the natives down south. It must be remembered that the food-supply available for the niggers on the north coast was unlimited … This, taken in conjunction with their long association with the Malays, may be the explanation of the superior type of the aborigines of the north coast of Australia.[49]

---

41  W.C. Willshire, *A Thrilling Tale of Real Life in the Wilds of Australia* (Adelaide: Freason & Brother, 1895), p. 17; Willshire, *The Land of the Dawning*, p. 15.
42  Willshire, *The Land of the Dawning*, pp. 16, 34, 42, 65, etc.
43  Willshire, *The Land of the Dawning*, p. 67.
44  Daly, *Digging, Squatting and Pioneering Life*, p. 262.
45  Willshire, *The Land of the Dawning*, p. 7.
46  M. Flinders, *A Voyage to Terra Australis*, vol. 2 (London: G. & W. Nicol, 1814), p. 205.
47  F.W.L. Leichhardt, *Journal of an Overland Expedition in Australia from Moreton Bay to Port Essington* (London: T. & W. Boone, 1847), p. 455.
48  D. Lindsay, 'Mr D. Lindsay's Explorations Through Anaheim's Land', *South Australian Parliamentary Papers*, 239, (8 February 1884), p. 15.
49  Searcy, *In Australian Tropics*, p. 36.

Wildey concurred.[50] Alongside this picture of superior strength was the accompanying notion of Northern Territory Aborigines as powerfully evil, crafty or fiendish who were depicted as cannibals,[51] child murderers[52] and brutish aggressive savages.[53] In Dawe's *The Golden Lake*, Kalua and his priest Wanjula are cowardly, crafty and vicious and the population superstitious and simple, although the beautiful Lusota is an exception.[54] Louis de Rougemont, who for the most part had a favourable opinion of the Aborigines, was critical of the role of Aboriginal women whom he saw as completely exploited by the males.[55] The belief in the primitiveness and savagery of the Aborigines was assumed by all authors in the writing from this period.

Contrasted to the 'wild blacks' were the 'tame' assistants and Dawe, Cossins and Favenc all emphasised the role of the Aboriginal guide in the narrative: Jimmy, 'King of the Murrumbidgee',[56] Marna,[57] and in Favenc's *The Secret of the Australian Desert*, Billy Button assists Morton, Brown and Charlie to find the answer to the riddle of the disappearance of the Leichhardt expedition. The construction of Aborigines could be considered merely a literary device[58] in contrast to the more realistic portrait of the guides, but it is difficult to separate the two. The reader is left with Favenc's picture of Aboriginal savagery and violence. Cheryl Frost cited *The Bulletin* comment: 'One notes with interest how unconsciously Mr Favenc takes the bushmen's view of relationships with the blacks'.[59]

Implicit in all the accounts written about the Territory from this period is a casual acceptance of violence in race relations. Paterson's fictional account of the Territory described punitive expeditions conducted by the pastoralist, Considine:

---

50   Wildey, *Australasia*, p. 114.
51   E. Favenc, *The Secret of the Australian Desert* (London: Blackie, 1894), pp. 64–65.
52   Cossins, *The Wings of Silence*, pp. 1–2, 187.
53   Bowes, *Comrades*, p. 219.
54   Dawe, *The Golden Lake*, pp. 213f, 266.
55   L. de Rougemont, *The Adventures of Louis de Rougemont As Told by Himself* (London: George Newnes, 1899), pp. 102–3.
56   Dawe, *The Golden Lake*, p. 33.
57   Cossins, *The Wings of Silence*, pp. 186–87.
58   R. Wighton, *Early Australian Children's Literature* (Surrey Hills, Victoria: Casuarina, 1979 (1963)), p. 35.
59   Red Page quoted, C. Frost, *The Last Explorer: The Life and Work of Ernest Favenc* (Townsville: James Cook University Foundation for Australian Literary Studies, Monograph 9, 1983), p. 60.

'I kep' the wild blacks from scarin' 'em to death, and spearin' of 'em, as is their nature to, and I got speared myself in one or two little shootin' excursions I had.'

'Shooting the blacks?' interpolated Gordon.

'Somethin' like that, Mister. I did let off a rifle a few times, and I dessay one or two poor, ignorant black feller-countrymen that had been fillin' my cattle as full of spears as so many hedgehogs—I dessay they got in the road of a bullet or two. They're always gettin' in the road of things.'[60]

Searcy in the section on shooting for sport commented: 'On one occasion I nearly bagged a nigger'.[61] His casual descriptions of other Europeans' attitudes to Aborigines are equally chilling: 'In one instance, so a man told me who was concerned in it, a whole nigger camp was wiped out'. Searcy noted another practice which 'seemed awfully brutal to me' when a man commented: 'When I want to be particularly severe ... I cut the top off a sapling and sharpen the remaining stump, bend it down and drive it through the palms of both hands of the nigger'.[62] Searcy used euphemisms and phrases which disguised the reality of what he was talking about. 'Potting', 'bagging', 'interfered with', 'wiped out', 'bad for the health of',[63] rather than killing, murdering or shooting, all combine to make a superficial reading of this book seem less offensive than it is. But these callous attitudes were widespread. Crucial to the development of Favenc's story, 'The Hut-Keeper and the Cattle-Stealer', is disbelief in the notion that anyone could feel serious remorse for ruthlessly slaughtering Aboriginal families.[64] In *Comrades* violence is seen as natural and inevitable.[65] Macdonald had his heroes shoot Aborigines on sight and only once in *The Lost Explorers* was there any suggestion of deviation from this behaviour when Bob pleads that 'It seems almost like murder' to shoot an Aborigine silhouetted against the skyline who is gesticulating and warning the party not to proceed.[66]

---

60  Paterson, *An Outback Marriage*, pp. 147–48.
61  Searcy, *In Australian Tropics*, p. 297.
62  Searcy, *In Australian Tropics*, p. 174.
63  Searcy, *In Australian Tropics*, p. 113.
64  E. Favenc, *Tales of the Austral Tropics* (London: Osgood, McIlvaine, 1894), p. 133.
65  Bowes, *Comrades*, pp. 78, 208.
66  Macdonald, *The Lost Explorers*, p. 278.

Although Willshire had been the first writer to concentrate upon the subject of Territory Aborigines and Spencer and Gillen had produced *The Native Tribes of Central Australia* in 1899, it was Jeannie Gunn who achieved widespread popularity with her description of the Aborigines from Elsey Station in *The Little Black Princess of the Never-Never*. Written for children, the book described Jeannie's relationship with a young Aboriginal girl, Bett-Bett. Jeannie herself was the only European in the narrative which was almost entirely centred around the Aboriginal community. Up to this point in the literary construct of the Territory, Aborigines had not been described in any way that suggested anything like humanity. This now changed with the writing of *The Little Black Princess*.

Jeannie Gunn wrote of her relationship with the Aboriginal women that she 'was the pupil, and they were the teachers'[67] and her praise for them was practically unconditional:

> I never laughed at their strange beliefs. I found them wonderfully interesting, for I soon saw that under every silly little bit of nonsense was a great deal of good sense. At first it appears great nonsense to tell the young men that fat turkeys and kangaroo tails will make them old and weak; but it does not seem so silly when we know that it is only a black-fellow's way of providing for old age.[68]

Until *The Little Black Princess*, there had been no instances describing friendship between Europeans and Aborigines in the literature of the Northern Territory.[69] Aborigines were shown to have forged other relationships with Europeans; particularly with fugitive convicts, and as helpers or assistants to explorers, police and pastoralists. As sexual partners, Aboriginal women have been identified by European women as

---

67  Gunn, *The Little Black Princess*, pp. 27–28.
68  Gunn, *The Little Black Princess*, p. 14.
69  Henry Reynolds has looked at the inter-relationship between Aborigines and settlers in exploration and development throughout the colonisation of the continent in *With the White People*. Inter-racial friendship does not appear in Northern Territory literature in this early period before Jeannie Gunn and indeed rarely after. John Lewis's account of his relationship with Nanyena and Carl Warburton's descriptions of Koperaki, Chapter 4, suggest a degree of mutual intimacy. After the publication of W.E.H. Stanner's *White Man Got No Dreaming: Essays 1938–1973* (Canberra: The Australian National University, 1979), with the moving account contained in 'Durmugam: A Nangiomeri', anthropologists begin to admit emotional ties with the subjects of their study. Recent literature tends to emphasise the divisive nature of Territory racial relations, although Robyn Davidson seems to evidence a friendship with Mr Eddy, *Tracks* (London: Granada, 1981), and *Travelling Light* (Sydney: Collins Australia, 1989).

'sisters in subordination—and labour'[70]—but the occasions have involved either the Aborigines or the Europeans abandoning their own set of values for that of the other culture.

At the conclusion to the story, the 'orphaned' Bett-Bett returns to her own country and people, to fulfil her obligations to kin and clan, which Jeannie ascribed to the Aboriginal bush hunger.[71] Jeannie felt 'strangely lonely' but she recognised that it was an inevitable part of her relationship to the Aborigines of Elsey. In the end they belonged to another world. Goggle Eye died, and Bett-Bett returned to the bush. Jeannie Gunn coped with and described the interface between the European and Aboriginal worlds with sensitivity and perception, and she was the first Territory writer to do so.

Despite this there is an absence of an account of violence toward the Aborigines around Elsey. Searcy mentioned Aeneas Gunn in the context of 'potting niggers' yet Jeannie is quiet about this.[72] Searcy was referring to Gunn's earlier stay in the Territory but perhaps some of the practices he followed then, he either did not do now or did not tell Jeannie about. Accounts have been collected from Aboriginal people from the Elsey area which describe the 'Sanguine Scot', John ('Jock') MacLennon, as encouraging inter-group rivalry and condoning the murdering of Aborigines. MacLennon armed his Aboriginal station hands and if a 'bush black' was shot, no questions were asked.[73] Although Jeannie Gunn had acknowledged that, 'The white man has taken the country from the black fellow ... until he is willing to make recompense by granting fair liberty of travel, and a fair percentage of cattle ... cattle killing, and at times even man killing, by blacks will not be an offence against the white folk',[74] a 'nigger hunt' was considered a vital part of Jeannie's bush education:

---

70   D. Spender, *Writing a New World: Two Centuries of Australian Women Writers* (Sydney: Allen & Unwin, 1988), p. xvi.
71   Gunn, *The Little Black Princess*, p. 105.
72   Searcy, *In Australian Tropics*, p. 29.
73   F. Merlan, 'Making People Quiet in the Pastoral North: Reminiscences of Elsey Station', *Aboriginal History* 2, 1 (1978), pp. 2–3.
74   Gunn, *We of the Never-Never*, p. 185.

and it was a forgone conclusion that our 'nigger hunt' would only involve the captured with general discomfiture; but the Red Lilies being a stronghold of the tribe, and a favourite hiding-place for 'outsiders', emergencies were apt to occur down the river', and we rode out of camp with rifles unslung and revolvers at hand.[75]

This raises the question, how much did Jeannie Gunn know about Elsey Station's policy to reduce cattle spearing? The juxtaposition of the ideas of a 'nigger hunt' and 'recompense' for European occupation suggests that Jeannie Gunn was ignorant of the Elsey Station practices of arming station Aborigines to shoot Aboriginal 'trespassers'. Whether Jeannie was shielded from these practices or whether coincidentally or intentionally they did not occur in the period of her occupation of Elsey cannot be ascertained.

A peculiar aspect of Jeannie Gunn's writing which suggests a conscious or unconscious acknowledgment of the dislocation between the bushman myths and the actuality of race relations, is the complete polarisation of European and Aboriginal experiences in the two books. *The Little Black Princess* is almost exclusively about her relationship to the Aboriginal people of Elsey. In contrast, *We of the Never-Never* hardly mentions an Aboriginal presence at all. Jeannie was already proclaiming the finiteness of the bush, in the Northern Territory, by 1902. This sense of the end of the frontier is apparent in other texts from the period as well. The 'half-caste' hero of W.S. Walker's *The Silver Queen* declaimed to his Aboriginal followers, 'We can neither prevent nor resist a further encroachment of civilisation'.[76] It is true that in a comparison with Harriet Daly, a great deal seems to have taken place in the Northern Territory. The image of the bush of the Northern Territory populated by wild white men contrasts that of Daly's where the bush is full of wild black men. By the turn of the century, Jeannie Gunn's bush, although equally large, seems populated by large moving groups of Europeans, and to a much lesser extent, Aborigines, but never constituted in the same place at the same time.

In *We of the Never-Never* there is a surprising absence of the work performed by Aborigines. They are described as in the garden, chopping wood and carrying out other sundry tasks, but where it might be expected that they would be described employed as stockworkers, there is a surprising shortage of information. Searcy has already mentioned the Northern

---

75   Gunn, *We of the Never-Never*, pp. 182–86.
76   W.S. Walker, *The Silver Queen: A Tale of the Northern Territory* (London: Ouseley, 1909), pp. 330–31.

Territory pastoral industry's dependence upon Aboriginal labour[77] yet there is a dearth of information about their role on Elsey Station. The Quiet Stockman is the horsebreaker, Dan, the Head Stockman is the font of information on the behaviour of cattle, and the Dandy does such sensitive manual work as digging graves. The Aboriginal stockworkers—'boys'—are described variously as having a separate camp 'their lubras with them'[78] and of imitating the Chinese drovers[79] but the reader could well feel that they are a minor adjunct to the business of running a pastoral property. It is curious that Jeannie gives such little detail on this, when she has written extensively of the Aboriginal role in the household. Perhaps this absence can be explained by the fact that much of the station work involved Aboriginal women and European men which possibly did not occur when she went out mustering. The main jobs in the pastoral industry which would usually have been performed by women, are then taken on by men because of the presence of a European woman. Jeannie appears to have stayed in and around the main camp while other groups came and went so the behaviour she observed may not have been typical.

Although the settlers of the Northern Territory sought to come to terms with the Aboriginal populations, that was only part of the process towards forging European settlement in the north. In the Northern Territory of the nineteenth century, Europeans were very much in a minority. The geographer W. Howchin commented that, 'The great want is the development of suitable industries and an increase of population'.[80] The tropical Northern Territory, it was feared, was much more suitable for Asian rather than Anglo-European settlement: 'The tropical country was in every way better suited to the Chinese than to men of European stock'.[81] Some commentators feared that land-hungry Asiatics would take over the place by force but for others, cheap indentured Asian labour offered both the population and the labour the Territory required. *The Australian Crisis* (1909) was written, Kirmess claimed, to alert Australia to 'the dangers to which the neighbourhood of overcrowded Asia exposes the thinly populated Commonwealth of Australia'.[82] The fear, in this case, was

77  Searcy, *In Australian Tropics*, p. 173.
78  Gunn, *We of the Never-Never*, p. 123.
79  Gunn, *We of the Never-Never*, p. 166.
80  W. Howchin, *The Geography of South Australia* (Melbourne: Whitcombe & Tombs Ltd, 1909), pp. 308–9.
81  Strang, *The Air Scout*, p. 412.
82  Kirmess, *The Australian Crisis*, p. 5.

Japanese.[83] Kirmess described a clandestine settlement of Japanese in the Northern Territory, the logistics of which were possible because of the 'marvellous organising talent of the race'.[84] Australia is ultimately forced to accede to Japanese imperialism; a pawn sacrificed to maintain Britain's diplomatic relationship with Japan. In a similar vein, *The Air Scout* (1912) described a Chinese invasion of Australia through the Northern Territory. Foiled by British and Australian pluck, using the modern technology of air reconnaissance, the ending is much happier than Kirmess's novel:

> With the huge war indemnity exacted from China a new Port Darwin was created, to become one of the busiest trading ports and one of the strongest fortresses in the world. Vast sums were expended on the development of the unoccupied lands of the Northern Territory, which was raised in the course of time to the full dignity of a federal state in the Commonwealth.[85]

But racial tension appeared to underlie the settlement of the Northern Territory. The fears of the Queensland, Victorian, New South Wales and, to a lesser extent, South Australian colonies of cheap Asiatic labour were echoed in the Northern Territory at the same time as the chronic labour shortage was recognised as an impediment to economic prosperity. The importing of indentured labour for work on the railway and the free entry of Chinese on the Territory diggings meant that as well as an Aboriginal presence, Europeans also had to deal with a large Chinese presence. The literature argued that the Chinese were not to be trusted because, in the stereotype, they were dirty, prone to gambling and perhaps even more frightening, industrious and capable of making profit where Europeans could not.

If there is little evidence in the literature of friendship between Aborigines and Europeans, there is even less between Chinese and Europeans. However, there was a certain ambivalence. Searcy for example reflected the Territory view that they were useful for the economic development but to be treated with caution: 'it was their virtues, not their vices, we had to fear'. Searcy found the Chinese contradictory[86] and made the usual

---

83   Kirmess makes it clear that his fears had been shared by other commentators to the point that Australians had become cynical when, despite the report, 'nothing happened', Kirmess, *The Australian Crisis*, p. 33; This worry does not appear to have been justified in the case of the writers however, Kirmess's twin concerns for a White Australia and an unpopulated north would increasingly be taken up by writers on the Northern Territory, see Part Two and the 'empty north' debate for more detail.
84   Kirmess, *The Australian Crisis*, p. 26.
85   Strang, *The Air Scout*, p. 428.
86   Searcy, *In Australian Tropics*, p. 331.

racially stereotypical 'Chinese jokes' about lack of hygiene, avariciousness, 'amusing' customs and dress but respected their honesty, business acumen and abstemiousness.[87] Sowden was even less tolerant.[88] Jeannie Gunn praised her Chinese cook, although she noted that it was difficult to control her domestic staff, both Aboriginal and Chinese.[89] Although in practice there was evidence of a certain stability, if not equity, in relations between Aborigines, Asians and Europeans, there was a definite sense that if the Asians were given any opportunity at all they would achieve total ascendancy.

But in the process of defining European settlement against a landscape of physical hostility, where the European population was outnumbered by Chinese and Aborigines, gender politics dominates in the writing.[90] This is particularly apparent in the writing of Daly and Gunn but also a feature of other writers. *We of the Never-Never* is concerned largely with the tension experienced between men and women in the bush and, like *Digging and Squatting*, supports the notion of the bush as an escape for men from women. *We of the Never-Never* opens with the trip from Darwin by train and then horseback to Elsey Station. The male station hands attempt to block the arrival of a woman by sending misleading telegrams. Despite this, Jeannie arrives and in a short time has managed to charm even the crustiest bush misogynist. The bushmen of the settlement along the rail line approved of Jeannie, largely because of her height

> 'You'll sometimes get ten different sorts rolled into one,' he said finally, after a long dissertation.' But, generally speaking, there's just three sorts of 'em. There's Snorters—the goers you know—the sort that go rampaging round, looking for insults, and naturally finding them; and then there's fools; and they're mostly screeching when they're not smirking—the uncertain-coy-and-hard-to-please variety you know,' he chuckled, 'and then,' he added seriously, 'there's the right sort, the sort you tell things to. They're A1 all through the piece.'
>
> The Sanguine Scot was confident, though, that they were all alike, and none of 'em were wanted; but one of the Company suggested: 'If she was little she'd do. The little 'uns are all right,' he said.

---

87  Searcy, *In Australian Tropics*, pp. 334–46.
88  Sowden, *The Northern Territory*, p. 64.
89  Gunn, *We of the Never-Never*, p. 51.
90  M. Dewar, *Snorters, Fools and Little 'Uns: Sexual Politics and Territory Writing in the South Australian Period* (Darwin: State Library of the Northern Territory, Occasional Papers, 32, 1992), for more on this.

But public opinion deciding that 'the sort that go messing round where they know they're not wanted are always big and muscular and snorters'...[91]

Jeannie was nicknamed 'little 'un' and Aeneas becomes the 'Man-in-Charge' or 'Maluka' (boss). Women were, in a charitable view, acceptable if small (and helpless). If women were tall or strong they were likely to be opinionated or assertive. Jack the 'Quiet Stockman', who rarely talked, felt repelled by women because they were not men:

> Jack has always steered clear of women, as he termed it. Not that he feared or disliked them, but because he considered that they had nothing in common with men ... 'They never seem to learn much either,' in his quiet way, summing up the average woman's conversation with a shy bushman: a long string of purposeless questions, followed by inane remarks on the answers.[92]

But it is apparent that even small and helpless women exert a great power. The alcoholic 'Tam-o'-Shanter'[93] fled from Jeannie who realised how 'he must have hated women'.[94] The presence of a woman meant the enforcement of washing and shaving.[95] The single European male inhabitant of Elsey who did not mind Jeannie's arrival was the 'Dandy'[96] (who was so-called because he liked to wear clean clothes[97]). Another practice that was curtailed or at least inhibited by the presence of a European woman was the practice on pastoral stations of Aboriginal women working by day mustering cattle and at night as sexual partners for the European men. Male writers Sowden,[98] Searcy[99] and Paterson[100] noted how widespread the practice was; Harriet Daly and Jeannie Gunn, out of delicacy or ignorance, never mention it.[101]

---

91  Gunn, *We of the Never-Never*, pp. 5–6.
92  Gunn, *We of the Never-Never*, p. 48.
93  Deborah Bird Rose suggests plausibly that the legacy of a lifetime of violence towards Aboriginal people in the pastoral industry left a guilt and depression that could not be assuaged and cites the instance of Tam (Jock McPhee) and his associate Young as a case in point; D.B. Rose, *Hidden Histories: Black Stories from Victoria River Downs, Humbert River and Wave Hill Stations* (Canberra: Aboriginal Studies Press, 1991), p. 34.
94  Gunn, *We of the Never-Never*, p. 26.
95  Gunn, *We of the Never-Never*, p. 56.
96  Gunn, *We of the Never-Never*, p. 41.
97  Gunn, *We of the Never-Never*, p. 1.
98  Sowden, *The Northern Territory*, p. 42.
99  Searcy, *In Australian Tropics*, p. 173.
100 Paterson, *An Outback Marriage*, p. 150.
101 Reynolds and McGrath point out that the practice of using young girls as Aboriginal stockworkers in the Northern Territory pastoral industry was common from the 1880s onwards; Reynolds, *With the White People*, p. 205; A. McGrath, *'Born in the Cattle': Aborigines in Cattle Country* (Sydney, Allen & Unwin, 1987).

While Sowden, Searcy and Paterson describe what might be termed a working relationship between men and women in the bush, the inequality of such relationship is attested to in works such as Dawe's *The Golden Lake* which described the result of such a relationship:

> My mother loved the white man; but he was a beast who thrashed her till her spirit was broken, and then drove her from him with threats to kill if she should return. Then was she forced to fly to the wilderness. She journeyed on many days, till, falling sick with exhaustion, I was born. And the white man's blood was in my veins, and I was hated by my people. And they made a law that I should die, because they also hated the white man. One night I stole from the camp and took to the desert, I, a boy.[102]

This perspective was not only evident in the romances. The journalistic account support the widespread sexual abuse of women as a perquisite of the European colonial situation. Police Constable Willshire stated bluntly:

> Men would not remain so many years in a country like this if there were no [Aboriginal] women, and perhaps the Almighty meant them for use as He has placed them wherever the pioneers go.[103]

The bushman's ambivalence towards women noted by Jeannie Gunn was articulated clearly in the writing of Willshire. Willshire displayed extreme hostility and tension in his accounts of Aboriginal women. Women the author approved of—and they were always young—are referred to as 'maidens'[104] or 'virgins'.[105] Older women were simply 'old gins'.[106] He considered Aboriginal women as a commodity to be used even if of 'irregular shape and poor looking'.[107] In Willshire's Arcadia of free love, sexual intercourse is a kindness towards ugly women. But there is an anomaly in this picture. Willshire, known as 'Oleara' by the Aborigines, portrayed himself apart from the sexual freedom. Oleara's decision to remain sexually aloof was challenged through the narrative. Some time after leaving his guide, the young and beautiful Chillberta, Oleara departed 'the little village of Okeeleebeetanna' and headed up into the hills where he found a large cave where:

---

102 Dawe, *The Golden Lake*, p. 169.
103 Willshire, *The Land of the Dawning*, p. 18.
104 Willshire, *A Thrilling Tale*, pp. 25, 36.
105 Willshire, *A Thrilling Tale*, pp. 9, 13, 23, etc.
106 Willshire, *A Thrilling Tale*, pp. 19, 35, 36, 37, 43, etc.
107 Willshire, *A Thrilling Tale*, p. 13.

he was met by a young women [sic], perfectly nude; around her head she wore a wreath of orange and lilac blossoms, from her neck hung an unique necklace of quondong stones, through her nose stuck a snow white bone, and her ribs and thighs were adorned with stripes of red ochre, bordered with pine-clay and charcoal. She was called the Duenna of the Harem … She told me she would show me a nice lot of young girls, and hoped I would not be infatuated with any of them, which I assured her was quite foreign to my thoughts … we stooped to enter a large well-lighted cave, containing 25 native girls from 12 to 20 years of age … The Duenna asked the chief if a few of the girls might 'incarine', that is, sing a song to the white before he left. The chief agreed, when four of the girls including the one who knew Oleara, came forward and sang a most weird and passionate song.[108]

Oleara retained his chastity even when pursued by the lovely Marmatruer to Okeeleebeetanna. Mysteriously this chapter is called 'Omnia Vincit Amor' (love of what?). Oleara never consummated his romances (at least not in the narrative).

The following pattern, with the elements of pursuit, death, pornography and capitulation, contains all the elements of gender relations as expressed by Willshire in *The Land of the Dawning*. The language used is that of the hunt. This incident is typical.[109] Willshire finds a 'beautiful savage maiden … graceful as a stag' who screamed and fled at the sight of the police party. She was captured by some of Willshire's Aboriginal police, although she was 'as wild as a buffalo'. She made a final attempt to escape that night and was caught just as she prepared to jump into a river. Willshire commented appreciatively, 'It was a phenomenal run'. She is given to the Aboriginal tracker who caught her for sexual use. Willshire then rationalised the rape and her subsequent capitulation as, 'This wild damsel was now over head and ears in love with the tracker who caught her. With downcast eyes and pretty blushes she listened to his stories of other lands with fertile vales and dewy meads'.[110] His descriptions of exploitation and rape are chilling, but the very acceptance of his behaviour indicates that for some, Territory Aboriginal women were regarded as less than human. It is not to

---

108 Willshire, *A Thrilling Tale*, pp. 25–26.
109 See for example Willshire, *The Land of the Dawning*, pp. 40–42 and p. 61, which describes the same sequence of events.
110 Willshire, *The Land of the Dawning*, pp. 47–48.

be wondered then, that European women were feared and despised since it is unlikely that the kind of behaviour described by Willshire could ever be condoned by them.[111]

But in this period, interaction between the sexes, as described in the writing, was contradictory. As well as the gross exploitation represented in Willshire's account, there was equally a strong tradition of powerful assertive women. Ernest Favenc, for example, wrote about women in the Territory bush with some sympathy. 'The Mystery of Baines' Dog' describes Mrs Brown, terrified by the appearance of former lover Dick Baines, who threatens to show Brown 'old letters and photographs' revealing their relationship. Brown visits Baines at his old hut to plead with him and, 'His axe was leaning against the wheel, and I picked it up ... I struck him down ... found the letters and ... left the spot'.[112] The truth is revealed (through the identity of Baines's dog) to one man who agreed that justice had been done and that there was no need to make public the killer of Dick Baines. This story indicates a real sympathy for Mrs Brown and an acceptance of women fighting violently to protect themselves.

In 'The Stolen Colours', a rather trivial story about romance and rivalry between European stockmen over the hand of a pastoralist's daughter, Agnes Elliott, Favenc recognised that courtship had as much to do with male ego as anything else:

> Men do not love women so deeply as they hate their rival in the affections of those women. Marriage is more often the result of a man's determination to avoid injury to his own armour propre than of anything else.[113]

At the same time there is still a complete acceptance of traditional values. In *The Secret of the Australian Desert*, the main character Morton remarked, 'the man who lifts his hand—or nulla nulla—against a woman is unworthy the name of a British sailor'.[114] Favenc's fantasy, *Marooned on Australia*, described two survivors from the wreck of the *Batavia* who encounter the lost civilisation of the Quadrucos ruled by the exotic Princess Azolta and Prince Zolca, although Azolta is kept out of the action at one point

---

111 Peter Forrest attributes the bushman's misogyny solely to the curb on sexual exploitation of Aboriginal women by the presence of a white woman; P. Forrest, *They of the Never-Never* (Darwin: State Library of the Northern Territory, Occasional Papers, 18, 1990), pp. 8–9.
112 Favenc, *Tales of the Austral Tropics*, pp. 117–19.
113 Favenc, *Tales of the Austral Tropics*, p. 212.
114 Favenc, *The Secret of the Australian Desert*, pp. 64–65.

because she has to stay at home and mind the children.[115] Perhaps Favenc was influenced by his wife, with whom he is known to have written in collaboration[116] which accounts for the absence of hostility that has marked some of the other Territory writing from this period.

Like Favenc, Louis de Rougemont's description of his relationship with Yamba denotes a kind of respect. Shipwrecked, de Rougemont meets Yamba: 'marvellously intelligent … she seemed to discover things by sheer intuition or instinct'.[117] Yamba is strong and brave and saves his life on several occasions. European women also enter the narrative in the form of two sisters held as naked captives (although not sexually molested[118]), whom de Rougemont rescues. The faithful Yamba does all the hard work, leaving the two sisters time to sing, dance and perform amateur theatricals in the camp until the sisters drown attempting to hail a passing ship.[119] It was a commonly held view that Aboriginal women were the drudges of society. Harriet Daly considered the Aboriginal women 'downtrodden'[120] and de Rougemont concurred: 'beasts of burden, to be felled to the earth with a bludgeon when they err in some trivial respect'.[121]

*An Outback Marriage* by Banjo Paterson gives a different perspective from either the Willshire or de Rougemont construction of gender relations. The Territory is presented as a place of refuge for men and women wishing to live outside the law. Paddy Considine is revealed as a cattle rustler and Margaret (Peggy) Donahoe's income is augmented by presents of opals from the miners:

> 'Where on earth did she get all those opals?'
>
> 'Ho, blokes gives 'em to 'er, passin' back from the hopal fields. In the rough, yer know! Hopal in the rough, well, it's 'ard to tell what it'll turn out, and they'll give 'er a 'unk as sometimes turns out a fair dazzler. She's a hay-one judge of it in the rough, too …'[122]

---

115 E. Favenc, *Marooned on Australia being the Narration by Diedrich Buys of his Discoveries and Exploits in Terra Australis Incognita* (London: Blackie, 1905 (1896)), p. 192.
116 Frost, *The Last Explorer*, p. 28.
117 De Rougemont, *The Adventures of Louis de Rougemont*, p. 97.
118 De Rougemont, *The Adventures of Louis de Rougemont*, p. 208.
119 De Rougemont, *The Adventures of Louis de Rougemont*, p. 251.
120 Daly, *Digging, Squatting and Pioneering Life*, p. 69.
121 De Rougemont, *The Adventures of Louis de Rougemont*, p. 179.
122 Paterson, *An Outback Marriage*, p. 177.

Why the blokes give the opals to Donahoe is never explained. Paterson is much more open when describing Considine's sexual peccadillos. Paterson describes Carew's and Gordon's first introduction to his Aboriginal stock workers, Maggie and Lucy:

> 'Those are nice-lookin boys,' said Carew. 'I mean the two new boys just coming in.'
>
> 'New boys!' said the old man. 'Them! They're my two gins. And see here, Mister, you'll have to keep off hangin' round them while you're camped here. I can't stand anyone interferin' with them. If you kick my dorg, or go after my gin, then you rouse all the monkey in me. Those two do all my cattle work …'[123]

Considine's attachment to Maggie and Lucy appears strong. When he hears news of his inheritance, he is anxious about whether they can accompany him to England. Carew is startled by the request but considers it: 'Fashion just now to make a lot of fuss over Australian chappies, whatever they do. But two black women—rather a tall order'.[124] There is a strange suggestion that this attraction is rather more one-sided. Considine wonders whether he could 'take Maggie and Lucy there' because 'as man to man, you wouldn't arst me to turn them loose, would you?'[125] Considine uses terms which suggest he considers Maggie and Lucy as possessions rather than as women in a relationship with him. But Maggie and Lucy seem to be able to assert their own terms in this association. Considine explains how he came to marry Peggy Donahoe:

> I hadn't long got the two gins; and just before the rains the wild geese come down in thousands to breed, and the blacks all clear out and camp by the lagoons … It's the same every year—when the wild geese come the blacks have got to go, and it's no use talkin' … one night I come home after being out three days and there at the foot of the bunk was the two gin's trousers and shirts … they'd run away with the others.
>
> So I goes after 'em down the river to the lagoon, and there was hundreds of blacks; but these two beauties had heard me coming, and was planted in the reeds, and the other blacks, of course, they says, 'No more' when I arst them. So there I was, lonely.[126]

---

123 Paterson, *An Outback Marriage*, p. 150.
124 Paterson, *An Outback Marriage*, p. 158.
125 Paterson, *An Outback Marriage*, p. 157.
126 Paterson, *An Outback Marriage*, p. 159.

Considine then goes to Pike's Pub where he met Margaret Donahoe and after a week's drinking wakes up to discover they have been married by a missionary who 'chanced along'. But the marriage is unhappy as Considine does not like Margaret's inability to change her lifestyle after marriage:

> [I] don't like her goin's on, and I takes the whip to her once ... one day a black man from this place ... says to me ... 'Old man ... Maggie and Lucy come back'. So then I says, 'and it's sorry I am that ever I married you ... I'm off'.[127]

Maggie and Lucy fulfil their spiritual and familial obligations annually irrespective of the demands of Considine. Margaret Donahoe refuses to give up her 'goin's on' and the marriage disintegrates. Considine then, while maintaining an aggressively machismo stance of a man surrounded by women, is revealed more subtly as depending upon women. He is unable to survive without them. Paterson's images of the women in contrast are very strong. Maggie, Lucy and Peggy Donahoe are all portrayed as women who are resourceful, independent and able to survive in the harsh circumstances better than most men.

Both Searcy[128] and Sowden[129] acknowledged the reliance of the pastoralists upon Aboriginal women's labour but it was not only Aboriginal women who were represented as indomitable and courageous. William Walker's heroine, Millie Heseldine, is strong because of the natural health of the Territory: 'the eucalyptus-saturated air ... the well-grown girl, every nerve, sinew, and muscle alive and alert with motion and enjoyment'.[130] Searcy described Mrs Tommy, 'a tall handsome well made woman, and a splendid equestrienne'.[131] Like the Aboriginal women, Mrs Tommy was presented as the powerful force in the partnership, ready and reckless to use force if required. In this period, when women are represented as strong, it is only in male terms; their ability to ride, shoot and assert themselves sexually are the parameters of their power. Femininity equates with weakness.

---

127 Paterson, *An Outback Marriage*, p. 159.
128 Searcy, *In Australian Tropics*, p. 173.
129 Sowden, *The Northern Territory*, p. 42.
130 Walker, *The Silver Queen*, p. 42.
131 Searcy, *In Australian Tropics*, pp. 176–77.

The literature from this period gives us an interesting picture of male-female interaction in the early European settlement. White women are bitterly resented and feared by men as powerful agents who interfere with the freedom of a lifestyle of not washing, getting drunk or sexually abusing women. Aboriginal women, although acknowledged as good workers, are considered open targets for sexual exploitation. Within this framework, it is perhaps easier to see why tensions between sexes occupied such a prominent place in the writing.

This then formed the beginnings of the literary construction of the Northern Territory. Jeannie Gunn's *We of the Never-Never* with its negation of the Aboriginal contribution, its emphasis on (European) 'bush characters' and its celebration of a masculine lifestyle marked a turning point in the description of the Territory. Trevor James noted that, 'The new note is the affectionate acceptance of the land and the hardship it imposes'.[132] The literary tradition of 'Gunn's Territory' would continue unabated for another eighty years or more and provide many of the significant icons and myths by which the Territory described itself and is recognised as different from the rest of Australia.

---

132 James, 'From Exploration to Celebration', p. 11.

# 3

# LOOKING FOR GOLD

The potential of the Territory to generate wealth both for the individual and the nation was a major preoccupation for the writers of the early twentieth century. In contrast to the earlier writers who had attempted to assure their readers of the degree to which civilisation had been transplanted in the north, the writers after the First World War laid greater emphasis on the culture of the frontier itself. This was presented as an indigenous product of the Territory: adventure-loving, violent, impatient with rules and bureaucracy, casual and frequently excessive:

> So here goes, with a loose rein and a long stirrup, for we have many a miles till our last camp. Sometimes we will be 'close-up perishing', we have many a tough sandhill to climb, blacks will give us trouble, and the camel team will go into a disastrous panic. Never mind, we'll climb each hill as we get there ... marvellously happy ... two Australian bushmen at their best.[1]

The frontier lifestyle was presented as exclusively masculine. Much of the source of the personality and character of the bushman was derived from their contact with the landscape. In the literary construction, it is the landscape which moulds the character and rewards those individuals with financial success. In this period, the Territory is presented as a vast untapped supply of mineral wealth waiting to be discovered.

---

1   M. Terry, *Sand and Sun: Two Gold-Hunting Expeditions with Camels in the Dry Lands of Central Australia* (London: Michael Joseph, 1937), p. 21.

Dominating Territory writing this century prior to the Second World War were the seemingly contradictory notions of nationalistic celebration of the bush lifestyle and a desire to open up and civilise the outback through industry. In this period these constructions battled it out. The men of the outback were warm and friendly (at least to other European men): 'The hospitality extended to all who peregrinate in the Never Never, Back-o'-Beyond, Lonely Lands, or West-o'-sunset—call the Big Spaces what you will'.[2] This period of writing represents the flowering of the romantic notion of the bushman of the Northern Territory. Virile, perhaps dishonest, the Territory male was laconic[3] and sometimes omniscient,[4] the best bushman in the world.[5] But by the 1920s there was a self-consciousness of the bushman tradition, particularly as enshrined in literature. Bob Wright, the hero of J. Armour's *Burning Air*, had 'read books on exploring, and his ambition was to get out into the wilds of Australia'.[6]

In the writing, though, the Territory bushmen are 'strong and resourceful chaps ... brown as their parched native earth'[7] and endowed with tenacity and grit: 'I'll never give in'.[8] They are invariably men of strength and character, 'lean but sturdy, his strong smiling face bronzed to the colour of mahogany, his long moleskin-clad legs bowed lightly from a life spent in the saddle ... he was a son of the vast open spaces of the great "outback"'.[9] It took 'men of grit and courage to live and work out there ... hard men'[10] 'with grey-blue, devil-may-care eyes, ever alert as if seeking adventure behind every bush or rock'.[11] Descriptions sometimes contained epithets such as 'ever fearless in danger', 'a man of fearless character', or simply 'Our Pioneer'.[12] The heroes' prowess with guns and ability to fight were also the mark of a manly adventurer. Willis, 'The usual bush township loafer', sneers at the boyish Jim Westcott. After Jim dislocates Willis's arm in a fight the expeditioners who have hired Jim, all congratulate themselves on

---

2   Capt. K. Harris, *'Kangaroo-Land': Glimpses of Australia* (Cleveland, Ohio: Kilroy Harris Traveltalks, 1926), pp. 24–25.
3   C. Warburton, *Buffaloes* (Sydney: Angus & Robertson, 1934), pp. 44–45.
4   W. Hatfield, *Buffalo Jim* (London: Oxford University Press, 1938), p. 114.
5   Sayce, *The Valley of a Thousand Deaths*, p. 29.
6   J. Armour, *Burning Air* (London: Hodder & Stoughton, n.d. c. 1920s), p. 16.
7   Armour, *Burning Air*, p. 59.
8   I.L. Idriess, *The Cattle King* (Sydney: Angus & Robertson, 1984 (1936)), p.11.
9   J.M. Downie, *Mutiny in the Air* (London: Blackie, n.d.), p. 39.
10  J.C. Downie, *Galloping Hoofs: A Story of Australian Men and Horses* (London: Thomas Nelson, 1953 (1936)), p. 76.
11  C. Warburton, *White Poppies* (Sydney: Angus & Robertson, 1937), p. 3.
12  M.M.J. Costello, *Life of John Costello* (Sydney: Dymock's, 1930), pp. 105–6, 112.

gaining such an asset.¹³ There was almost an acknowledged childishness in the bushman's simplicity and love of adventure: 'the Bushman is always a boy at heart'.¹⁴

These fearless honest chaps were contrasted to the villains in these adventure yarns who frequently looked as though they should be in the city. 'Hector took an instinctive dislike to him because his eyes were so shifty. Compared with the alert, purposeful stockmen, Peter Crooks looked like those loungers who waste their time idling around back-country hotels.'¹⁵ Cities were synonymous with low-life idling: 'the average city fellow of to-day is ruined … He has everything done for him, doesn't know what real hardship or real hard work is like. The cities have spoilt the young men of today'.¹⁶ The bush, in contrast, provided a way for men to improve themselves: 'many a dead-beat and bad starter from the southern States made to the wild country in a final effort at rehabilitation'.¹⁷ The salubrious nature of the outback was stressed by the writers: 'The Bush is a wonderful tonic. It tones up the system in every possible manner'.¹⁸

But although the novelists were largely interested in presenting a paradigm of manliness, at the same time there are indications that the Australian bushman had begun to be regarded more critically by the journalistic, biographical writers. The image of the typical Territory white man had become slightly tarnished since the days of Jeannie Gunn. Knut Dahl noted:

> The Australian bushman is of a virile type. His face is bearded up to the eyes, his arms and chest are hairy like those of an orang-outang, and he is bow-legged from much riding … not over-scrupulous as to the means employed to gain his ends.¹⁹

---

13  Hatfield, *Buffalo Jim*, p. 96.
14  M. Terry, *Across Unknown Australia* (London: Herbert Jenkins, 1925), p. 142.
15  C. Sayce, *The Golden Valley* (London: Blackie, n.d. c. 1924), p. 31.
16  Downie, *Galloping Hoofs*, p. 77.
17  Warburton, *White Poppies*, p. 35.
18  M. Terry, *Untold Miles: Three Gold-Hunting Expeditions Amongst the Picturesque Border-Land Ranges of Central Australia* (London: Selwyn & Blunt, n.d. c.1932), p. 15.
19  K. Dahl, *In Savage Australia* (Boston: Houghton Mifflin, 1927 (1926)), p. 253.

G.H. Sunter described a type of bushman the Aborigines dismissed as a 'plurry loafer'.[20] But the naivety evident in the portrayal of the bushmen by the majority of writers of this period was undermined most conclusively by Xavier Herbert. While *Capricornia*'s portrayal of the people of the bush was not without irony, Herbert's description of the bushman sitting around the camp-fire singing 'Waltzing Matilda'[21] confirmed for the reader that Andy McRandy, Jack Ramble and Joe Mooch were true Australians. At the same time they were drunkards, anti-authoritarian, exploiters of Aboriginal women for casual sex and great mates. Despite this, or because of it, they recognise the qualities of Aboriginal society and are critical of the automatic assumptions of European superiority.[22] The chaste white heroes of literature before the war could never be presented with the same confidence again.

But the overwhelming mythology that consumed the Territory writers throughout this century was the belief that the Territory contained fabulous mineral wealth. The thread of pursuit of a Lasseter-type reef dominated many of the stories. B. Cronin's heroes find the 'remains of fabulous riches' in *The Treasure of the Tropics* (1928). Alick from E.V. Timm's *The Valley of Adventure* (1926) put it simply. 'Everybody knows that the Northern Territory of Australia is rich with all sorts of minerals—gold, silver, copper, tin, and lead.'[23] Edwin Grew and Marion Sharpe agreed.[24] Conrad Sayce's heroes almost always found gold—*Golden Buckles* is fairly typical. Sayce made the search for a hidden gold reef (told to others by dying or delirious men) the plot for *The Golden Valley*, *The Valley of a Thousand Deaths* and *In the Musgrave Ranges*. Theo Price's hero in *God in the Sand* discovers quartz 'veined and encrusted with pure gold'.[25] In Ian Miller's *The Lost Reef*, Bill Meldrum and his dog Bluey find a lost map showing Lasseter's Reef and travel to Central Australia on a gold seeking expedition. In Arthur Russell's *The Caves of Barakee*, Mr Freeman modestly told the boys that in his youth he found a series of caves in Central Australia. 'My boys, one of the caves contained, I should say,

---

20  G.H. Sunter, *Adventures of a Trepang Fisher: A Record Without Romance Being a True Account of Trepang Fishing on the Coast of Northern Australia; and Adventure Met in the Course of the Same* (London: Hurst & Blackett, 1937), p. 83.
21  Xavier Herbert's *Capricornia* (Sydney: Angus & Robertson, 1979 (1938)), p. 330.
22  Herbert, *Capricornia*, p. 325.
23  Timms, *The Valley of Adventure*, p. 144.
24  E. Grew & M. Sharpe, *Rambles in Australia* (London: Mills & Boon, 1916), p. 282.
25  T. Price, *God in the Sand* (Sydney: P.R. Stephensen, 1934), p. 84.

well over ten million pounds' worth of gold.'²⁶ John Hoskin's grandfather left a letter detailing finds of 'innumerable outcrops of pure gold ... not specks, but lumps of gold' in Val Heslop's *The Lost Civilization* (1936). Armour's *Burning Air* found valuable radioactive ore, James Downie's *The Treasure of the Never-Never* and, of course, Idriess's *Lasseter's Last Ride* described the discovery of Lasseter's reef. *Hell's Airport*, by the pilot on the Lasseter expedition, was first published in 1934. William Hatfield's *Buffalo Jim* (despite the title) was, in a large part, a description of an expedition to Central Australia to look for a fabulous gold reef. Michael Terry's *Sand and Sun* and *Untold Miles* dealt with his gold-seeking expeditions in Central Australia. M. Lynn Hamilton's science fiction novel of 1932 set in the Northern Territory described a hidden kingdom of disgruntled geniuses run by Colonel Ord. Hamilton's hidden country contained mineral wealth almost beyond description:

> Alluvial gold might be had for the trouble of picking it up ... there was tin, copper, and wolfram besides, and a huge seam of coal ... valuable sapphires and topazes—some of the rough stones larger than duck eggs.²⁷

The attitude shared by many of the landscape writers to the natural environment was paradoxical. Many looked optimistically towards a glorious future when the landscape would be transformed as a result of white settlement. The natural environment was presented in terms of its future potential: 'This tract of country, though now entirely devoid of men or animals, is of such a character that it will some day support a thriving population'.²⁸ Penryn Goldman looked forward to the day when 'THE DEAD HEART OF AUSTRALIA ... will be re-born'.²⁹ Armour prophesied (correctly) that the mining of radioactive ore would lead to urban Territory development:

> science and industry would transform those hills. Around them roads would run. Motor-cars would dash to and fro. The merry voices of children would be heard playing among the stones. Then above the stones ... would be bridges, towers and buildings and the whole life of a city. On these hills and valleys a city must spring up—a city that would claim the best from the rest of the world.³⁰

---

26  A. Russell, *The Caves of Barakee* (London: The Boy's Own Paper Office, 1936), p. 18.
27  M.L. Hamilton, *The Hidden Kingdom* (Melbourne: Wentworth-Evans, 1932), p. 36.
28  Sayce, *The Valley of a Thousand Deaths*, p. 27.
29  P. Goldman, *To Hell and Gone* (London: Victor Gollancz, 1932), p. 142.
30  Armour, *Burning Air*, p. 106.

E.V. Timms's *Valley of Adventure* finished with John Chisholm predicting that, 'Sanctuary Island will be a great gold-mine, and the green tunnel a highway of industry ... Men and machinery will transform the valley'.[31] Idriess noted that, 'when the white man came ... he would cover the land with wells and lakes in the form of station tanks; he would make many blades of grass grow where one grew now'.[32] This idea of carving the future prosperity of the Territory from an inhospitable landscape was the white man's burden:

> They felt they were face to face with the power of untamed nature—the desert and the savage inhabitant of it—and that even they were units in an army of progress which was conquering that nature and making it minister to the needs of civilised man.[33]

Although many journalists and novelists promoted the idea of mineral wealth transforming the Territory, there were dissenting views. Eric Baume speedily published *Tragedy Track* in an effort to stop the rush to the Granites Goldfield which led many hopefuls to their ruin after Ernestine Hill's glowing articles for Associated Newspapers. Herbert's *Capricornia* mocked the prophecies of Territory riches through development and emphasised the role newspaper writers had played:

> There aint no need for this here railway at all ... There's plenty of empty space to fill up down south yet. This railway's only the whim of a few transplanted cocknies [sic] that hate to see places without tram-lines in 'em, and of engineers that want jobs, and of manufacturers that want to sell things to the men employed on the buildin', and a few newspaper editors and other blowbags that dunno what they're talkin' about and don't care so long's they talk ... it's an utterly useless land.[34]

European wanted to impose order because there was a sense that the Territory landscape had a primitive, uncontrollable quality. As with the earlier writers there was a sense of ambivalence. Elsie Masson described going to the Territory as a journey in both time and space:

---

31  Timms, *The Valley of Adventure*, p. 237.
32  I.L. Idriess, *Lasseter's Last Ride: An Epic in Central Australia Gold Discovery* (Sydney: Angus & Robertson, 1980 (1931)), p. 73.
33  J. Bushman, (Sayce) *In the Musgrave Ranges* (London: Blackie, n.d.), p. 91.
34  Herbert, *Capricornia*, p. 318.

Those that go there undergo a strange experience—not only do they travel many hundred of miles by sea, but also they journey sixty years into the past, into the old Australia ... which has long passed away in the south but which still lingers in the wild, intractable Northern Territory.[35]

Carew, in Carl Warburton's *White Poppies*, extended this to a landscape of fantastic possibilities: 'the Northern Territory, a portion of the oldest continent on earth, might it not contain some surviving monster of prehistoric age?'[36] Dahl found the Territory landscape was incomprehensible: 'Here is no dusky summer night, nor any winter, but a burning day and a red sun that slakes itself in the far horizon like a red-hot iron plunged in water'.[37] Dahl, like Masson, consciously articulated this sense of spatial and temporal dislocation of landscape: 'We had entered, as it were, a different world down here on the Daly'.[38]

As in the earlier period, the women wrote most enthusiastically about the natural world, although they emphasised the human element rather than the ideal of wilderness. Jessie Litchfield asserted an aggressive chauvinism, 'the pride the residents of the Territory feel in their harbour is understood—a pride compared with which that of a Sydneysider is weak and puerile'.[39] Edwin Grew and Marion Sharpe were equally laudatory of Darwin, 'our last memory of Australia ... it was Port Darwin that we were most loth to leave, for we somehow felt that Australia had kept her best till last'.[40] Ernestine Hill noted, with peculiarly urban similes, that waterfalls were a 'tourists' delight' and that 'Walt Disney ... never conjured a gayer fantasia'. The flying fox, she believed, has a voice 'like a squabble between Mickey Mouse and Donald Duck'. Hill described bower birds nesting 'with a zest worthy of suburbia' and remarked that 'no department store ever evolved anything like paperbark'.[41]

---

35  E. Masson, *An Untamed Territory* (London: Macmillan, 1915), p. 24.
36  Warburton, *White Poppies*, p. 85.
37  Dahl, *In Savage Australia*, p. 104.
38  Dahl, *In Savage Australia*, p. 142.
39  J.S. Litchfield, *Far North Memories* (Sydney: Angus & Robertson, 1930), p. 9.
40  Grew & Sharpe, *Rambles in Australia*, pp. 291–92.
41  E. Hill, *The Territory* (North Ryde, New South Wales: Outback Classics, 1985, (Angus & Robertson, 1951)), pp. 18–25.

But if there was a sense that it was the role of the European to impose a settled order upon the landscape, there was equally the belief that the hardships of the country forged the character of the inhabitants. All the writers depicted the environment as potentially life-threatening to Europeans. The landscape was depicted as hostile, exotic and terrifying:

> Already they were on the fringe of the wild and unknown Never-Never … All fully realised the savage wildness of the locality over which they were flying. All knew that under the glittering, blue, glass-like surface of the Arafura Sea, lurked countless shoals of man-eating sharks and other hideous monsters of the deep; that the stretches of swampy, mosquito-infested jungle were alive with crocodiles, buffaloes, and giant pythons; and that all through this wild and sparsely populated Never-Never country, grinning death and peril stalked abroad and lurked in the shadows in countless forms and guises, by night and by day.[42]

George Sunter depicted a hostile Northern Territory coast with frequent reference to crocodiles, giant clams, box jelly fish, giant squid, whales and shark,[43] while Michael Terry's books, particularly *Sand and Sun*,[44] depicted graphically the dangers of the Centralian desert. Hatfield noted that the landscape contained 'a cruel beauty. Deceptively alluring', a 'false promise' to travellers who are left only 'the mocking sand'.[45] Frank Clune's chapter 'Blood on the Spinifex' from *The Red Heart*[46] leaves the reader in no doubt that the Territory is dangerous country to all but the brave and the canny. Much of the success of Ion Idriess's *Flynn of the Inland* rested upon the assumption of the dangers and hazards inherent in life in the isolated outback. Central Australia, particularly for the new-chum, became synonymous with almost certain death: 'the heart of the country, the Dead Heart, as the Aussies themselves call it … A dry scorchin' wilderness that sends white men mad with thirst or loneliness if they ain't bumped off by the wild niggers!'[47] But despite the harshness of the environment, the authors were keen to point out that the landscape had the power to exercise an almost spiritual attraction over the bushmen. Idriess noted of Lasseter that, 'uncanny … he was of this land and always

---

42  Downie, *The Yellow Raiders* (London: The Children's Press, n.d.), pp. 129–30.
43  Sunter, *Adventures of a Trepang Fisher*, pp. 22–3, 29–31, 38, 44, 102–3, etc.
44  See for example, Terry, *Sand and Sun*, Chapter 7, 'A Forced March' and Chapter 8, 'The Desert Cheated'.
45  W. Hatfield, *Australia Through the Windscreen* (Sydney: Angus & Robertson, 1936), p. 126.
46  F. Clune, *The Red Heart: Sagas of Centralia* (Melbourne: Hawthorne, 1944), pp. 31–40.
47  Downie, *Mutiny in the Air*, p. 31.

would be'.⁴⁸ There was a sense that the bush made you a better person: 'not ordinary men … men of the desert'.⁴⁹ The landscape formed a testing ground: 'a country for men, not weaklings'.⁵⁰

The authors felt a kind of spirituality inherent in the landscape and evoked the image of religion. Hatfield described Lily painted against the backdrop of the 'Paradise River' with Eden-like descriptions of 'the filtered greenness … through the tangled pandanus overhead'.⁵¹ Ernestine Hill employed the same Arcadian descriptions: 'all green glades and grottoes, ivy-climbing creepers, the willowy droop of paper-barks over white sand … Trailing clouds of glory shrill cockatoos flew screaming in flocks above us, white, green, black, crimson, and the dawn coloured galah'.⁵² Idriess imbued the landscape with imagery suggesting ancient religions. The Olgas were 'like an old-time city of domed temples piled one upon the other'⁵³ and 'the dome' of 'Ayers Rock' like 'some old-time temple'.⁵⁴ Errol Coote found 'Mount Olga' 'looked like a group of mosques'.⁵⁵

There was, as with the earlier writers, a distinction made between the town and the bush. If the writers were sometimes ambivalent or cautionary towards the physical environment, the settlements of the Northern Territory were described critically by many of the writers. R.H. Milford described the inhabitants of Darwin:

> Many of the living corpses of Darwin in a comatose state of alcoholism. Blacks, half-castes, pearlshell-divers, government officials (mentioned in their order of merit) and others—all stagger or lurch unevenly about in the poisoned air as if each movement of their bloated, beer-soaked bodies was going to be their ultimate …⁵⁶

---

48  Idriess, *Lasseter's Last Ride*, p. 82.
49  Sayce, *In the Musgrave Ranges*, p. 9.
50  Sayce, *The Golden Valley*, p. 58.
51  W. Hatfield, *Black Waterlily* (Sydney: Angus & Robertson, 1935), pp. 167–68.
52  E. Hill, *The Great Australian Loneliness* (Sydney: Angus & Robertson, 1991 (North Ryde: Harper Collins, 1940)), p. 155.
53  Idriess, *Lasseter's Last Ride*, p. 72.
54  Idriess, *Lasseter's Last Ride*, p. 90.
55  E. Coote, *Hell's Airport and Lasseter's Lost Legacy* (Hawthorndene, South Australia: Investigator Press, 1981 (1934)), p. 111.
56  R.H. Milford, *Australia's Backyards* (Sydney: Macquarie Head, 1934), p. 9.

Darwin's reputation, 'like a shop with all its soiled goods in the window; … one hears the worst of it, but none of the best of it, long before one arrives there'[57] meant that some writers were pleasantly surprised.[58] Charles Conigrave considered outsiders too critical of Darwin[59] pointing out it was Australia's 'front door' to Asia.[60]

But Darwin was portrayed almost universally as a town based on a strict hierarchy of class with the Administrator at the top and the Aborigines at the lower end of the social scale. Malcolm Ellis wrote ironically of pompous officials who saw themselves as 'potentates'.[61] Hatfield outlined this idea in his characters of Jim Westcott and Morton Dale. Jim thought Darwin exotically beautiful[62] but he 'could hardly believe such a small town could be so caste ridden'[63] and English aristocrat, Morton Dale, ignored 'all the imagined classes' of Darwin.[64] G.H. Wilkins was affronted by the rudeness and parochial insularity of Darwin residents.[65] Henry Hall was annoyed by the pompous formality of the dress requirements of the dining room of the hotel.[66] Ernestine Hill thought Darwin the, 'Shabbiest seaport of the Australian coast … there were only two [European] classes—those paid to stay there and those with no money to go',[67] although she rejoiced in the romantic mix of nationalities and peoples in the town:

> To come into Darwin … is to tiptoe across the bounds of possibility into an opium dream … Government officials, immaculate in white; Larrakeahs and Wargaits, their skins gleaming like glossy back taffeta riding bicycles about under the banyan trees; Chinese ladies with pantaloons and blue umbrellas; swarthy Filipinos, Fijian fuzzy-wigged, and grave doric beauties … these are some of the characters in Darwin's musical comedy.[68]

---

57 P. Bridges, *A Walk-About in Australia* (London: Hodder & Stoughton, 1925), p. 236.
58 M. Dorney, *An Adventurous Honeymoon: The First Motor Honeymoon Around Australia* (Brisbane: John Dorney, n.d. c. 1927), p. 82.
59 C.P. Conigrave, *North Australia* (London: Jonathan Cape, 1936), p. 117.
60 C.P. Conigrave, *Walk-About* (London: Dent, 1938), p. 210.
61 M.H. Ellis, *The Long Lead* (London: T. Fisher Unwin, 1927), p. 164.
62 Hatfield, *Buffalo Jim*, pp. 197–98.
63 Hatfield, *Buffalo Jim*, p. 203.
64 Hatfield, *Black Waterlily*, p. 66.
65 C.H. Wilkins, *Undiscovered Australia: Being an Account of an Expedition to Tropical Australia to Collect Specimens of the Rarer Native Fauna for the British Museum, 1923–1925* (London: Ernest Benn, 1928), p. 137.
66 H. Hall, *Our Back Yard: How to Make Northern Australia an Asset Instead of a Liability* (Sydney: Angus & Robertson, 1938), p. 62.
67 Hill, *The Territory*, p. 6.
68 Hill, *The Great Australian Loneliness*, pp. 136–37.

The other towns and settlements of the Northern Territory fared little better in the descriptions than Darwin. Ellis described the sleepiness of Alice Springs,[69] and although Fred Blakely liked Katherine, he found Pine Creek uncomfortable.[70] Lewis's description of the Yam Creek digging included claim jumping and corrupt police officials.[71]

A class-conscious Darwin contrasted strongly to the free and easy camaraderie which denoted the personal relationships of the bush dweller in the literature. Although this idea of striking contrast between urban and bush Territory had been touched on by most writers, it was Herbert in *Capricornia* who explored this theme most fully since it was Mark Shillingsworth's refusal to acknowledge the caste system that began the long sequence of events which make up the narrative of the novel. Although Herbert, like other authors,[72] supported the idea that Darwin was a fascinating blend of polyglot people from all backgrounds, the novel also suggested that there was very little mixing between groups. Indeed it was precisely Mark Shillingsworth's refusal to acknowledge the shibboleth of Darwin society that make him an outcast.

In an interesting reversal of the idea that the landscape transformed the individual into the lean, rugged bushman, Herbert described the process by which the cheerful, egalitarian Shillingsworth brothers are transformed into petty class-conscious bureaucrats. The brothers arrive at Port Zodiac where, 'Their bearing was that of simple clerks not Potentates, as it was their right that it should be as Capricornian Government Officers'. The brothers realise rapidly that they have a social standing at Port Zodiac which must be maintained. Oscar Shillingsworth lies about their background and is supported by Mark.

'They did not lie boldly, nor for lying's sake. They felt the necessity forced on them by the superiority of their friends.' But Mark was unable to maintain the fiction of their social standing and, 'One night … he told the truth about his father. Forthwith he was accepted as a brother'.[73] Mark's refusal to take up the white man's role resulted in his becoming

---

69  Ellis, *The Long Lead*, pp. 224–25.
70  F. Blakely, *Hard Liberty* (Sydney: George G. Harrap, 1938), pp. 238, 244.
71  J. Lewis, *Fought and Won* (Adelaide: W. K. Thomas, 1922), pp. 103–9.
72  For example, R.S. Sampson, *Through Central Australia* (Perth: Sampson Brokensha, 1933), pp. 23–24; Hill, *The Territory*, pp. 4f.
73  Herbert, *Capricornia*, pp. 8–18.

socially outcast from the other public servants. This in turn allowed him the freedom to initiate sexual relations with Aboriginal women and hence become the progenitor of Norman Shillingsworth.

Even in the outposts of European settlement there was clearly a great deal of stress laid on appearances. Social standing was determined not only by employment but also by the social position enjoyed in wider society. Ellis looked at Alice Springs society and its response to a Vice Regal visit.[74] Litchfield looked at Territory society and remittance men because the bushfolk are 'made up of all types of men'.[75] This is a repeated theme, that in the bush there are men of all social strata but one's place in society is subordinate to the fraternity of the bush. This being the case, it is to be wondered then that social position is so frequently mentioned, not only by Litchfield, but Sayce too larded his stories with references to public schools[76] and remittance men.[77] Perhaps faced with the threatening landscape of the Territory, writers were reluctant to let go of the sustaining structures of the civilised world, including the class and caste system.

But as in the earlier period, class difference was overshadowed (theoretically at least) by the obligations of mateship. Mateship was a theme which continued to permeate Territory writing, as it did in the earlier period. Sayce made much of mateship and its obligations. Tom, the rough bushman, and Tynan, the young new-chum Doctor, look after each other all through *Golden Buckles*. M'Shane [sic] and Stan become mates after they save each other's lives.[78] Equally, Sleat's failure to observe the obligations of mateship alerted the reader that he was really bad: 'In the unwritten bushman's code, the desertion of a mate is the worst of all crimes, and Dick had shunned Sleat as a man would shun a loathsome reptile'[79] so it is no surprise that Sleat turns out to be a drunkard and a murderer. In Armour's *Burning Air* Jim Fisher and Roy Mitchell are mates who agree to go prospecting in Central Australia together.[80] The most obvious consequence of mateship, which will be explored by later writers, is that

---

74  Ellis, *The Long Lead*, p. 228.
75  See for example Litchfield, *Far North Memories*, pp. 27, 29, 88, 194.
76  Where for example the trigger for 'Ballanda' remembering some of his past occurs when the narrator whistles 'an old school song' and makes a football, C. Sayce, *The Splendid Savage: A Tale of the North Coast of Australia* (London: Thomas Nelson, n.d. c. 1925), pp. 160–61; Sayce, *The Valley of a Thousand Deaths*, p. 108.
77  Sayce, *The Valley of a Thousand Deaths*, p. 59.
78  Sayce, *The Valley of a Thousand Deaths*, p. 50.
79  Sayce, *The Valley of a Thousand Deaths*, p. 238.
80  Armour, *Burning Air*, p. 22.

it forms a barrier to heterosexual relationships. In *Capricornia*, Heather, although daunted by the discovery that Mark has been having sexual relations with Aboriginal women, remains faithful. Heather lost out in her relationship with Mark, not because of the infidelities with Aboriginal women, but because Mark had a stronger relationship with his mate,[81] 'Chook' Henn, and his love of adventure. Heather recognised this clearly: 'I can't do anything with him with Chook about'.[82] But mateship was necessary in the bush where European women were few and a mate was someone you could depend upon for survival: 'every man present had experienced the worth of a comrade; some among them owed their lives to the devotion of a "cobber"'.[83]

White settlement in the Territory meant government from a distance by clerks and bureaucrats. Without a local representative government, claimed Ellis, time and Federal money was only wasted, 'devising new and increasingly futile remedies for Northern emptiness'.[84] Hall agreed.[85] Jessie Litchfield noted that all Territorians hated to be administered from distant Federal authorities.[86] Conigrave agreed that the control of the Territory by Canberra had led to 'anomalies' and 'mistakes'.[87] Whatever the cause, the Northern Territory had proved no greater benefit for the Federal administration than it had for the South Australian. Tom, the bushman from Conrad Sayce's *Golden Buckles*, blamed the Australian attitude to the north: 'Central Australia is being exploited, not settled'.[88] But for other commentators, it was not so simple. A. Grenfell Price expressed the situation in an unusual metaphor:

> The history of Australia presents, on the whole, a magnificent example of the successful reaction between an incoming people and a favourable environment. The Northern Territory, almost alone, has remained a vast iceberg of failure, unmelted by the soft warm waters of neighbouring success.[89]

---

81  This theme of heterosexual love as subordinate to mateship would be picked up by Tom Ronan, *Vision Splendid* (South Yarra: Currey O'Neil, 1981 (Cassell, 1954)).
82  Herbert, *Capricornia*, p. 358.
83  I.L. Idriess, *Flynn of the Inland* (North Ryde: Angus & Robertson, 1990 (1932)), p. 206.
84  Ellis, *The Long Lead*, p. 181.
85  Hall, *Our Back Yard*, p. 49.
86  Litchfield, *Far North Memories*, p. 26.
87  Conigrave, *North Australia*, pp. 117–18.
88  C. Sayce, *Golden Buckle* (Melbourne: McCubbin, 1920), p. 59.
89  Price, *The History and Problems of the Northern Territory*, p. 2.

Carl Warburton expressed the problem more colloquially. A theme of the novel *White Poppies* centres around the neglect that the two cattlemen feel the Territory has suffered[90] and becomes their justification for allowing an opium plantation:

> What is the hoodoo that hangs over the Northern Territory?
>
> ... Before my departure from the south, an experienced man told me that here was but one way to conquer the tropics—to work, and keep on working, and not to fall victim to the dread complaint of hot climates—lethargy ...
>
> It is not the man's fault altogether ... Once up here he is forgotten, and feels he is. The country has been referred to as the 'Land of Lost Souls'; I think a more appropriate name would be 'The Land of Forgotten People' ... I should like to cut this country out of the Commonwealth, induce the Old Country to take over, or else govern it from Darwin in our own way. Surely we have sufficient men with brains and ability to do so. Why should we be under the domination of southern politicians who have not the foggiest idea of the country and its peculiar requirements, who throw us a sop now and then to keep us quiet.[91]

Despite the reality of economic endeavour in the north, more and more people came to the Territory as it became easier for people to travel with the improvements in technology and communication. These latter-day pioneers seemed preoccupied with crossing the Territory in a variety of diverse and difficult means including car, bicycle and camel.[92] In 1929 the railway from Adelaide was through to Alice Springs and almost immediately tourists began to arrive in Central Australia. A cyclist passing through on the road to Darwin noted the 'many signs of the difficulties that the motor-cars were meeting. Water crossings had been corduroyed and bushed'.[93] The travellers came for a variety of reasons[94] and many wrote about their experiences, such as Edwin Grew and Marion Sharpe's *Rambles in Australia* (1916), Captain Kilroy Harris's *'Kangaroo-Land'*:

---

90   Warburton, *White Poppies*, p. 39.
91   Warburton, *White Poppies*, p. 174.
92   Croll recorded this anecdote from Hermannsburg which illustrates the kind of traffic that went through even in isolated missionary settlement: Marie 3 ½ prayed on going to bed: 'Please God, don't send any more visitors and then we can undress at the fire.' ... Ruth 5 'God doesn't send visitors. They just come and when they've seen everything they go away again', Robert Henderson Croll papers, La Trobe Library, ms 8910, 1236/1, 13 June 1941.
93   Blakely, *Hard Liberty*, p. 243.
94   See L. Riddett, 'Passing Through: Travellers the Victoria River District, 1899–1960'. *Northern Perspective* 10, 1 (1987), p. 1, for more on this.

*Glimpses of Australia* (1926), Muriel Dorney's *An Adventurous Honeymoon: The First Motor Honeymoon Around Australia* (1927), Penryn Goldman's *To Hell and Gone* (1932) or Lord and Lady Apsley's *The Amateur Settlers*. In fiction, Alexander Macdonald's *The Mystery of Diamond Creek* (c. 1930) described the crossing of the Northern Territory by 'Murray's Mastodon Tank car, model A, which carried the expedition throughout the entire journey of one thousand miles'.[95] In the end, the travellers seemed to come—not to arrive, but for the actual experience of getting there.

The bushmen, it seems, had to be tough not only because of the hazards of the environment but because European settlement in the tropics was considered a graphic and biological oddity.[96] Geographers continued to debate the issue at length frequently linked to the White Australia Policy. Walter Howchin's *The Geography of South Australia* (1909) and *The Geology of South Australia* (1918) were used as standard texts for forty years.[97] J.W. Gregory, Professor of Geology in the University of Glasgow, in *The Menace of Colour* (1925), specifically devoted one chapter to 'Australia and its Northern Territory'.[98] 'Coloured' immigration to the north of Australia was feared to be the thin end of the wedge. J.S. Parer stated, 'The Northern Territory is the front door to Australia, and on its development rests the high ideal of all true Australians. A "White Australia" and this alone, is worth every effort which is in our power'.[99] A. Grenfell Price's *White Settlers in the Tropics* is probably the best known on this topic. *White Settlers* was published in 1939 and posed such questions a 'Why in general have the whites failed? Are they beginning to make progress? Can they hope for ultimate success?'[100] Geographers raising these kinds of issues unconsciously supported the frontier notion of the perilousness yet urgent necessity of European colonisation of the north. From the earliest period of non-Aboriginal settlement of Australia there had been a sense of urgency about a populated north. During the period leading up to World War II this amounted to a national obsession. Walter Bromhead proposed

---

95   Macdonald, *The Mystery of Diamond Creek*, p. 319.
96   J.W. Gregory, *The Menace of Colour: A Study of the Difficulties due to the Association of White and Coloured Races, With an Account of Measures Proposed for their Solution, and Special Reference to White Colonization in the Tropics* (London: Seeley Service, 1925), p. 14; A.G. Price, *The History and Problems of the Northern Territory, Australia* (Adelaide: A.E. Acott, 1930), pp. 55–56.
97   N.H. Ludbrook, 'Howchin, Walter', *Australian Dictionary of Biography*. vol. 9, B. Nain, and G. Serle eds, (Melbourne: Melbourne University Press, 1981 (1983)), p. 377.
98   Gregory, *The Menace of Colour*, pp. 150–72.
99   J.J. Parer, *The Northern Territory: Its History and Great Possibilities* (Melbourne: J.J. Parer, 1922), p. 78.
100  A.G. Price, *White Settlers in the Tropics* (New York: American Geographical Society, 1939), p. 1.

a volunteer 'Australian militia' or 'Pioneering Legion' based at Darwin or Arnhem Land.[101] J.N. MacIntyre,[102] Hastings Young,[103] M.H. Ellis,[104] Frank Cotton,[105] Sydney Upton,[106] Fred Blakely,[107] C.P. Conigrave,[108] T. Ranken,[109] R.S. Sampson[110] and David M. Dow all believed, 'Australia should fill up her empty north'.[111] But Xavier Herbert mocked the typical fears. 'No ... there's no fear of any sort of invasion here, except in the way of a politician now and then and a few of them newspaper blowbags.'[112]

The landscape of the Northern Territory, at this time, as represented in the literature, was somewhat paradoxical. The bushman's free ethos of a rugged adventurous life as described by writers like Idriess, Clune, Sayce, Armour, Dahl, Sunter or Warburton contrasted oddly to the image of the parochial, inefficient and pretentious standards of living in the Northern Territory towns described by Herbert, Ellis, Blakely, Wilkins or Conigrave. There was already, in contrast to the earlier writers, a sense that the 'real' Territory lay outside the settled borders. The landscape had the potential both to generate wealth and mould the character of the bushmen, at least in theory. Yet the image of the bushmen was already beginning to tarnish and the novelty value of living in the back of beyond was severely challenged by the arrival of the travellers. The general consensus was that the Territory still lacked an economic base which could generate capital and ensure a population of sufficient size to deter the interests of Australia's northern neighbours. This view was not to change in the immediate future.

---

101 W.S. Bromhead, *Shall White Australia Fail?* (Sydney: Angus & Robertson, 1939), p. 222.
102 J.N. MacIntyre, *White Australia: The Empty North the Reasons and Remedy* (Sydney: Penfold, 1920), p. 5.
103 D.H. Young, *A White Australia Is it Possible? The Problem of the Empty North* (Melbourne: Robertson & Mullens, 1922), p. 110.
104 Ellis, *The Long Lead*, Preface.
105 F. Cotton (Porkobidni), *Porkobidni's Plan: The Development of the Northern Territory* (Sydney: no publisher given, 1933), p. 3.
106 S. Upton, *Australia's Empty Spaces* (London: Allen & Unwin, 1938), p. 124.
107 Blakely, *Hard Liberty*, p. 152.
108 Conigrave, *North Australia*, p. 247.
109 T. Ranken, *Fire Over Australia* (Sydney: Angus & Robertson, 1938), p. 110f.
110 Sampson, *Through Central Australia*, p. 3.
111 D.M. Dow, *Australia Advances* (New York: Funk & Wagnall, 1938), p. 44.
112 Herbert, *Capricornia*, p. 321.

# 4

# RACE RELATIONS

In the period leading up to the Second World War, Aborigines are presented in the writing not merely as antagonists to the march of progress, but as a 'stone-age' relic from a prehistoric past. This change in focus seems to have originated from developments in the social sciences.[1] Scientists of all persuasions came to the Territory to explore new frontiers of anthropology, genetics, environmental science and biology: 'From now on the rules of the game will be very strict, for the days of anthropology have arrived, and the Native will become an important subject, lifted from the abject state we doom him to as "just a nigger"'.[2] As one writer noted: 'There's always one o' these professors ready to have his leg pulled if a buck reckons he's King Mick out on his sandhill. They cause more trouble with the blacks than anything else'.[3] The 1920s and 1930s had brought an increased awareness of the Northern Territory and in particular, of its Aboriginal population.

Issues of racial discrimination and sexual exploitation were a major concern of writers who found a particular focus on the 'half-caste problem'.[4] The 'half-castes' of their novel were defined only in terms of their European fathers, as writers minimised or ignored their Aboriginal families. All these novelists shared the assumption that 'Aboriginality' was an inherited genetic taint that has the power to assert itself under the

---

1   Flora Eldershaw noted, 'Scientific observation has always been an abundant source for the landscape writer.' F. Eldershaw, 'The Landscape Writers', *Meanjin* 11, 3 (1952), p. 228.
2   F. Blakely, *Hard Liberty* (Sydney: George G. Harrap, 1938), pp. 156–57.
3   W. Hatfield, *Desert Saga* (Sydney: Angus & Robertson, 1933), p. 167.
4   For more detail on this see T. Austin, 'Cecil Cook, scientific thought and "Half Castes" in the Northern Territory 1927–1939', *Aboriginal History* 14, 1 (1990), pp. 104–22.

stimulus of the landscape and association with other Aboriginal people. The first of these writers is probably the least well-known today. Conrad Sayce in *Comboman* (1934) and (to a lesser extent in) *Golden Buckles* (1920) promulgated the then popular notion about 'the half-caste'—that although educated as a European, at first exposure to the primitive, blood will out. *Comboman* described Robert Grey's efforts to bring up his 'half-caste' child, Stanley, as a European by ruthlessly denying him any contact with his family and sending him to school in Adelaide. All proceeds well until Stanley returns to the Northern Territory as a sixteen year old youth, where, despite his good looks and confident manner, it becomes immediately obvious to the reader, as well as to Grey, that Stanley's heredity will manifest itself. Sayce illustrates this by a description of a series of incidents: Stanley's cowardice and cruelty is established by a description of how he loves to torture animals; watching Aborigines plucking emu feathers from a long dead carcase, Stanley can barely restrain himself from flinging himself down and joining them; at the sight of brumby stallions fighting, Stanley begins to foam at the mouth and nearly bites his father.[5] Finally, Grey realises he is beaten when he returns home after an absence to find Stanley has sneaked off to corroboree with his family:

> There was no trace of intelligence in those eyes. The fire of life was fierce, primitive, black. The savage music was rousing only savage blood … The missionaries were right … He's only a black bastard after all … and I … I'm only a Comboman.[6]

The continuing popularity of *Capricornia* and its masculine construction of Norman Shillingsworth's Northern Territory has overshadowed William Hatfield's female character on the same theme, outlined in *Black Waterlily* (1935). Herbert and Hatfield were politically committed to arguing for justice and representation for Aboriginal people (particularly those with non-Aboriginal kin) and their novels suffer as literature from the soap-box style of their protagonists. Both authors argue vehemently that children from Aboriginal and non-Aboriginal descent should be brought up to respect both sides of their cultural heritage:

> what I've always maintained about half-castes … They should be left in the camp to grow up as blacks unless their father claims them and has them brought up in a white home from infancy. It's cruel madness to send

---

5   C. Sayce, *Comboman: A Tale of Central Australia* (London: Hutchinson, n.d. c. 1934), pp. 252, 254, 269.
6   Sayce, *Comboman*, p. 286.

policemen out to drag them from their black mothers and bring them up with the idea they are white, or as good as white, then turn them out into the world to compete with white men who hate them as competitors on the labour-market and loathe them socially …[7]

But despite Hatfield's fame with his contemporaries at the time of the publishing of his novels, few Territory writers are remembered now as well as Herbert.

Many writers felt inspired as a part of the privilege of their contact with Aborigines to record information of a vague ethnographic nature. Warburton, for example, described Aboriginal camps, customs, material culture and other social and religious practices.[8] Sunter described many Aboriginal hunting techniques and considered the Aborigines, 'the finest bushmen in the world'.[9] Writers who were not dependent upon Aboriginal skills presented a less sympathetic picture of Aboriginal life, but still felt qualified to record ethnographic data. Wilkins recorded ceremonies.[10] Michael Terry outlined a few Aboriginal hunting methods, some examples of material culture and methods of communication but did not bother to distinguish between different Aboriginal groups. They were simply the 'Blacks'. He did not identify individuals by name, only using a physical characteristic. He did not recognise any language beyond defining 'bogey' as 'Aboriginal' for swim.[11] Terry's sensitivities covered a vague awareness of Aboriginal spirituality. Camping at a waterhole in the Tanami a member of Terry's party observed at its being deserted, 'I suppose the cows [Aborigines] have some religious beliefs about it being sacred'.[12] Terry justified the Coniston massacres on the grounds that, 'We know that no nation retains idle lands once a stronger people desire possession. However, we may try to alter it in the future, might has been right'.[13] As well as recording ethnographic information, most of the writers included their personal attitudes toward Aborigines as well. In many cases, they used the ethnographic information as a justification of their own attitudes of racial and cultural superiority.

---

7   Hatfield, *Black Waterlily*, p. 125.
8   Warburton, *Buffaloes*, pp. 54, 93, 108–15, 134f, 207f.
9   Sunter, *Adventures of a Trepang Fisher*, p. 59.
10  Wilkins, *Undiscovered Australia*, pp. 183f.
11  Terry, *Across Unknown Australia*, pp. 174–86.
12  Terry, *Sand and Sun*, p. 74.
13  M. Terry, *Hidden Wealth and Hiding People* (London & New York: Putnam, n.d. c. 1941), p. 235.

Dominating all the texts was the conviction that Aborigines were intellectually inferior to Europeans. R.B. Plowman noted that Aborigines displayed 'primitive reasoning'[14] but Plowman was confident that the Aborigines did not have 'the intelligence of a white man'. Hall agreed: 'the Territory natives are comparable with children who are not quite normal … most unreliable when not under the eye of a white man'.[15] Conigrave considered the Aborigines intellectually inferior to Europeans.[16] Litchfield commented that an Aborigine, 'is childish as a rule, with the mental development of a boy of ten or twelve'.[17] Hatfield too, in *Buffalo Jim*, saw Aborigines as simple children of nature: 'A bit of sweet food and tobacco, without a spot of alcohol, and their whole bodies, let alone their crude features, positively radiate happiness'.[18] Dahl saw the Aborigines as totally amoral: 'For tobacco they would sell or do anything'.[19] Basedow regarded the Aborigines as contradictory: 'simple but unapproachable, humble but dignified, barbarous but kind-hearted, and ungrateful but generous'.[20] T.E.A. Healy depicted the Europeans as victims of Aboriginal whim:

> Europeans pretend that the natives are their servants, but the natives do not assist with the pretence and order their lives without any regard for their masters and mistresses … The spurious, ill-fitting garment of civilisation which they wear is shaken off when the impulse comes to roam. There is no word of explanation, none of regret. Just a word to missus; 'I been go walkabout'.[21]

Edwin Grew and Marion Sharpe agreed with Healy.[22] But Mary Bennett was more critical of the system: 'The Aboriginal Compound at Kahlin exists to supply the white people with cheap labour'.[23]

---

14  R.B. Plowman, *Camel Pads* (Sydney: Angus & Robertson, 1935), p. 156.
15  Hall, *Our Back Yard*, pp. 95–96.
16  Conigrave, *North Australia*, p. 201.
17  Litchfield, *Far North Memories*, p. 55.
18  Hatfield, *Buffalo Jim*, p. 215.
19  Dahl, *In Savage Australia*, p. 39.
20  H. Basedow, *Knights of the Boomerang* (Sydney: Endeavour Press, 1935), p. 17.
21  T.E.A. Healy, *And Far From Home* (London: Michael Joseph, 1936), p. 124.
22  Grew & Sharpe, *Rambles in Australia*, p. 274.
23  M.M. Bennett, *The Australian Aboriginal: As a Human Being* (London: Alston Rivers, 1930), p. 120.

Particularly popular was the view that Aborigines were cannibals. Both fiction and non-fiction writers helped to perpetuate this mythology.[24] Most of Sayce's *Comboman* is concerned with Robert Grey's son Stanley, as Grey was never much interested by his elder child, a daughter named Koomilya. The Aboriginal group to which Grey is related wish to initiate him and hold a long ceremony involving dancing and drugs and culminating in a rich feast. Grey is attracted by the good smell of food in the barbecue pits:

> Grey looked again. Framed in blackened leaves, he saw a face. It was scorched and shrivelled, but undoubtedly the face of a child. A wisp of fair hair had escaped the heat and still clung to the childish head. It was the face of Koomilya.[25]

Litchfield,[26] Wilkins,[27] Blakely,[28] Basedow[29] and others[30] all confidently maintained that Aborigines routinely killed and ate people, particularly children of mixed Aboriginal and non-Aboriginal heritage. Herbert soundly debunked this popularly-held notion in *Capricornia*. Mark Shillingsworth, in drunken paternalistic pride feared that Marowallua would kill their child as he 'believed the lubra sometime killed their halfcaste babies. He might have guessed that they did not do it very often in Capricornia, where the halfcaste population was easily three times greater than the white'.[31]

---

24 Cannibalism, frequently seen as the ultimate crime against humanity, as Arens has demonstrated, can rarely be proved in human history despite the numerous accounts of its practice; W. Arens, *The Man-Eating Myth: Anthropology & Anthropophagy* (New York: Oxford University Press, 1980 (1979)). Michael Pickering has carried out a similar study in Australia, which suggests that Arens's conclusions are upheld for Aborigines as well. In other words, despite the confidence in this construction, Pickering has shown that 'the great majority of reports of cannibalism by Aborigines have their basis in, at one end of the scale, innocent misunderstandings and misinterpretations, based on conjecture and presumption, of phenomena which did not involve the act of cannibalism, and, at the other end of the scale, in deliberate attempts to denigrate and dehumanise Aborigines as a prelude to denying them basic rights, usurping their lands and destroying their culture.'; M. Pickering, 'Cannibalism Amongst Aborigines? A Critical Review of the Literary Evidence', Bachelor of Letters thesis, The Australian National University, 1985, p. 115.
25 Sayce, *Comboman*, p. 117.
26 Litchfield, *Far North Memories*, p. 58.
27 Wilkins, *Undiscovered Australia*, pp. 171, 175, 177–78, etc.
28 Blakely, *Hard Liberty*, p. 242.
29 Basedow, *Knights of the Boomerang*, pp. 224–29.
30 Students interested in pursuing this theme are referred to Pickering's Appendices which give a detailed breakdown for cannibal references in Australian literature relating to Aborigines, Pickering, 'Cannibalism Amongst Aborigines?'.
31 Herbert, *Capricornia*, p. 25.

There is a suggestion that Aborigines believed that the European were also cannibals or at least grossly concerned with the dead. Aboriginal bones provided a local cash crop for the Litchfields who 'got five pound per dozen for blackfellows' skulls'.[32]

> We usually bought any dead bodies from the niggers, paying them a bag of flour for the 'dear departed'. We used to bury the corpse in an anthill, and when all the flesh had been eaten from the bones, we sent the skeleton to museums, and received up to ten pounds each for them.[33]

Dahl, too, collected skulls.[34] When Pat Ritchie brought in a leprosy patient, he described the sorrow of the family and evident belief that the mission was removing Aboriginal people to kill them.[35]

A widely-held view that Aboriginal children of European fathers were at risk of being killed and eaten, was a powerful propaganda message justifying the removal of such children from their mothers (which was the Government policy of the time). Despite the widespread representation of Aborigines as powerless or primitive, C.E.M. Martin's *The Incredible Journey* (1923) is a fairly sympathetic portrayal of two Aboriginal women, Iliapa and Polde, who travel great distances over difficult terrain to rescue Iliapa's son, Alibaka, from the clutches of the evil and exploitative European man, Simon. Maternal love is absent from almost all of the depictions of Aboriginal women and thus the portrait of Iliapa is an extraordinary departure. Absence of Aboriginal maternal love is, of course, another justification for taking children away from their mothers. Unusually,[36] Martin actively criticises the policy: 'A fellow can't be allowed to steal a child from a black mother, any more than from a white one'.[37] The female character in Herbert's book who emerged as a powerful protagonist is Tocky, daughter of Connie Differ

---

32   Litchfield, *Far North Memories*, p. 149.
33   Litchfield, *Far North Memories*, p. 110.
34   Dahl, *In Savage Australia*, p. 158.
35   P.H. Ritchie, *North of the Never-Never* (Sydney: Angus & Robertson, 1934), p. 77.
36   Martin's view is quite extraordinary in the writing and preceded Hatfield's criticism by more than a decade. Despite growing doubts of Aboriginal policy, even in the post-war period, few writers actually criticised this practice of removing children. See for example, 'Yorkie' J. Walker, *No Sunlight Singing* (London: Hutchinson, 1960), Chapter 6, some forty years after Martin, who even then, suggests it is the manner and nature of the institutionalisation that is at fault rather than the practice. After the policy was discontinued, F.X. Herbert, *Poor Fellow My Country* (Sydney: Collins, 1975), is critical, as is Aboriginal writer, B. Cummings, *Take This Child ... From Kahlin Compound to the Retta Dixon Children's Home* (Canberra: Aboriginal Studies Press, 1990), Chapter 8.
37   C.E.M. Martin, *The Incredible Journey* (London: Jonathan Cape, 1923), p. 268.

and Aboriginal Protector, Humbolt Lacy. Herbert portrayed Tocky as the bringer of bad luck.[38] Much of the misfortune in Tocky's life occurs because of the predation of European males upon Aboriginal girls. Her birth, which was the outcome of a seduction by an Aboriginal 'Protector' of a young girl in his charge, leads to Connie's dismissal and enforced marriage to the no-good Peter Pan. Tocky murders Frank, it is implied, because he attempted to come into her tent for sex.[39] Generally the female 'half-castes', with the exceptions, perhaps, of the saintly Connie Differ and Fat Anna, are portrayed as simple, superstitious and often violent.[40] Connie dies—perhaps because of a constitutional weakness, perhaps because she runs away from the institutionalised care. Herbert recognised that the Government administration did not work for the benefit of the Aborigines, but seems to imply that its failure was a result of the sexually exploitative nature of European men or the misfortune of individuals, rather than an inherent fault in the Government policy.

For the purposes of the adventure story, Aborigines were still presented as threatening. E.V. Timms's *The Valley of Adventure* is set against a backdrop of 'primitive savagery of this unknown jungle land, where every shadow was a menace and a sound became a warning or a death-cry'.[41] In the 'Boy's stories' of the brothers Downie, apart from one or two trusted souls employed as menials, such as Jackie who saved the group in *Mutiny in the Air*,[42] Aborigines were frequently the source of danger to the heroes. The 'Kaiditcha' men who are pursuing Bill Meldrum and Moorara in Miller's *The Lost Reef* are terrifying, murderous and omniscient.[43] Aborigines as enemies were generally portrayed as terrifying, bestial and treacherous:

---

38  Herbert, *Capricornia*, p. 191; The theme of harbouring a jinx is a constant in Herbert's writing. For example Herbert, *South of Capricornia*, Chapter 25, 'Machinations of a Jinx' where the jinx is identified and unnamed; *Soldiers' Women* (Sydney: Angus & Robertson, 1961), with the character of Pudsey Bat; *Poor Fellow My Country*, with the character of Prindy.
39  Herbert, *Capricornia*, p. 393f.
40  Herbert, *Capricornia*, e.g. Yeller Jewty's violence to Nawnim pp. 42, 49, Tocky's ambivalence to Norman p. 384.
41  Timms, *The Valley of Adventure*, p. 45.
42  Downie, *Mutiny in the Air*, p. 234.
43  I. Miller, *The Lost Reef* (London: Oxford University Press, n.d.), p. 18; the subject matter and style suggests that this was published in the 1930s.

Their black, ape-like features glistened with perspiration; their deep-set cunning eyes learned with the lust to kill ... He knew he could expect little mercy from such savages. For in the back of his mind were the tales he had heard of these notorious Arnhem Land warriors—and he knew that a fate probably worse than death awaited him.[44]

But gradually in this period, in the process of writing about the Territory, Aborigines became less important to the writers than the landscape. The courage of the European settlers was pitted, not against hostile natives, but against the landscape itself. As Sayce pointed out, 'the most terrible disasters of the desert are caused, not by wild and fiendishly cruel natives ... but by grim nature herself. Nature was their greatest, their most merciless, their most unconquerable enemy'.[45]

Aborigines were still included, but they were not usually presented as central to the plot or action: 'the Australian aboriginal was a poor specimen of humanity at the best, and his resistance would be more noise than effective at close quarters'.[46] Writers sometimes celebrated battles of the past but in this period,[47] civilisation was felt to have left its mark on even the wild Aborigines of the Territory. Hatfield has one bushman declaring about his rifle: '*I'll* never use it. Brought it to fend off wild niggers, and the only savages I've seen since I left Gawler, were here in town, biting my ear for *tickpence*!'[48]

Hatfield's *Desert Saga* was anomalous in that it aimed to present the narrative from the Aboriginal perspective. But the hero, Grungunja, appeared to share attitudes more Biblical than Aboriginal. (His slaying of his enemy, Kamarandoo, was almost a replication of the David and Goliath story.[49]) Having escaped death on several occasions, Grungunja explained his Christ-like immortality to the priest of the Alice Springs Gaol. The missionary rebuked him for such talk and pointed out that he had been imprisoned for the sin of cattle spearing. Grungunja answered with dignity and authority, 'the white man took my country, killed my kangaroos, let their cattle drink my water and eat my grass,

---

44 Downie, *The Yellow Raiders*, p. 122.
45 Sayce, *In the Musgrave Ranges*, p. 111.
46 Macdonald, *The Mystery of Diamond Creek*, p. 163.
47 For example, E.H. Earnshaw's *Yarragongartha* (Sydney: by the author, 1930), described the attack on Barrow Creek Telegraph Station and Yarragongartha, who helped the white men with the subsequent reprisal.
48 Hatfield, *Buffalo Jim*, p. 185.
49 Hatfield, *Desert Saga*, p. 32.

every blade of it. Is that not a sin? Should they not be put in here too?'[50] Another writer who deliberately attempted to describe Aboriginal culture in a mythological framework that echoed the Biblical narrative was Theo Price in his romantic *God in the Sand* (1934). An ethnologist, Errol Courtney, dying alone in the desert, is confronted by a vision of a beautiful European woman who sings for him the legends and stories of the Aborigines. In this period, Aboriginal spirituality was a little known quantity. Sensitive writers recognised Aborigines held beliefs, but did not know what they were. In the absence of further information, the writers interpreted Aboriginal spirituality the only way they knew and in this period it retained a decidedly Biblical flavour.

But most of the authors agreed that association with non-Aborigines brought about a debasement of Aboriginal culture. C.E.M. Martin pointed out that association with non-Aboriginal people led to a breakdown of the gerontocracy and that the young men flouted traditional law.[51] But for the writers, Aboriginal association with Europeans frequently implied not simply a change, but a physical and moral degeneration. Stuart McDonald noted, 'The really primitive aborigine is a gentleman in disposition and kindly-hearted. But put him in trousers, put a pipe in one of his hands and a glass in the other and he is, more often than not, a lazy, crafty knave'.[52] Basedow deplored, 'The tendency in these days is for the natives to drift to the white people's settlements and hang about them in a state of unutterable beggary'.[53] Ellis agreed.[54] Sayce noted of one miscreant that he had 'villainy by associating with' a white man.[55] Aborigines were considered acceptable only when they lived in remote areas not wanted by European settlers. Tom, the stockman from *Golden Buckles*, advised the new-chum, 'If you're in these parts long, Jim, you'll learn that the plain, straight-out wild nigger is far better than the educated one. A half-caste is the worst of the lot'.[56] There was approval, even in the adventure stories, for Aborigines who were at home in hostile barren country where a white man would starve to death.[57] The remote Aborigines were: 'different from

---

50   Hatfield, *Desert Saga*, p. 148.
51   Martin, *The Incredible Journey*, p. 53.
52   S. McDonald, *Ungamillia (The Evening Star): A Romance With a Central Australian Background* (Sydney: Deaton & Spencer, 1933), p. 12.
53   Basedow, *Knights of the Boomerang*, p. 13.
54   Ellis, *The Long Lead*, p. 234.
55   Sayce, *The Valley of a Thousand Deaths*, p. 78.
56   Sayce, *Golden Buckles*, p. 64.
57   Sayce, *The Valley of a Thousand Deaths*, p. 189.

the camp blacks who hang round stations. They'll likely be station blacks themselves some day, for the wild nigger's dying out'.[58] Grungunja's son, Ngurlbunnya, took eagerly to stock work and in a short time was 'calling his father a dirt desert nigger, a "Myall"'[59] Idriess portrayed the 'myall' Aborigines graphically as at one with the landscape:

> Their whole physique expressed great endurance. Each man had a front tooth knocked out; chest and shoulders were cicatriced by warrior weals, and his naked body, was greased with goanna fat … By degrees, women came towards the camps … Their legs were conspicuously more shapely than the general spindle shanks of the aboriginal, and the young girls' breasts were plumply developed. Rains had broken the drought in this country and all were waxing fat on the plentiful animal and plant food that quickly appeared.[60]

In contrast he depicted Aborigines in close association with Europeans as comic objects of derision.[61] Although European contact was seen as bad, Sayce noted that it improved standards of Aboriginal hygiene[62] and Charles Chewings too believed European contact lifted Aborigines 'out of their naturally squalid habits of living'.[63] But Europeans were not encouraged to be too familiar with Aborigines. 'Buffalo Jim' Westcott ran into trouble with other members of the expedition in Central Australia for trying to learn Aboriginal words.[64]

But approval for the 'wild blacks',[65] may have come not simply from their isolation from European settlement, but in the belief that they were becoming extinct. It was still believed in this period right up to the Second World War that the Territory would soon be rid of its Aboriginal population. Books such a James Devaney's *The Vanished Tribes* (1929) constructed an 'Aboriginal' world where the inhabitants somehow melt away: 'Not understanding, bewildered and lost, they have passed like the sunset'.[66] Ernestine Hill wrote, 'A few more years, and there

---

58  Sayce, *In the Musgrave Ranges*, p. 82.
59  Hatfield, *Desert Saga*, p. 131.
60  Idriess, *Lasseter's Last Ride*, p. 33.
61  Idriess, *Lasseter's Last Ride*, p. 17.
62  Sayce, *In the Musgrave Ranges*, p. 36.
63  C. Chewings, *Back in the Stone Age* (Sydney: Angus & Robertson, 1936), pp. 149–54.
64  Hatfield, *Buffalo Jim*, p. 115.
65  Sayce, *The Valley of a Thousand Deaths*, p. 140.
66  J. Devaney, *The Vanished Tribes* (Sydney: Cornstalk, 1929), p. 234.

will be no more corroboree'.⁶⁷ Commentators such as Elsie Masson,⁶⁸ G. Buchanan,⁶⁹ Ellis,⁷⁰ and Chewings,⁷¹ believed that the Aborigines were dying out, although Basedow stated that it was not necessarily inevitable.⁷² Both Blakely and Ellis saw the survival of Territory Aborigines as a chance to alter the record of colonial settlement elsewhere. Blakely stated that although 'it is too late for a general scheme to protect and preserve all our Natives', a special effort should be made with the Aborigines of Central Australia as, 'these tribes are a possession of international importance, the sole remaining link with the Stone Age, and … the direct offspring of original man'.⁷³ Dorney, too, stressed that the Aborigines were 'not beyond the stone age'.⁷⁴ Of all the writers, Ellis had perhaps the clearest picture of European incursion in the Territory and articulated the heart of the insoluble problem—the competition between Europeans and Aborigines over land.⁷⁵

Conflict between Aborigines and outsiders for the resources of the landscape is a part of these texts and frequently the means by which the protagonists can demonstrate their heroism. Conrad Sayce, particularly, had a high level of racial violence in his texts; that these books were aimed at children seems inappropriate to modern sensibilities. Sayce presents it as biologically inevitable that a white man was able to subjugate the Aborigines because, 'he was a true member of the race which has subjected other races to its rule all over the world. He had an instinctive understanding of the native mind'.⁷⁶ Sayce described the hero, Stan, driving out a camp of Aboriginal people from Narrawing station by burning their huts, threatening to shoot them and cracking stockwhips at them.⁷⁷ The Europeans noted that 'Arrkroo, the Hater' roused the 'Warraguls' to kill the European intruders because he feared that once the news of the presence of gold in the Musgrave Ranges was publicised,

---

67   Hill, *The Great Australian Loneliness*, p. 185; Tom Griffiths also makes this point. T. Griffiths, *Hunters and Collectors: The Antiquarian Imagination in Australia* (Melbourne: Cambridge University Press 1996), pp. 190f.
68   Masson, *An Untamed Territory*, p. 150.
69   G. Buchanan, *Packhorse and Waterhole* (Facsimile edition, Carlisle: Hesperian Press, 1984 (Sydney, Angus & Robertson, 1933)), pp. 84, 110.
70   Ellis, *The Long Lead*, p. 248.
71   Chewings, *Back in the Stone Age*, p. 155.
72   Basedow, *Knights of the Boomerang*, p. 15.
73   Blakely, *Hard Liberty*, p. 185.
74   Dorney, *An Adventurous Honeymoon*, p. 51.
75   Ellis, *The Long Lead*, p. 250.
76   Sayce, *The Valley of a Thousand Deaths*, p. 109.
77   Sayce, *The Valley of a Thousand Deaths*, p. 198.

'the warraguls would be driven out of this, their last great stronghold'.[78] At the conclusion of the book there is little doubt for the reader that Arrkroo's prediction will prove correct. Mick, from the same text, burnt an Aboriginal man 'Eagle' with a red-hot branding iron. When Eagle attempted to retaliate Mick tied him up and flogged him. The only real curb to Mick's excessive violence was the knowledge that he was a white man and hitting 'a man when he's down, nigger or no nigger'[79] is not the white man's way. Mick was by no means presented as the villain of the story, although arguably Eagle was the hero since he saved the life of young Saxon Stobart three times and finally gave his life protecting the Europeans. As the book finishes, Mick plans to return to the Musgrave Ranges: 'I'm with you … Boss Stobart, whether it's gold or niggers you're after'.[80]

Even in the biographical texts there is an acceptance of silence in race relations. Aubrey Wisberg and Harold Waters's *Bushman At Large* (1937) contains a chapter on the Northern Territory with a description of a reprisal for the supposed murder and rape of two missionaries on the Arnhem Land coast:

> A lone lubra's lazily shifting eyes were the first to spot us. Her shrill scream of consternation, astonishment, and fear awakened the camp. A shot cracked. Her cries were abruptly silenced. The blacks streamed from under their gunyahs. A few had spears in their hands. They offered fine targets against the bright water … The whole camp turned tail and fled, screaming with panic. One black paused to hurl a boomerang. It whistled past my head. I made it a point of honor to avenge the insult. I took careful aim. My honor was in no way impaired.
>
> The lubras and children tailing after them as best they could, the aborigines retreated to the water's edge. We followed them with the relentless, indomitable destruction of a juggernaut. Men, women, children fell victims to our sweeping gunfire.
>
> For the murdered whites we had taken almost a hundred black lives in exchange. Young Tim Hall had a slight spear wound. Beyond that we had no other injury.[81]

---

78  Sayce, *In the Musgrave Ranges*, p. 267.
79  Sayce, *In the Musgrave Ranges*, pp. 193–206.
80  Sayce, *In the Musgrave Ranges*, p. 283.
81  A. Wisberg & H. Waters, *Bushman At Large* (New York: Green Circle, 1937), pp. 24, 26.

Although Costello had noted incidents of hostility towards Europeans[82] which sometimes resulted in death,[83] there was a much greater sense that it was the Aborigines rather than the Europeans who were at risk. Sunter described 'Carl Annam', who with his Aboriginal wife was reported to have 'galloped after blackfellows shooting them down like dogs'.[84] Even Hatfield suggested that 'friction with the natives' was a cause for worry in the rush to the Granites gold fields, not on compassionate grounds, but because, 'They wanted no more of that sort of thing, with the aftermath of public outcry and official inquiry'.[85]

This period represents the beginning of the identification of Aborigines with occult powers. Before this, although writers mentioned the supernatural powers Aboriginal 'witchdoctors' exercised within their own community (for example Jeannie Gunn's description of bone pointing), by this period, Aboriginal power has now overflowed into the non-Aboriginal domain. Idriess suggested that the reason for Lasseter's death was because he touched a sacred object:

> 'At any rate,' said Blakely slowly, 'from the moment we took the stick, the curse began to work.'
>
> 'Yes, your enterprise could never succeed.' He turned as he opened the door. 'Who actually laid his hands on the stick first?' he asked in a low voice.
>
> 'Lasseter,' said Sutherland.
>
> 'He will never come back,' said the man, and was gone.[86]

Michael Terry mentioned the arcane '"black arts" no white man may ever master'.[87] Warburton said of T'Kala that 'Many white men credited him with extraordinary … and unnatural powers'.[88] Sayce's Aborigines were frequently capable of telepathic communication.[89] Although this perception was developed more fully in later periods (Bill Harney, later Xavier Herbert), for now, the writers concentrated upon documenting cultural rather than spiritual practices.

---

82   Costello, *Life of John Costello*, p. 164.
83   Costello, *Life of John Costello*, p. 175.
84   Sunter, *Adventures of a Trepang Fisher*, p. 155.
85   Hatfield, *Buffalo Jim*, p. 152.
86   Idriess, *Lasseter's Last Ride*, p. 68.
87   Terry, *Across Unknown Australia*, p. 188.
88   Warburton, *White Poppies*, p. 13.
89   Sayce, *The Valley of a Thousand Deaths*, pp. 15–16; Sayce, *The Splendid Savage*, p. 107.

Above all, the writers were concerned with controlling Aboriginal behaviour, largely as a means of restricting any impediments to European settlement and industry. A distant and uninterested administration in the Territory had left Aboriginal health and housing to Church authorities who frequently established settlements in remote and isolated areas. Almost every 'scientific' expedition from this period used mission stations as bases for operations: Wilkins, Dahl, Thomson, Porteus, Croll, Blakely-Lasseter and so on. A few writers depicted the mission stations sympathetically. Hatfield's character 'the Doctor', who is in charge of a mission station in *Black Waterlily* (recognisable as Oenpelli), is noted for his sincerity and rapport with the Aborigines. When Gilbert roused the tribe to violence, the Doctor refused to carry arms and said solemnly, 'If ... they can raise a hand against me, my work has been in vain, and it were better that I die'.[90] Wilkins too supported missionary work as a way of modifying Aboriginal cultural practices so that they would 'lose their superstitious beliefs and refrain from the gruesome and horrible customs of their tribe'.[91] Archer Russell claimed that the poor health record evident in missionary settlements was not the fault of the missions but of 'public apathy and Governmental neglect'.[92]

But generally most commentators did not approve of missionary work to the Aborigines.[93] The mission stations, seen to have the advantage of cheap rent and slave labour, were resented by the secular population of the Northern Territory.[94] Hermannsburg station was regarded by many as a training ground for spies[95] and German-born missionaries were forced to register as aliens.[96] This scenario was repeated during the Second World

---

90   Hatfield, *Black Waterlily*, p. 272.
91   Wilkins, *Undiscovered Australia*, p. 179.
92   A. Russell, *A Tramp-Royal in Wild Australia: 1928–1929: Being tile Record of a 'Walkabout' among the lone Cattlemen and Cameleers of Australia's Vast and Little-Known Central Wonderland, Together With Notes on the Aboriginal, the Physical Features, and the Fauna and Flora of the Desert Home. Done in the Vagabond Spirit under the Urge to Adventure, and With the Will to See the Country as it is* (London: Jonathan Cape, 1934), p. 194.
93   Patrick Wolfe, looking at Central Australia, suggested that at least a part of this condemnation was to do with the belief that, 'the moral order of the Arunta, which, though it could not compare with white morality, was unequivocally preferable to the degeneracy which followed acculturation'; Wolfe, 'On Being Woken Up', p. 200.
94   See M. Dewar, 'Strange Bedfellows: Europeans and Aborigines Arnhem Land Before World War II'. MA (Hons), University of New England, 1989, Chapter 7, for examples of this in the Arnhem Land region.
95   Skipper Partridge quoted, A. Grant, *Camel Train and Aeroplane: The Story of Skipper Partridge* (Dee Why, New South Wales: Frontier Publishing, 1989 (1981)), pp. 109–10.
96   T.G.H. Strehlow, *Journey to Horseshoe Bend* (Sydney: Angus & Robertson, 1969), pp. 12–13.

War when Rex Battarbee was appointed to watch over the activities of the mission.[97] Elsie Masson felt that mission training was relatively useless in comparison to practical work on the pastoral properties.[98] Although Dahl attached himself to the Jesuit mission 'Uniya' on the Daly,[99] he was critical of its work.[100] Croll thought that the missionary influence deprived Aborigines of their own spiritual life at the same time exposing them to the risk of disease and death in settlement life.[101] Terry thought missions to the Aborigines useless because he did not believe the Aborigines capable of understanding a spiritual message.[102] Sunter thought the conditions poor on Goulburn Island mission[103] and cited the case of a brutal man who justified himself on the grounds that missionaries used similar techniques.[104] Conigrave thought the missions unsuccessful because of the 'pull and attraction of the bush'.[105] In 1934 medical Doctor Charles Duguid was shocked by the attitudes of some of the members of the Australian Inland Mission who referred to the Aborigines as 'niggers' and opined frankly that their work was with the European pastoralists and that the Aborigines, '[ha]ve never been any good and never will be'.[106] Theo Price cited Arnhem Land anthropologist Lloyd Warner's criticism of missionary work in the Northern Territory.[107] Typical of the secular attitude to missionary work was Herbert's depiction of the mission station Tocky and Christobel are sent to. Herbert lampooned the ostensibly well-meaning but ineffectual missionary, Mr Hollower, and the other mission staff: assistant Brother Bleeter, his wife, 'devoted spinsters, Sisters Wings and Harp' and Pacific Island assistants. Hollower was writing *God In The Silver Sea* oblivious to the fact that his nickname was 'Ol' Lucifer'. At night, locked in the dormitories, the girls gathered together naked in the heat to sing rude songs about him to the refrain of hymns.[108]

97  C. Duguid, *Doctor and the Aborigines* (Adelaide: Rigby, 1972), p. 146.
98  Masson, *An Untamed Territory*, p. 141.
99  Dahl, *In Savage Australia*, p. 35.
100 Dahl, *In Savage Australia*, p. 37.
101 R.H. Croll, *Wide Horizons* (Sydney: Angus & Robertson, 1937), p. 134.
102 Terry, *Across Unknown Australia*, p. 101.
103 Sunter, *Adventures of a Trepang Fisher*, p. 146.
104 Sunter, *Adventures of a Trepang Fisher*, p. 183.
105 Conigrave, *North Australia*, p. 205.
106 Duguid, *Doctor and the Aborigines*, p. 97.
107 Price, *God in the Sand*, p. 15.
108 Herbert, *Capricornia*, pp. 248–51.

Dissatisfied with missionary administration, most writers felt qualified to use their texts as vehicles for putting forward their ideas for Aboriginal administration. Terry[109] and Chewings[110] advocated a tightening up of the system which was felt to be too laissez-faire. Blakely advocated reserves but added that they must be inviolate from incursions by outsiders, whether they be 'missionaries or prospectors'.[111] Gordon Buchanan noted that 'the white man has his duty to do'.[112]

In this period also, the last massacre of Aborigines by police in the Northern Territory occurred at Coniston Station. Authors were only just beginning to question the justice of imposing European concepts of morality and legal process on the Aborigines and their possible continuing role in Australia society. This recognition was rather late in coming, not only because of the predominantly European perspective of the authors, but because it was only in this period that commentators realised that Aborigines were not going to become extinct. Justice for Aborigines became an issue for some writers. Elsie Masson noted that, 'too often the savage black who commits an act of violence is simply avenging equal outrages done to his own race by the savage white'.[113] With reference to the Caledon Bay massacres,[114] Conigrave commented that there was 'urgent need of a drastic change in the present system of bringing natives to trial in a white man's court'.[115] Hatfield's Aboriginal character Gilbert gave an impassioned account of his thoughts concerning treatment of Aborigines by Europeans from Darwin.[116]

J.S. Needham wrote:

> The aborigines are expected to obey our laws and are judged by them, and their laws are not considered in our courts. The trouble is that no one has told them what is expected of them and the judges are themselves

---

109 Terry, *Across Unknown Australia*, p. 101.
110 Chewings, *Back in the Stone Age*, pp. 149–54.
111 Blakely, *Hard Liberty*, p. 186.
112 Buchanan, *Packhorse and Waterhole*, p. 117.
113 Masson, *An Untamed Territory*, p. 177.
114 The Caledon Bay and Woodah Island killings were a focus of interest to many writers in this period and later but much of this I have covered, M. Dewar, *The 'Black War' in Arnhem Land: Missionaries and the Yolngu 1908–1940* (Darwin: North Australia Research Unit, The Australian National University, 1992).
115 Conigrave, *North Australia*, p. 222.
116 Hatfield, *Black Waterlily*, pp. 241–42.

ignorant of the customs, traditions and laws of the natives. No full or true justice is to be expected while this double ignorance is allowed to prevail.[117]

The authors sometimes expressed a fear that contact with Aborigines could culturally subsume the European settlers; probably an oblique reference to Europeans engaging in sexual relations with Aboriginal women. Sayce maintained the necessity of living like a white man: 'I had heard and read about white men ... who had gradually adopted native life and customs, and had become very degraded'.[118] An elderly bushman warned the young Saxon Stobart that, 'Many a good lad has gone to the dogs through having too much to do with niggers'.[119] Jim Westcott was criticised for 'his familiarity with the natives'.[120] For it was an accepted tenet that Aboriginal women were open for sexual exploitation. 'The lubra has no moral ethic whatever' Ernestine Hill asserted confidently.[121] In contrast she noted that many European men who had been having sexual relations with Aboriginal women were deeply ashamed and '"went bush" rather than meet me'.[122] Herbert noted the same sentiments. Mark Shillingsworth could not face Heather, 'knowing that while white women might forgive a man any amount of ordinary philandering they are blindly intolerant of weakness for Black Velvet'.[123] This was in fact untrue, although Herbert was at pains to minimise the distinction. Heather stated passionately to Norman, 'all men are comboes [sic] one way or ... another. What's difference black lubra or white?'[124] That white women do forgive European men for Aboriginal lovers is asserted by Conrad Sayce, one of the most vehemently racist authors from the period. In *Golden Buckles* Ida is told that Jim has fathered a baby with Ruby, his Aboriginal mistress. When Ida hears the new she is angry and hurt. Jim, for reasons known only to himself, fosters this belief despite the fact that it is untrue. Jim becomes angry with Ida for not recognising that this is the way that true men live in Central Australia and flounces off saying, 'I'm going north.

---

117 J.S. Needham, *White and Black in Australia* (London: Society for Promoting Christian Knowledge, 1935), p. 167.
118 Sayce, *The Splendid Savage*, p. 82.
119 Sayce, *In the Musgrave Ranges*, p. 36.
120 Hatfield, *Buffalo Jim*, p. 130.
121 Hill, *The Great Australian Loneliness*, p. 230.
122 Hill, *The Great Australian Loneliness*, p. 230.
123 Herbert, *Capricornia*, p. 36.
124 Herbert, *Capricornia*, p. 359.

I'm going back to be with men'.[125] Ida proves her love (and incidentally saves Jim's life when he was dying of thirst) by ignoring his past sexual associations and travelling to Central Australia to be with him.

But if most Europeans in the Northern Territory had difficulty accommodating an Aboriginal presence, they were not favourably inclined to the other nationalities that settled in the Northern Territory. The Asian residents were particular targets for European disapproval, although their capacity for work in the tropical climate was grudgingly admired. Sunter praised Japanese working skills although he believed their presence on the Territory coast caused trouble because of their sexual relations with the Aborigines.[126] Wilkins noted that the Japanese worked under more difficult conditions than Europeans would tolerate.[127] Conigrave commented that 'the mixture of races' in Darwin lowered the standard of living.[128] Edwin Grew and Marion Sharpe commented,

> the entrance to Darwin is the Chinese quarter, all tumble-down tin shanties, unsightly and comfortless, and very poverty-stricken looking with shrill children screaming and playing in the dust. Its appearance gave one an inkling why Australians would rather dispense with the cheap and efficient Chinese labour than leaven the population of their great clean land with people who could thrive contentedly in a little colony of pigsties.[129]

Many writers criticised other nationalities for their treatment of Aborigines, particularly Elsie Masson[130] and Dahl.[131] But other writers feared the economic threat that Asians posed to the European residents. Ellis commented upon the economic and cultural hold the Chinese exercised in Darwin.[132] Blakely[133] and Sampson agreed.[134] Warburton recognised that Europeans had not always dealt justly with the Chinese.[135] Journalist T.E.A. Healy summed up the mood of the community: 'On the

---

125 Sayce, *Golden Buckles*, p. 151.
126 Sunter, *Adventures of a Trepang Fisher*, pp. 83, 163f, 172.
127 Wilkins, *Undiscovered Australia*, p. 212.
128 Conigrave, *North Australia*, pp. 111–12.
129 Grew & Sharpe, *Rambles in Australia*, p. 278.
130 Masson, *An Untamed Territory*, p. 152.
131 Dahl, *In Savage Australia*, p. 75.
132 Ellis, *The Long Lead*, pp. 165–66.
133 Blakely, *Hard Liberty*, p. 252.
134 Sampson, *Through Central Australia*, p. 24.
135 Warburton, *White Poppies*, p. 148.

first afternoon in Darwin I sat on the hotel veranda. I had seen the filth of Chinatown, smelt the execrable drains, visited all the town in ten minutes drive. For some reason I felt completely desolate'.[136]

In the earlier period of writing, women, both European and Aboriginal, were frequently presented as strong, capable characters. In this later period women become less powerful and are portrayed as superficial. Increasingly hostility is reported from European women towards Aboriginal women. In many novels from this period, women are not even mentioned. As Ernestine Hill noted, in the Northern Territory 'white women were rare'.[137] H.W.H. Stevens in his *Reminiscences of a Hard Case* (1937) states that the only drawback to working at the British Australia Telegraph (BAT) office in Darwin 'was the scarcity of ladies' society'.[138] There are no women at all in Sayce's *The Splendid Savage*, *The Golden Valley* and *In the Musgrave Ranges*. Apart from an old Aboriginal woman who is nearly burnt to death by Dick and Stan, women do not come into *Valley of a Thousand Deaths* either. Women are equally absent from E.V. Timms's *The Valley of Adventure* or Bernard Cronin's *The Treasure of the Tropics*. J.M. Downie's *The Flying Doctor Mystery* does not mention women. W. Hatfield's *Desert Saga* has a few female characters, but the main protagonists are male. Aboriginal women, although portrayed in the novel as both saintly and loving, are completely subject to male domination.[139] In Armour's *Burning Air*, Blackwood's missing daughter Rae hardly comes into the story (apart from being Jim's inspiration as 'an angel' and her complaint that, 'men are all the same. They think they have hard times but women have harder') except in purely masculine racist terms. Jim foils what he believes to be an attempt by Raska, the 'Afghan', to rescue her (little knowing it was really his mate in disguise): 'He had beaten the Asiatic, yet he was furious at the fellow for daring to carry off the white girl'.[140] Idriess suggested, in his reconstruction of Lasseter's last days, that Lasseter incurred the enmity of the Aborigines by his spirited and courtly defence of Lerilla from the savage wife beater, Gadgadgery.[141]

---

136 Healy, *And Far From Home*, p. 121.
137 Hill, *The Territory*, p. 10.
138 H.W.H.S[tevens], *Reminiscences of a Hard Case* (Singapore: Lithographers, 1937), p. 6.
139 Hatfield, *Desert Saga*, p. 76.
140 Armour, *Burning Air*, pp. 147, 152, 202.
141 Idriess, *Lasseter's Last Ride*, p. 150.

The Territory is depicted almost without exception as a man's country. Idriess has Kidman thinking 'sympathetically' of the first women 'who would come gradually into this country under present conditions'.[142] Kidman's wife is depicted as staying at home, bringing up the children and insisting Kidman attend church. When Kidman returns on a brief visit to Kapunda to hear the cockatoo shrieking 'Hullo father', he construes this as 'ominous'. 'It was. A baby girl'.[143]

As with the earlier writers, women are depicted as contributing to (if not the sole cause of) the maintenance of the social hierarchy. Jessie Litchfield described some of the women of the tin fields at West Arm: the lairy Mrs. Tress, whose outfit prepares us for her sexual promiscuity: 'bright orange blouse, a violet skirt, emerald green belt, red stockings, and black buttoned boots ... The whole ensemble was topped off with a gaudy Japanese umbrella'.[144] Mrs. Wilson, on the other hand, is too good, 'undeniably a "wowser". One could read her character in the square-toed, thick soled boots she wore, in her thick black woollen stockings, and in her stiff black hat'.[145] Ernestine Hill wrote with admiration of the pioneering Sargents of Stapleton Station with their large family, 'mostly girls', whose matchless abilities for self-sufficiency make them 'the right type of settler'.[146] *Larapinta* tells us what the 'right type' is like. When the nasty Jack Latcher criticises Beth, it is on the grounds that she is too empty headed and concerned with shallow interests, unlike Margaret who can cook over a camp fire, set bones, sew wounds, cut hair and round up cattle.[147] Edwin Grew and Marion Sharpe paid tribute to the role of women on the Northern Territory frontier:

> The part to be played by women in the future of the Northern Territory is a very important one. It is a hard thing for a man to go into exile with his cattle and his black retainers, but if Australian or European women will consent to share the hardships, and the rough life, and the loneliness, in order to make a home for their men; bringing to it, as opportunity offers, the atmosphere and the comforts of civilisation, the problems of opening up the inland country is helped considerably on its way ...[148]

---

142 Idriess, *The Cattle King*, p. 85.
143 Idriess, *The Cattle King*, p. 121.
144 Litchfield, *Far North Memories*, p. 179.
145 Litchfield, *Far North Memories*, p. 182.
146 Hill, *The Great Australian Loneliness*, p. 136; the actual story of one of the 'girls' has been written by E. Meaney, *Esther: The True Story of An Australian Country Girl* (Batchelor, Northern Territory: Esther Meaney, 1988 (1987)).
147 R.B. Plowman, *Larapinta* (Sydney, Angus & Robertson, 1939), p. 105.
148 Grew & Sharpe, *Rambles in Australia*, p. 274.

Herbert does not describe the female characters in the same detail as males but characterisation is not Herbert's metier. His male characters, too, exist to support a narrative. But like Litchfield, Herbert's European women are marked by a preoccupation with the trappings of society. When Mark Shillingsworth calls on his brother to ask for a loan, Oscar is entertaining his fiancée, Jasmine Poundamore, and her sister Heather. Mark is overawed by the

> taking of afternoon tea in a style quite foreign to him. At first he thought that they were drinking beer, because their beverage was brown and was served with ice in glasses. It was tea. And he found to his discomfort that a strange combination knife-fork was given him with which to eat cakes so small that he could have put six in his mouth at once … in using it he had to expose his grubby-nailed hand … He sweated and fumbled and blushed …[149]

When Mark returns to find Heather alone on another occasion, they share 'a manly sort of afternoon tea'.[150]

Beyond apportioning a vague and anonymous blame, rarely during this period did authors look at the circumstances which generated the 'half-caste' population. Philippa Bridges used the situation as evidence for the need for more European women.[151] But European women were seen as curbing men's natural behaviour. Like Gunn, Litchfield found that European women were thought to 'cast an evil spell over the camp, that it would never be successful until we left'.[152] The texts display less hostility between the sexes in this period, although there are clearly problems inherent in the masculine construction of the Territory lifestyle. Elsie Masson noted that although a man travels north to, 'The prospect of better work, or the fascination of life in a more primitive community … The wife, on the other hand, goes because he goes, and not because the life appeals'.[153] White women were increasingly portrayed as suffering heroines in the Territory story. Ernestine Hill lyricised, 'I have met women … nomads of the Never-Never, to whom, with their loved ones always

---

149 Herbert, *Capricornia*, p. 32.
150 Herbert, *Capricornia*, p. 34.
151 Bridges, *A Walk-About in Australia*, p. 185.
152 Litchfield, *Far North Memories*, p. 88.
153 Masson, *An Untamed Territory*, p. 25.

close beside them, the loneliness meant little ... Hard lives—but among them all, never yet have I met a woman who was unhappy'.[154] Archer Russell noted:

> Wonderfully capable and noble-hearted are these women of the far-back places ... Theirs is a courage that cannot be measured ... Year after year, unsung, unknown, they live their lonely lives, uncomplaining, never wincing, always cheerful. Mother and housekeeper, doctor and nurse, governess and cook, and stockbanger often—such are some of the bush wife's occupations and in none of them is she dismayed, by none of them is she beaten. You women of the city—what do you know of loneliness and discomfort?[155]

Women were seen most often as controllers of the domestic sphere and some writers found it difficult to instil glamour or interest in the roles. T.E.A. Healy pointed out that it was difficult for women to look after the household because of the shortages of basic commodities.[156] Masson noted that women played a significant role in socialising Aborigines into European society through the training of domestic servants.[157] Bridges agreed.[158] Hall patronisingly commented upon the difficulties faced by women settlers:

> My experience has been that the average man dumps his home at the most convenient spot—near a spring, a well, a good natural waterhole, a dam, or a tank. A little later he wonders why his wife and children are not happy and contented. But bring the average woman to a new home, with a good background and a pleasing outlook. Be it ever so humble, she loves it on sight and at once visualised the beauty of a better home in such surroundings. And is, therefore, a better and happier help mate. I ask all my women readers: Is that not so?[159]

A brief mention of European women as potential sexual partners for Northern Territory men was hinted at. Nursing Sister Pircy Leonard from Warburton's *White Poppies* commented, emphasising a certain dumb chivalry in relations between sexes in the bush:

---

154 E. Hill, 'In the Bough Shade', L. Brown, B. de Crespigny, M.P. Harris, K.K. Thomas, P.N. Watson, *A Book of South Australia: Women in the First Hundred Years* (Adelaide: Rigby, 1936), p. 244.
155 Russell, *A Tramp-Royal in Wild Australia*, p. 167.
156 Healy, *And Far From Home*, p. 124.
157 Masson, *An Untamed Territory*, p. 50.
158 Bridges, *A Walk-About in Australia*, p. 226.
159 Hall, *Our Back Yard*, pp. 32–33.

Yes, she was glad she had come—this was a man's country. The men treated the womenfolk so differently, too. In their rough, travel-stained khaki, broad-rimmed hats, riding half-broken, plunging horses, they seemed fearsome enough—rough, uncouth, pitting brute strength against brute strength. But in the presence of women they changed somehow. At first shy-eyed and dumb, twirling their hats in strong fingers and shuffling feet shod in high-heeled riding-boots, they show an old world deference and courtesy. Afterwards, the shyness is replaced by a straight-eyed, breezy camaraderie, but the manners remain knightly. Like the knights of old, they ride away with a laugh, far into the unknown deserts, facing dreadful privations and death. Why? Perhaps to win fortune, to lay at their lady's feet.[160]

Or perhaps because of sexual tension, for as Lyn Riddett has demonstrated in her analysis of the role of the Australian Inland Mission nursing sisters, 'The importance of white women to the north rested largely on their potential as breeders'.[161] A view of European women's sexual relationships was presented in R.H. Milford's *Australia's Backyards* (1934) in a chapter revealingly titled 'The Adulteresses of Darwin' which formed a striking contrast to the more domestic or chivalric construction favoured by the majority of authors. Milford was scandalised by the women of Darwin:

> the average white woman has developed the fetish, that in the Territory she must never 'work'. Therefore, while always having at her command an army of 'niggers' … beneficently supplied by the various 'protectors' … Satan finds mischief for idle hands to do …
>
> time is spent in scandalising their enemies and friends—there is really no difference here—on a major scale, alcoholic parties, and bridge. The night period is given up largely to joy-riding in motor cars with gentlemen who are seldom their husbands. Not only at night either …[162]

In the light of this view of the Northern Territory as the decadent tropical north of sexual licence, it is surprising how little mention was made during this period of the bushman's practice of cohabiting with Aboriginal women, although Dahl commented that, 'A bushman in Northern Australia without a black woman was a rare exception'.[163] Dahl described incidents of brutality, kidnapping and sexual exploitation, and

---

160 Warburton, *White Poppies*, p. 113.
161 L. Riddett, 'Guarding Civilization's Rim: The Australian Inland Mission Sisters in the Victoria River District 1922–1939', *Journal of Australian Studies* 30 (September 1991), p. 39.
162 Milford, *Australia's Backyards*, p. 10.
163 Dahl, *In Savage Australia*, p. 254.

actually witnessed the rape of a ten year old girl.[164] Wilkins was shocked when sexually propositioned by a young Aboriginal girl but acknowledged that, 'Such ideas are prevalent throughout a great part of the territory'.[165] Of Aboriginal and European sexual liaisons he commented, 'The result, however deplorable, is natural, and no statute made by man has power to stop it'.[166] Blakely particularly reserved his contempt for the 'Combo' (a man who acknowledges his Aboriginal mistress) suggesting that the problem was not widespread but restricted to a degenerate few: 'This man is for ever destroying the morals of the Natives, and he is the original creator of the half-caste problem. Take a census of the half-castes, and it will surprise you how few white men should be dealt with'.[167] Milford agreed that the 'moral turpitude can be laid at the door of the white males' for the 'immense number of half-castes', although, unusual in any construction of the Territory sexual relations, he also suggested that a white Darwin woman had a 'half-caste' baby.[168] Some writers concentrated on the tangible products of such liaisons, preferring to ignore the circumstances which created them. Croll advocated full citizens rights for the children of such unions with 'greater facilities for education'.[169]

Although the journalistic writers such as Blakely, Wilkins, Dahl, Croll, Milford and Litchfield[170] mention sexual relations between European men and Aboriginal women, until *Capricornia*, the novelists were coy in their descriptions. Sayce had difficulty reconciling the reality. He coped by noting that Aboriginal women were only sexually attractive to bad white men, like Sleat.[171] They were physically repulsive to decent, manly ex-public school chaps like Stan and Dick: 'The women were the usual lot to be found in a blacks' camp, dirty chattering monkeys … with here and there an old toothless hag, so hideous that Stan was fascinated by the grotesque face and withered form'.[172] In *Comboman* Robert Grey is revolted by Pralta:

---

164 Dahl, *In Savage Australia*, p. 254.
165 Wilkins, *Undiscovered Australia*, p. 160.
166 Croll, *Wide Horizons*, p. 144.
167 Blakely, *Hard Liberty*, p. 186.
168 Milford, *Australia's Backyards*, p. 9.
169 Croll, *Wide Horizons*, p. 146.
170 Litchfield, *Far North Memories*, p. 57.
171 Sayce, *The Valley of a Thousand Deaths*, p. 99.
172 Sayce, *The Valley of a Thousand Deaths*, p. 199.

> Light from the smoking lamp ... shone mercilessly on this woman whom he had made the mother of his children. Judged by every canon of his training, she was repulsive. It was unbearable to think that her blood flowed in the veins of the baby cuddling in his arms.[173]

After *Capricornia*, novelists became more interested in looking at the circumstances surrounding Aboriginal and European sexual liaisons, although in this period the subject matter was largely left to the non-fiction writers. Even in Herbert's *Capricornia*, which was by comparison with Sayce a striking interpretation of sensitivity and humanity, Norman Shillingsworth's mother is little more than a name in the text. As in the *Comboman* construction, it is the European father, who is seen as the dominant influence upon the child.[174] This view is also repeated in *No Footprints in the Bush* where Arthur Upfield depicts McPherson as the dominant influence over Rex whose Aboriginal mother, Tarlalin, died before the action of the novel.[175]

Th chief influence upon the writing in this period came from the scientists who promulgated the notion that the Northern Territory was a living museum display of mankind's prehistoric past. There were a few dissenting voices, mainly from the writers who had extensive experience living and working in the bush such as Sunter or Warburton, but for the most part the travellers and public servants in the Territory perpetuated the notion of infantile, primitive Aborigines. The central subject of the narratives was the celebration of a distinctive Territory culture created by European males pitting themselves against the wilderness. This mythic culture of the Never-Never and its popularity as the 'real' Australia functioned as a metaphor justifying European occupation. Aborigines were regarded as so primitive and morally degenerate that they could not see the mineral wealth that Europeans needed to develop the land.

Territory writing was to take another turn after the publication of *Capricornia*. Herbert's treatment of the tabu subject of Aboriginal and European sexual relations and his scepticism regarding the moral integrity of the European bushman brought a frankness to the writing

---

173 Sayce, *Comboman*, p. 25.
174 This interesting bias in the text of *Capricornia* has been explored more fully, E. Lawson, 'Oh Don't you Remember Black Alice? or How Many Mothers had Norman Shillingsworth', *Westerly* 3 (1987), pp. 29–40.
175 A. Upfield, *No Footprint in the Bush* (Harmondsworth, Middlesex: Penguin, 1949 (1940)), pp. 68f; similarly, Bon's mother also is dead, p. 104.

and paved the way for such people as Harney, Walker and Ronan. Although the confidence with which Gunn and Willshire could assert the gentlemanliness of the Australian bushman was weakened by Herbert's irony, there remained a strong tradition of Territory writing which lauded the rough nobility of the bush. In the pre-World War II period, writers such as Sayce, Armour, Downie, Hatfield, Clune and Idriess glorified the romantic ideal of the noble white bushman. Although many of these writers continued to write throughout the 1940s and even later, their formative styles were established in the pre–World War II period. The pre-war period represents a simplistic approach to subject matter where the Territory was the land of adventure, populated by brave bushmen and tricky savages.

# 5

# THE ATOMIC TERRITORY

In the arts, 'outback iconography' became important nationally and internationally in the period immediately after the Second World War.[1] The Territory firmly became 'outback' for the writers at a time when, paradoxically, it least resembled it: 'Outback Australia started to become much better known and it seems the idea of there being an internal anthropological frontier came to an end'.[2] Anthropology was by now, however, a firm component of any writing. A measure of the pervasive association between the Northern Territory and the social sciences in the post-war period can be seen in *Outbreak of Love* (1957) where Martin Boyd lampooned the earnest and impoverished anthropologists 'who had just returned from three months' primitive sex observation in the Northern Territory'.[3] The literary focus on Aborigines as interpreted by anthropologists was firmly established: A.P. Elkin, for example, wrote the prefaces for the writing of H.E. Thonemann of Elsey Station, Bill Harney, Ronald Berndt, Russel Ward, Roland Robinson and others.[4] Although Harney gently jibed at scientists' lack of understanding of the material they collected,[5] he directly acknowledged their influence.[6]

---

1   H. McQueen, *The Suburbs of the Sacred* (Ringwood: Penguin, 1988), p. 168.
2   N. Peterson, '"Studying Man and Man's Nature": the History of the Institutionalisation of Aboriginal Anthropology', *Australian Aboriginal Studies*, 2 (1990), pp. 13–14.
3   M. Boyd, *Outbreak of Love* (Ringwood: Penguin, 1984 (1957)), p. 240.
4   T. Wise, *The Self-Made Anthropologist: A Life of A.P. Elkin* (Sydney: Allen & Unwin, 1985), p. 195.
5   W.E. Harney, *North of 23°: Ramblings in Northern Australia* (Sydney: Australasian, n.d. c. 1943), p. 115.
6   Harney, *North of 23°*, p. 31.

After the war and in direct contrast to the previous period, writing about the region meant writing about Aborigines: 'it seems to me … that the native is inseparably bound up with the Territory. It seems impossible to discuss the one without the other'[7] remarked the Doctor in Vic Hall's *Bad Medicine*. The writing adopted a tone akin to propaganda as the literature promoted the Aboriginal assimilation policy and a new openness in dealing with Aboriginal sexual exploitation. But the confidence in the ideas appeared only on the surface and it is apparent that many of the writers were aware of the contradictions within not only the Territory but Australian society as a whole. Randolph Stowe commented, 'all that is written about the colour question is written by white men for white men only … What is needed, of course, is an aboriginal writer'.[8]

Before the war, explorers and travellers came to the Territory looking for adventure and excitement. After the war, artists of all kinds—painters, film-makers, dancers and writers—made the pilgrimage to seek direct inspiration from the landscape and contact with the Aboriginal Territorians. Missionary writing gained a new lease of life, flourishing under the renewed interest in Aboriginal matter and, particularly in the 1960s and 1970s, autobiographical books describing field experience in the Territory proliferated.

The 'Aboriginal assimilation' policy came under scrutiny from the general public as writers sought to describe the Territory solution to the 'Aboriginal problem'. The virtual destruction of Darwin by Japanese bombing in the Second World War and the subsequent military build-up made redundant the notion of the remoteness and inviolateness of a Territory landscape populated by wild Aborigines. The catalyst for the change in official attitudes to Aborigines was, ironically, the wartime involvement of Aborigines with the army. The army employed large numbers of Aborigines in support services and for many of the new arrivals from the south it was to be their first contact with large numbers of Aborigines. In contrast to the pastoral industry, conditions for Aboriginal workers in the defence force were less exploitative although they did not receive equal wages.[9] The role of Aborigines within the army was seen at the time to have been highly successful. In retrospect, though, it set the agenda for

---

7   V.C. Hall, *Bad Medicine: A Tale of the Northern Territory* (Melbourne: Robertson & Mullens, 1947), p. 273.
8   R. Stow, 'Negritude for the White Man', M. Reay ed., *Aborigines Now* (Sydney: Angus & Robertson, 1964), p. 6.
9   Wise, *The Self-Made Anthropologist*, p. 164.

the assimilation program of the 1950s in so far as the government-run Aboriginal settlements, inspired by the war-time army labour camps,[10] were run on hierarchical institutionalised lines.[11] Sir Paul Hasluck, twelve years Minister for Territories in the Menzies Government, enacted new legislation designed to assimilate Aborigines into the dominant European culture. The Welfare Ordinance of 1953—the classification of Aborigines according to the amount of 'white' in their progenitors—reached national prominence following the case of Albert Namatjira. National interest focussed on the Northern Territory.

Among intellectuals and academics, the debate concerning Australian society and the bush tradition reached a peak in three publications of the 'radical nationalists': Vance Palmer's *The Legend of the Nineties* (1953), A.A. Phillips's *The Australian Tradition* (1958)[12] and Russel Ward's *The Australian Legend* (1958).[13] John Docker noted the reassertion of the older values: 'For the radical nationalists ... Australia's true spirit, of independence, egalitarianism, tolerance, sardonic humour, hospitality, had been created by a small group of pioneers, of nomads, pastoralists and, for Palmer, selectors'.[14] By 1964, Donald Horne's *The Lucky Country*

---

10   J. Long, *The Go-Betweens: Patrol Officers in Aboriginal Affairs Administration in the Northern Territory 1936–74* (Darwin: North Australia Research Unit, The Australian National University, 1992), p. 167.
11   Julie T. Wells, 'The Long March: Assimilation Policy and Practice: the Darwin area 1939–1967', PhD thesis, University of Queensland, 1995, although Robert Hall suggests that the Army was guided in its policy by the administration in Darwin; Robert A. Hall, *The Black Diggers: Aborigines and Torres Strait Islanders in the Second World War* (Sydney: Allen & Unwin, 1989), p. 135.
12   Arthur Phillips noted that both he and Russel Ward chose the title, 'The Australian Tradition' for their respective works but that as Phillips's book 'was rather faster through the press', Ward chose instead 'The Australian Legend'. This coincidence Phillips saw as 'symptomatic of a developing trend of thought ... in ... Australian culture', A.A. Phillips, *The Australian Tradition: Studies in a Colonial Culture* (Melbourne: Longman Cheshire, 1980 (1958)), p. xxiv.
13   At this time, a contrasting note to the radical nationalists was provided by John Pringle, Scottish ex-editor of the *Sydney Morning Herald*, who after five years residence penned his version of Australian culture and society, *Australian Accent*. Pringle found D.H. Lawrence's *Kangaroo* a 'profound' book about Australia and appreciated his enthusiasm for a vigorous, if misogynist, democratic ideal. The book was presented from a markedly Sydney perspective; Pringle noted, 'There is nothing in it about the Dead Heart or the Outback'. Despite Pringle's conscious determination to avoid the outback nationalist cliches, he found painter Sidney Nolan's Ned Kelly series 'of the Australian centre, with the bare red ranges stretching to infinity, symbolise this feeling of man's loneliness in a hostile land'. J.D. Pringle, *Australian Accent* (Adelaide: Rigby, 1978 (1958)), p. 124.
14   J. Docker, 'Culture, Society and the Communist Party' in A. Curthoys, and J. Merritt, eds *Australia's First Cold War 1945–1953, Vol 1: Society Communism and Culture* (Sydney: Allen & Unwin, 1984), p. 185.

examined the nationalist tradition in more critical terms.[15] This focus on Australian nationalism in turn brought a renewal of interest in the Territory bush themes.

Some of the contradictions inherent in this period of Australian cultural history appear in the writing about the Northern Territory. Before the war, the protagonists of Territory writing were depicted as in a state of conflict with the landscape. The Territory was seen as hazardous; in seeking to exploit the economic potential of the environment there was a sense that the settlers were at risk from the physical and mental geography. The post-war Territory was apparently more benign, at least from the non-Aboriginal perspective. Overtly there was a commonly voiced rejoicing at the technological and physical mastery over the environment. Similarly there was an apparent celebration of the incorporation of Aborigines within the European legislative system. Gender tension once again entered the literary agenda, but mostly centring around the sexual exploitation of Aboriginal women—the construction Herbert had so clearly outlined in *Capricornia*.

The writing in the immediate post-war period can be seen to share a number of assumptions and characteristics. The science and technology of the atomic age was thought to have much to offer both the Territory and its inhabitants through the exploitation and control of the environment. Since by now it has become apparent that Aborigines are not going to become extinct, they must be given the education and opportunity to live exactly as Europeans do; it is recognised that this will be a slow process and must be carried out in stages. Specifically, children of Aboriginal mothers and European fathers must be rescued from the squalor of the camp and placed in institutions to ensure that they do not retain any ties to their Aboriginal family or adopt any attitudes that may be construed an Aboriginal rather than European; Church financed institutions that undertake this task, however, are regarded with suspicion and distrust by the secular population. European women, the home-makers, form a model of emancipation for their oppressed Aboriginal sisters.

Ironically, the literature about the Northern Territory, while arising from nostalgic celebration of the true Australia and the bush ideal, had the effect of raising issues that were relevant to a more pluralistic view of

---

15  'Australia is a lucky country run mainly by second-rate people who share its luck', D. Horne, *The Lucky Country* (Ringwood: Penguin, 1971 (1964)), p. 220.

Australian society. While writers were attracted to the subject of the Northern Territory as the geography of outback Australia, what they described was an organised system of outback administration which actively discriminated against the language, culture and society of the indigenous people. Some writers, such as Alan Marshall and Frank Hardy, deliberately set out to expose this situation for public scrutiny. Other writers, attracted by the Territory outback as artistic inspiration, while ostensibly articulating the Australian bush ideals, found themselves as reluctant critics of Federal Aboriginal policy. Throughout all the changes of this period, the Territory managed to hold its position as the place of dreams and myths fundamental to all Australians. Tom Ronan noted: 'The Northern Territory … is a roughly rectangular piece of country bounded on the north by the Menace of Asia and on the south by the Kidman Legend'.[16]

In the period after the Second World War, many ex-servicemen found the Territory a source of inspiration. Writers, artists, journalists and film-makers all came north seeking the 'real' Australia. Territory men, including artist, Eric Joliffe, writer and adventurer, Syd Kyle Little, bushman and writer, Bill Harney, and journalist and writer, Douglas Lockwood.
Source: Reproduced with permission Northern Territory Library, Harney /McCaffery Collection PH510/42.

---

16  Tom Ronan, *The Mighty Men On Horseback: Sketches and Yarns* (Adelaide: Rigby, 1977), p. 71.

During the 1960s, particularly following the British nuclear testing at Maralinga in South Australia, there was a growing sense of the important role that the remote areas of Australia would play assisting our allies in the Cold War. Immediately after the war, in the texts our principal ally was Britain rather than the United States of America. In Capt. W.E. Johns's *Biggles in Australia* (1955) British secret agents attempt to keep developments in the Australian uranium industry secret. M.E. Patchett's *The Venus Project* (1963) centred around a Russian rocket, tracked by Woomera to its landing in Arnhem Land. By the time of Edward Lindall's *The Last Refuge* (1972), the heroes were working with the American CIA to foil a communist plot.

Leith Barter has demonstrated the fervour with which Territorians pursued a uranium find in the 1950s.[17] This may not have assumed the mythic proportions of the Lasseter quest but it is certainly a feature of the period and mineral finds of all kinds continue to feature in the texts. Henry C. James's *Gold Is Where You Find It* follows the wanderings of Dead Sweet Joe Stephenson in his quest to find gold. Oil is discovered in Kenneth Moon's *The Fire Serpent Mystery*. In *Biggles Works it Out*, the chase for Von Stalheim began after the theft of half a ton of gold from Berula mine in the Northern Territory on the edge of the Great Sandy Desert. At one point in *Terry in Australia*, Bengt Danielsson had Mr White look for radioactive ore while Terry looked for gold. An edited version of Fred Blakely's manuscript about the Lasseter expedition was published entitled, *Dream Millions*, claiming 'new light on Lasseter's Lost Reef'.[18] Pat Malvern's *Secret Gold* described two boys who fly north to Central Australia and stumble across a gold deposit.[19]

Uranium gave the Territory an international significance, for in the writing the region was seen as critical in an international context. Alan Aldous's *Danger on the Map* (1947) suggests that control over the Territory's vast uranium deposits was crucial to global stability:

---

17   See L.F. Barter, 'The 1950s Uranium Boom in the Northern Territory', *Journal of Northern Territory History*, 2 (1991), pp. 16–27 for his analysis of post-war optimism for the potentiality of uranium as income generating for the Northern Territory.
18   F. Blakely, *Dream Millions: New Light On Lasseter's Lost Reef*, M. Mansfield, ed. (Sydney: Angus & Robertson, 1972).
19   I am assuming this book to be around 1940s or later, although its plot of aviation, missing fathers, mysterious Mike's lost memory and bag of gold could equally belong to the period before the war; P. Malvern, *Secret Gold: A Story of Two Boys Who Found Wealth in the Heart of the Australian Desert* (London: Sheldon, n.d.).

Knowledge of atomic power practically means world domination for whoever holds that knowledge. It is safe with stable, conscientious and humane statesmen. But what about if this power gets into the hand of power-lusting men?[20]

Uranium was linked to science and progress. When uranium was accidentally discovered by young Donald on Diana Downs, he pleaded with his father, old fashioned Mr Tendrill who believed working on the land more important that studying science at University, 'if we do make a lot of money out of a big uranium find … could we use it to build up the place scientifically? I mean, things have hardly changed here in a hundred years so far as the raising of cattle is concerned'.[21]

Phyllis Power's 'Outback' series contains a plethora of references to mineral discoveries. Mary in *Lost in the Outback* finds gold accidentally when she is changing a tyre, 'You had luck spotting this bit; it should keep you in pocket-money for a while'.[22] Again, Mary in *Nursing in the Outback* (1959) suspects that she and Sister Hannah are lost in uranium country, but the pair find an opal field after they have been kidnapped by gold smugglers.[23] In *Adventure in the Outback* (1957) Bert and Al discover that the cattle rustlers are secretly looking for uranium with a geiger-counter, 'usually they're after gold', but after the boys discover copper and uranium-rich ore, the novel ends happily with the family pegging a claim on the station at 'Prince's Soak'.[24] In Lucy Walker's romance *The Man from the Outback*, the rationalisation for the marriage between 'Half Moon' station owner, Kane Manners, and the seventeen year old Mari was provided by the secrecy needed because of uranium prospecting:

> 'Mari,' Kane said quietly, I'm sorry I kissed you like that. Put it down to excitement and relief, will you? I've known for a fortnight they've found uranium and miles of pitch-blende on Half Moon and known all this week the Government was about to announce the news to the public. I've had to keep it to myself or the stock market would have rocketed … just try and understand why I had to keep you … a prisoner. I thought marriage was the best way to tie you up'.[25]

---

20  A. Aldous, *Danger on the Map* (Melbourne: Cheshire, 1947), p. 199.
21  A. Aldous, *The Tendrills in Australia* (London: Chatto & Windus, 1959), p. 151.
22  P.M. Power, *Lost in the Outback* (London: Blackie, n.d.), p. 84.
23  P.M. Power, *Nursing in the Outback* (London: Blackie, 1959), pp. 106, 128, 189.
24  P.M. Power, *Adventure in the Outback* (London: Dent, 1957), pp. 111, 113, 135.
25  L. Walker, *The Man from Outback* (London: Collins, 1974 (1964)), p. 248.

Nevil Shute's novel of the future *In the Wet* noted the huge population increases possible in Australia after the irrigation of marginal land in the Northern Territory with the development of 'nuclear distillation of sea water in the North, around Rum Jungle, and that's getting cheaper and cheaper'.[26] Non-fiction writers too were preoccupied. Ross Annabel's *The Uranium Hunters* described the mood: 'Darwin was getting more uranium-happy every week as the rush gained momentum'.[27] Alan Moorehead chose the name of Australia's new uranium mine for the title of his book on the Territory, *Rum Jungle* (1953). Equally, Frank Clune's *The Fortune Hunters: An Atomic Odyssey in Australia's Wild West, and Things Seen and Heard by the Way in a Jeep Jaunt* published in 1957 also reflected the preoccupation.

The cover notes of nursing sister Ellen Kettle's book on medical services to the Territory Aborigines in the 1950s, *Gone Bush* (1967), emphasise the pervasiveness (and incidentally the masculinity) of the image. The commentary states that the book 'should open our minds to an understanding of their urgent needs and a sympathy for this primitive race so suddenly brought face to face with men of the atomic age'.[28] The idea that in the Territory, the stone age and the atomic age were brought face to face was an appealing one but support for this bright future was not entirely unanimous. From South Australia came a lone voice of dissent when Charles Duguid resigned in protest from the Aborigines Protection Board after the decision to take over the Reserve land of the Pitjantjatjara for the development of a British Government testing station for guided missiles.[29] But generally there was a feeling of economic optimism: 'There was an intangible atmosphere permeating the whole Territory that gave a warning of frenzied development to come … There was but one way for the Northern Territory to go—up, up and still up'.[30]

The landscape, as well as providing the means for material wealth, continued to be seen by authors as 'uncanny' or mystical with the power to construct character. Ross from Adelaide, in Michael Barrett's *The Gold of Lubra Rock* is detected immediately, 'obviously not a Territory man'.[31] The extremes of climate, the geographical hazards and its Aboriginal population located

---

26   N. Shute, *In the Wet* (London: The Book Club, 1954), p. 187.
27   R. Annabel, *The Uranium Hunters* (Adelaide: Rigby, 1971), p. 6.
28   E. Kettle, *Gone Bush* (Sydney: F.P. Leonard, 1967).
29   Duguid, *Doctor and the Aborigines*, pp. 151–52.
30   R. Court, *North of Alice* (London: New English Library, 1971), p. 123.
31   M. Barrett, *The Gold of Lubra Rock* (London: Robert Hale, 1967), p. 13.

Northern Territory settlement spatially and metaphorically. The Northern Territory was still seen as remote, perched on the rim of the continent and very vulnerable to Asian immigration:

> Look, there's New Guinea right on top of us … Then there's Indonesia. Millions more. Millions and millions. And the Japs and the Chinks—just waiting—just waiting! One day they'll all pour down. Everybody knows. What is there here? No people and all the minerals in the world.[32]

Although by this time most of the Territory had been colonised, Arnhem Land remained inaccessible; the landscape was imbued with mystical significance and adventure. Arnhem Land was the setting for Alan Aldous's *Danger on the Map* and home to international masterminds seeking world domination, Dutch treasure, savage Aborigines and uranium-rich ore. When Biggles came to tackle international spying on Australia's uranium deposits, he was warned by an old timer, 'Arnhem Land. If you want a spear in your gizzard that's the place to go'.[33] Bert's uncle in *Adventure in the Outback* warns him that Arnhem Land is 'where the last of the really wild aborigines roam' and that 'some queer stories' are told about a 'ruined city' that is said to glow at night which even the police fear.[34] Coralie and Leslie Rees described 'Ruined City' in Arnhem Land: 'taboo to the blacks' with bottomless holes and ancient rock columns.[35] In *Northward the Coast*, Lang Bowman's trek across Arnhem Land to the coast takes the party through crocodile infested rivers inhabited by hostile and sexually aggressive Aborigines.[36] Lindall implies that Arnhem Land, even in this period, is still a place you can disappear into.[37]

This post-war period saw a renewed interest in the Territory, but unlike the period before the war, the focus was upon Central Australia rather than the north coast. Despite 'Arnhem Land' remaining an evocative symbol of uncharted territory, most of the writing was located in Central Australia. Douglas Lockwood's 'Front Door' (Darwin) was a rather more prosaic image than the 'Dead Heart'[38] (Alice Springs). In Nevil Shute's *A Town Like Alice*, Alice Springs provides the context by which the

---

32   G. Cotterell, *Tea At Shadow Creek* (London: Eyre & Spottiswoode, 1958), p. 250.
33   Capt. W.E. Johns, *Biggles in Australia* (London: Hodder & Stoughton, 1955), p. 85.
34   Power, *Adventure in the Outback*, p. 34.
35   C. & L. Rees, *Spinifex Walkabout: Hitch-Hiking in Remote North Australia* (Sydney: Australasian, 1953), p. 225.
36   E. Lindall, *Northward the Coast* (London: Heinemann, 1966), pp. 142f, 195f.
37   E. Lindall, *The Last Refuge* (Melbourne: Gold Star, 1972), p. 71.
38   J.K. Ewers, *Tale From the Dead Heart* (Sydney: Currawong, 1944), p. 5.

outback was judged. Alice Springs 'is a bonza town'[39] (unlike Darwin[40]). Darwin was still suffering from the devastation of the Japanese air raids that had virtually destroyed the town.[41] Writers express a nostalgia for pre-war Darwin[42] and emphasise the derelict state of the city: 'Darwin was something special, it was the entrance to the continent and … Australia's arsehole. There was a beguiling air of failure and frustration about it'.[43] Darwin, was sometimes seen as dangerous[44] and described in terms of hazards and extremes of climate.[45]

There was a belief that Central Australia formed the ethereal heartland of Australians. Coralie and Leslie Rees found the Aboriginal spiritual presence more apparent in the landscape of Central Australia. They saw Central Australia as 'lands eloquent with living light and strange primeval contours'.[46] Prospector Dead Sweet Joe Stephenson could always feel 'the desert was still pulling at him'.[47] Queen Elizabeth during one of her visits to the Northern Territory commented, 'After this visit, no one will be able to suggest to me that Central Australia is a dead heart. From now on, I shall always look upon it as a living heart, beating with confident energy'.[48] Alice Springs was considered physically more attractive, with tourist potential:[49] 'a town of trim tropical green and white bungalows, with flourishing private gardens and orange-trees which in spring load the air with heavy-scented blossom … The Alice has its dignity'.[50]

But although Darwin had lost its pre-eminence as the point of focus for the writers, it still had a kind of atmosphere in the texts provided by its cosmopolitan nature. Darwin, as previously, was presented as a kind of melting pot of different races but the lines of demarcation separating the groups appeared to be breaking down. Many writers included

---

39  N. Shute, *A Town Like Alice* (London: Pan, 1961 (1950)), p. 148.
40  Shute, *A Town Like Alice*, p. 158.
41  A. Moorehead, *Rum Jungle* (London: Hamish Hamilton, 1953), pp. 75–76.
42  K. Mitchell, *Doctor in Darwin* (Sydney: Horwitz, 1960), pp. 37–38; Idriess, *Track of Destiny*, p. 77.
43  Cotterell, *Ten At Shadow Creek*, p. 253.
44  Although the danger of the landscape are not emphasised as they are in other periods, there is still the idea that outside the urban centre, this violation and geographical hazard mean a fight for survival e.g. J. Iggulden, *Dark Stranger* (London: Macdonald, 1965) and the description of the boat trip.
45  M. Barrett, *Traitor At Twenty Fathoms* (London: Collins, 1963), p. 5.
46  Rees, *Spinifex Walkabout*, pp. 238, 254.
47  H.C. James, *Gold Is Where You Find It* (London: Harrap, 1949), p. 234.
48  Reply made by Queen Elizabeth II to an address of welcome during the Royal visit to Alice Springs in 1963, quoted, F. Flynn & K. Willey, *The Living Heart* (Sydney: F.P. Leonard, 1979 (1964)).
49  H. Griffiths, *An Australian Adventure* (Adelaide: Rigby, 1975), p. 127.
50  Rees, *Spinifex Walkabout*, p. 240.

a description of the inter-racial mix of Darwin.[51] Phyllis M. Power,[52] Edward Lindall,[53] Elspeth Huxley,[54] Geoffrey Cotterell[55] and Captain W.E. Johns all provided an almost identical description of Darwin:

> eight o'clock saw Biggles, by himself, aiming his way through the scented tropical night to the harbour, rubbing shoulders with as strange an assortment of humanity as could be found in any port on earth, east or west. Stockmen in sombreros; Chinese vendors of potato chips; pearlers; black boys on bicycles; Greek merchants, and seamen of every colour and race under the sun—Malays, Indonesians, Cingalese, Maoris, and Melville Islanders who had paddled their canoes across sixty miles of shark-infested water to go to the cinema and watch white screen stars doing things that must have been incomprehensible to them.[56]

Hamey described a multicultural mix over a Christmas dinner.[57] For Walker, Darwin's promise of inter-racial tolerance was the dream sustaining both Polly and her daughter Mary.[58] But the multi-cultural aspect of Darwin did not commend itself to all visitors: 'Darwin is the only Australian port of entry where the general tourist is likely to see aborigines. The aborigine is primitive man, and primitive man does not look his best huddling in squalor on the edge of town'.[59] Despite the multicultural message, the legacy of the war is still apparent in much of the writing, particularly in regard to the representation of Japanese in the writing.[60]

---

51  The Darwin melting pot construction had been celebrated by Paterson some sixty years earlier: 'Palmerston is unique among Australian towns, inasmuch as it is filled with the boilings over of the great cauldron of Oriental humanity. Here comes the vagrant and shifting population of all the Eastern races. Here are gathered together Canton coolies, Japanese pearl divers, Malays, Manilamen, Portuguese from adjacent Timar, Kobe; all sorts and conditions of men ... The Chow and the Jap and the Malay consider themselves quite as good as any alleged white men ... There is an Eastern flavour over everything ...' A.B. Paterson, 'The Cycloon, [sic] Paddy Cahill and the G.R.' in Headon, *North of the Ten Commandments*, p. 213.
52  Power, *Adventure in the Outback*, p. 30.
53  Lindall, *Northward the Coast*, p. 30.
54  E. Huxley, *Their Shining Eldorado: A Journey Through Australia* (London: Chatto & Windus, 1967), p. 262.
55  Cotterell, *Tea At Shadow Creek*, p. 203.
56  Johns, *Biggles in Australia*, p. 83.
57  Harney, *North of 23°*, p. 97.
58  Walker, *No Sunlight Singing*, pp. 77, 90–91, 176.
59  P. McGuire, *Westward the Course: the New World of Oceania* (Melbourne: Oxford University Press, 1946 (1942)), p. 166.
60  See M. Dewar, 'Blowing Rusty Bugles: the War and Territory Writing', *Northern Perspective* 18, 2 (1995), 65–73.

IN SEARCH OF THE NEVER-NEVER

Cover *The Little Black Princess of the Never-Never* (adapted for use in schools, Melbourne: Robertson and Mullens, 1945).

Jeannie Gunn separated her experiences. *We of the Never Never* is almost exclusively about her European experiences in the Territory. In *The Little Black Princess* Jeannie documented her relationship with the Aborigines from the Roper River area, in particular her friendship with the young girl, Bett Bett. At the same time she created the ethnic stereotype of lovable, unpredictable, infantile black servants.

Illustration and text from *The Little Black Princess* (same edition).

Cover and spine *Comrades* by Joseph Bowes (London: Hodder and Stoughton, 1912).

Territory writing developed rapidly into the boys' adventure genre where the heroes were all plucky white men fighting the treacherous 'blacks'. But Aborigines became subsequently less important in the texts mirroring their political and social status in an increasingly 'white' Australia. By the 1920s even the 'savages' were European.

Cover *The Splendid Savage* by Conrad Sayce (London: Thomas Nelson, n.d. c. 1925).

*A black figure leapt into the open and fell.*

"*The blacks unloaded these for me.*"

In the novels Aborigines were alternatively stereotyped as a deadly foe to be conquered and shot or a race of menials to be exploited for their labour: *The Splendid Savage* by Conrad Sayce (London: Thomas Nelson, n.d. c. 1925) pp. 49 and 191.

IN SEARCH OF THE NEVER-NEVER

Cover *The Red Heart* by Frank Clune (Melbourne: Hawthorne, 1944).

In the writing the Northern Territory was a mythic region where adventurers rode on horseback to find gold and all the crooks came from the cities. Increasingly the Territory landscape became important as the spiritual and corporeal life force of the nation. The region was constructed in the writing as the 'heart' of Australia. Once voiced, this image persisted.

Cover *The Crocodile Club* by Kaz Cooke (Sydney: Allen & Unwin, 1992, cover design Redback Graphix).

Reproduced with permission.

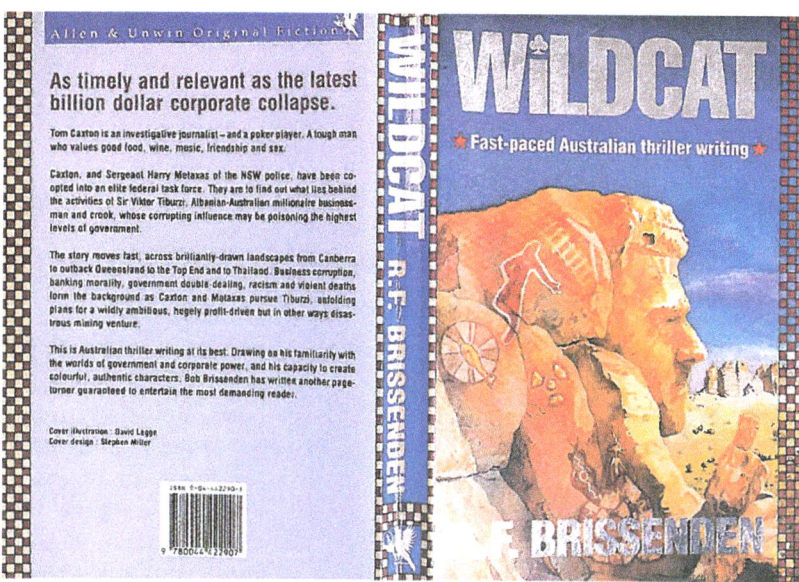

Cover *Wildcat* by Bob Brissenden (Sydney: Allen & Unwin, 1991, cover illustration David Legge, cover design Stephen Miller).

Reproduced with permission. Note the images used in the artwork. Cover notes point out that the 'rock art' is not Aboriginal.

Bob Brissenden (second from left) and party undertaking field research in the Gulf region June 1987.

After the passing of the *Aboriginal Land Rights (NT) Act 1976*, Aborigines, land and spirituality were inexorably linked. While the region was still constructed as a frontier, proximity to Asia and environmental issues became more important. Most writers used these elements to heighten drama in Territory writing. Drugs, Asia, land rights, sacred sites, environmental issues and big business all battle it out in *Wildcat* by Bob Brissenden.

Source: Photograph reproduced courtesy Trevor Hosie.

By the decade of the 1930s, the image of the threatening wild Aborigine had almost, but not quite, disappeared from the text. Despite both title and illustration, the book was mainly about a gold-finding expedition. Title page and illustration *Buffalo Jim* by William Hatfield (London: Oxford University Press, 1938).

Xavier Herbert, 1984.

Probably the Territory's greatest writer, in *Capricornia* (1938) Xavier Herbert published a novel which raised issues of Aboriginal identity and justice while at the same time debunking the dream of the noble chaste white bushman. In *Poor Fellow My Country* (1975) published some forty years later, he reinvented a Territory populated by doomed Aborigines of magic and power where landscape was the provider of spirituality for Aborigines and Europeans alike.

Source: Photograph reproduced with permission, Northern Territory Library, Wetter Collection, PH350/16.

The building of Port Darwin brought more than colonists and livestock. The writing of early settlers, like Harriet Daly, attempted to promote financial interest in the region. Settlers saw the Aborigines as an obstacle to profit and something to be removed. Colour engraving of Port Darwin, Northern Territory, 1873, by J. Carr (engraving J.C. Armytage).

Source: Reproduced with permission, Museum and Art Gallery of the Northern Territory PR 00004.

A century later, European notions of Aboriginal culture had become a reason to come to the Territory. Uluru and Kakadu became popular tourist destinations and visitor figures skyrocketed. In the literature Aboriginal land was constructed as both spiritual and accessible. Some of the characters had only to cross the country before they became aware of Aboriginal heritage. They did not need to meet any Aborigines; by this time the landscape alone was sufficient inspiration. Patrick Hockey, 'Tennant Creek come to Obiri', 1985.

Source: Reproduced with permission, Museum and Art Gallery of the Northern Territory GA 00559.

In contrast to the image of Darwin as an exotic multicultural port, the image of the small, parochial public service town that had been noted so critically by writers from the previous period persevered. The Reeses found a 'swarm of civil servants' had taken over from the leisurely 'old-timers' who yearned for the Darwin of the past and feared it had become 'a town for civil servants and air-travellers, white duck, white-collar pioneers'.[61] Harney noted the divisions in Darwin between government and non-government workers, 'people being judged not by their ability so much as by the "set" or party to which they belonged'.[62] Cynthia Nolan noted the luxurious Darwin Hotel overlooking the sea where one could sit at tables on the lawns, 'but not in shorts or without a tie'.[63] Lean rugged Lang Bowman contemptuously described Alan Kemick: 'one of Darwin's leading businessmen, a social lion, a man of money and considerable power' who drives an expensive car and worries about the neatness of his dress.[64]

In this period particularly, Darwin was frequently regarded in the context of the inclement extremes of the Wet-Dry tropics of the Top End. The 'Wet' marked the passage of time for those who could not leave the Territory. In Sumner Locke-Elliott's play *Rusty Bugles*, the men measured the length of time of service by the number of wet seasons endured. Mac warned Rod, the newcomer, 'Wait until you've done a Wet, mate. Just wait. I done four'.[65] The discomfort of the Territory climate was emphasised to Biggles too: 'hell in the wet ... every kind of biting bug making yer life miserable, blacks waiting for a chance to stick a spear in yer ribs, living on ironclads [canned food] and native tucker ... hell all the time'.[66] Nancy Polishuk was told, 'If you're ever going to swim in the Daly, just remember these things: Crocodiles, sharks, stingrays, whirlpools, snags, mud, tidal bores'.[67] In *Master of Ransome* Sam warned Sara of the Wet, 'Turkish bath weather. Knocks most of 'em to pieces ... That's when tempers get frayed in the north, young 'un'.[68] The approach

---

61 Rees, *Spinifex Walkabout*, p. 162.
62 Harney, *North of 23°*, p. 178.
63 C. Nolan, *Outback* (London: Methuen, 1962), pp. 110–11.
64 Lindall, *Northward the Coast*, pp. 11f.
65 S. Locke-Elliott, *Rusty Bugles* (Sydney: Currency Press, 1980 (University of Queensland Press, 1968)), p. 12.
66 Johns, *Biggles in Australia*, p. 84.
67 N. Polishuk & D. Lockwood, *Life on the Daly River* (London: Adventurers Club, 1963 (1961)), p. 35.
68 L. Walker, *Master of Ransome: A Romance* (London: Collins, 1974 (1958)), p. 59.

of the Wet drives the party across Arnhem Land in *Northward the Coast*.[69] The texts in the period preceding the war suggested a Darwinian model of natural selection; that the harshness of conditions and climate weeded out those without sufficient backbone to endure the rigours. After the war, there seemed to be a more psychoanalytic construct; that the extremes of the climate showed you what you were really like, stripped of the veneer of urban society.[70] Sometimes this realisation took the form of a heightened sexual awareness.[71]

But if there were doubts expressed in the writing at this time that Darwin was still the exotic and mysterious Territory where anything could happen, it was only a reflection of the questioning and analysis of the whole European experience in the bush. The age of innocence had, in large measure, passed and the reckless joy in the colonial experience was viewed by commentators much more cynically. Cynthia Nolan quoted the bushman who exclaimed, 'Glad I'm not in the cities. Here at least we don't think about how many hours a day we put in';[72] an ironical shift where the dislike of cities seems, by this stage, confined to a hostility towards labour regulations. The whole thrust of Tom Ronan's *Vision Splendid* was to suggest to the reader that the true bushman had either gone or was very old. Ronan portrayed the bushman of the 1920s and 1930s as independent, courteous, hard-working and mostly honourable,[73] although he allowed that they occasionally exhibited a cheerful dishonesty.[74] Olaf Ruhen writing about the same period in *Naked Under Capricorn* had a similar construction. But the cynicism of the post-*Capricornia* 1950s writing also acknowledged that the bushmen were socially inept, sexually exploitative, miserly, unlucky and alcoholic.[75] Ronan mocked the stereotype:

---

69   Lindall, *Northward the Coast*, pp. 130, 176, 228.
70   Implicit in all Edward Lindall's novels, but also James Vance Marshall and Joan Woodberry. See also W. Watkins, *Sun, Sand and Blood* (Melbourne: Gold Star, 1972) (originally published as *Soliloquy in the Simpson*), A. Chester, *When the Blood Burns: A Novel of the Flying Doctor Service* (Perth: Patersons, n.d.), etc.
71   Again, Edward Lindall's novels; M. West, *The Naked Country* (London: New English Library, 1970 (1660)), p. 97; J.V. Marshall, *The Children* (London: Michael Joseph, 1959), p. 50; Carol and David's sexually 'frigid' marriage when in the city, J. Glennon, *The Heart in the Centre* (Adelaide: Rigby, 1960); or more unpleasantly in the contrasting behaviour of Larry and Brad, P.A. Knudsen, *The Bloodwood Tree* (London: Frederick Muller, 1962), etc.
72   Nolan, *Outback* p. 9.
73   Ronan, *Vision Splendid*, pp. 35–40.
74   For example, Marty cheating at two-up, or the nobbling of the horse at the 'Ladies Bracelet' at the Border races, Ronan, *Vision Splendid*, pp. 77, 86, 232.
75   Ronan, *Vision Splendid*, pp. 132, 195, 242, 259; O. Ruhen, *Naked Under Capricorn* (North Ryde: Angus & Robertson, 1989 (1958)), pp. 101, 115, 209.

> In the poetry books ... the station hand is a young, handsome bloke, rides like Billy Waite, fights like Les Darcy, always in and out of town at dances and races, and finishes up marrying the boss's daughter and getting his picture in the Pastoralists' Review. Most of the Territorians'd sooner get a Jacky to take the edge off their horses, do their fighting with a waddy when the other bloke ain't looking, and think they're lucky if they can get their arms around a few greasy old goanna-eatin' gins.
>
> 'I,' concluded Mr. Blivens, 'am a typical Territorian'.[76]

But if the honourable bushman could no longer be found in the literary or documentary writings, he remained alive and well in adventure stories, women's romantic fiction and children's books. Lucy Walker, doyenne of the Australian romance, set her books in the outback'. The cover notes of *Master of Ransome* tell us that: 'Sara's story is a fascinating and romantic story, with its background the real Australia'.[77] It is hard to know geographically where this real Australia is, since there are references to Alice Springs, Darwin, Adelaide and Perth, but the reader is told that Ransome Station is in the 'North of Australia', 'The place of fascination and mystery; of crocodiles, pandanus, floods and droughts. The place where, a hundred years ago, they said white men could not live and stay sane'.[78] The bushman is epitomised by the station owner Greg Camden, whose face is 'bronzed', 'eyes were blue', says little, but has an 'unflinching gaze'.[79] The heroine Sara recognises that the freedom of the bushman was created by the landscape:

> she guessed the reason for this freedom was because of the tremendous amount of initiative and independence each man on a cattle station was called upon to show in his work every day. She knew enough of station life ... to know there were hazards and enterprises in the everyday march of events that men without individuality and enterprise would never be able to face. Lonely struggles hanging to the horse's tail across swollen rivers in the Wet. Endurance treks across shadeless, barren, waterless plains in the Dry. They were the least of it. Stallion hunts, stampeding cattle, cattle thieves ... not to mention sickness and accident in remote and unapproachable places.[80]

---

76   Ronan, *Vision Splendid*, p. 190.
77   Walker, *Master of Ransome*, cover notes.
78   Walker, *Master of Ransome*, p. 17.
79   Walker, *Master of Ransome*, p. 24.
80   Walker, *Master of Ransome*, p. 45.

Formula writers emphasised the rugged and the masculine: 'dry and leathery-face men, unshaven, some with cigarettes drooping from their lips … they had craggy jaws and pale blue eyes which were set in brown skins earned and wrinkled by the sun'.[81] The Northern Territory of men and horses has become the province, ironically, of romance.[82] Mateship has been supplanted by heterosexual love. Not only in women's romances like Eileen Finlay's *Journey of Freedom* (1950), Madelyn Palmer's *Dead Fellah!* (1961), the Lucy Walker series, or Karen Miller's *Flying* Doctor[83] series but also in men's adventure romances such as Alan Chester's *When the Blood Burns* (n.d.), Geoffrey Cotterell's *Tea at Shadow Creek* (1958), Jack Danvers's *The Living Come First* (1961), Charles Frances's *The Big One* (1963), James Glennon's *The Heart in the Centre* (1960), Peter Knudsen's *The Bloodwood Tree* (1962) or Morris West's *The Naked Country* (1960).

All of Edward Lindall's adventure stories have a strong romantic theme which follows an identical formula. There is a tough misanthropic hero, usually a bushman of some sort, placed in proximity with a woman, usually from the city, and they are initially hostile towards each other. As they face rigours of the Territory environment (and assorted villains) they begin to feel attracted to each other and eventually become sexual and romantic partners: Lang Bowman begins as misogynist, lean, laconic and tough[84] but by the end of the trek to Arnhem Land he and Ruth have fallen in love; Sam Warden dislikes the palaeontologist's niece, Morgan Lithgow, but after they have been abandoned in the desert they fall in love and decide to continue to look for fossilised remains rather than return to civilisation;[85] crocodile shooter Greg Landers initially thinks ex-waitress Taffy to be too superficial but after being hunted by killers they eventually find each other;[86] the Northern Territory Native

---

81  Barrett, *The Gold of Lubra Rock*, p. 13.
82  This construction of a 'romantic' heterosexual *Outback* continues popular. See for example, D. Cork's *Outback Rainbow* (London: Mills & Boon, 1977) where Nicky Reay eventually wins the heart of laconic misogynist cattle station boss Jarratt Buchan; ten years later, K. Allyne's *Carpentaria Moon* (London: Mills & Boon, 1987) the only real change has occurred in the heroine's occupation. Eden Challinor is no longer a secretary or housekeeper, but has come to 'Arrunga River' as 'Tourist Manager'.
83  Only some of the many 'Flying Doctor' romances appear to be actually set in the Northern Territory. Karen Miller's series describe a fictional base 'Raggy Point Flying Doctor Service and its little Northern Territory Hospital'; K. Miller, *Flying Doctor Urgent* (Sydney: Horwitz, 1963), cover notes; K. Miller, *Call For the Flying Doctor* (Sydney: Horwitz, 1962); K. Miller, *Flying Doctor Disappears* (Sydney: Horwitz, 1963). K. Mitchell's Flying Doctor series is almost all set outside the Territory (with the exception of *Doctor in Darwin*), as is Michael Noonan's Flying Doctor series.
84  For example, it takes Lang Bowman several weeks of sharing a camp site and 125 pages before he can bring himself to call Ruth by name, Lindall, *Northward the Coast*, p. 125.
85  E. Lindall, *The Killers of Karawala* (New York: William Morrow, 1962).
86  E. Lindall, *A Lively Form of Death* (London: Constable, 1972).

Welfare Patrol Officer in charge of the Walgut (a mysterious and remote desert tribe) believes anthropologist Vanessa Jordan will cause trouble, but after being abandoned in the desert by hostile claim jumpers they survive happily together.[87] In a similar frame, Edward Lindall's *The Last Refuge* is an account of terrorism in north Australia by a group of ex-university radicals who are violently opposed to American interests in north Australia. The Peking-supported group kill for the pleasure of it while mouthing Chairman Mao to each other. The book ends with the successful undercover ASIO agent rescued by the CIA agent to live happily ever after in 'the State of Capricorn', after the Northern Territory has been sold to the United States of America as the fifty-first state.[88] But Lindall's construction was repeated by others. It was no longer considered appropriate to have a dream-woman who waited back in the city for the bushman. By now the dream-woman has become a partner in the field and an actual protagonist in the writing.

Before the war, the ideal of the bushman was simple mateship. But in this later period mateship brings a great deal of misfortune to the characters of *Vision Splendid*. Toppingham and Marty were such good mates that even when down on their luck and broke during the Depression, they both refused work because they believed it would leave the other stranded.[89] Toppingham lost his chance to marry Stephanie because he missed the appointment through looking after his drunken mate, Billy Jaggers.[90] In Walker's *No Sunlight Singing*, bush mates appear as little better than partners in crime, perpetrating ugly acts of violence upon the Aborigines of the station. The bushmen are an anarchic vigilante group whose violence brings about the deaths of Polly and Paddy. Talking to mates about sex with Aboriginal women is a shared masculine ritual and part of the pleasure gained lies in the boasting of conquests:

> 'Well, for mine,' said Dick, 'anybody can have the whites, or the half-castes either for that matter. The blacks'll do me. With these white sheilas you never know where you are. You might muck around all night, just about blowin' a gasket, and then end up gettin' scrubbed. With a gin you can bowl her over any time you want, any way you like'.[91]

---

87  E. Lindall, *A Gathering of Eagles* (Sydney: Collins, 1970).
88  Lindall, *The Last Refuge*, p. 155f.
89  Ronan, *Vision Splendid*, pp. 219–20.
90  Ronan, *Vision Splendid*, pp. 255–59.
91  Walker, *No Sunlight Singing*, pp. 31, 160f, 176.

Harney defended the practice as virile and natural: 'In a land where white women were as rare as a rocking horse in manure, and the Aboriginal girls ever around, what other subject should one expect to find around the camp fire of a group of lusty young men'.[92] Inter-racial violence, both sexual and non-sexual, continues to form a part of the text, but unlike their pre-war counterparts, the heroes are often disgusted by or removed from the action.[93]

Children's stories continue to stress the adventure and the romance of the Territory lifestyle and Aborigines, though usually subordinate to the action, are at least mentioned. Richard Graves's *Spear and Stockwhip* (1950) described the adventures of 'Stones' Flint who runs away from school and becomes a drover with a group of other lads. A perceptible difference in the representation of post-war Aborigines with their pre-war counterparts is that 'Darkie' and 'Baroopa' are permitted to be courageous and intelligent. Darkie is the son of an ANZAC hero and, at the end of the book, his Aboriginal mother states that the boys must learn responsibility and 'have a greater education'[94] before taking up life as pastoralists. Olaf Ruhen's *Corcoran's the Name* (1956) is similar as is Leslie Rees's *Panic in the Cattle Country* (1974). Phyllis M. Power, although giving her Aboriginal character a strange pidgin English to speak and referring to them as 'Abos', nevertheless points out that Ivy is quite capable of looking after the clinic[95] and that the Prince family is heavily reliant upon Timboora's exceptional skill in the pastoral industry.[96] Tom Prince tells the lads that the reason that he has an amicable relationship with his Aboriginal workers is because he respects their sacred sites.[97]

Other writers print a more straightforward racism. Ronald Barr, in an echo of the earlier novels of the nineteenth century, like Michael Terry before World War II, describes the Northern Territory, in particular Arnhem Land, as the site of the remains of ancient civilisations. The heroes of *Warrigal Joe* (1946) face the 'cannibal blacks in Arnhem Land' to explore

---

92  W.E. Harney, *Content to Lie in the Sun* (London: Robert Hale, 1958), p. 50.
93  For example, the finding of the body of the hanged Aborigine, M. Barrett, *Stranger in Galah* (London: Longmans Green, 1958); the reactions of the locals to Bart Hall's hired aggressors, Court, *North of Alice;* the ugliness of Dr Stephen Lithgow's attitude to Big Harry, Lindall, *The Killers of Karawala*, etc.
94  R.H. Graves, *Spear and Stockwhip: A Tale of the Territory* (Sydney: Dymock's Book Arcade, 1950), p. 161.
95  Power, *Nursing in the Outback*, p. 170.
96  Power, *Adventure in the Outback*, p. 65.
97  Power, *Adventure in the Outback*, p. 82.

the hidden 'Lost City' with ancient tombs and cryptic writing.[98] As well as the treasure of the Lost City, the explorers also find 'a rich harvest of bullroarers and other relics' which they pack up carefully to deposit in the Devon Museum.[99] Allan Aldous's *Doctor With Wings* (1960) although appearing on the surface to be preoccupied with modernity, concentrating as it does on the impact of technology upon the outback, contained much the same message of European racial superiority inherent in the Territory lifestyle as the pre-war writers. Aldous, like Danielsson, emphasises the 'Americanisation' of Alice Springs with its social role model that of a 'Wild West Town':

> 'Trouble is,' said the doctor driving the car, 'we get too many American Western films. The abos go for them in a big way. Lazy lot most of them. Lounge around waiting for tourists to give 'em five bob for posing for them while they click away their roll of Kodachrome.'[100]

But some of the children's stories contained a less cliched interpretation of race relations. Erle Wilson's *Churinga Tales* ends with the coming of the white man. The little boy asks his uncle what happens after this. "'*That* is a story our Churinga can't tell you," his uncle replied, and the little boy thought his voice sounded very sad. "But some day you may know.'"[101] Bengt Danielsson's *Terry in Australia* is an account of a visit of a British family to a pastoral property near Alice Springs. This book offered a less compromising interpretation of the Territory than suggested by Graves, Barr, Aldous or Johns. The book attempted to raise some of the implications of European settlement of the Northern Territory by looking directly at 'Aboriginal policy' which dispossessed people from their land under pastoral lease restricting their access to ritual country.[102] Madeleine Duke's *The Secret People*, similarly, attempted to deal with some of the prejudices and assumptions made about Aboriginal society.[103]

---

98   D. Barr, *Warrigal Joe: A Tale of the Never-Never* (Melbourne: Cassell, 1946), pp. 10–11, 72.
99   Barr, *Warrigal Joe*, p. 236.
100  A. Aldous, *Doctor with Wings* (Leicester: Brockhampton Press, 1961 (1960)), pp. 11–12.
101  E. Wilson, *Churinga Tales: Stories of Alchuringa—the Dream-time of the Australian Aborigines* (Sydney: Australasian, 1950), p. 94.
102  B. Danielsson, *Terry in Australia* (London: Allen & Unwin, 1961 (1958)), pp. 70–71.
103  But British physicist, Dr Madeleine Duke, like Bengt Danielsson, was not an Australian and the indigenous children's literature remained much less critical of race relations in the Northern Territory, M. Duke, *The Secret People* (Leicester: Brockhampton, 1967).

Writers confronted by the settlement of the once wild Territory resorted to mysticism in their analysis, in an effort to make the situation simpler for children. Joan Woodberry's *Come Back Peter* suggested that the outback had ceased to exist as a geographical place and was more a mental concept. Paul noted:

> His mother thought that this was the Outback—the Never-Never—but he knew that … the Outback did not start here. The men had gone Outback, but wherever they were, the Outback itself still existed beyond the horizon. You never got to the Outback; it was always in front of you, beyond you, beckoning, tantalising, and when it could, destroying.[104]

The tensions frequently apparent in Territory writing appear in the children's literature. Danielsson, Woodberry, Rex Ingamells's *Aranda Boy* and James Vance Marshall's *The Children* (1959) and *A Walk to the Hills of the Dreamtime* (1970) all present a disturbing picture of Territory life where the implications of European settlement for Aborigines, loneliness and hardship are not described in terms of the heroic pioneers but hark back to a grimmer, Lawson-like tradition of the threatening nature of the landscape.

In this period, the mythic theme that the landscape of the Territory contained an unlimited mineral wealth—uranium, gold, copper, opals—just for the finding continued with renewed enthusiasm buoyed by hopes of the atomic age. The Central Australian landscapes becomes increasingly identified as the physical embodiment of Australian nationalism. Economic optimism and iconic nationalism unite in the same landscape but representation of the people of the region present a more compromising picture of the Territory in the Australian context.

---

104 J. Woodberry, *Come Back Peter* (Adelaide: Rigby, 1969), p. 55.

# 6

# SEX AND THE DREAMTIME

In the post-war period, the largely unrelated topics of Aboriginal culture and gender tensions preoccupied the writers. As subjects, they tended to be mutually exclusive. The area writers were most attracted to was that of Aboriginal spirituality but there was a more general enthusiasm by white writers to explore the whole notion of Aboriginality. Sex and sexual relations were more problematic and focussed upon gender roles, exploitation and redefining the nuclear family post–World War II.

Although in this period there were no Aboriginal writers in a position to explore the Northern Territory as a literary subject, non-Aboriginal writers filled the gap, writing accounts purporting to be from an Aboriginal perspective. William Hatfield had written *Desert Saga* in 1933, in which he attempted to describe the events of first contact in Central Australia. Bill Harney's *Brimming Billabongs* (1947) was a post–World War II effort by a non-Aboriginal writer to present a picture of contemporary Aboriginal life and its interactions with the European community. Harney's book was followed closely by another book in which a non-Aboriginal set out to write an Aboriginal biography in the first person. H.E. Thonemann's *Tell the White Man: The Life Story of an Aboriginal Lubra*[1] was published in 1949 and described the story of Buludja of the Mungari from near the Elsey Station area. Rex Ingamells's *Aranda Boy* (1952)[2] told the story of Gurra, an Arrernte from Central Australia. Douglas Lockwood's *I, the Aboriginal* (1962) and *We, the Aborigines* (1963) are further examples of

---
1   H.E. Thonemann, *Tell the White Man: The Life Story of an Aboriginal Lubra* (Sydney: Collins, 1949).
2   R. Ingamells, *Aranda Boy: An Aboriginal Story* (Melbourne: Longman Green, 1952).

a non-Aboriginal attempt to construct Aboriginal life experience.[3] Paul Carter[4] points out that it is, of course, not possible for a non-Aboriginal author to offer an authentic Aboriginal perspective.[5] The writing served the function of informing the reader while at the same time licensing the author to portray non-Aboriginal behaviour from a different perspective. Today this device of 'Aboriginal' writing by non-Aboriginals is much less popular (although it is not unknown[6]). This writing generated a construction, that although seen as authentically Aboriginal, was in fact no more so than Jeannie Gunn's *The Little Black Princess* had been two generations earlier. The 'Aboriginal' writing continued to support the attitudes and assumptions apparent in the 'non-Aboriginal' writing.

Certainly the interest in Aboriginal culture and spirituality was a preoccupation of the period where serious writers attempted to justify and incorporate 'Aboriginal' experience within a non-Aboriginal 'scientific' framework. Roland Robinson published several collections of Aboriginal mythology after working with communities in the Northern Territory but they contained the 'scientific' seal of approval. *Legend and Dreaming* (1952), for example, contained an introduction by A.P. Elkin; *Wandjina* (1968) had an acknowledgment to R.M. Berndt. Robinson's *Aboriginal Myths and Legends* (1966) contained material collected by Strehlow. The influence of the social sciences is apparent—not *only* anthropology but psychology as well. Robinson wrote revealingly of his interest in Aboriginal mythology,

> The innocent fairy-tale has a surface innocence. It is a surviving vestige of primitive myth, an image thrown up from the unconscious ... Where does imagination start but from primeval images still known in Man's barbaric heart.[7]

---

3   This literary device is less common, although can still be seen in the contemporary period, for example in the writing of B. Wongar or Ted Egan's 'Gurindji Blues'.
4   P. Carter, *Living in a New Country: History, Travelling and Language* (London: Faber & Faber, 1992), p. 69.
5   Although not everyone agrees with Carter: D. Headon, 'Beyond the Years of the Locust: Aboriginal Writing in the 1980s—Part One', *Meridian* 7, 1 (1988), pp. 13–22 and 'Beyond the Years of the Locust: Aboriginal Writing in the 1980s—Part Two', *Meridian* 7, 2 (1988), pp. 128–44; see Part Four, Chapter 7 for further discussion on this point.
6   For example, the recent biography of Aboriginal writer Jack Davis; written by non-Aboriginal Keith Chesson who wrote, 'Jumping from my own written passages to direct quotations from Jack lost a great deal of continuity and there was a conflict of style. I have fused the two, and adopted a first-person narrative throughout, in an effort to achieve a more even pace and style.'; K. Chesson, *Jack Davis: A Life Story* (Melbourne: Dent, 1988), p. 3.
7   R. Robinson, *Aboriginal Myths and Legends* (Melbourne: Sun Books, 1968 (1966)), p. ix.

It is difficult to know if this interest in Aboriginal spirituality was more concerned with perceived psychological truths of humanity or an actual interest in Aborigines. Whatever motivated the writing, there was a lot of it. In this period most 'serious' authors of the Territory managed to publish at least one collection of 'Aboriginal' mythology. Anthropologist Norman Tindale published an account for children of the coming of 'the most primitive human being in the world today'—the Aborigines, or 'Negritos'—to the continent of Australia.[8] Tindale said,

> When my daughter was young, I used to tell her stories about the aborigines … When my son was born … I had to tell the stories again … My daughter and my son remembered the outlines of some stories and we put them down, and between … us the whole story series grew up into the book 'The First Walkabout'.[9]

C.P. Mountford also published several accounts of Aboriginal mythology, as did Alan Marshall.[10] In Erle Wilson's *Churinga Tales* (1950) the uncle clutches the 'magic charm' (the 'Churinga') and thinks, 'Surely … something of the legend and tales of an ancient race might be kept alive a little longer by telling them in the age-old way to a child by a fire'.[11] Some of the construction of Aboriginal mythology took a very odd form: Bruce and June MacPherson's *The Magic Boomerang* (1963) is noteworthy as a picture book of three dolls photographed against the Centralian landscape. The two white dolls, Jenny and Sue, help Kinjiwa, an Aboriginal doll, find his magic boomerang. The spirit of 'Ayer's Rock' (Uluru) in gratitude promised to 'watch over you and guide you wherever you go'.[12] Even considering the dearth of good children's fiction published in this period,[13] it is surprising that these collections should have proved popular.

---

8   N.B. Tindale & H.A. Lindsay, *The First Walkabout* (Melbourne: Longmans Green, 1954), p. ix.
9   Norman B. Tindale interview n.d., Hazel de Berg 65, Canberra, National Library of Australia.
10  A. Marshall, *People of the Dreamtime* (Melbourne: Hyland House, 1978 (1952)); S. Bozic in conjunction with A. Marshall, *Aboriginal Myths* (Melbourne: Gold Star, 1972).
11  E. Wilson, *Churinga Tales: Stories of Alchuringa—the Dream-time of the Australian Aborigines* (Sydney: Australasian, 1950), pp. 11–12.
12  B. & J. MacPherson, *The Magic Boomerang* (Sydney: Young Australian, 1963).
13  H.M. Saxby claimed, 'In the thirty years of social change, educational advancement, and literary development, it would be comforting to be able to claim that children's books in Australia have kept pace with the most progressive and worth-while movements in our society. A glance at the list of children's books published in 1941 and that for 1969–70 indicates immediately that much has been achieved. Which all sounds like reason for self-congratulation until the fine metal is weighed against the dross', H.M. Saxby, *A History of Australian Children's Literature 1941–1970* vol. 2, (Sydney: Wentworth, 1971), p. 215.

After the Second World War, all Australia seemed interested in Aborigines. Tom Ronan lamented that the heroism of the European pioneer had been subsumed by this interest:

> He saw ... that a man named B. Lannigan had died in Fossicker's Creek from fever. Poor old Barney! In Canada or Texas they'd write songs and poems about a man like him. In Australia the southern papers would sooner devote their news columns to an account of some full blood abos, who'd been made a parson or learned to play the piano.[14]

But in the literature, the new bushmen had a place for Aborigines, and not necessarily as subordinate. Block Bryan who was portrayed by Ronan as the true bushman, (competent at his job, can fight and win against any man, unlucky in love) is criticised for his recognition of Aboriginal stock workers.[15] Harney's bushman is haunted by an Aboriginal spirit.[16] In this period there is the beginning of the belief that non-Aboriginal people are outsiders in the Territory. Writers express a fear that the landscape has the power to cause moral and physical degeneration. The debilitating or slackening influence of the environment is, at one level, a euphemism for sexual contact with Aborigines. In *Rusty Bugles* when Vic is refused leave, his mates are made anxious because of his resignation, 'It's a pleasant way to rot in the sun sitting on an anthill'.[17] Ronan too noted the fear that the Territory landscape could somehow subsume the European culture; that it provided a degenerating, slackening influence.

> It's the greatest land in the world bar Scotland. But if you don't guard yourself it will get you. It hates the white man because he is trying to alter a way of life that hasn't changed since the Ice Age. And it takes its revenge of him by tempting him to forswear his own God and follow the creed of 'no matter' and 'bye and bye' ... The north has got better men than you; better men than me ... So don't let yourself get careless in the little things. That will help you to keep up to the mark in the big ones.[18]

The bushman's heroic experiences cannot by now be separated from Aborigines but a new dimension in this interaction, is the beginning of recognition that Aborigines have rights to the land that may override any of the new-comers' claims. Ronan particularly, felt the Territory to be

---

14   Ronan, *Vision Splendid*, p. 250.
15   Ronan, *Vision Splendid*, pp. 292, 297.
16   Harney, *North of 23°*, p. 84.
17   Locke-Elliott, *Rusty Bugles*, p. 79.
18   Ronan, *Vision Splendid*, p. 16.

Aboriginal, rather than non-Aboriginal land. *Vision Splendid* finished on a mournful note that despite technological improvements in opening up the country:

> the 'North'—the 'Never-Never'—Australia's Backyard, its unwanted child-the 'Land of Anomalies'. All it wants to make it flourish is the sort of faith that will make people come here, not to make a pile and get out—they won't anyway: make a pile, I mean—but come here to stay.
>
> No one seems to do that. No one bar the old black fellow. And that is why the black fellow will win out in the end.[19]

This fear, that the Territory was not really the place for white people, had been expressed in the earlier novels but few put it as explicitly as did Ronan. The notion of 'giving it back' is mentioned. Cynthia Nolan quoted a bushman moodily saying: 'I dunno ... the way Australia's going the bloody politicians'll wreck this country. It'd be better to give it back to the aborigines, with apologies'.[20] Coralie and Leslie Rees suggest to Pastor Albrecht: 'Giving Australia back to the black man?'[21]

The incorporation of Aborigines within the cultural context seems to have come about in part because of a heightened awareness of their presence through the occupation of the Northern Territory by armed forces during the war, but also because of the recognition that the Aborigines were not dying out. The post–World War II period, then, saw white Australians attempting to place Aborigines into some kind of understandable context. Although the assimilation program initiated in 1939 had been interrupted by the war, in the post-war period the process of white Australia attempting to accommodate Aboriginal Australians in a political sense had begun. An important part of this process was reflected in the depiction of Aborigines in literature. In children's literature, comics and thrillers, the Northern Territory was still portrayed as populated by wild Aborigines, an image which persisted for a surprisingly long time. Edward Lindall's *Northward the Coast*, for example, depicts the Aborigines as corroboree dancing primitives who work themselves into a hypnotic frenzy of ecstasy and lust.[22] Poet Milan Vodicka wrote:

---

19  Ronan, *Vision Splendid*, pp. 191, 347.
20  Nolan, *Outback*, p. 101.
21  Rees, *Spinifex Walkabout*, p. 264.
22  Lindall, *Northward the Coast*, pp. 194–5.

> In the tropical wet-season when it heavily rains
> and the future with nature grows near—
> still in slow progress of new frontier, the Aboriginals
> remain of Pintubis tribe, boomerang and spear.[23]

The plots of both James Vance Marshall's novels, *The Children* and *A Walk to the Hills of the Dreamtime*, rely upon the Territory being the home for tribes of wandering nomads who have no contact with Europeans: 'Among the secret water-holes of the Australian desert his people had lived and died, unchanged and unchanging, for twenty thousand years'.[24] But the post-war period brought writers to the Territory who were interested in documenting the changing political status of Aborigines and at the same time attempting to 'understand' the 'Aboriginal problem'. The 'stone age' legacy persevered as a clear indicator that white Australians were still struggling to contextualise the Aboriginal experience.

Recognition of the injustices of the colonial legacy were expressed by a small number of writers who painted an equivocal picture of race relations. In *Adventure in the Outback*, for example, the Aborigines from 'Prince's Soak' pastoral lease attack uranium prospectors who trespass on a sacred site. The Police Officer Molloy comments 'disgustedly', 'I hate having to arrest these wild chaps because they don't really understand what it's all about, but at the same time they can't be allowed to go throwing spears at people'.[25] In *Terry in Australia* the actions and attitudes of the pastoralist, White, are explicit criticism of the newcomers lack of sensitivity to Aborigines' prior claim to the land. Granny points out to him, 'we are their guests'.[26] The recognition of Aboriginal spirituality and rights to land were not, however, overriding concerns of the majority of authors who still continued to view Aborigines as examples of 'primitive man', that is, with no concept of property rights.

In this period, Aboriginal skills are presented as something that clever white people could pick up quite quickly. Mary learns an Aboriginal language in a matter of days,[27] and 'Warrigal Joe' has all the skills of the Aboriginal bushmen.[28] Non-Aboriginal bushmen can also appropriate

---

23 M. Vodicka, '1869–1969', *Track to Rum Jungle* (Ilfracombe, Devon: Stockwell, 1970), p. 63.
24 Marshall, *The Children*, pp. 26–7.
25 Power, *Adventure in the Outback*, p. 118.
26 Danielsson, *Terry in Australia*, pp. 135f.
27 Power, *Lost in the Outback*, p. 99.
28 Barr, *Warrigal Joe*.

Aboriginal spirituality. Keith Willey commented that after death, old bushmen go to 'the blackfellow dreaming place'.[29] Edward Lindall's heroes have learnt the secrets of survival from the Aborigines. But it is not only in the popular accounts that assume that it is a relatively straightforward matter to acquire Aboriginal expertise. That kind of assumption is also inherent in the many collections of Aboriginal mythology; a European author, it is presumed, can simply listen to the stories from Aboriginal informants and then write them down, polishing the language a bit prior to publication to make it understandable to a European audience. In the previous period, the protagonists learnt to be true bushmen just from interaction with the landscape; by now, Aborigines are responsible for influencing Europeans in their relationship to landscape:

> I found that blanket branded 'Alice Springs'
> and made my bed with it in stones and sand
> where like a lyre the casuarina sings
> across a region like a shrivelled hand.
>
> And I, too, lost it in some place, for them
> possessions wearied me, and it seemed best
> to travel light and clean as other men
> who tramped toward a campfire in the west;
>
> who came and made their fires beside those scant
> water-holes where thin acacias dream
> and painted finches drink, or the hesitant
> red-gold-ringleted lorikeets swoop and scream.[30]

Writer were fond of juxtaposing elements of European technology from the 'Atomic Age' with Aborigines from the primitive 'Stone Age'. M.E. Patchett's *The Venus Project* with the wildly implausible plot of fish people from Venus hijacking Russian space ships and flying to Australia, relished the contrast: 'What a picture! Here we are chewing like stone-age men in the middle of stone-age country, and just over there is the ultimate triumph of our civilization waiting for us!'[31] But even Beth Dean and Victor Carell remark upon the skill of 'A Stone Age man in his own environment, pitting his skill, patience and speed against nature

---

29  K. Willey, *Joe Brown's Dog, Bluey* (Adelaide: Rigby, 1978), p. 115.
30  R. Robinson, 'Deep Well', part one, 'The Desert', *Deep Well* (Sydney: Edwards & Shaw, 1962), p. 53.
31  M.E. Patchett, *The Venus Project* (Leicester: Brockhampton, 1963), p. 56.

for his daily needs'.[32] They note that 'experts' on Aborigines no longer assert that they are a dying race: 'their culture—their age old beliefs and customs ... all these are dying ... and will, in a few more too short years, vanish altogether and be lost to us forever'.[33] Frederick Macartney's poem 'Didjeridoo' expresses much the same sentiments.[34]

This belief in the death of Aboriginal culture (as opposed to the Aborigine themselves) was noted by some of the commentators. Unlike the pre-war writers who were more willing to ascribe supernatural powers to Aborigines, in this period there tends to be a disparagement of mystical leanings. A part of this is the notion that Aborigines are politically, socially and spiritually powerless. It is inconceivable, therefore, in this period that Aboriginal spirituality could have any impact upon non-Aboriginal people. Leslie and Coralie Rees report peanut farmer Bill Parry 'disparaged the power of the "singing"'. '"Of course there's nothing in it," he said. "The blackfellow thinks there is—they're very superstitious."'[35] A view, incidentally, he was not able to pass on to his sons by Aboriginal mothers. Bill Parry Junior has become a feared traditional 'Lawman' on the Daly River.[36]

The inevitability of assimilation was reinforced by the image of Aboriginal culture as degenerate. Woodberry's Irish servant Biddy in *Come Back Peter* mourns that, 'Nobody could make the magic any more'.[37] Mahrdei, Kyle-Little's charismatic witchdoctor in *Whispering Wind*, though dominating much of the narrative, is dead by the end of the book.[38] Again in the sense of something past or forgotten, the children of Ann Wells's *Men of the Honey Bee* are not particularly spiritual, but the old father, Daragulil, is represented as a gifted telepathic.[39] Elspeth Huxley, visiting the Tiwi, found that the 'Pukamani has shrivelled to a half-hearted caper held at the weekend so as not to interfere with working hours'.[40] Willinja the Sorcerer in Morris West's *The Naked Country* laments that:

---

32   B. Dean & V. Carell, *Dust for the Dancers* (Sydney: Ure Smith, 1955), p. 39.
33   Dean & Carell, *Dust for the Dancers*, p. ix.
34   F.T. Macartney, *Hard Light and other verses* (Surrey Hills, Victoria: Gallen, n.d.), p. 20.
35   Rees, *Spinifex Walkabout*, p. 200.
36   D. Ritchie, 'Social History of the Darwin Hinterland Coastal Plains'. PhD in progress, Deakin University.
37   Woodberry, *Come Back Peter*, p. 16.
38   Kyle-Little, *Whispering Wind: Adventure in Arnhem Land* (London: Hutchinson, 1957), p. 240.
39   A.E. Wells, *Men of the Honey Bee* (Adelaide: Rigby, 1971), p. 19.
40   Huxley, *Their Shining Eldorado*, p. 271.

so far there was no young man fit and ready to undergo the ritual death and assume the burden of his power and knowledge. Perhaps there never would be. More of the young bucks were drifting away to the white man's towns, to the homesteads and to the prospector's camps ... one day there were only old ones left, shrivelled women squatting in the sand, toothless ancients mumbling at lily roots because they could no longer eat the strong meat of the hunters'.[41]

Ion Idriess, perhaps not surprisingly, is still reiterating his pre-war formula of Aboriginal telepathy and magic, which is the main thread of *The Vanished People* (1955).[42] But despite this, most of his examples are from the Kimberley, Cape York or New Guinea and the book is disjointed and difficult to follow. Edward Lindall's *Northward the Coast* does not actually state that Aborigine are magical, although Mary is more sensitive to Ruth's warmth for Lang when there is little evidence of this to anyone else.[43] To European commentators in this period, Aboriginal magic is synonymous with either a remote 'Dream time' past or simply ignorance. In *Adventure in the Outback*, Uncle Tom tells Bert, 'Anything the abo doesn't understand is immediately put down to magic'.[44]

Europeans are sometimes presented as saving the Aborigines from their dark spiritual world:

> I was taken from a blacks' camp only just in time to save me from the fear of black magic, but I learned enough to know that it haunts the black man all his life. No white man can understand it—its power, its terror! It was a horrible thing to my mother. She could never escape it, not even at her death. Sometimes my wife and I are afraid we might go back to the tribe. Only your kind treatment of us—treating us as white people—and our reading keeps us from it.[45]

---

41  West, *The Naked Country*, p. 112.
42  Particularly Chapters 8–19, I.L. Idriess, *The Vanished People* (Sydney: Angus & Robertson, 1955).
43  Lindall, *Northward the Coast*, p. 107.
44  Power, *Adventure in the Outback*, p. 122.
45  F.J. McLeod, *Womba: An Aboriginal Stockboy in the Cattle Country in the Heart of Australia* (Melbourne: Georgian House, 1951), p. 67.

Other writers too emphasised a construction of Aboriginal 'traditional' life that was unpleasant or violent, particularly towards women.[46] Although only a limited value was placed by the writers on the practice and customs of remote Aborigines, there remained a tendency to disparage Aborigines who were clearly adopting aspects of European society. (The only exception to this arises from the assistance Aborigines gave the Australian service people during the war.[47]) Johnny Jingo in *Danger on the Map* illustrates the duality. Johnny is portrayed as an infantile idiot for much of the novel, but he change dramatically after the party is forced to march across Arnhem Land:

> He was no longer the grinning, amiable black ready to do the Dook's bidding at much as the raising of a finger. He was now the black fellow in his own domain, alert, cunning and filled with a strange natural dignity. His primal aboriginal blood was dominant in the wilderness; it was the blood of his ancestors, long used to scratching existence from a barren land and contending for very life with their natural enemies, drought, snakes, crocodiles and hostile tribes.[48]

Ian Mudie's Northern Territory poems, particularly 'Ambo, Alligator River Tribesman' also attempted to show the fracture between Aboriginal and non-Aboriginal societies.[49]

Aborigines living apart from European settlement were seen as cleverer, more interesting or, at very least, happier than those in close proximity. In *Peter Devlin: Buffalo Hunter* (1973), when the boys protest about the lack of wages and poor conditions experienced by Aborigines in the Northern Territory pastoral industry, the practice is defended on the grounds that Aborigines were much happier and better off than now, 'they had a greater dignity than most of the mob that now hang around the

---

46 Douglas Lockwood's description of Aboriginal life as dominated by fear of sorcery, *I, the Aboriginal* (Adelaide: Rigby, 1962), pp. 145f; Ellen Kettle's construction of widespread violence and child killing, *Gone Bush*, p. 15f; the Chauvels' version of female puberty rituals, C. & E. Chauvel, *Walkabout* (London: W.H. Allen, 1959), pp. 239f, descriptions of ritual 'rape' of the adolescent girl, Illuta, with the 'huge blunt sword' by the three men, or the descriptions of cannibalism in this novel by a non-Aboriginal attempting an 'Aboriginal' perspective, J. Patrick, *Inapatua* (Melbourne: Cassell, 1966), pp. 67, 89, etc., although Gillian Cowlishaw's anthropology thesis has suggested that Aboriginal religious ideology allowed the domination of women by men; G. Cowlishaw, 'Women's Realm', PhD thesis, University of Sydney, 1979.
47 C. Barrett, *Up North: Australia Above Capricorn* (Melbourne: Robertson & Mullens, 1942), p. 22.
48 Aldous, *Danger on the Map*, p. 145.
49 I. Mudie, *The Blue Crane* (Sydney: Angus & Robertson, 1959).

fringes of the towns and get boozed up on the wages they earn'.⁵⁰ Coralie and Leslie Rees considered the Aborigines from the more remote areas as inheritors of a purer cultural tradition.⁵¹

But more than simply praising a remote Aboriginal lifestyle, the authors described Aborigines who were not living a 'traditional' life, in terms that suggested they were bad or morally despicable. The old bushman, Joe, in Keith Willey's *Joe Brown's Dog, Bluey*, found the bush Aborigines with 'their spare, tough bodies and the equally unyielding quality of their natures, the living expression of the desert which he loved' yet disapproved of the 'hangers-on in towns and cattle stations'.⁵² Dean and Carrell found the Aborigines of Bagot Compound in Darwin, 'idle, gambling, and thirsty for strong drink'⁵³ while on the Daly they merely subsist on white rations.⁵⁴ John Greenway said contemptuously,

> I was soon to travel … among the fringe-dwelling aborigines who squatted on the edges of white settlements. Mostly they were beaten people—beaten, I think, not so much by the whites as by themselves. I could never bring myself to laugh along with their old men, forty years exiled from their tribes to save their penes from the stone knife, when they bragged with their characteristic high giggle, 'I nebber bin cut. Dey nebber catch me!' The nebber bin cut. Rubbish they were thought to be by the desert people, and rubbish they were.⁵⁵

But this dislike of Aborigines selectively adopting European practices posed a logistical and unresolvable problem for the authors who were also influenced by the current assimilation policy. Few writers actually challenged the assumption that the assimilation of Aboriginal culture within a broader white Australia society was beneficial to Aborigines, although for many the support was qualified. Douglas Lockwood found that being in a party which made first contact with the Pintubi 'one of the most exciting episodes of my career in the Australian outback'.⁵⁶ Tom Ronan asserted that Aboriginal association with the pastoral industry was

---

50   P. Buddee, *Peter Devlin: Buffalo Hunter* (Adelaide: Rigby, 1973), p. 40.
51   Rees, *Spinifex Walkabout*, p. 232.
52   Willey, *Joe Brown's Dog, Bluey*, p. 4.
53   Dean & Carell, *Dust for the Dancers*, p. 75.
54   Dean & Carell, *Dust for the Dancers*, p. 96.
55   J. Greenway, *Down Among the Wild Men: The Narrative Journal of Fifteen Years Pursuing the Old Stone Age Aborigines of Australia's Western Desert* (Melbourne: Hutchinson, 1973), p. 179.
56   D. Lockwood, *The Lizard Eaters* (Melbourne: Cassell, 1964), p. 5.

beneficial.⁵⁷ Rex Ingamells did not question the assumption that contact with white people improved the lot of Territory Aborigines, but stressed that the Europeans must be 'good' and 'help' Aborigines.⁵⁸

But other writers were not so optimistic. Charles and Elsa Chauvel recognised that association with Europeans had not improved life for many Aborigines.⁵⁹ Locke-Elliott put it more simply. After a loud clap of thunder Sammy says, 'The boongs reckon that's the sound of the gods getting wild'. Ot answers him, 'Jeez, they got enough to be angry about'.⁶⁰ Cynthia and Sidney Nolan were critical of European administration of the Aborigines which they asserted maintained a double standard.⁶¹ In *No Sunlight Singing* the system of employing Aborigines was depicted as little better than an open mandate for physical and sexual abuse of the labour force.⁶²

But if some were pessimistic about the ability of the Federal or Territory administration to oversee the mechanics of the assimilation policy, that left only the Church to do better. Generally the missions were wholesale advocates for the assimilation policy. Father Gsell employed the iconoclastic approach of paying a 'bride price' to acquire female children for the mission by intimating that he required a wife.⁶³ Gradually by control of the access to material goods and marriage partners, the mission was able to assume all the main functions of the Tiwi community: food, health, education and eventually spiritual beliefs. Secular writers tended to be somewhat trenchant in this period about the role of the missions. Tom Ronan was critical of the influence of the mission stations, arguing that Mission Aborigines 'treated any white man in authority with a sort of servile familiarity'.⁶⁴ Although Harney deplored the conditions the missionary settlements created,⁶⁵ he had an implicit faith in the assimilation program which he saw as tied up with success at conversion.⁶⁶ But whether missionary or government agent, the agenda was still the same. Non-Aboriginal people hoped to achieve equality by promoting a nationally homogenous culture above the concerns of minority groups.

---

57  Ronan, *Vision Splendid*, p. 215.
58  Ingamells, *Aranda Boy*, p. 89.
59  Chauvel, *Walkabout*, p. 256.
60  Locke-Elliott, *Rusty Bugles*, p. 88.
61  Nolan, *Outback*, p. 80.
62  Walker, *No Sunlight Singing*, p. 159.
63  F.X. Gsell, *'The Bishop with 150 Wives': Fifty Years as a Missionary* (Sydney: Angus & Robertson, 1956), pp. 85–6.
64  Ronan, *Vision Splendid*, p. 55.
65  Harney, *North of 23°*, p. 154.
66  Harney, *North of 23°*, p. 123.

MICKEY DEWAR

Title page and illustration *Danger on the Map* by Allan Aldous (Melbourne: Cheshire, 1947).

In the period after the Second World War Allan Aldous wrote several books which were located in the Northern Territory. Presaging the era of the assimilation policy, in his writing and other novels from this period, Aborigines were strictly constructed as menials who needed to be taught the European way.

Separating children from their Aboriginal families to be raised in missions or government institutions was generally seen as a good thing. Although the Reeses disapproved of Alice Springs's 'degenerate Rainbow Town, which was a mile of galvanised-iron shacks housing much of the aboriginal and part-aboriginal population',[67] they felt that Croker Island's 'part-white' Methodist mission 'had the air of a holiday resort'. The Reeses described a child who waited in excited anticipation for a visit from her mother. When her mother stepped from the plane the child exclaimed in disappointment: 'That's not my mother ... That's only a gin'.[68] 'Yorkie' Walker was more critical. *No Sunlight Singing* depicted quite a different picture from the 'holiday resort' atmosphere of the Reeses' experiences. The Quiveseys, in charge of 'Kuralla' 'half-caste' mission, are portrayed as vainglorious petty tyrants who work their charges ceaselessly, the whole role of the mission being to turn out housemaids for European Territorians.[69]

---

67   Rees, *Spinifex Walkabout*, p. 241.
68   Rees, *Spinifex Walkabout*, pp. 167–9.
69   Walker, *No Sunlight Singing*, p. 102.

'Half-castes' were seen as something very separate from Aborigines and their non-Aboriginal heritage tended to be emphasised. The act of physically removing children from their mothers was mirrored in the writing as authors sought to distance the 'half-castes' from their Aboriginal families. The Reeses were told by the Director of Native Affairs, Frank Moy, that 'half-caste' has a 'bad taste' and why not use 'part-white'? He then told them that it was no hardship for the mother to part with their children because 'there wasn't a great deal of affection for *coloured* children by aboriginal mothers'.[70] Commentators wrote about 'the real aborigines', finding 'part aborigines' in some, as not authentic.[71] 'Half-castes' found themselves part of a political and legislative anomaly which became the theme of several books. Jack Danvers's *The Living Come First* has as its main character Johnny Austral who had an Aboriginal mother and a European father. It is clear from the text that Johnny's frustrations are in a large part due to not being accepted as a European. Johnny tells his sweetheart:

> 'What gets me, Cherry, is that it's so rottenly unfair. The white race made us, and now the white race won't have us. My father was some roaming swaggy who wandered into an abo camp with a couple of bottles of plonk. I was the result. The responsibility rests on him, not on my mother. She was a poor, dumb lubra who didn't know any better. The whites made me, and now the whites kick me in the face'.[72]

Unlike the family in *No Sunlight Singing*, it is apparent that there is no Aboriginal alternative for Johnny to embrace. The parameters of the book suggest there is only the lifestyle of a European or going to the bad. Johnny's foster father states, 'half-castes often *are* inferior ... We know half-caste boys often become thieves or drunks, and many half-caste girls sluts'.[73] Johnny is dealt with in a vacuum as it were, with no blood family on the scene, European or Aboriginal. Mick, in F.J. McLeod's *Womba* is similarly presented as 'abandoned'.[74] Nugget in *Country of the Dead* has a family, but they are of limited help to him. He finds solace with the old Aboriginal men yet is destined to be disappointed because 'The old fellas must all die soon ... The desert is not the same. Soon the white men will bring the cattle out here, too. Then the dancing-grounds will

---

70   Rees, *Spinifex Walkabout*, pp. 163, 166.
71   F.T. Macartney, *Proof Against Failure* (Sydney: Angus & Robertson, 1967), p. 96.
72   J. Danvers, *The Living Come First* (Melbourne: Heinemann, 1961), p. 25.
73   Danvers, *The Living Come First*, pp. 233–4.
74   McLeod, *Womba*, p. 88.

not be any more'.⁷⁵ Jet in the Peter Devlin series too appears to have no family and must stand alone: 'You're a bridge, Jet. You share two worlds'.⁷⁶ This kind of construction, of Aboriginal children completely without family, is similar to Jeannie Gunn's of Bett-Bett, and suggests Aboriginal parents were uncaring. This kind of assumption justified the widespread institutionalisation thought appropriate for many Aboriginal children with European kin.

In the writing is a suggestion that 'half-castes' 'are a potential challenge to the very terms, and terminology, of the colonial encounter'⁷⁷ and could become a threat to non-Aboriginal settlement in a way that Aborigines were not:

> The bitches breed like rabbits when they get mated with a white man … You mark my words: before long this country would be stiff with yellerfellers, give them their way. And the yellerfeller will run the white man into the ground one day. Lying, sneaking, thieving rats the lot of them.⁷⁸

Although it is clear that the post-war assimilation policy had a strong hold on Territory attitudes both personally and in policy, many of the writers use language which stresses the transitory aspect of the implementation (in itself a recognition that it was not achievable). Leslie and Coralie Rees quote Frank Moy, Director of Native Affairs, who stated that, 'Neither whites nor blacks are evolved enough for' unsegregated schooling.⁷⁹ Elspeth Huxley, in a revealing choice of metaphor, stated that the object of the settlement at Snake Bay on Melville Island was, 'to wean the aborigines away from the breast-milk of dependence on to a sieved money economy'.⁸⁰

After the period covering roughly the first half of the century, where women rarely entered the writing and the emphasis was almost entirely on the masculine experience, the reader of post-war Territory writing is likely to encounter more mention of women in the writing. Children's literature of this period still tended to ignore or minimise the role of women, although Phyllis M. Power was an exception. Sister Hannah is capable and confident, Mary is a brilliant and courageous pilot who can

---

75   L. Rose, *Country of the Dead* (Sydney: Angus & Robertson, 1959), p. 180.
76   P. Buddee, *Peter Devlin: Range Rider* (Adelaide: Rigby, 1973), p. 170.
77   T. Donaldson, 'Australian Tales of Mystery and Miscegenation', *Meanjin* 50, 3 (1991), p. 341.
78   Ruhen, *Naked Under Capricorn*, p. 95.
79   Rees, *Spinifex Walkabout*, p. 165.
80   Huxley, *Their Shining Eldorado*, p. 270.

fix any machinery. Mrs Snowdon drives a truck competently, tutors the boys in correspondence and can leap quickly into a tree when pursued by an angry steer. 'Just watch the lubras ride, they're even better than the men, and don't they just love the work' says Al to the new-chum Bert.[81] Mary Patchett too had a female as well as male hero in her *Festival of Jewels* (1968) which described two children who foiled international jewel robber on the road to Darwin. But as in the earlier depictions of women in Northern Territory writing, assertiveness and success were largely judged by an ability to assume a masculine role.

Captain W.E. Johns has no women in his Territory 'Biggles' books—less because of the outback mythology than because Johns apparently believed 'Boys hate the introduction of girls into their stories'.[82] Joan Woodberry's female characters in *Come Back Peter* are almost universally unable to function in the Territory outback. Paul's mother is on the edge of a nervous breakdown after the premature death of her son Peter. Johnnie Moran's mother is sick and unable to cope while her husband is away. The Irish maid, old Biddy, is nostalgic for her early days on the station. James Vance Marshall's *A Walk to the Hills of the Dreamtime* has a female protagonist who is locked in a cross-cultural struggle with a magical Aboriginal elder after the two children have been found by an Aboriginal group wandering lost in the desert. Although Sarah wins the cross-cultural debate with the assertion of the power of the Christian magic, she loses her life in the process. Richard Graves's *Spear and Stockwhip* contains few references to women, although of the only female mentioned Tom remarks admiringly, 'they're tough, these northern women'.[83] Bengt Danielsson's *Terry in Australia*, like Phyllis Power's 'Outback' novels, has very positive female role models. Granny and Elizabeth rescue Terry and his father after their vehicle breaks down. Granny wins the Alice Springs Queen's Birthday shooting competition and the tall tales competition with her stories of the sea and dynamiting cattle rustlers from an aeroplane.[84] But Danielsson's book perhaps reflects the Swedish cultural influence rather than Australian.

White women, when they are mentioned in adult literature, are frequently depicted in the role of guardians of order and social form. Aboriginal women, in keeping with the theme of the depiction of

---

81 Power, *Adventure in the Outback*, p. 63.
82 Captain W.E. Johns quoted, R. Boston, 'The Cavalry of the Air Flies Once More', *Guardian Weekly*, 19 July 1992, p. 23.
83 Graves, *Spear and Stockwhip*, p. 113.
84 Danielsson, *Terry in Australia*, pp. 59, 82, 100.

intra-Aboriginal relationships generally, are described in ways that suggest a down-trodden aspect. This is often mentioned as a contrast to the emancipation that European women in the post-war period are supposedly enjoying. Sexual relations between Aboriginal women and European men once again emerge as a topic of literary discussion, with writers tending to focus either on the exploitative or accepted nature of these relationships. But it was still a widespread belief that the 'outback' conditions were too harsh for a European woman. But the main point of note really, is that women actually do appear in the writing. This fact notwithstanding, Cynthia Nolan commented dryly, 'A quite erroneous opinion, generally held in the cities, is that wives on these outback stations are eager to have a visit from another white woman'.[85] Cynthia Nolan noted that a white female visitor was frequently resented since it meant 'unnecessary extra efforts'. The implication of this is that the arrival of a female visitor meant that the station woman had to then reveal the suppressed womanly side of her personality and demonstrate competence at female arts rather than conforming to a masculine competence as 'one of the boys'.

Two accounts of the Territory bushmen in this period show a revival of the Jeannie Gunn image with a strong emphasis on the process by which the women acclimatise to the harsh outback conditions. Elisabeth George described the life of Henrietta Pearce and the ways she adapted to bush life in *Two At Daly Waters* learning to cook, camp out, coming to appreciate Aboriginal society and cope with the harshness of climate.[86] Nancy Polishuk declared at her first sight of their block of land on the Daly River, 'I feel like a real pioneer now'. She is surprised when she spends six weeks in Darwin after the birth of her son Peter to find herself 'pining and sighing wistfully for the Daly'. *Life on the Daly River* stresses the extremes of the climate and much of the book is taken up by a description of the big flood of 1957.[87] These two books once more establish European women in the pioneering mould but equally there is a preoccupation with description of domestic routine[88] which reflects the priorities of gender roles in the post-war period. Henrietta Drake-Brockman's play, *Men Without Wives*, also celebrates the battling pastoralist's wife in the character of Mrs. Bates and

---

85   Nolan, *Outback*, p. 92.
86   E. George, *Two At Daly Waters* (Melbourne: Georgian House, 1945), pp. 30f, 33, 44, 56, 76, 98f, 125.
87   Polishuk & Lockwood, *Life on the Daly River*, pp. 47, 69, 73f.
88   For example George, *Two At Daly Waters*, pp. 30f; Polishuk & Lockwood, *Life on the Daly River*, pp. 46f.

her 'heart of gold' as opposed to Mrs. Abbott from the town who has yet to learn the lessons of the landscape.[89] In a less serious mode, this theme of the city woman who follows her husband to the Territory and learns to survive the experience occurs in the romantic novel as well.[90]

The usual way European women were presented was a pioneering homemaker. Harry Griffiths, missionary with the Methodist Inland Mission, summed up the general feeling in a tribute to 'the handful of European women' who came north 'to make a home for husband and family'.[91] The stereotypical view of European Territorian women was provided by Dean and Carell who approvingly described Margaret Dodds, a school teacher from Mainoru station, who gave her Aboriginal housemaids English lessons,[92] or 'quiet unassuming' Mrs Lear, 'in complete charge of the station' and 'often alone'.[93] Harry Griffiths admired the way Mrs McGoogan, station manager's wife, insisted that everyone dressed nightly for dinner. She trained her Aboriginal staff to wait on the table in black dresses, white aprons and caps for special occasions. This, Griffiths stated, had the function of showing 'the Territory-born how the "other half" lived'.[94] Women's observance of social rituals had the effect of alienating that section of society which did not observe them. In *Vision Splendid* when Toppingham helps a drunken Marty at the Border races, he is too late and too dirty to attend 'a party at which ladies were to be present'.[95] Ronan subscribed to the traditional pre-war Territory values where mateship and a love of adventure were idealised above heterosexual relationships. Billy Jaggers, from *Vision Splendid*, allowed Ronan to lampoon the bushman's traditional disgust for women in the Territory:

> He'd thought he'd be sorry to leave the Territory, but when things got that way at a place like Big Knob that a man couldn't walk ten yards on a dark night without being half strangled by a clothes-line full of pants and petticoats, it was time to give the bush away completely.[96]

So it is an irony when he is robbed of all his savings by his sister.

---

89   H. Drake-Brockman, *Men Without Wives: and Other Plays* (Sydney: Angus & Robertson, 1955).
90   Such as, for example, Coralie Baker and her Flying Doctor husband Noel in Miller's *Flying Doctor Disappears*.
91   Griffiths, *An Australian Adventure*, p. 68.
92   Dean & Carell, *Dust for the Dancers*, p. 49.
93   Dean & Carell, *Dust for the Dancers*, p. 89.
94   Griffiths, *An Australian Adventure*, p. 77.
95   Ronan, *Vision Splendid*, p. 83.
96   Ronan, *Vision Splendid*, pp. 292-3.

Ted Strehlow payed tribute to the strength of the bush woman in the portrayal of the character of the wife of the owner of Horseshoe Bend station, Ruby Elliot.[97] She is described as powerful and resourceful but with the ability to accommodate Aboriginal experience[98] and the power to revitalise and regenerate men she came into contact with, both Gus Elliot and also the dying Carl Strehlow.[99] In keeping with the prevailing stereotype, her competence in the saddle and at station work was seen in no way to threaten her feminine power. Playwright Suzanne Spunner has seen in Strehlow's construction, a rationalisation of Strehlow's own personal circumstances of the abandonment of his first wife, for his younger new love, Kathleen.[100] But Strehlow's Ruby Elliot was clearly an unusual case. Other writers emphasised the pedestrian nature of Territory gender relations. Elspeth Huxley described heterosexual activity in Alice Springs: 'The art of pleasing men seems to lie more in glossing over or disguising sex than in emphasising it … Most of the women … accept, their lot, count their blessings and let it go at that'.[101] Tom Ronan described why such liaisons sometimes failed: 'one of those marriages where the wife couldn't live in the north, or the husband earn a decent living anywhere else'.[102]

A contrast to the picture of a few brave women enduring the harsh outback conditions can be found in the romantic fiction. Lucy Walker's description of Ransome Station is almost overwhelming in the number of women described: the heroine Sara, the scheming cousin Julie, Greg's sister, Marion, the avaricious Mrs Camden, the housekeeper Mrs Whittle who is acknowledged ruler of the house; even the ringers are married. There is no place for Aboriginal and non-Aboriginal sexual liaisons in women's romantic fiction. Despite the number of European women present in the story, there is evidence of a masculine ritualistic code of behaviour.[103] Clearly it is a part of romantic Territory mythology that women occupy a special position located apart from the world of gambling, drinking and stockwork which appear to be exclusively masculine pursuits. Women are only visible when they are in the kitchen. Part of the pleasure for Sara

---

97  Interestingly, like Jeannie Gunn, Ruby Elliot is never referred in the text by her own name, but always called Mrs Gus Elliot.
98  Strehlow, *Journey to Horseshoe Bend*, p. 201.
99  Strehlow, *Journey to Horseshoe Bend*, pp. 129, 157.
100 S. Spunner, 'The Ingkata's Wife', draft typescript, 1990.
101 Huxley, *Their Shining Eldorado*, p. 311.
102 Ronan, *Vision Splendid*, p. 339.
103 Walker, *Master of Ransome*, p. 107.

on Ransome Station arises from the fact that the drudgery of household management is performed by mentally infantile but cheerful Aboriginal assistants.[104] This transparent quality of women is evident in Walker's *The Man from the Outback* as well. Although the taciturn but wildly attractive hero, Kane Manners declared at Mari's arrival that, 'No white woman has been on this station for twenty years'[105] as the novel progresses, in blatant contradiction, the reader is introduced to many women, white and black.

When a European woman was portrayed in literature, aside from the Jeannie Gunn plucky station woman, it was usually as a controller of the domestic sphere. This was heralded by the Christian missionaries as feminist emancipation since 'girls brought up and educated on the mission tend to become more independent when it comes to marrying: they insist on choosing their own husband'.[106] Even Ann Wells's *Men of the Honey Bee*, published comparatively recently, expressed with confidence that European contact had resulted in Aboriginal emancipation. Darangui, who learns English and becomes a school teacher, declares to his brothers after a dispute over who will marry Lindirij after Maingala's death: 'There is coming a new law in this country, and in this new law a woman has the right to her own decision in a matter such as this'.[107]

The 1950s emphasis on home and housework was the predictable response of Australian society to renegotiate the nuclear family and resettle women out of the workforce after the relatively free conditions they experienced during the war. Lucy Walker gives Mari, the white heroine of *The Man from Outback* (the antithesis of romance!), a full page description of the electrical appliances and layout of the kitchen at NinnaWarra.[108] This was set against a backdrop of disdain for 'traditional' Aboriginal culture. Europeans, particularly European women, asserted with great confidence a dislike of Aboriginal gender relations and the notion that conforming to white Australian social norms was of great benefit to Aboriginal women. Hilda Wurst of Hermannsburg argued that: 'Before they were influenced by Christian teaching the women were very downtrodden'.[109] Elsa Chauvel described 'MinMin' 'a superb young native' 'I hoped she would marry one

---

104 Walker, *Master of Ransome*, p. 38.
105 Walker, *The Man from Outback*, p. 16.
106 Rees, *Spinifex Walkabout*, p. 230.
107 Wells, *Men of the Honey Bee*, p. 202.
108 Walker, *The Man from Outback*, p. 12.
109 Rees, *Spinifex Walkabout*, p. 259.

of the [European] stockmen, for then her life would be easier'.[110] In this atmosphere of male Aboriginal sexual exploitation, it is interesting that *Northward the Coast* is the only book from this period which suggests that European women were at the risk of sexual abuse from Aboriginal men.[111] But then Lindall is one of the few authors in this period who mentions the sexual relationships of European women at all.[112]

Women idealised as domestic home-makers meant that discussions of sex in literature tend to be limited either to a purely masculine ritual or as expressed by women's relationship to children. This period marked a certain coyness in discussion of matters relating to sex (with European women). In Locke-Elliott's *Rusty Bugles*, the play dealt only obliquely with European heterosexual relations (perhaps not surprisingly given Locke-Elliott's own sexual orientation). There are no female characters but they are present as idealised figures (Rita Hayworth)[113] or as girlfriends or wives. But this sexual idealisation of European women was comparatively rare in the writing. Film stars prove more reliable than the real-life women. The scene where Mac's daughter, Alice, writes that her mother is pregnant again is full of pathos as after the congratulations, everyone realise that Mac could not be the father.[114] The cheerful Ot, who keeps a garden and does everyone else's work to earn enough money to get married, forgoes his leave when his girlfriend Dawn writes that she has married someone else.[115]

Although European women's sexual behaviour was not an issue under discussion in this period, in contrast, Aboriginal women's sexual behaviour was of primary interest to many of the writers. White women were depicted as controlling Aboriginal women's sexual behaviour, particularly with European men. Mrs McGregor in *Vision Splendid* had a reputation as a 'gin shepherd' and locked the housemaids in the bathroom each night

---

110  Chauvel, *Walkabout*, p. 191.
111  Lindall, *Northward the Coast*, p. 183; the possibility that Aboriginal tracker, Merara, raped Barbara Winning is raised, R.W. Hunter's *The Innocent Savage* (Sydney: Horwitz, 1963 (1960)), but we, the readers, know he is innocent.
112  Although the women usually become the lovers of the heroes, by the later Lindall, *Northward the Coast* and *Death and the Maiden* (London: Constable, 1973), white women are portrayed as sexually vulnerable to the predations of males, particularly Death and the Maiden where the heroine is raped by Billo the (white) station hand.
113  Locke-Elliott, *Rusty Bugles*, p. 28.
114  Locke-Elliott, *Rusty Bugles*, pp. 32, 33.
115  Locke-Elliott, *Rusty Bugles*, p. 74.

which had the result that it was difficult to keep male staff.[116] Mrs Foster from *No Sunlight Singing* turned a blind eye to the sexual exploitation of Aboriginal female staff, but sent them to Darwin if there was any tangible evidence of sexual relations.[117] After Marriner married a European woman in *Naked Under Capricorn*, his wife Monica is vindictive towards his Aboriginal family and eventually, taking advantage of Marriner's absence from the station, drives them from their country. Sexual relationships are presented in the texts as a way for Aboriginal women to gain power. The terrorists of Lindall's *The Last Refuge* (who for the most part are moving in a Northern Territory that seems almost entirely devoid of an Aboriginal population) approve of the custom of the Aborigines who use 'wife lending' as a means of watching over the activities of a stranger.[118] Harney suggested that European men could also be 'Gin shepherds', jealously guarding the Aboriginal women they had sexual relations with.[119]

The two sides to the issue of sexual relations between Aboriginal women and European men, the contract or exploitation dichotomy, were again explored by the writers of this period. The relationship between European stockmen and black women was a major theme in Ronan's *Vision Splendid*. Despite an initial embarrassment Toppingham eventually joined the rest of the men on the station[120] and took an Aboriginal mistress, Lily. He was first startled and then amused when he realised that she had come to him, not out of desire, but because of her husband Jimmy's insistence and that she required payment of goods such as tobacco, dresses, beads, tea and sugar for her services.[121] But Toppingham questioned his attitudes after his (European) love, Stephanie, married the boss:

> as a question of ethical values, was there much difference between a white, educated, civilized woman who'd sell herself permanently for a share of A.J. Bruno's wealth, and a lubra who'd sell herself temporarily for a few sticks of tobacco.[122]

But Ronan's depiction of male and female interaction emerges as gentle and sensitive when contrasted to Walker's accounts of vicious exploitation and rape. Walker takes the view (which was also so apparent

---

116 Ronan, *Vision Splendid*, p. 111.
117 Walker, *No Sunlight Singing*, p. 146.
118 Lindall, *The Last Refuge*, p. 76.
119 Harney, *North of 23°*, p. 76.
120 Ronan, *Vision Splendid*, p. 57.
121 Ronan, *Vision Splendid*, p. 64.
122 Ronan, *Vision Splendid*, p. 270.

in the writings of Willshire) that sexual relationships were conducted on European terms as part of the perquisites of white domination of the Territory. No heterosexual relationship (with perhaps the exception of Paddy and Polly) is presented in *No Sunlight Singing* as anything more than necessity—bartering sex for financial security. The station owner, the 'Pig', forces Polly into a sexual relationship; Jimmy trades sex with Mary for secrets; David Foster trades alcohol for sex; Meg prostitutes herself for methylated spirits because she is forced to by her pimp, and Mary offers sex (and abandons her friendship with Meg) so that her daughter can assume the privileges of white exemption from the Welfare Ordinance.

In Olaf Ruhen's *Naked Under Capricorn*, the characters of Marriner and Dallas exemplify the accommodating as well as the exploitative relations with Aboriginal women in the writing. Marriner is a good man, although weak. He has an excellent relationship with the Aboriginal community on whose land he has settled, but he does nothing when he discovers the naked body of Maudie with a bullet in her spine, murdered by Dallas because she was pregnant with his child.[123] Dallas's exploitative and violent brutality towards Aboriginal women eventually leads to his death at the hands of Aborigines from Marriner's station. The ensuing police reprisal brings about the deaths of several close friends of Marriner's as well as his son, Henry. *Naked Under Capricorn* implies that although there can be sexual relationships of companionship and trust between European men and Aboriginal women, the majority of relationships do not take this form. Women are deeply resented if they do not comply with sexual demands. Donnegan in *Unlucky Dip* confirms this and calls Lucy 'that little yellow bitch' whom he might have 'had' but 'she thought it might be funny to keep us both stringing along'.[124]

Even within the less exploitative framework, there is a sense of a fundamental boundary being crossed by those involved in inter-racial sex. Once European men have had Aboriginal lovers, they are portrayed ambiguously as being too ashamed or perhaps unwilling to return to sexual relations with European women. Not only Mark Shillingsworth, but in *Vision Splendid* Tony Carlow commits suicide rather than face his fiancée, the Honourable Margaret,[125] and Toppingham is afraid to engage in 'even the mildest flirtation with a white woman after the life he had

---

123 Ruhen, *Naked Under Capricorn*, p. 101.
124 M. Henry, *Unlucky Dip* (London: Cassell, 1960), p. 174.
125 Although perhaps Carlow had contracted venereal disease; Ronan, *Vision Splendid*, p. 66.

been leading for the last twelve months'.[126] Or perhaps European men do not want white women after they have had Aboriginal lovers; Keith Willey's bushman, Joe Brown, only wants relationships with Aboriginal women because they are less demanding.[127] Olaf Ruhen's character, Mo, explains that the bushman remain in the bush because of the sexual bonds he forms with Aboriginal women: 'No matter what brings the white man here, it's the black woman that keeps him here'.[128]

The literature of the Territory in the post-war period mirrored the preoccupations of the times. Assimilation was justified by the writers on the grounds that it was a physical, moral and cultural improvement for Aborigines to live as Europeans. At the same time, the obvious problem with such a policy are inherent and the contradictions are mirrored in the writing. Thonemann's character, Buludja, gives a stilted speech on the topic:

> When you taught us to break down our rigid customs you did not make us adopt the better ones of yours. You exploited us, made us live in a manner contrary to our upbringing, and then punished us for not keeping your laws and for keeping our own. The result has been that we keep neither, as one is against our teaching and the other against your instructions, and you call us outcasts or degenerates. Our moral beliefs have been swept aside and we have been compelled to live in an atmosphere so strange that we fail to comprehend its meaning.[129]

Even the Reeses, who approve of the philosophy, can see that a cultural gulf created by the little girl who sees her mother as 'only a gin' and the substandard living conditions of 'rainbow town' in Alice Springs, are not unqualified improvements in Aboriginal standards of living. Ronan escapes dealing with the issue directly by nostalgically harking back to a pre-war Territory but by implication suggests that he has reservations with the notion that Aborigines must renounce their own culture and identity. Walker is uniformly grim on the realities of assimilation where the loyalty of Meg to the old woman with leprosy is contrasted starkly by the pressure on Mary to renounce any friendship or obligation outside European society.

---

126 Ronan, *Vision Splendid*, p. 74.
127 Willey, *Joe Brown's Dog, Bluey*, p. 8.
128 Ruhen, *Naked Under Capricorn*, p. 115.
129 Thonemann, *Tell the White Man*, p. 103.

Against the backdrop of assessment of the Federal Aboriginal policy, and in contrast to the absence of any mention in the pre-war period, runs a resurgence of sexual tensions which exist on all levels. It is ironic that the misogyny of the bushmen of pre-war literature, with the almost total absence of women, should, in the post-war period become the stuff of which women's romances are made. The political emphasis on woman as home-maker and controller of the domestic sphere is asserted directly and unequivocally. Aboriginal women are seen to gain advantage in relations with Europeans that seem little more than legitimised prostitution. In *No Sunlight Singing*, Mary's marriage to ensure her daughter's future is protected by gaining citizen's rights is the logical extension of the wholesale belief that domestic bondage in European society is infinitely preferable to the 'down trodden' state (as perceived by non-Aboriginal writers) of Aboriginal society. Finally and most crucially in this period, the novelists are attempting to grapple with the notion of sexual liaisons between Aboriginal women and European men. In this period, the depiction of women as free sexual agents is regarded as threatening to the role of women as idealised home-makers. Any construction of sexual relations outside marriage, therefore, emphasises the exploitative and negative aspects.

There was a peculiar ambiguity about the way non-Aboriginal writers viewed Aborigines in this period. While there was lip-service paid to the complexity and spirituality of Aboriginal culture in the collections of Aboriginal myths and legends, at the same time there was a cynicism towards Aboriginal powers which had not been apparent in the pre-war period. The writing therefore no longer emphasised Aboriginal telepathy, ceremonies or tracking skills which had been taken for granted in the earlier adventure narratives. But there was a new optimism expressed by the writers that there would be a new equality in black/white relations.

In this period Territory writers were preoccupied with an exploration of both Federal Aboriginal policy and gender roles. Their underlying concern was an attempt to evaluate the assimilation policy of the Commonwealth Government. In the 1950s, the lionising of Albert Namatjira and his subsequent fall from grace, focussed attention (probably more than any other single case) on white Australia's treatment of the Aborigines. In the post-*Capricornia* era, writers sought to explore the issues raised by Herbert and the exploitative nature of many of the sexual relationships between European men and Aboriginal women was emphasised. Together with the cultural complacency, inherent in the society that promoted 'Aboriginal assimilation' was the beginning of anger at the racial prejudice exhibited in the post-war Territory. Harney, Ronan, Lockwood and Walker attempted to articulate the Aboriginal case, but at this stage, Territory Aboriginal writers were still silent. Alongside the scepticism about the benefit of the Atomic Age for Aboriginal culture, there is evidence of keen interest on the part of the writers towards Aboriginal mythology and spirituality. In contrast, the relationship to landscape was seen as less significant. This was to change after the 1970s.

# 7

# WELCOME TO WILDERNESS

The 1970s brought an increased concern for environmental issues, cultural plurality, feminism, and a reform Government in Canberra. At the same time Gough Whitlam espoused a policy to promote excellence in the arts in an international context.[1] These changes were reflected in the ways the Northern Territory came to be represented in literature. Writers tended to focus on the geographical locations offered by Kakadu and Arnhem Land in the Top End, and Uluru and the desert in the Centre. Continuing the trend established by post-war writers in the wake of the war-time destruction of Darwin, the emphasis remained on Central Australia. But it was the Aboriginal theme that was of primary concern to European writers—not as in the previous period relating to the sexual or political implications of European contact but as a source of an intrinsic view of the world and hence a new interpretation of the Territory landscape and wilderness:

> … the bush, or as we now say, the Land,
> the three quarters of our continent
> set aside for mystic poetry.[2]

In this period, the notion of white Australia's rights to the land were questioned, although in spite of the Referendum of 1967 and the Federal Court Judgement in the case of *Milirrpum and Others v Nabalco and the Commonwealth of Australia*, the concept of *terra nullius* was not

---

1   J. Davidson, 'Mr Whitlam's Cultural Revolution', *Journal of Australian Studies* 20 (May 1987), pp. 84–5.
2   L.A. Murray, 'Louvres', Headon, *North of the Ten Commandments*, p. 223.

overturned until the 1992 High Court decision in the Mabo case.[3] In the Northern Territory, the *Aboriginal Land Rights (Northern Territory) Act 1976* conferred on Aborigines the right to claim certain land if they could demonstrate common spiritual affiliation. This legislation transformed Aboriginal spirituality from an anthropological construct to a political and legal reality. In one stroke Aboriginality was redefined in yet another non-Aboriginal construction. Humphrey McQueen noted that, 'Environmental and anti-war movements established the mental space in which European Australians could reconceive of tribal Aboriginal as noble savages'.[4] Stephen Muecke has argued that the western version of Aboriginal culture has 'imposed unnecessary limits on being Aboriginal'.[5] Nowhere is this more evident than in the construction of 'Aboriginality' evident in the writing.

The change in national mood was reflected in the Territory writing. Writers such as Robyn Davidson, Thomas Keneally, Bruce Chatwin and Lindy Chamberlain, produced epic and influential works in a Territory setting which attempted to define and relate the Territory frontier experience to the rest of Australia. There was a sense of excitement in the Northern Territory: 'from all over the world people blew into town—adventurers, bums, academics, musicians, eccentrics and thinkers. It was out on the network that, in Alice, something remarkable was happening'.[6]

The writing shared the following assumption and characteristics. The Northern Territory was seen to provide access to wilderness and formed a focus for those associated with the conservation movement.

Aborigines were perceived to provide a role model for Europeans by showing the way to live harmoniously with the environment. It is by now accepted in the literature that the European settlers of the Northern

---

3   Michael Dodson, (then) the Director of the Northern Land Council, articulated the shift in attitude: 'A few years ago the buzz word, when dealing with Aboriginal people, was "consultation". Now after Mabo, it's "negotiation".'; M. Dodson, 'The Aboriginal and Torres Strait Islander Social Justice Commission', Anthropology Seminar Program, Northern Territory University, 3 March 1993.
4   McQueen, *Suburbs of the Sacred*, p. 92.
5   S. Mueke, 'Lonely Representations: Aboriginality and Cultural Studies', B. Attwood & J. Arnold, eds, *Power, Knowledge and Aborigines*, Special edition of Journal of Australian Studies, (Bundoora, Victoria: La Trobe University Press in association with the National Centre for Australia Studies, Monash University, 1992), p. 40.
6   Davidson, ' Alice Springs', *Travelling Light*, p. 120.

Territory have always practised a policy of deliberate genocide towards the Aboriginal inhabitants. Uluru has been made the spiritual nucleus for all Australians while Darwin has reinforced its role as Australia's Asian city.

It is paradoxical that in this period the Northern Territory is still presented as a frontier. The significance of this frontier is that it must be experienced as the rite of passage to wilderness. Economic potential is no longer the preoccupation—rather it is accessing the wilderness which is seen to be spiritually renewing. To Jeannie Gunn the Territory wilderness, although beautiful, formed a testing ground for the moral worth of a character and was seen as something to be subdued and survived. The only consolation in the difficult existence was the communication and fellowship with other bushmen. Three quarters of a century later in the writing of Davidson or Chatwin, the wilderness itself is spiritually renewing, sustaining and satisfying but it is the interaction with the Territorians on the 'frontier' which forms the ordeal which needs to be survived.

Kakadu has become the place Australians dream of making pilgrimage to and writers themselves are attracted by these icons. Cliff Hardy, Peter Corris's hard-boiled fictional detective, noted the suburban dream ironically, 'One day, Vanessa, I'll sell the agency and we'll drive around Australia. I've always wanted to see Kakadu'.[7] Mainstream writers often express the need to experience the Territory. Lyn Riddett commented that writers often express the view that the Territory is, 'Touching a well-spring of uses … In Australia today, culturally, you need to know [not only] … the icons, Uluru, Kakadu, but need to experience them'.[8] Australian nationalist and bard John Williamson united some of these images in his 1992 CD 'This is Australia Calling'. The title track tells how the spirits from Uluru are sending a warning to all of Australia to conserve our natural resources. At the same time Williamson (or perhaps the spirits) urges people to end the 'gloom and doom' talk of the economic recession and get the country 'rolling'. The new Northern Territory message of environmental awareness through Aboriginal spirituality is entwined with the old one of the economic potential of the country.

---

7    P. Corris, *Beware of the Dog: A Cliff Hardy Novel* (Sydney: Bantam, 1992), p.137.
8    Lyn Riddett, interview, Northern Territory University, 31 July 1992.

Also the sense of movement was a theme explored in much of the writing in this period. The geographical remoteness of the Northern Territory was once again emphasised and as in the works of many earlier writers, passage to the Territory is almost as important as arrival. For the newcomers, there was the notion of a quest. 'Most of us are pilgrims of one kind or another, although what we are truly in homage to might not come clear until our pilgrimages are done' begins John Bryson's account of Lindy Chamberlain's ordeal in Central Australia.[9] In descriptions of Aborigines, there was the evocation of predefined and cyclical travel through the image of nomads. Brue Chatwin was foremost in this construction. But themes centred on movement through space are a major part of nearly all construction of the Territory. Robyn Davidson's *Tracks* is the story of a journey. John Hooker's *The Bush Soldier* never makes it to the Territory although the whole book is devoted to trying to get to Alice Springs. John Spicer's *Catchpole* only just makes it. Evan Green's characters cannot wait to leave it in *Alice To Nowhere*. The Chamberlains' travel through the Territory are interrupted by the tragedy at Uluru. Christopher Wood's *Dead Centre* is one long pursuit. The dramatic climax of Herbert's *Poor Fellow My Country* occur during the long trek across country by the ill-sorted party. Andrew McMillan's *Strict Rules* is an account of a rock band's tour of the Territory. David Foster's *Mates of Mars* travels north from Alice Springs to Arnhem Land then east to the Gulf. B. Wongar's characters are forever travelling into more remote areas to escape pursuers. Russell Guy's character is always 'going to Darwin'.[10] Suzanne Spunner's *Dragged Screaming to Paradise* not only looks at travel but is written in three 'movements'. Charmian Clift's three short articles on the Northern Territory are included under the heading, 'Wanderings'. The significance of depicting non-Aboriginal subjects as transient is perhaps a reflection of the deeper insecurity non-Aboriginal people feel in the Northern Territory. The Northern Territory is not a home, but a place to come to or go from. Territory authors often admit that they went there, not purposefully, but to get away from something or as a place en route to somewhere else.[11]

---

9   J. Bryson, *Evil Angels* (Ringwood: Penguin, 1986 (1985)), p. 10.
10  For example R. Guy, *What's Rangoon To You is Grafton to Me* (North Ryde, New South Wales: Angus & Robertson, 1991), pp. 33, 40, etc.; Oddly enough when Guy actually sets a short story in the Northern Territory he describes a traveller who has difficulty leaving.
11  For example Morris Lurie commented: 'I didn't really go *to* Alice Springs, I went *away* from home. But the outpost feeling of the place, the remove from my reality, suited my purpose'; Morris Lurie, letter to the author, 8 August 1992; Suzanne Spunner who found Darwin, 'An entry point into Australia, an exit point out of Australia … you do feel you could sail and get somewhere else …', Interview, Suzanne Spunner, Fannie Bay, Darwin, 30 July 1992.

In this period, experience of the physical landscape of the Northern Territory, particularly the desert, is regarded as a source of inspiration and fulfilment. The landscape retains the power to build character: 'the bush make the bushman have a different outlook, way of looking at life'.[12] In the texts, many of the characters, in process of travelling and arrival, realise the true nature of their inner-most selves:

> Living in Sydney you could fool yourself ...
>
> But here, against the hard actuality of the desert, he felt oddly, disturbingly impotent. It was as if the country's very harshness had stripped him of all pretence. How could he ever pit himself against the inviolate desert? And yet, paradoxically, the land here spoke of fulfilment. Perhaps you have to dominate it first to succeed, Stephen thought.[13]

The harshness of the environment necessitates that pretext is redundant and reality exposed. In *Mates of Mars*, David Foster's Territory is a place where people are forced to confront their own strengths and weaknesses when the band of martial arts experts converges on the small Aboriginal community of Neverfuckinlose. Thus, Steve learns bladder control, Bruce is accepted as an equal and Sven the womaniser is brutally punished. Cyril is overtaken by his nemesis but Jade and Vincent manage to escape. Jade is depicted as outside of an essentially masculine world and Vincent, unlike the others, is at home in Neverfuckinlose: 'Vincent can't swim but he can admire the Nankeen heron. Paradise. He could live here. He doesn't want to go back to Sydney'.[14] But it is not only Vincent's capacity to appreciate the landscape which saves him. In Sydney, he is the foreigner, the outsider, and in a paradoxical reversal, it is Vincent who is most at home in the Territory. The Northern Territory, as writers stress, is a place where values are inverted. In John Bryson's Territory, the innocent are found guilty, the godless are spiritual and the police conspire to break the law.[15]

The belief that the Northern Territory landscape both shapes and reveals true personality is a long-standing tradition in the writing.[16] The characters in the texts frequently experience personality changes

---

12  R. Ansell & R. Percy, *To Fight The Wild* (Perth: Fremantle Arts Centre Press, 1980), pp. 101–2.
13  J. D'Ath, *The Initiate* (Sydney: Collins, 1989), pp. 34, 63.
14  D. Foster, *Mates of Mars* (Ringwood: Penguin, 1991), p. 241.
15  Bryson, *Evil Angels*, p. 508.
16  The problem is that in the contemporary period the Territory landscape moulds a character no longer popular: 'tough, exploitative, rough-and-ready, intolerant of liberal wimps down South ... Sadly, these virtues are demode'; David Foster, letter to the author, 3 December 1991, p. 2.

after exposure to the Territory landscape. Facing the environment reveals the inner nature of the character. Frequently this is manifested as a protagonist portrayed as stronger, tougher and often with heightened sexual powers.[17] The construction in *Dead Centre* is fairly typical. Mary, who had always taken a rather passive role before coming to Australia, finds herself actively pursuing the mystery of her husband's disappearance. After being abandoned in the desert, she catches sight of her reflection, 'her face seemed strange ... she looked like another woman—perhaps she had become one'.[18] When Mary is reunited with her husband, he seems so unlike himself that at first she doubts that it is him. Up until now their sexual relationship has always been one of indifference but after their experiences in Central Australia their sex life is transformed. David explains, 'It's probably difficult for you to believe but I found myself out here ... for the first time in my life I really feel at peace with myself'.[19]

The changes wrought by exposure to the environment can be revelatory, leading to fulfilment or conversely they can lead to despair depending upon whether the characters are to be developed as heroes or villains. In *Death Down Under* Sybil noticed how the 'harshly beautiful Outback environment' of Central Australia drew the film crew together: the unattractive Charlie Date 'had become a friend' and the gossipy outgoing Alice Fleming 'had become subdued and thoughtful'.[20] Robyn Davidson found the hostilities and the difficulties of Alice Springs giving her strength, a 'psychological fortress',[21] and at the same time the landscape was 'magical and life-affirming'.[22] In Heather Grace's *Heart of Light* (1992) the unifying and spiritual nature of the landscape heals wounds and consolidates friendship and strength.[23]

---

17  More than simple romance is the implication that the environment somehow reduces people to their most basic drives: Virginia and Maguire after they have been pursued by villains, P. Cornford, *The Outcast* (Sydney: Collins, 1988), p. 265; Lydia and Alfie Candlemas inexplicably demonstrate a heightened interest in sex after they come to the Northern Territory in Herbert's *Poor Fellow My Country*, pp. 150f, 547f, etc.; Adam in M. Page's *A Nasty Little War* (Adelaide: Rigby, 1979); Kate and Nick in A. Sayle, *The Last Frontier* (London: Century Hutchinson, 1986), etc.
18  C. Wood, *Dead Centre* (London: Michael Joseph, 1980), p. 212.
19  Wood, *Dead Centre*, pp. 224–5.
20  C. McNab, *Death Down Under* (Sydney: Allen & Unwin, 1990), p. 199.
21  Davidson, *Tracks*, pp. 47, 78.
22  Davidson, *Tracks*, p. 37.
23  H. Grace, *Heart of Light* (Fremantle, Western Australia: Fremantle Art Centre Press, 1992), pp. 142–3.

The writers affirm that perceptions of the Territory landscape are inexorably bound up with a sense of self. After Rod Ansell was stranded up the remote Fitzmaurice River for two months, he wrote, 'identity is a strange thing. With no one to talk to, you begin to lose your feeling of who you are'.[24] In contrast, the family in Goldsworthy's *Maestro* acquired a new identity as Territorians after living in Darwin.[25] Betty-san, in Yamamoto's short story, initially felt alienated and rejected by the environment, but the suggestion is that it was her own life she was rejecting.[26] Bill Marshall-Stoneking has Ezra Pound talking in his sleep, giving a roll call of names for places in Australia. The Central Australian desert is the antithesis of containment. In his imprisonment Pound has recurring dreams of the Australian landscape.[27]

Playwrights stress the effects of the landscape on their characters. Nowra's interpretation of *Capricornia* centres around the fact that Norman cannot truly know who he is until he is confronted by his past in the Territory landscape. In *God's Best Country* Tweetie says, 'I don't know what happened to my little brother, but he doesn't live here any more. It's someone else—someone completely different'. Her husband Boy answers, 'It's this bloody country … It changes everyone'.[28] Simon Hopkinson's play *Buffaloes Can't Fly* typically asserts that the hardships of the lifestyle and hostility of the landscape strip away the pretences and devices by which the characters hide themselves, revealing the paradox that it is Reg who cannot cope while Laura assures Jack that she will survive.[29]

But some of the changes wrought by the landscape upon the subjects of the texts are unwelcome and many of the Territory writers point out that some people cannot cope under the stresses of the hostile environment. As in Jeannie Gunn's construction, outback becomes the testing ground for the moral and physical strength of the character. Davidson noted that the Territory produced a tolerance for strange or aberrant behaviour.[30] The effect on the Darwin residents of the enigmatic and epigrammatic Maestro of Peter Goldsworthy's novel is minimised because 'Darwin was

---

24 Ansell & Percy, *To Fight the Wild*, p. 109.
25 P. Goldsworthy, *Maestro* (North Ryde: Angus & Robertson, 1989), pp. 21–2, 100.
26 M. Yamamoto, 'Betty-san', *Betty-san*, trans. Geraldine Harcourt, (New York: Kodansha, 1983), pp. 62, 66.
27 B. Marshall-Stoneking, *Sixteen Words For Water* (North Ryde, New South Wales: Angus & Robertson, 1991), p. 27.
28 G. Francis (L. Browne), *God's Best Country* (Sydney: Currency Press, 1987), p. 22.
29 S. Hopkinson, *Buffaloes Can't Fly* (Montmorency, Victoria: Yackandandah Playscript, 1981), p. 50.
30 Davidson, *Tracks*, p. 163.

the terminus … the Top End of the road. A town populated by men who had run as far as they could flee'.[31] These sentiments were echoed by Andrew McMillan, that Darwin was 'the end of the line'.[32]

Outside the urban centres, the behaviour becomes even more aberrant as Europeans cope with the strain of living as a cultural minority. The stresses of living in an Aboriginal community are explored in Thomas Keneally's *Towards Asmara*.[33] Lee Cataldi's poem 'If You Stay Too Long in the Third World' deals with the same topic.[34] Other writers, too, have noted that many non-Aboriginal people cannot cope with the isolated conditions of the remote settlements. Chatwin lampooned 'Gym Bore', a community adviser, who, although attractive to women, was like a 'policeman' who purports to present an unrealistic and 'silly' 'Aboriginal' viewpoint.[35] Other characters appear to be in a limbo where the landscape is an environment representing a complete absence of a moral order. The amoral landscape is at least as threatening as the isolation, harshness or danger of the physical world. In David Foster's *Mates of Mars*, the European adviser flees at the start of the Wet taking the key to the store with him.[36] In part, Herbert suggests that some of the more bizarre reversals of standard practice at the Leopold Inland Mission by David and Father Glascock arise as a result of its isolation from the European Christian society.[37]

Continuing the trend that had begun in the post-war period and typified by the 'Town Like Alice' image, the attention of writers in this period remained away from Darwin and focussed literary interest in Alice Springs as a source of 'Australianness'. In his map of Australia, Dick Francis left out Darwin but showed Alice Springs.[38] As previously mentioned, the central theme of Robert Spicer's *Catchpole* is the journey to Alice Springs. The climax of the novel presents two versions of Central Australia, one folksy and environmentally aware, the other cosmopolitan and touristy, but both endings are happy.[39] Andrew McMillan suggests that the Aborigines share a similar construction with a focus on Central Australia:

---

31 Goldsworthy, *Maestro*, p. 17.
32 A. McMillan, *Strict Rules* (Sydney: Hodder & Stoughton, 1988), p. 131.
33 T. Keneally, *Towards Asmara* (London: Hodder & Stoughton, 1989), pp. 60–81.
34 L. Cataldi, *The Women Who Live on the Ground: Poems 1978–1988* (Ringwood: Penguin, 1990), pp. 54–5.
35 B. Chatwin, *The Songlines* (New York: Viking, 1987), pp. 46–7.
36 Foster, *Mates of Mars*, p. 267.
37 Herbert, *Poor Fellow My Country*, pp. 1325f.
38 D. Francis, *In the Frame* (London: Michael Joseph, 1976), map.
39 R. Spicer, *Catchpole* (Forest Hill, Victoria: Animo, 1989), pp. 184–98.

To the Top Enders, the desert is a wild, tough place that breeds wild, tough people. The tribesmen of Arnhem Land have a certain fear of the men from the desert, a grudging respect for warriors. 'They're wild, that desert mob, eh?' they say with a degree of awe that's never reciprocated. 'Fierce eh?'

To the desert people, the Top Enders are merely 'fish eaters', inherently different, softer mob whose sense of discipline is comparatively lax.[40]

Ann McGrath noted that Central Australia, with Uluru at its 'symbolic centre of the Australian nation', has proved a national and spiritual icon for all Australians.[41] Writers emphasise the age of the rock and its significance to Aboriginal people.[42] Annette Hamilton commented,

For the Rock itself has become one of the prime symbols of Australian national consciousness ... [it] has come to stand for everything that is most remarkably, peculiarly and significantly Australian. Going to the Rock has come to constitute a kind of pilgrimage into the deepest realms of national cultural identity.[43]

But just as Alice Springs represents a kind of spiritual centre for all Australians, then Darwin is defined within an Asian context. The proximity of 'Asia' in the writing represents either the multicultural and exotic or a threatening 'yellow peril' (and occasionally both, for example Moffitt's *Death Adder Dreaming*). For Ian Stewart in his fantasy novel of the future, *Reunion*, Darwin has become the economic capital of Australia with its own currency and transplanted Asian population. Darwin as a 'Hong Kong–style city' has only been made possible by the change in attitude in the Territory administration towards Asian immigration.[44] To a lesser extent, Stewart's novel *An H-Bomb for Alice* also supports this construction of the Northern Territory in the shadow of Asia. Yamamoto's character Nakako emphasised the tolerance of Asia and cosmopolitan aspect of Darwin: 'For some reason people came here from

---

40  McMillan, *Strict Rules*, p. 138.
41  A. McGrath, 'Outback Mythologies, Historians and Other Travellers', paper for the Australian Historical Association Conference, Darwin, 1991, pp. 4–6.
42  Bryson, *Evil Angels*, p. 2; Davidson, *Tracks*, pp. 135–38; B. MarshallStoneking, *Lasseter—the Making of a Legend* (Sydney: Allen & Unwin, 1985), p. 108, etc.
43  A. Hamilton, 'Spoon-feeding the Lizards: Culture and Conflict in Central Australia', *Meanjin* 43, 3 (1984), p. 376.
44  I. Stewart, *Reunion* (Sydney: Gordian, 1988), p. 234.

all over the world'.⁴⁵ The plot of Wongar's allegorical novel *The Trackers* described an Asian architect whose dream was to build a bridge linking Australia and Asia.⁴⁶

But alongside the construction of the exotic is the stereotype of Asia as source of drugs and populated by sadistic torturers. Bob Brissenden's *Wildcat* is set in the Northern Territory and Thailand. *The Kangaroo Connection* (1980) also stresses the proximity to Asia in terms of the drug traffic. The villains are sinister 'Malays' who ram burning bamboo shoots up Charles Landers's nose and forcibly remove his girlfriend's bra.⁴⁷ The anti-Asian bias is modified slightly by Kimini who turns out to be a hero, of sorts. He is an undercover Japanese leader of an international World Organisation of Peace and Security (acronym WOOPS) rendered harmless since his castration during his last visit to the Northern Territory during World War II. John Hooker's *The Bush Soldiers* also combines the Northern Territory, World War II and proximity to Asia. The novel postulates a successful Japanese invasion of the continent after the cowardly military and civilian response to the bombing of Darwin.⁴⁸ Ian Moffitt's *Death Adder Dreaming* has Asian villiains.⁴⁹ Eric Willmot's *Below the Line* described Australia in the next century as a continent divided along a 'Brisbane line' where the north is populated by Aborigines and Indonesian immigrants. When the heroine Angela finally makes it north to the capital Larakia (Darwin), she discovers that 'it seemed to have changed very little except for its name. Even the people on the street looked the same with about the same racial mix'.⁵⁰ A perspective common to many texts in this period is that Darwin is already an Asian city by virtue of its population and geographic location.

But although writers from this period are, like those of the previous period, attempting to articulate their personal reactions, there is an apparent need to define the Territory in relation to the rest of the world. In this period, the Northern Territory is presented as a region of international controversy and many of the writers use the American base, Pine Gap, at Alice Springs

---

45   M. Yamamoto, 'Chair in the Rain', *Betty-san*, p. 122.
46   B. Wongar, *The Trackers* (Collingwood: Outback Press, 1975).
47   N. Watkins, *The Kangaroo Connection* (Rabaul, New Guinea: Camwat, 1980), pp. 129f.
48   J. Hooker, *The Bush Soldiers* (Sydney: Collins, 1984), pp. 34, 77, etc., although the heroes never actually make it to the Northern Territory and the book finishes as they are heading towards Alice Springs.
49   Not only are they murderers but the reader is alerted that they are really bad because they also log rainforests in Sarawak, I. Moffitt, *Death Adder Dreaming* (Sydney: Pan, 1988), p. 172.
50   E. Willmot, *Below the Line* (Sydney: Hutchinson, 1991), p. 179.

or the Ranger uranium mine in Kakadu as setting for the activities of spies, terrorists or similar international intrigue. David Foster saw Alice Springs as 'Australia's dead heart, the Red Centre of the continent' and 'Pine Gap ... among the world's first targets of a Soviet nuclear attack'.[51] Jan McKennish's *A Gap in the Records* combined this concern and a feminist outlook in a novel centred around the women's protest at Pine Gap in November 1983.[52] John Clive's thriller, *Barossa*, also uses the theme of the Territory's vulnerability to nuclear attack.[53] Christopher Wood's thriller *Dead Heart* has Australian government agents, the CIA and operatives for a mysterious multinational all travelling around the Northern Territory trying to spy on each others' activities. The military base at Tindal is the focus of concern of Philip Cornford's *The Outcast*. Damien Broderick's *The Dreaming Dragons: A Time Opera* has the CIA puzzled by evidence of Rainbow Serpents from outer space dwelling three kilometres below Uluru and only accessible through a 'space gate' controlled by an autistic Aboriginal boy called Mouse.[54] Leslie Platt's *Survival 3* describes a secret rocket base in the desert; Michael Page's *A Nasty Little War* has both the CIA and the KGB attempting to foil a Communist Chinese invasion; Joan O'Hagan's *Against the Grain* has the Australian Government in collusion with the Americans over a contract to supply uranium if the discovery of a new drought-resistant wheat strain can be suppressed, while in Ian Stewart's *An H-Bomb For Alice*, Alice Springs, along with the American base at Pine Gap, is the target of Russian terrorists.[55] Selina in Kaz Cooke's *The Crocodile Club* perhaps best summed up the general attitude in these texts: 'Who wants the Americans on their side? All you get is a whole lot of nuclear-targeted bases and your wheat market shot to buggery'.[56]

Apart from international terrorism, the Territory is also presented as a focus for crimes of all kinds—drug smuggling, kidnapping, murder and larceny. To Dick Francis, Central Australia, 'baked, deserted, and older than time', is the headquarters for art forgeries sold throughout Australia and New Zealand.[57] Bob Brissenden's *Wildcat*, although more down

---

51  Foster, *Mates of Mars*, p. 196.
52  J. McKennish, *A Gap in the Records* (Melbourne: Sybylla, 1985).
53  J. Clive, *Barossa* (London: Granada, 1982 (1981)), p. 53.
54  D. Broderick, *The Dreaming Dragons: A Time Opera* (Carlton: Norstrilia, 1980); 'Perhaps the Rainbow Serpent is an intelligent computer ... perfectly preserved until now by the Vault's force shields', p. 108.
55  I. Stewart, *An H-Bomb For Alice* (Feltham, Middlesex: Hamlyn, 1981), pp. 171f.
56  K. Cooke, *The Crocodile Club* (Sydney: Allen & Unwin, 1992), pp. 187–8.
57  Francis, *In the Frame*, p. 131; although as Headon et al. point out, the locals are presented as benign and incapable of violence: 'Northern Territory', p. 13.

to earth, also includes secret Government agencies in a plot involving international drug smuggling. Clare McNab's murder mystery, *Death Down Under*, is solved in Central Australia. The series of kidnappings in John Clive's *Barossa* is politically motivated by events in the Northern Territory.

As in the earlier periods, descriptions of a Northern Territory culture are frequently presented in the form of an opposition whereby the rigid social hierarchy of the Northern Territory town is used to throw the freedom and splendour of the landscape into sharp relief. Kaz Cooke's portrayal of Darwin is immensely detailed in her delineation of her characters' social status. At the top of the hierarchy are 'the Crocodile Club'—a controlling mafia of 'government and the mining companies and the old-timer public servants … Profit driven, amoral, plundering, wall-eyed, greedy complacent old blokes with hardened arteries and bat-shit where their soul should be'.[58] Her description of the festivities at the Sailing Club associated with the arrival of a federal minister provide an intricate description of the different groups and their interrelationship.[59] The urban centres of the Territory have become a focus for writers not only providing a contrast to the bush or wilderness but also as illustrations of the growing ugliness of European settlements.

Although the focus on Alice Springs had begun in the previous period, some writing in the modern period in contrast to the writing immediately after the war was extremely critical of conditions in the town. Michiko Yamamoto's character Betty-san commented bleakly, 'Alice Springs made Darwin seem a metropolis'.[60] Morris Lurie's short story, 'Inside the Wardrobe' depict Alice Springs as a place to leave, full of lonely, misplaced people, voyeurs on life.

With the exception of the earliest South Australian period, descriptions of the Territory are imbued with a nostalgia for a remembered past and this period of writing is no exception. Writers who share a long association with the region, regret the changes that have taken place. Tom Cole in *Hell West and Crooked* sketches his return to Arnhem Land forty-five years later: 'Only the ghosts were there'.[61] Herbert describes Darwin where the

---

58 Cooke, *The Crocodile Club*, p. 72.
59 Cooke, *The Crocodile Club*, pp. 161f.
60 Yamamoto, *Betty-san*, p. 17.
61 T. Cole, *Hell West and Crooked* (Sydney: Collins, 1989 (1988)), p. 356.

casual hierarchy of 'Port Palmerston'[62] is contrasted to the contrived but unacknowledged racial delineation evident in modern day 'Elizabeth'.[63] Peter Goldsworthy delicately blends nostalgia for the atmosphere and architecture of pre–Cyclone Tracy Darwin with a lament for the lost innocence of his childhood.[64] Although Robyn Davidson presented an ugly view of Alice Springs in *Tracks*, when she returned in 1989 she thought it much worse.[65] But rather more strangely, this nostalgia is not confined to those writers who actually remembered a past Territory. Younger contemporary writers whose experience in the Territory is only brief, have somehow absorbed this regret. Bruce Chatwin looked for an Alice Springs of the past[66] and Andrew McMillan noted regretfully the changes in Alice Springs and Darwin.[67] Charmian Clift noted the atmosphere of nostalgia.[68]

This nostalgia for a Territory past is not confined to the European subjects of literature. Throughout all of B. Wongar's books about the Territory is the pervasive theme of the rape of the land by European mining activities. Since Aboriginal spirituality is so closely tied up to the land, the destruction of the landscape becomes synonymous with the genocide of a people. In the short story 'Mogwoi, the Trickster', Wongar describes what happens when an Aboriginal man faces death:

> After all that has happened to Riratjingu land and the people, it would not be easy to face the ancestors. The tribal water holes are levelled, but even if there are any to be found around here I would not like to wait there and be reborn; after all, what is there left to spring into life for when even the hills and the rocks have been taken away from the country. I am going to be Mogwoi, the trickster spirit, moving around this world, and from time to time I will call on all those I met in life to make their time uncomfortable too.[69]

This theme of the landscape made totally bereft of life is repeated again in many of the short stories: 'The Miringu' which describes the return of a man to his country after a long prison term, only to find that there

---

62  Herbert, *Poor Fellow My Country*, pp. 221–5.
63  Herbert, *Poor Fellow My Country*, pp. 1452–6.
64  Goldsworthy, *Maestro*, p. 146.
65  Davidson, 'Alice Springs', p. 130.
66  Chatwin, *The Songlines*, p. 32.
67  McMillan, *Strict Rules*, pp. 6, 130.
68  C. Clift, 'The Centre', *The World of Charmian Clift* (Sydney: Collins, 1989), p. 204.
69  B. Wongar, *The Track to Bralgu* (Boston: Little, Brown, 1978), p. 12.

is nothing left, 'No tribe could survive here; the animals have left and even the crabs are sunk in their mudholes never to come out again'.[70] In 'Girigiri, the Trap', the 'trees are like bones' and 'the whole island looks like a skinned carcass'.[71] In the novel *Walg*, an allegorical fantasy describing the impact of European settlement on Aboriginal people, the nostalgia is for the land itself. White people are represented as destroying the land in their effort to mine uranium. The sacred sites, the geographical features and the life found within the region are shown to be ripped apart by the European invaders.

This image of European invaders as destroyers is reiterated in poetry which echoes the refrain of the alienation of the white Territorians from the landscape.[72] Lee Cataldi's 'The Women Who Live on the Ground' from the book of the same name emphasises the different worlds ('another planet') of Aboriginal and non-Aboriginal Australians. Tony Scanlon expresses disgust at non-Aboriginal occupation of the Territory and again uses a space metaphor to stress the difference between cultures. As in Cataldi's work, he has no doubt who the aliens are:

> ask then for directions to the Last Frontier
> and black hands will wave away south, or west—
> 'Not here, mate,' they will say, 'this is Suck City'.
> In their eyes is the truth of the ravished north,
> of the Dreamtime raped brutally by alien men,
> remoter from the true North than Andromeda:
> pastiche pioneers, Durack according to Disney.[73]

While Europeans seem to use the destruction of landscape as a metaphor for, or even as synonymous with, destruction of Aboriginal culture, Aboriginal voices focus on the depopulation that has occurred among the communities. Lazarus Lamilami recalled with regret that as a young child the missionaries moved in and took over the ceremonial grounds on Goulburn Island, thus changing the political and spiritual focus of the Goulburn Island people forever.[74] Gagudju elder Bill Neidjie wrote poignantly and simply expressing the sadness for all things gone:

---

70   Wongar, *The Track to Bralgu*, p. 45.
71   Wongar, *The Track to Bralgu*, p. 68.
72   Although 'I Grieve for the Spirit of Strehlow' and 'Olive Pink Flora Reserve, Alice Springs' pay tribute to the inter-relationship of landscape with two non-Aboriginals; D. Johnson, *The Jewel Box* (Springwood, New South Wales: Butterfly Books, 1990), pp. 38, 43.
73   T. Scanlon, 'On the Last Frontier', *Rain At Gunn Point* (Armidale: Kardoorair, 1990), p. 62.
74   L. Lamilami, *Lamilami Speaks* (Sydney: Ure Smith, 1974), p. 90.

> First people come to us,
> They started and run our life ... quick.
> They bring drink.
> First they should ask about fish, cave, dreaming, but ...
> they rush in.
> The make school ... teach.
> Now Aborigine losing it,
> losing everything.
> Nearly all dead my people,
> my old people gone.[75]

Deborah Bird Rose's *Hidden Histories* documented the Aboriginal view of the destructiveness inherent in the coming of the Europeans to the country around Victoria River. In 1988 Ronald Berndt published this account of the consequences of European contact for the people living on the Buffalo Plains area east of Darwin:

> That brother and that sister made a big country, with plenty of people. There were many people there who had married their sisters. But many of them are now gone: many people died from measles—you can see their bones everywhere![76]

But just as European settlement changed Aboriginal life, so the Territory landscape changed the Europeans.

As in the earliest writing, the Northern Territory, with its capital in Darwin, is described increasingly in an Asian context. Novels begin to define north Australia as linked economically, if not culturally, with the islands to the north. There is an assumption that the Territory enjoys a special relationship to Asia somehow beyond the national ties.[77] In this Australian-Asian union, the writers stress that the Northern Territory, by reason of its geographical location, is in a more privileged position than elsewhere in Australia. As one writer has commented, 'Darwin ... it's the end of Australia but potentially the beginning of somewhere else'.[78]

---

75  A. Fox, S. Davis & B. Neidjie, *Kakadu Man: Bill Neidjie* (New South Wales: Mybrood, 1985), p. 37.
76  F. Wadedi, '3. Death of the People at Marabibi', Berndts, *The Speaking Land*, p. 27.
77  This assumption does not seem to be solely confined to the literature. Juan Federer has noted that this feeling of a 'special' relationship between the Territory and Asia is widespread amongst Territorians, if unjustified; J. Federer, 'The Northern Territory's "Foreign Affairs": From Outback to Integration Frontier', Centre for Southeast Asian Studies Seminar Series, Northern Territory University, 16 May 1990.
78  Spunner, interview.

Aborigines now take on a much more powerful position in the mythology of the writing and are presented as guardians of truth, spirituality and, above all, country. To be Aboriginal in the contemporary period of writing, implies a certain spirituality, manifested both in a special relationship to land but also intrinsically.[79] Following the grim pessimism of the sexual exploitation of the previous period, Northern Territory race relations are described with Holocaust-like imagery embellished by elements of ritual and an alternative spirituality.[80]

As the writing progressed into the 1990s it can be seen that environmental issues are of paramount importance, although the characters are becomingly increasingly nihilistic about their interaction with landscape. Andrew McGahan's novel *1988* (1995) is an indicator. The enthusiastic post-hippies in 1970s time-warp Territory (Davidson, Keneally, Chatwin) have given way to earnest males determined to drink themselves into a prolonged state of mental, physical and emotional numbness. By 1995, sex—usually a preoccupation with Territory writers—has become a non-issue. Aboriginal representation in the Territory literature, at a height in the 1970s, diminishes. Aborigines continue as characters in the texts but writing about Aborigines by non-Aborigines decreases and the ethics of representation become increasingly complex as academic debate concerning Aboriginal proprietary rights over information achieves a popular currency. In the texts, Aborigines are frequently invoked, however briefly, as environmental custodians of the continent. There is a feeling globally that indigenous peoples can 'point the way to a solution for all people'.[81] Alongside this operates a rigorous de-anthropomorphising of the landscape. William Lines writes passionately in his conclusion to *Taming the Great South Land*, 'The Australian landscape is neither harsh nor gentle, indifferent nor compassionate, prime all cruel nor humanely forgiving, male nor female'.[82] With no sense of irony at all, Lines had introduced his discussion on the natural history of the continent with the words of Bill Neidjie:

---

79   For example, the many novels and short stories of B. Wongar; L. Chamberlain, *Through My Eyes* (Port Melbourne: William Heinemann, 1990); G. Webb's *The Numunwari* (Melbourne: Fontana, 1980); B. Chatwin's *The Songlines* (New York: Viking, 1987); Davidson's *Tracks*, D. Foster's *Mates of Mars* (Ringwood: Penguin, 1991); T. Keneally's *Flying Hero Class* (London: Hodder & Stoughton, 1991), to name only a few.
80   B. Wongar, *Walg: A Novel of Australia* (New York: Dodd, Mead, 1983), p. 32.
81   R Barsh, 'Indigenous Peoples, Racism and the Environment', *Meanjin*, 49, 4 (1990), p. 730.
82   W.J. Lines, *Taming the Great South Land: A History of the Conquest of Nature in Australia* (Sydney: Allen & Unwin, 1992 (1991)), p. 278.

> Rock stays,
> Earth stays.
> I die and put my bones in cave or earth.
> Soon my bones become earth …
> All the same.
> My spirit has gone back to my country …
> My mother[83]

Clearly there is a problem for non-Aboriginal writers both in the way they relate to the landscape and their relationship to Aborigines and Aboriginal authority. This kind of tension underpins the descriptions of the Northern Territory and find a focus for the debate. How Territorians relate to both each other and the landscape in the literature is the focus of the final chapter which looks at the writing up to the contemporary period.

---

83  Lines, *Taming the Great South Land*, p. 1.

# 8

# POOR BUGGER ALL OF US

With the current emphasis upon social pluralism, Aborigines are presented in the writing in the period after the 1970s with a surprising degree of unanimity.[1] In this construction of the Northern Territory, Aborigines are characteristically portrayed as spiritual beings with demonstrable magical powers capable of affecting themselves and others in ways that cannot be explained. Xavier Herbert's *Poor Fellow My Country* (1975), Lindy Chamberlain's *Through My Eyes* (1990), Grahame Webb's *The Numunwari* (1980), Bruce Chatwin's *The Songlines* (1987), Robyn Davidson's *Tracks* (1981), David Foster's *Mates of Mars* (1991), Damien Broderick's *The Dreaming Dragons* (1980), Len Davenport's *Sandshoe Kadaicha* (1977) and Thomas Keneally's *Flying Hero Class* (1991) all share this kind of construction. David Myers identified a similar progression in Australian films from this period generally. Films such as Igor Auzins's *We of the Never-Never* (1982), Peter Weir's *The Last Wave* (1977), Fred Schepisi's *The Chant of Jimmy Blacksmith* (1978) and Henri Safran's *Storm Boy* (1976) depict Aborigines as 'the initiates of a spiritual paganism and a religiosity that they draw from their closeness to the forces of nature'.[2] This kind of construction had been pioneered in Nicholas Roeg's cinema adaptation of James Vance Marshall's novel, *The Children*, filmed as *Walkabout* (1970).

---

1   Kaz Cooke's novel is an exception and her Aboriginal characters are witty, street-wise and pragmatic. This novel seems to be the only fictional account of the Territory from the contemporary period that does not include some mention of extra-sensory power or magic about Aborigines; K. Cooke, *The Crocodile Club* (Sydney: Allen & Unwin, 1992), pp. 95, 151, 166, 174, etc. In film, *Crocodile Dundee I & II* have a similar construction.
2   D. Myers, *Bleeding Battlers from Ironbark: Australian Myths in Fiction and Film 1890s–1980s* (Rockhampton: University of Central Queensland, 1992), p. 9.

After the 1970s, however, there was considerable debate concerning the role non-Aboriginal commentators could play in the writing of Aboriginal history. In this period, non-Aboriginal authors have frequently collected, transcribed and edited oral material elicited from Aborigines which has formed the basis for published work. Some literary critics consider that such material be regarded as the literary work of the Aborigines from whom the oral source material was obtained.[3] Bill Neidjie's world-view has been transcribed as a kind of free-form poetry and used as the basis for several texts.[4] Isobel White, Diane Barwick and Betty Meehan produced a collection of stories obtained by interviewing and recording Aboriginal women for their accounts of the circumstances of their lives.[5] T.G.H. Strehlow's *Songs of Central Australia* is a translation and interpretation of the mythology of the Arrernte peoples. Translations of Aboriginal myths and stories have been included in broader Australian anthologies.[6] Luise Hercus and Peter Sutton, Deborah Bird Rose, Peter and Jay Read, and the Berndts have published collections based on Aboriginal oral culture.[7] Not surprisingly many of the accounts published focus upon Aboriginal reaction to European settlement.[8] It has been pointed out that this raises the risk of, 'whites speaking with Aboriginal voices, as Aborigines'.[9] Possibly because of this European editorial intervention, but more probably because of the nature of oral accounts, the Northern Territory has an Aboriginal voice in the writing, but not Aboriginal writers. The Territory

---

3   See for example, David Headon's views on this: Headon, 'Beyond the Years of the Locust', pts 1 and 2.
4   B. Neidjie, *Story About Feeling* K. Taylor, ed. (Broome: Magabala, 1989); A. Fox, S. Davis & B. Neidjie, *Kakadu Man: Bill Neidjie* (New South Wales: Mybrood, 1985), and the previously mentioned quotation from Lines, *Taming the Great South Land*.
5   I. White, D. Barwick & B. Meehan, eds, *Fighters and Singers: the Lives of Some Australian Aboriginal Women* (Sydney: Allen & Unwin, 1985).
6   For example, E. Campion, *Living Here: Short Stories from Australasia 1938–1988* (Sydney: Allen & Unwin, 1988) begins with a story 'The Payback' by T. Tjapangarti of the Pintubi and trans. P.B. Tjampitjinpa & B. Marshall-Stoneking, pp. 4–5.
7   For example D.B. Rose, *Dingo Makes Us Human: Life and Land in an Aboriginal Australian Culture* (Melbourne: Cambridge University Press, 1991); Rose, *Hidden Histories*; L. Hercus & P. Sutton, *This Is What Happened: Historical Narratives By Aborigines* (Canberra: Australian Institute for Aboriginal Studies, c. 1986); R.M. & C.H. Berndt, *The Speaking Land: Myth and Story in Aboriginal Australia* (Ringwood: Penguin 1989 (1988)); P. & J. Read, *Long Time, Olden Time: Aboriginal Accounts of Northern Territory History* (Alice Springs, Northern Territory: Institute for Aboriginal Development, c. 1991), etc.
8   But limited by non-Aboriginal interpretation of events nonetheless as Tim Rowse's review of Rose's *Dingo Makes Us Human* points out, T. Rowse, 'Relative Politics', *Australian Book Review* 143, August 1992, pp. 6–7.
9   W.B. McGregor, 'Writing Aboriginal: Oral Literature in Print', *Meridian* 8, 1 (1989), p. 55.

has yet to find its Jack Davis, Ruby Langford, Oodgeroo Noonuccal, Elsie Roughsey, Jimmy Chi or Sally Morgan—all writers with a strong sense of both Aboriginality and 'place' inherent in their writing.

The Territory is considered unique by Australian writers because of the large Aboriginal population[10] and the interaction between Aborigines and Europeans is seen as 'vital if we are to have an australian [sic] culture, without it … we white australians can never take root in this country unless we understand such a landscape in a spiritual way like the aborigines'.[11] There is an increased emphasis upon the universality of experience rather than the cultural difference:

> We are all tribal people under the skin
> And we deny this at the expense/ of tearing ourselves in half …
> But the Dreaming lives in each of us.[12]

But there is a moral dilemma for some in the legitimacy of grafting an Aboriginal interpretation of the landscape onto writing by non-Aboriginals;[13] the philosophy 'cannot sustain us [European writers]'.[14]

Aboriginality itself is a complex question. There may be people who genetically satisfy the definitions of Aboriginal but who do not regard themselves as Aborigines.[15] Others who identify in their writing as Aboriginal but who do not satisfy the definition. The spectrum of values on this point is best illustrated by the changing attitudes by arbiters of literary criticism to the writer B. Wongar who retained a strong Territory focus. Initially considered as reminiscent of the Ern Malley hoax, this literary controversy surfaced during the 1970s when the writing of Wongar came to public notice. Wongar's collections of short stories, *The Track to Bralgu* (1978) and *Babaru* (1982), together with his novels *The Trackers* (1975), *Walg* (1983), *Karan* (1986) and *Gabo Djara* (1988), are set predominantly

---

10  For example, B. Wongar, letter to the author, 2 December 1991; Foster, letter to the author, 3 December 1991; Thomas Keneally, letter to the author, 2 March 1992.
11  Louis Nowra, letter to the author, 3 December 1991.
12  B. Marshall-Stoneking, *Sixteen Words For Water* (North Ryde, New South Wales: Angus & Robertson, 1991), p. 69.
13  Although non-Aboriginal writing presenting an 'Aboriginal' perspective has also been seen as 'constructing an historical framework for writing of the present' and of providing, in the literature, 'new perspectives on our racial past'; N.B. Albinski, 'Putting Value Back in the Land', *Meanjin* 46, 3 (1987), p. 375.
14  Foster, letter to the author, p. 2.
15  This happens in land claim evidence as was shown in the recent Finniss River Land Claim hearings.

in the Northern Territory. They describe the horrors of race relations in the region and were hailed as the 'new genre of "Aboriginalism" and ... brought ... [the author] international acclaim'.[16]

As B. Wongar's writing appeared so strongly political, concentrating mainly on the negative impact of European occupation of Australia on the Aborigines, it was somewhat of a shock when he was revealed as European.[17] Investigative journalism by the *Sydney Morning Herald* and *The Age* and an influential article by Robert Drewe in *The Bulletin*, revealed that the trail to Wongar led to Yugoslavian anthropologist Sreten Bozic.[18] Bozic himself had worked in Arnhem Land, the Kimberley and as a miner at Gove. In 1972 he had written *Aboriginal Myths* in collaboration with Alan Marshall. In 1974 he complained to *The Age* that he had been 'boycotted and discriminated against by publishers and Government authorities'. When contacted by *The Bulletin* in 1981 B. Wongar said, 'No, I am not Mr Bozic ... It is a touchy point ... There is some confusion about the names'. But Robert Drewe finished his article on B. Wongar with this paragraph:

> Wongar, the talented and mysterious Arnhem Land Aboriginal writer, went into hospital in Melbourne last month for major surgery. Before he did he told a friend on the telephone: 'When you ring me, ask for Mr Bozic. That's the name they know me by'.[19]

Latterly the debunking of Wongar as a literary hoax has lost currency,[20] although perhaps not entirely.[21] Michael Connor and David Matthews have called for an appraisal of his work apart from the issue of Aboriginality

---

16  B. Wongar, *Karan* (South Melbourne: Macmillan, 1986), cover notes.
17  Yet the clue was in the name; Patrick Wolfe has argued convincingly that the term 'Dream-time' was a colonial construct imposed upon Aboriginal society and quotes Elkin that 'Wongar' is used in northeast Arnhem Land to denote 'Dream-time'; Wolfe, 'On Being Woken Up', p. 203. It is hardly surprising then that 'Wongar' surfaces as a pseudonym chosen by a European to denote Aboriginality.
18  But if 'Wongar' means 'Dreaming', the semiotics of Wongar's other name are equally bizarre. 'Sreten Bozic', Terry Lane informs us, means 'Merry Christmas' in Serbo-Croat; T. Lane, *Hobbyhorses: Views on Contemporary Australian Society* (Crows Nest, New South Wales: Australian Broadcasting Corporation, 1990), p. 134.
19  R. Drewe, 'Solved: the Great B. Wongar Mystery', *The Bulletin Literary Supplement*, 21 April 1981, pp. 2–5.
20  For a bibliography of the Sreten Bozic / B. Wongar identity debate see R.L. Ross, 'The Track to Armageddon, B. Wongar's Nuclear Trilogy', *World Literature Today: A Literary Quarterly of the University of Oklahoma* (Winter, 1990), pp. 37–8, footnote 1.
21  In a recent review of B. Wongar's newest novel, *Marngit*, John Hanrahan commented, 'While admiring much that Bozic has written, I cannot ignore the fact that he is not an "insider" ... He will always be an outsider looking in, even if he does so with more knowledge sympathy and understanding than most of us'. J. Hanrahan, 'Wongar Still Poses Problems', *Australian Book Review*, 138, Feb/March 1992, p. 16.

and suggested that analysis of Wongar's work, 'has not often progressed beyond question of authorial identity and legitimacy'.[22] Literary critic Paul Sharrad commented in an article 'Does Wongar Matter?' that, 'identity, even though it must to some extent determine his credibility, matters less, however, than his social vision as revealed through the stories'.[23] Livio Dobrez suggested that Bozic's experience of growing up in a small Serbian village of Tresnjevica during World War II gave him a particular insight into Aboriginal suffering.[24] Other critics agreed.[25] Wongar was the first, but as the lines blurred between Aboriginal and European heritage, authors such as B. Wongar, Mudrooroo Nyoonga or Eric Willmot, came to be regarded on the basis of subject matter rather than racial identity. B. Wongar, in his allegorical stories of European colonisation of Australia, highlighted the atrocities and ugliness of dispossession. Wongar wrote:

> All my writing portrays black/white relationships. It is about the white man's difficulty to learn how great was the Aboriginal culture and how profound was their stewardship of land and caring for the environment …
>
> The great aspect of Aboriginal traditional culture is that by retaining the low population density the tribal people retained ecological stability through eons of time. The whole world could have benefited immensely from this heritage. Tragically, white people in Australia have bent over backwards trying to destroy it.[26]

Increasingly from the 1970s on, that emphasis would find popular expression in other writings.

But the depiction of people is important for by this time there is not sense of an unpeopled wilderness in the Northern Territory. The experience of the landscape cannot be separated from the Aboriginal experience, particularly in the early part of this period. Herbert, Davidson, Chatwin, Wood, Marshall-Stoneking, McMillan and Keneally relate to the landscape in a privileged way largely because of their relationship to Aboriginal people who provide the key to interpreting landscape. In *Kakadu Man* …

---

22   M. Connor & D. Matthews, 'In the Tracks of the Reader, in the Tracks of B. Wongar', *Meanjin*, 48, 4 (1989), p. 714.
23   P. Sharrad, 'Does Wongar Matter?', from *Kunapipi* 4, 1 (1982), pp. 37–50, quoted, Ross, 'The Track to Armageddon, B. Wongar's Nuclear Trilogy', p. 38.
24   L. Dobrez, 'What Colour is White? A European Experience of Aboriginal Australia', J. Hardy ed., *Stories of Australian Migration* (Kensington, New South Wales: New South Wales University Press, 1988), p. 132.
25   Ross, 'The Track to Armageddon', p. 35.
26   Wongar, letter to the author.

*Bill Neidjie* (where in the title, place is eponymous) Allan Fox suggested that it is necessary for Europeans to learn to understand the environment from the Aborigines:

> I can find no adequate work in English to describe the personalisation of the landscape by Aboriginals ... If we later Australians are only wise enough to listen, it may be that we will still have enough time to cure some of the environmental calamities initiated by our clumsy stewardship ... Bill is on about attitudes and values ... the future rests on ours.[27]

Alongside the image of Aborigines as custodians of the landscape, is the suggestion that Aborigines are perhaps more powerful than Europeans imagine. The role of the medicine man Buginja in the adventure novel *Wilderness* is ambiguous. Is he existing on the fringe of the European settlement or is he really controlling events? The hero Garret is only able to cure Amy with medicines learnt from the Aborigines.[28] Some of B. Wongar's Aboriginal characters have the superhuman power to transform themselves into different species and to magically transport themselves across the continent. In *Poor Fellow My Country*, Bobwirridirridi appears ('materialised') in the beginning of the narrative and he dematerialises at the end, telling Rifkah he is going to the sky to become a star.[29] Bobwirridirridi is neither born nor dies; he appears out of the landscape and ultimately returns there.

Many writers imply that for the sensitive European, close association and affinity with Aborigines in their country produces a corresponding cosmological assimilation. Herbert is interested in developing the theme of the spiritual influence that exposure to Aboriginal cultural values has on the Europeans. This influence is manifested in a change in their relationship to the environment. The characters depicted with the most sympathy, Jeremy Delacy and Billie Brew, both describe mystical experiences linked to landscape. They are possessors of an Aboriginal spiritual guardian, 'Lamala' or 'Yalmaru', who looks after them and promises to sustain them in an after-life experience.[30] This suggests that the spirit of the land will communicate with Europeans who show sufficient respect for landscape.[31] Davidson, too, experienced a vision of ghostly camels late one night

---

27   A. Fox, 'Australian Dreaming', Fox, Davis & Neidjie, *Kakadu Man*, p. 17.
28   R. Donaldson & M. Joseph, *Wilderness* (Melbourne: Icon, 1975), p. 15.
29   Herbert, *Poor Fellow My Country*, pp. 10, 1448.
30   Herbert, *Poor Fellow My Country*, pp. 1275, 1444.
31   Herbert, *Poor Fellow My Country*, p. 1463.

after drinking too much tequila[32] but it was through her relationship to Mr Eddie, an old Aboriginal man, learning the 'myths and stories' of the country that she 'began to see how it all fitted together'.[33]

But some non-Aboriginal writers believe they have developed a sensitivity to the 'Aboriginal' view of the landscape just by being there. After a few days in Central Australia, Bruce Chatwin can instinctively identify a Dreaming site because he 'knew it had to be'.[34] The writer suggests that affinity with Aborigine and environment can bring about a spiritual state whereby non-Aborigines can gain access to the Aboriginal cosmos. By the end of this period, direct exposure to Aboriginal culture is not as important as being receptive to the emanations of the landscape. The 'sacredness' of the landscape will be apparent to Europeans if they open their senses. Julie and Kass in Heather Grace's *Heart of Light* find 'magic' in the bush without actually meeting any Aborigines.[35] In *Death Adder Dreaming*, Rod can tell he is near a sacred site of ancient malevolence by the 'tingling delight' he feels as he is swimming.[36] In the finale of Amanda Sayle's *The Last Frontier* the lovers are united and, 'In the deep silence, they seemed to hear the murmur of Wanabi, the Rainbow Serpent, guardian of the last frontier. He was bestowing his blessing'.[37] This belief is not confined to fictional writers. Academic, David Tacey, recalled that he grew up in Alice Springs 'where the Aboriginal spirit of place is strongly felt' which he found to be 'an almost physical sensation' that even racist, insensitive people who disliked Aborigines were aware of.[38] In a recent publication he noted: 'I had few significant contacts with Aboriginal people ... but it was not the people so much as the Aboriginal land that had the real impact on me'.[39]

But most of the writers interpret their experience of the landscape, at least nominally, with reference to their interaction with Aborigines. The hostility of the physical environment astounds and intimidates the narrator in the play *Dragged Screaming to Paradise*. At the same time,

---

32  Davidson, *Tracks*, p. 42.
33  Davidson, *Tracks*, p. 174.
34  Chatwin, *The Songlines*, p. 105.
35  Grace, *Heart of Light*, pp. 142–3.
36  Moffitt, *Death Adder Dreaming*, p. 250.
37  Sayle, *The Last Frontier*, p. 286.
38  D.J. Tacey, 'Australia's Otherworld: Aboriginality, Landscape and the Imagination', *Meridian* 8, 1 (1989), pp. 48–65.
39  D.J. Tacey, *Edge of the Sacred: Transformation in Australia* (Melbourne: Harper Collins, 1995), pp. 13–14.

landscape proves to be the reason she comes to call the Northern Territory paradise. In common with many other writers, it is not the landscape by itself, but the landscape interpreted through the Aboriginal heritage that provides the impetus to stay here:

> But nothing, and certainly not your own ignorant expectations, can prepare you for the Living National treasure that is the Main Gallery at Ubirr [Kakadu]. Suddenly thousands and thousands of years fall away, and there in front of you is another culture ... It is immediately powerful and after you witness it, the landscape never looks the same again.[40]

Similarly, David, the missing engineer of *Dead Centre*, explained that his personal transformation only occurred after he came in contact with the Aborigines: 'Their way of life made complete sense to me ... Look at the rest of us, piling material possessions we don't really need, guzzling booze and anti-depressants'.[41] Similarly, the further Robyn Davidson moves away from her own culture, the more she feels alienated from it. 'I compared European society with Aboriginal. The one so *archetypally* paranoid, grasping, destructive, the other so sane. I didn't want ever to leave this desert.'[42] This construction of the veniality of European society is reinforced by the character of Stanley in Ian Moffitt's *Death Adder Dreaming* whose description suggests that Europeans working with Aborigines do so as a result of some personal inadequacy.[43] Further, that Aboriginal society offers a preferable world view:

> There is a sense that history is out of human control, is sweeping white society helplessly along with it, and that there is much to admire or even envy in a 'timeless' culture that has resisted this tide.[44]

But equally, the writers are anxious to point out that not every sojourner in the Territory comes to an equal appreciation of either the environment or Aboriginal culture. Thomas Keneally illustrates one reason for failing to access Aboriginal spirituality in his description of the community advisers of 'Fryer River' settlement.[45] Most travellers to the Territory are automatically excluded from the cabal of Aboriginal spirituality because

---

40  S. Spunner, *Dragged Screaming to Paradise* (Darwin: Paradis Production, 1990), 'The Third Movement: Paradise'.
41  Wood, *Dead Centre*, p. 227.
42  Davidson, *Tracks*, p. 195.
43  Moffitt, *Death Adder Dreaming*, p. 121.
44  J. Fiske, B. Hodge & G. Turner, *Myths of Oz: Reading Australian Popular Culture* (Sydney: Allen & Unwin, 1988 (1987)), p. 129.
45  Keneally, *Towards Asmara*, p. 77.

the experience of visitors is seen by writers as shallow and insincere. The character of Boy in *God's Best Country*, whom the audience is encouraged to dislike (a jogging public servant who believes Canberra the 'most beautiful place in Australia'), demonstrates his failure to relate to the landscape in contrast to the Aborigine of the station: 'I don't think I'll ever understand this place'.[46]

Insensitive newcomers have the power to destroy the landscape as a consequence of their inability to perceive it: 'you could weep for the desecration ... for the shoddiness'.[47] Herbert, in his conclusion to *Poor Fellow My Country*, noted bleakly the contribution of the visitor:

> A first-class road also ran up the river ... for the convenience of the tourist who ... came in droves ... along with bits of the pretty green ore that could be bought as souvenirs, were picture postcards of nuclear-bomb-blasts and of the ruins of Hiroshima ... Postcards of the Big House and its garden also were on sale ... Another Tourist Attraction of the locality was the Painted Caves.[48]

Herbert saw the Europeans as at war with the landscape. For Herbert, it was the newcomer who had the capacity to create and change the environment for the worse. Charmian Clift was similarly pessimistic.[49] Kaz Cooke and Suzanne Spunner agreed. Cooke depicted Darwin as a town with southern architecture and garden artificially maintained in the face of a hostile punishing climate,[50] and Spunner described the population of transplanted southerners acting out rituals inappropriate for the place or climate.[51] But for Davidson, the landscape of Central Australia emerged triumphant. This dynamic of conflict between the image of immensity and perfection of the landscape competing with the vileness of 'man' is the underpinning theme in this period.[52] Rick, the photographer, epitomised the outsider who had none of the appropriate attitudes or skills necessary for survival but even he, after a few days exposure to the bush, began 'changing ... letting the desert work on him, coming to a recognition of it, and of himself as a consequence'.[53]

---

46  Francis, *God's Best Country*, pp. 36–37, 39.
47  C. Clift, 'The Rock', *The World of Charmian Clift*, p. 207.
48  Herbert, *Poor Fellow My Country*, pp. 1452–3.
49  Clift, 'The Rock', p. 209.
50  Cooke, *The Crocodile Club*, pp. 78, 115, 150, 176–77, etc.
51  Spunner, *Dragged Screaming to Paradise*, 'Second Movement: Darwin'.
52  For example Davidson's abrupt change of mood: Davidson, *Tracks*, pp. 107–8.
53  Davidson, *Tracks*, pp. 138–43.

Some writers expressed a frustration and a lack of understanding at the cultural gap between Aboriginal and non-Aboriginal experience. The young school teacher in John Barclay's *The Bloom is Gone* commented,

> We've never asked the poor buggers anything. We took their land without asking. Now we take their children without asking and after we waste a few years of their lives we throw the young adults back, cocky, pseudo-educated, and hating our guts more than ever.[54]

There is a strong sense of futility of any communication between Europeans and Aborigines. At Neverfuckinlose, Bruce cannot understand Cyril's comment that Europeans are not liked, 'But I don't understand … The people here have been most friendly towards us. Always waving and smiling, except for one old woman who threw a turtle at my head'.[55] Communication of any kind seems impossible: '"We've tried everything" explains the coach driver … "We've shot them and we've given them everything they wanted. But nothing works."'[56]

A clue to whether the protagonist will be defined sympathetically or unsympathetically is given in their attitude towards Aborigines. Bruce Chatwin defined people almost exclusively in terms of their ability or capacity to interact with Aborigines: the saintly 'Arkady Volchok', who reveres them, the policeman who despises them, the 'Old Territorian' who exploits them financially.[57] Racial tensions appear to be pronounced in Alice Springs and underpin all descriptions of the town. In *Promise of Rain* Gail Morgan wrote, 'Violence here is as thick as the dust. People are puffed out with it, blown about no matter how much their hush puppies attempt to anchor them. They wear their long socks like poultices, in anticipation of injury'.[58] Robyn Davidson, answering the criticism that she painted 'a very negative picture of the Alice', asserts that in the recent period, the racism has not disappeared, merely become 'more cautious in its expression'.[59] Certainly the attitudes expressed by Wood in *Dead Centre* do not contradict Davidson. When Mary only narrowly fought off rape by Luri, the police were unsympathetic. They considered that Mary had put herself in a vulnerable position by getting into an Aborigine's car at night. Aborigines are described as either drunken and hopeless,

---

54  J. Barclay, *The Bloom is Gone* (Sydney: Australasian, 1977), p. 65.
55  Foster, *Mates of Mars*, pp. 244–5.
56  Foster, *Mates of Mars*, p. 198.
57  Chatwin, *The Songlines*, pp. 25f, 31, 33, 136.
58  G. Morgan, *Promise of Rain* (London: Virago, 1985), p. 109.
59  Davidson, 'The Mythological Crucible', p. 230.

'the living dead',[60] or as mystical nomads of the desert. Europeans, with few exceptions, are bigoted, violent and racist. Yamamoto commented of Alice Springs that, 'Aboriginals roamed the bare, straight streets, while the park was the haunt of drunken black men even in the daytime. They dressed much as the whites did, though in the shabbiest and plainest of clothes; they never appeared to work'.[61]

The authors document, yet stand apart from, the hostility between Europeans and Aborigines. Lindy Chamberlain commented that the attitude of Territorians was one of extreme prejudice towards Aborigines.[62] Eric Willmot, in *Below the Line*, suggested that the Aborigines of the Northern Territory preferred Indonesian control with a 'puppet' government led by an 'Aboriginal man as President'[63] to rule by southern white Australians. In *Wildcat* the reader is made aware that Tiburzi is a villain of the highest order by his persecution of the local Aboriginal community, mining of an Aboriginal sacred site and his enjoyment in killing endangered species.[64] Kaz Cooke depicts the Territory as the focus for a national prejudice[65] where the local politician can refer to the Aboriginal community as 'just a bunch of coons' with impunity.[66] Northern Territory politicians are also the villains of Moffitt's *Death Adder Dreaming*: 'Christopher Partridge ... former mining engineer ... cultivated the white backlash' and his father, a famous and venerable anthropologist, for good measure is revealed as a rapist.[67] It is generally accepted by writers in this period that European settlers attempted genocide in the Territory.[68] 'Historical novels' reconstruct the past according to this new revelation. Hugh Atkinson's *The Longest Wire* includes scenes of racial violence and rape perpetrated by the men building the Overland Telegraph Line. Whatever the allegorical truth, Atkinson's portrayal is not substantiated by historical evidence.[69] This shift represents a complete change in construction. In the earliest periods, writers such as Jeannie Gunn refused

---

60   Wood, *Dead Centre*, p. 227.
61   Yamamoto, 'Betty-san', p. 17.
62   Lindy Chamberlain, letter to the author, 4 December 1991.
63   Willmot, *Below the Line*, pp. 29–30.
64   R.F. Brissenden, *Wildcat* (Sydney: Allen & Unwin, 1991), pp. 150f, 243, 264.
65   Cooke, *The Crocodile Club*, p. 166.
66   Cooke, *The Crocodile Club*, p. 58.
67   Moffitt, *Death Adder Dreaming*, pp. 21, 195.
68   The 1990 United States produced film, *Quigley Down Under*, for example, had several scenes where men, women and children are rounded up by white stockmen. Quigley is hired to shoot out all the Aborigines and is left for dead by the fellow whites when he refuses to comply.
69   J. Bern, 'Blackfella Business Whitefella Law', PhD thesis, Macquarie University, 1974, pp. 74–5.

to acknowledge that Aborigines were killed and accounts of outback life suppressed this even in circumstances when the historical evidence was strong that it had occurred. Now it seems that the opposite is true. In the modern period writers assume that Aborigines were routinely poisoned and raped, even in circumstances when the historical evidence suggests otherwise.

It is now the popularly accepted view that the Northern Territory is a region dominated by racial tensions and extreme violence. The brutality to Aborigines by Europeans is a constant theme of all B. Wongar's writing. In *Gabo Djara* a European man notes, 'It was much cheaper to chuck a jar of strychnine into a water hole or put it in bags of flour. We often infected blankets with smallpox before giving them to the natives?'[70] *The Track to Bralgu* echoes this theme. In 'Poor Fellow Dingo' a dingo is rescued while an Aboriginal woman and her children are left to starve in the flood. The violence continues throughout the short stories, particularly in 'Willy-Willy Man', 'Buwad the Fly' and 'Dugaruru' in *Babaru*. This image of European oppression is presented vividly in Wongar's *Walg* where, in an evocation of Nazism, the Aborigines are forcibly involved in a eugenics program.[71] The eugenics, it transpires, are a way of disenfranchising future Aborigines from the landscape (under the rather dubious premise that under the tribal law of patrilineal succession the absence of male progenitors will debar future generations from their cultural inheritance) to pave the way for wholesale mineral exploitation and a uranium boom. The exploitation described in *Walg* takes place on a grand scale where at the uranium mine site, 'Gin Downs', the pre-adolescent Aboriginal girls are rounded up, chained, systematically brutalised and pack-raped to death, while the Europeans take bets on the number of men the girls can survive. When the eugenics program fails to produce results (because the 'abos breed differently' and without the necessary magic, the women remain infertile), the dead bodies of the women who fail to conceive are taken in truckloads to be buried in mass graves at the dump.[72] The racism in B. Wongar is systematised and coupled with the destruction of the environment.

---

70  Wongar, *Gabo Djara* (South Melbourne: Macmillan, 1988), pp. 93–4.
71  Wongar, *Walg*, p. 59.
72  Wongar, *Walg*, pp. 32, 54–6.

While the Europeans are identified as the destroyers, the corollary is that Aborigines (in the texts) have come to be associated with preservation of wilderness.[73] This is a theme of Wongar's *Walg*, where the whole landscape becomes barren through European contact and the survival of life is only possible through Aboriginal intervention. The juxtaposition of 'Aboriginality' and 'Conservation' is apparent in *Kakadu Man*. Bill Neidjie articulated his affiliation to the land in a way that is both appealing and understandable to Europeans:

> We need this earth to live because we'll be dead,
> we'll become earth.
> This ground and this earth ...
> like brother and mother.[74]

Although Lindy Chamberlain asserts that the physical landscape did not affect her writing,[75] in *Through My Eyes*, she repeatedly uses 'dingo' as a metaphor for wilderness[76] and suggests a spirituality that is linked to Aboriginal authority. Throughout popular fiction in this period, the association between Aborigines and conservation is strong. In Grahame Webb's *The Numunwari*, the hero, an Officer with the 'Northern Territory Wildlife Division', is passionately committed to conservation (and can only operate with the assistance of his Aboriginal friend and mentor, Oodabund), whereas the villains are poachers abetted by a time-serving public servant who wants to reintroduce crocodile shooting.

In contrast to writers from the earlier periods, Aborigines are almost universally presented as on a higher spiritual plane than the shallow Europeans. The Aboriginal hero Oodabund is omniscient in his ability to

---

73  Xavier Herbert is the only dissenting voice in this association of Aborigines and conservation. He actively attacked the Aboriginal administration of national parks in the Territory which he found unAboriginal: 'not much nearer to being blackfellows except in breed.' Herbert, *Poor Fellow My Country*, p. 1453.
74  Fox, Davis & Neidjie, *Kakadu Man*, p. 77.
75  Chamberlain, letter to the author.
76  Prior to the fatal attack, Chamberlain describes how she and her baby Azaria are watched by dingoes where other people are ignored by them. Onlookers describe dingoes biting children, chewing clothing and camping gear magically leaving no trace except paw-prints in the dust. The dingo that takes Azaria is not like the other 'mangy ones' but has a shiny coat and is in 'beautiful condition'. When Lindy realises her baby is gone, she runs behind the tent and gives chase to the dingo she sees there, but it is a false lead, it is yet another dingo. The dingoes appear and disappear without warning, terrifying the Chamberlains and others. The dingo becomes the metaphor for the terror and the loss but at the same time it is recognised as a free part of the wilderness. After Lindy has spent her first night at Berrimah prison in Darwin, she wakes early and, 'There in the early light of dawn, I saw a dingo in the distance facing toward me. It was free anyway'; Chamberlain, *Through My Eyes*, pp. 23, 36–46, 48, 287.

predict the behaviour of the giant crocodile, Numunwari.[77] Jackie Jackie, in *The Kangaroo Connection*, portrayed as hot-headed and unsophisticated for most of the book, mysteriously emerges as having the power to bring the dying Charles back to life: 'My father is Witch Doctor and I know many ways he would use now to help Charles'.[78] In Lindy Chamberlain's narrative, Aborigines are both sympathetic and telepathic.[79] Davidson, Chatwin and Keneally[80] also support this construction. Foster, like the other writers, emphasises the mysticism of Aborigines. Cyril, his Aboriginal protagonist, is not like other people with his very black, strange eyes, powers of detection, and complete absence of 'fear of pain'. Although Cyril looks young, he is the 'oldest man in Neverfuckinlose' and his enemies spy on him in the shape of birds.[81]

In the texts, European writers sometimes use the concept 'sacred site' as a means of linking European and Aboriginal mythology. Roland Perry, in *Blood is a Stranger* introduced what seems to be a very un-Aboriginal concept called a 'Bad Dreaming'. Burra tells Ken Cardinal: 'It's no coincidence that all the Bad Dreaming areas are where the biggest uranium ore-bodies are'.[82] Damien Broderick in *Dreaming Dragons* amalgamated images of the sacred site Uluru and sci-fi cliches to create a composite of intelligent-aliens-from-outer-space and the Rainbow Serpent. Nan Albinski has pointed out that *Dreaming Dragons* 'uses aboriginal legend and a central Australian setting, grounding images of rebirth firmly in a dead heart which is not a sinister wasteland, but the guardian of a treasure'; it is indeed a 'sacred site'.[83] For Billy Marshall-Stoneking, the Lasseter legend of a fabulous reef where the gold lies thick on the ground coalesces with a construction of an Aboriginal sacred site of fantastic power and known only to a small group of chosen Pintubi elders. Marshall Stoneking relates that when the group needs money, custodians travel to the site and return with gold to finance projects in the Papunya community such as the purchase of new cars.[84] This construction is consistent with the general accordance given by non-Aboriginal writers to the myth that Aborigines possess superior knowledge that allows them to harness the power and

---

77  For example Webb, *The Numunwari*, pp. 132f.
78  Watkins, *The Kangaroo Connection*, p. 165.
79  Chamberlain, *Through My Eyes*, pp. 73, 148–53.
80  For example, Keneally, *Outback*, pp. 16–35.
81  Foster, *Mates of Mars*, pp. 245, 283.
82  R. Perry, *Blood is a Stranger* (Richmond, Victoria: Heinemann, 1988), p. 88.
83  Albinski, 'Putting Value Back in the Land', p. 370.
84  Marshall-Stoneking, *Lasseter*, pp. 180–1.

sacredness of landscape. It is ironic that in the contemporary period, Lasseter's reef, the Depression dream of an impoverished Australia, has become by the 1980s an Aboriginal site of enormous mythological power capable of generating new Toyotas.

In contrast, Aboriginal writers do not overtly promote either the spiritual or the conservationist theme apparent in other writers. Aboriginal writing tends to be dominated by the theme of institutionalised racism and inequality. Although Bill Neidjie emphasised the role of country in Aboriginal spirituality, and has been linked to the conservationist ideal, he also had a political agenda:

> No-matter about that White-European,
> e can go with that one
> but must White-European got to be listen this culture
> and this story
> because important one this.[85]

Barbara Cummings's *Take This Child*, Merrill Bray's *Our Mob* and Charlie Perkins's *A Bastard Like Me* expose the system of state institutionalisation that was imposed on children whose mothers were Aboriginal and whose fathers were not. In Perkins's moving account of growing up, away from family and friends, he describes his increasing politicisation. His account of his youngest brother's death is suffused with the bitterness of inequality:

> we lost another brother, the youngest. We lost him a couple of years ago, in the desert. He was working about sixty miles south of Alice Springs. He, like me and many Aborigines today, had an unhappy life. He was drinking one day and carried on drinking into the night. In the middle of the night he walked off. He must have thought of walking back to Alice Springs ... no one really cared. He was 'just another bloody Abo'. In the darkness he must have crossed the road and kept walking. By the next day he was walking around in circles. He died in the desert, lost for five days. It is a pretty rotten way to die ...

> his white workmates in the camp did not even check on his whereabouts or report him missing until three days later ... The search did not begin until four days after he set out.[86]

---

85  Neidjie, *Story About Feeling*, p. 171.
86  C. Perkins, *A Bastard Like Me* (Sydney: Ure Smith, 1975), pp. 12–13.

Writers who identify as Aboriginal from outside the Territory, see the region as a focus for political and spiritual experiences[87] voicing pan-Aboriginal themes.

With respect to the role of women and gender relations generally in this period, the literary images and themes of the first period of Territory writing are to some extent regenerated. Aborigines may have had a reversal in their earlier status as a doomed race of childlike primitives, but women have yet to achieve a comparable transformation, in spite of the fact that, as in the earliest period, they are well represented as authors. Lyn Riddett noted a perception amongst writers that 'Darwin is a good place to touch feminism ... this is a community where women are perceived as acting strongly'.[88] Yet there are indications that this perception is not without contradictions. Where women are described as strong, it appears only to be measured by their ability to put up with the impositions of misogynist males. *The Australian* review of Sara Henderson's book suggests that kind of ambiguity.[89] This construction, so apparent in Robyn Davidson, is also apparent in Heather Grace's *Heart of Light*.

Drama, in contrast, emphasises the strength of women. Although initially Laura in *Buffaloes Can't Fly*, is presented as prissy and superficial, by the end of the play she has proved herself a much stronger and more adaptable character than her husband Reg. Fat Anna in Nowra's *Capricornia* is a very powerful character indeed. She is able to enter prisons without a key and when threatened by O'Connell states she will declare him to be 'combo' if he does not let her farewell Norman properly. When his back is turned she jokes with Norman suggesting O'Connell has a tiny penis.[90] *Dragged Screaming to Paradise* is a monodrama and has a lone woman narrating the action of the play. *The Ingkata's Wife* focuses upon a sympathetic appraisal of the life of Kathleen Strehlow. But the strength of the roles given to women on the stage is not repeated in the novels. This strength has not

---

87   For example, the Northern Territory, and particularly Uluru in Central Australia, is often seen as a spiritual centre for all Aboriginal people. Ruby Langford and other Aboriginal women in the community raise money to travel there. When Ruby arrives at Uluru she thinks of 'how someone had said it was the magnetic centre and meeting place of all the dreaming tracks'; R. Langford, *Don't Take Your Love to Town* (Ringwood: Penguin, 1988), pp. 234f; Mudrooroo wrote a series of poems set around Central Australia as metonymic for national race relations; Mudrooroo, 'Uluru', 'The Olgas', 'Yulara', 'Uluru II', *Meanjin* 52, 2 (1992), pp. 259–61.
88   Lyn Riddett, interview.
89   M.R. Liverani, 'Romance Aplenty, Perilously Short on Common Sense', *The Australian Weekend Review*, 1–2 August 1992, p. 6.
90   L. Nowra, *Capricornia* (Sydney: Current Theatre Series, 1988), p. 95.

been translated into the cinema. The women of *Priscilla: Queen of the Desert* (Stephan Elliott 1994), with perhaps one exception, are depicted unsympathetically.

In the same way that in the period after the war emphasis upon the role of woman as home-maker brought about a corresponding rejection of Aboriginal women's roles outside of the home, with a focus upon the exploitative nature of inter-racial sexual relations, this period shows tensions of another kind. For many of the female writers, feminism is an issue.[91] At the same time feminism is seen as intimidating. When women step beyond what is seen as their appropriate behaviour, the punishment is usually rape. Robyn Davidson's friendliness (or assertiveness?) makes her the candidate 'as the next town rape case'. Eventually Davidson leaves the hotel to begin work at the camel farm. The final impetus to go comes about after she returns to her room one night to find someone has defecated on her pillow. She writes,

> One does not have to delve too deeply to discover why some of the world's angriest feminists breathed crisp blue Australian air during their formative years, before packing their kangaroo-skin bags and scurrying over to London or New York or any place where the antipodean machismo would fade gently from their battle-scarred consciousnesses like some grisly nightmare at dawn. Anyone who has worked in a men-only bar in Alice Springs will know what I mean.[92]

In Betty Roland's *Beyond Capricorn*, Anna travel by herself to the Northern Territory to meet a man she hardly knows who has offered marriage. Anna is nearly raped by her prospective in-laws after she arrives at the cattle station to find her fiancée, Archie Livingstone, in gaol. Christopher Wood's hero Mary is nearly raped twice. In the first instance, it is because of the hatred that Aboriginal activist Luri feels toward her both for being European and for her relationship to her husband whom Luri believes is involved in a conspiracy to defraud the 'Pitjata' Aborigines. The second instance is a pack rape, only thwarted by the fortuitous timing of an Aboriginal terrorist attack on remote Simmon's Creek roadhouse. The description of the roadhouse bar with its polaroid snaps adorning the wall of 'men with their trousers down and their buttocks pointed at the camera; either that

---

91  Robyn Davidson, Kaz Cooke, Heather Grace, Gail Morgan, Lee Cataldi, Jan McKennish and Suzanne Spunner all include either a female character described as a feminist or discussion relating to feminism.
92  Davidson, *Tracks*, pp. 33–5.

or fingering their genitals' sets the scene for the inevitable confrontation. Mary flees the group and locks herself within the flimsy cabin (invoking the image of Barbara Baynton's 'The Chosen Vessel'):

> Mary strained her ears, she could feel her heart thumping. She was in a prison at the mercy of the men outside. They could do what they liked with her, the nearest police station was over a hundred miles away. Men made their own laws in this outback wilderness. And they were laws for men, not women.[93]

In *The Kangaroo Connection* Gail Manning is tied to a chair and forcibly undressed.[94] Selina in *The Crocodile Club* is offered the choice of sexually gratifying Franklin, the corrupt politician, or death.[95]

White women are punished by rape, sexual abuse or vilification when they break away from the domestic stereotype. In a reference to Robyn Davidson, Lindy Chamberlain and Kathleen Strehlow, Spunner's character of the Ingkata's wife screams at the audience,

> You didn't like the Camel Girl and you don't like the Dingo Mother and you sure as eggs don't like me. You didn't like her because she was young and single and wanted to be left alone; and you wouldn't believe her because she was a mother but she wouldn't cry on cue, and you can't stomach me because I'm a widow and I won't stop greiving [sic].
>
> Why shouldn't I draw the curtains and stay inside out of the heat? I never liked the kitchen anyway.[96]

In contrast, Aboriginal women are commended for their qualities of strength and loyalty. Lee Cataldi's poem '*kuukuu kardiya* and the women who live on the ground' is fairly typical of the view. White women are 'femmocrats' with handbags as fat as bank accounts, contrasting the Aboriginal women who 'move lightly'. White women dominate by force with a shrillness that belies their lack of authority, while the Aboriginal women endure patiently with a real strength.[97] European women have become the scapegoat for racial tension in the Northern Territory. In the contemporary construction they are increasingly blamed for European hostility towards Aborigines. Herbert was influential in establishing this construction:

---

93 Wood, *Dead Centre*, pp. 129–35.
94 Watkins, *The Kangaroo Connection*, p. 131f.
95 Cooke, *The Crocodile Club*, p. 132f.
96 Spunner, 'The Ingkata's Wife', p. 49.
97 Cataldi, *The Women Who Live on the Ground*, pp. 36–8.

it's this Black Velvet business … Those poor [white] women! You can see the humiliation in their eyes … and also the meanness in their tight mouths … What's the use of a lady trained at the best ladies' school to a man who has to battle with this harsh country and needs a woman only to cook his tucker and root like an animal after watching animals root all day? … The first choice is the obvious one, the women with their roots in the soil itself … the Aboriginal women … and I don't doubt that many, given the chance, would become something of ladies in their own right … and still be able to go out and bring in your dinner from the bush …[98]

Almost universally, European women are portrayed as utterly horrible in the writing of B. Wongar. In the short story 'Goarang, the Anteater' from *The Track to Bralgu*, the female scientist is depicted as sexually abusing the anteater in ways that suggest a bestial attraction through her daily manipulation of the thermometer in the anteater's anus and the stroking of his spines. The nursing sister in *Walg* is instrumental in maintaining the eugenics program by the rounding up of Aboriginal women. Carol, the wife in *The Tracker*, set out a program of 'westernisation' for her Asian husband, Dao Ba Khang, in music, dress and food and permits him to have anything to do with, or read anything about Asia, as it is unacceptable to white Australian sensibilities. As Dao's skin inexplicably darkens and he becomes the target for vicious racial prejudice, he becomes paradoxically more attractive to European women; the receptionist makes smacking noises with her lips and notes that 'It makes you look erotic'.[99] Dao noted critically of his secretary:

> The girl's breasts were flabby. She wore a brassiere but it was hanging loose, showing space in its cups. The brassiere had probably lost its shape so the girl had stuffed it with a handful of … Dao could not whether it was cotton wool or paper tissue. But did it really matter? He felt like a man who has just opened an oyster shell and instead of a pearl, finds a worm. This is what this would is like, he thought.[100]

Unlike the portrayal of European women in the poetry, literature and drama of this period Aboriginal women are presented as sensitive, brave and intelligent; the protagonist of *Walg* typifies the image. In Betty Roland's *Beyond Capricorn*, Djindara is a model of competence, loyalty and support for her lover Booroola and contrasted by the foolish albeit well-meaning Anna who needs Mark to rescue her. Even in satire, Aboriginal

---

98  Herbert, *Poor Fellow My Country*, pp. 54–5.
99  Wongar, *The Trackers*, p. 19.
100 Wongar, *The Trackers*, pp. 22–3.

women are presented as intelligent, articulate and culturally cohesive.[101] Aboriginal women are also the preferred sexual partners. In *Poor Fellow My Country*, Jeremy's lover is Nan and not Rifkah. In *Beyond Capricorn*, Mark tells Anna the facts of life: 'dark girls have a way with them and once a man has tasted black velvet, "gone combo" we call it up here, he doesn't fancy another kind'.[102] But if the heroes are not partnered with Aboriginal women, then their lovers are often intelligent Asian women,[103] again contrasted with their strident European counterparts.[104]

Some of the writers are superficially approving of particular European women when their behaviour conforms to specific parameters. Chatwin marvels at Marion and believes it 'was no exaggeration to say she looked like a Piero Madonna' and ponders the enigma of Australian women, 'so strong and satisfied'.[105] In what must surely be an unconscious extension of the idea that Aborigines are children, the Madonna is an image invoked for certain European women who work with Aborigines. Xavier Herbert considered Rifkah the epitome of womanhood[106] so when Father Glascock tells Monsignor Maryzic that Rifkah wants to 'dedicate her life to looking after Aborigines', Monsignor Maryzic answers, 'Der Jewish voman is always mutter first. She is der mutter of mutters. Der Mutter of Gott vos Jewess'.[107]

Despite the ambiguity of their presentation, European women are depicted as enthusiastic heterosexual partners. Bruce Chatwin greatly admires Marion, the female anthropologist who looks 'innocent' and wears 'skimpy' 'rags'.[108] In Kaz Cooke's novel, wives are dominated by husbands and sexual slurs are applied as a matter of course, but there is no suggestion of any alternative.[109] Many women suffer sexual violence, but

---

101 The character of Chloe is archetypal; Cooke, *The Crocodile Club*, p. 94.
102 B. Roland, *Beyond Capricorn* (London: Collins, 1976), p. 85.
103 Gentle Asian spouses are a feature of Brissenden's *Wildcat*; Stewart's *Reunion*; Moffitt's *Death Adder Dreaming*.
104 Again Aboriginal writing seems to conflict with this stereotype. Eric Willmot's *Below the Line* has a strong and courageous white heroine; Charles Perkins' *A Bastard Like Me* although pointing out the prejudice of white girls, clearly respects his wife Eileen and gives a portrait of her as loyal and intelligent.
105 Chatwin, *The Songlines*, p. 112.
106 Xavier articulated this idea to his wife Sadie, 'Rifkah represents all that is sweet in womanhood. She is beautiful, gentle', letter to Sadie, 11 October 1968. See also letter 6 September 1968; quoted, *Xavier Herbert*, de Groen & Pierce, pp. 266–70.
107 Herbert, *Poor Fellow My Country*, p. 1335.
108 Chatwin, *The Songlines*, pp. 34, 49, etc.
109 At the conclusion to the story Selina may not be married to Jock, but they finish up as enthusiastic lovers; Cooke, *The Crocodile Club*, pp. 79, 141, 155.

a strong theme of romance remains present in the narratives; in *Tracks*, Robyn Davidson forms a sexual liaison with her photographer; in *Beyond Capricorn*, Anna marries her rescuer, Mark Gillespie; in *Dead Centre*, Mary is re-united with David; in *The Kangaroo Connection*, Gail finishes up with Charles; the narrator in *Dragged Screaming to Paradise* negotiates her presence in Darwin almost entirely through and against her husband and *The Crocodile Club* ends with Selina Plankton in bed with Jock.

Sexual partnering is a major theme of *Poor Fellow My Country* where Lydia, Bridie and Alfie are victims of lust for Jeremy, the old 'scrub bull'. Herbert once commented that the crisis in Jeremy Delacy's life occurred when he realised he had misunderstood his relationship with his wife Nanago.[110] Nan declared,

> I am not mistress … I am servant … You know I love you. But I am Aboriginal woman. I am servant to man I love. White woman who is boss don't love her husband. Only partner … Always I am servant of Jeremy Delacy. Time I can't be his servant, I don't want to live.[111]

Although Jeremy Delacy emerge as incapable of consummating a successful relationship with either Rhoda, Alfie, Rifkah, Lydia or as it transpires, Nan, the women do not appear in contrasting roles of strength. Rhoda remarries but her family fails to live up to her exacting standards, Alfie returns to her husband, Lydia to her father and Rifkah passes seemingly as easily from Delacy to Father Glascock and to Pat Hannaford as Nan once passed from Jeremy's brother to Jeremy. It is, in a small way, an affirmation of woman as survivor that the character of Bridie Cullity, who alone manages to achieve her desire to successfully bear Jeremy's child, remains tough, assertive and most significantly, alive, at the end of the narrative.

In the popular fantasy literature, the pattern is very much the same. Jade is the least developed character in *Mates of Mars* and women are pictured as sexually exploited and physically abused. Bob Brissenden's *Wildcat* and Grahame Webb's *The Numunwari*, both of which demonstrate a commitment to contemporary Aboriginal politics and spirituality, do not feature women in the narrative. In Webb's *The Numunwari*, a tough female anthropologist appears and disappears on the first four pages.

---

110  X. Herbert, interview, with the author and Ann McGrath, 'The Singapore Restaurant', Darwin, during the Finniss River Land Claim Hearings, 1980.
111  Herbert, *Poor Fellow My Country*, pp. 1282–3.

Oodabund's daughter Nancy, although clearly competent, is at the mercy of her father and her husband's wishes, even after death, and Mac's faithful wife Anne has a very minor role apart from cooking delicious barramundi dinners and worrying about her husband.[112] Yamamoto's character Nakako, in her short story 'Powers', echoes the sentiments of Spunner's *Dragged Screaming to Paradise*:

> Ryuji had been sent out by a joint mining venture. A Japanese company man first and last, he'd transported everything with him—his life and work—to be reassembled in this foreign land. He had lost nothing. Whereas Nakako had stripped herself of everything. And now, in league with this one man, she was going to make a complete home.[113]

But if European women have not achieved a comparable role with men in the literature, there has been an improvement in the European perception of intra-Aboriginal gender relations. Although a post-war interpretation is still current, Andrew McMillan, for example, suggests of Aboriginal women that, 'their role is one of subservience', other authors offer a new construction consistent with contemporary gender politics.[114] Robyn Davidson suggests that within the Pitjantjara, males and females hold positions of equal importance: 'While men and women have separate roles, necessitated by environment, these roles are part of a single function—to survive—and both are mutually respected'.[115] Marion, the female anthropologist in Chatwin's *The Songlines*, expressed a similar perspective:

> She told me how Aboriginal women have song cycles of their own and therefore, different sites to be protected. Few people had realised this until recently: the reason being that the women were that much tighter with their secrets than the men.[116]

Esther tells Lucy in *Promise of Rain*, 'We have our own corroborees'.[117]

This position was given thorough treatment by anthropologist Dianne Bell in her influential *Daughters of the Dreaming*:

---

112 Webb, *The Numunwari*, pp. 49, 90, 135, 137, 247.
113 M. Yamamoto, 'Powers', *Betty-san*, p. 120.
114 As Bain Attwood has suggested in his 'Portrait of an Aboriginal as an Artist: Sally Morgan and the Construction of Aboriginality', *Australian Historical Studies* 25, 99 (October 1992), pp. 302–18, and was demonstrated in Part Two, Chapter 3, authors, particularly those writing about Aborigines, are affected by trends in the social science disciplines.
115 Davidson, *Tracks*, p. 170.
116 Chatwin, *The Songlines*, p. 49.
117 Morgan, *Promise of Rain*, p. 119.

> Through a study of Aboriginal women's ritual activity I hoped to answer questions which had nagged me since I began anthropology ... In some studies of Aboriginal religion I had read that women were deemed to be of less cultural importance than men ...
>
> Having learnt something of women's ritual realm, having seen that their independence and autonomy of action were not illusory, I was forced to come to terms with the dynamics of women's culture and its interrelations with, not subsumation by, that of men ...
>
> I re-read the work of the desert ethnographers Baldwin Spencer and Francis Gillen and Mervyn Meggitt and although the words were familiar, the images were not. They saw women as denied access to the spiritual domain, as ritually impoverished, as pawns in male political power plays. Something was awry.[118]

This interpretation, that male anthropologists saw subservience because they could not gain access to the 'women's ritual realm' and therefore were ignorant of Aboriginal women's separate spiritual and cultural life, is extremely interesting as it marks a complete reversal of ideas on this subject. Up until this point, all the earlier Territory writers had agreed as to the inferior position of Aboriginal women. This differing in construction of Aboriginal society most clearly reflects the changing status of European women.[119] Unconscious of any irony, Davidson asserts, 'If there is sexism amongst Aborigines today, it is because they have learnt well from their conquerors'.[120] This view of the changing status of Aboriginal women perhaps influenced the way sexual relationships were portrayed in the literature and accounted for the comparative absence of descriptions of exploitative relationships that had so dominated the texts of the previous period. Writers tended towards the view that many of the relationships, particularly those arising in the Northern Territory pastoral industry, could perhaps have been more mutually beneficial than had been described in the previous decade.[121]

---

118  D. Bell, *Daughters of the Dreaming* (Melbourne: McPhee Gribble, 1983), pp. 23–4.
119  Phil Kaberry, for example, suggested this construction of intra-Aboriginal relationships some forty years earlier and it was simply ignored; P. Kaberry, *Aboriginal Woman: Sacred and Profane* (Farnborough, Hants.: Greg International, 1970 (London: George Routledge, 1939)).
120  Davidson, *Tracks*, p. 170.
121  McGrath, *Born in the Cattle*, Chapter 4, suggests, for example, that there is no simple exploitative model which is appropriate for the wide spectrum of relationship formed.

The developments of the last two decades represent both continuity and change in the literary model of the Northern Territory. Writers continue to assert that the real Territory lies outside the urban centres. Most of the writers describe the Northern Territory as frontier.[122] The notion, which had been a theme in previous periods, that the wilderness landscape had the power to renew and transform personality, was regenerated in parallel with new themes of environment, conservation and wilderness protection. Central Australia maintained its position within Australian iconography as crucial to an understanding of national character and identity. Darwin was confirmed as Australia's Asian city. The identification of both Aborigines and Territory landscape with the supernatural and magic appear heightened. Women are present as individual angry voices, but no concerted female response is indicated to rival the predominantly masculine tone which persists in Territory writing. The European writers maintain the dominant interpretation of landscape, although appear less secure than at any other period and ostensibly seek direction from an Aboriginal authority, Aboriginal mysticism, travel and misogyny.

Throughout the period of this study, the majority of the authors (with some rare exceptions) have shared a universality of approach. They have attempted to write about national issues within the context of the personal. There have been few published works, either novels or plays, that have not been autobiographical. Even Xavier Herbert (the closest thing to literature in Territory writing) retained a strong autobiographical slant within his writing. What does this mean? Somehow the author's individual story has come to articulate the region. In both European and Aboriginal publications the landscape, the politics and the personal are amalgamated and there is a sense of attempting to 'document' the true Australia in the descriptions of the Territory. Where this will lead Territory writers in the future is anyone's guess. There is an increasing scepticism towards the view that landscape alone can provide salvation for the individual. Nonetheless, the region's proximity to Asia, active indigenous presence and repeated assertion of frontier lifestyle of masculine extremes guarantee that the Territory will remain relevant to the Australian experience.

---

122 For example, without any kind of prompting by me, Peter Goldsworthy, Louis Nowra and David Foster in correspondence all defined the Northern Territory as different from the rest of Australia, because it is a frontier.

# SELECT TERRITORY BIBLIOGRAPHY

A Collection of Writing by Members of the Fellowship of Australian Writers Northern Territory Section. *Colours of This Land*. Darwin: published by the Authors, 1988.

A Lady Long Resident in New South Wales. (Barton, C.) *A Mother's Offering to her Children*. Milton, Queensland: Jacaranda Press, 1979 (1841).

Ackermann, J. *Australia From a Woman's Point of View*. Melbourne: Cassell, 1981 (Cassell, 1913).

Adair, D. *Death Rides the Desert*. London: Hutchinson, n.d.

Adamson, B. *Frank Clune: Author and Ethnological Anachronism*. Melbourne: Hawthorn Press, 1944.

Albrecht, P.G.E. *Hermannsburg: A Meeting Place of Cultures Personal Reflections*. Casuarina: Nungalinya, 1981.

Alcorta, F.X. *Darwin Rebellion 1911–1919*. Darwin: University Planning Authority, 1984.

Aldous, A. *Danger on the Map*. Melbourne: Cheshire, 1947.

Aldous, A. *The Tendrils in Australia*. London: Chatto & Windus, 1959.

Aldous, A. *Doctor with Wings*. Leicester: Brockhampton Press, 1961 (1960).

Allyne, K. *Carpentaria Moon*. London: Mills & Boon, 1987.

Annabel, R. *The Uranium Hunters*. Adelaide: Rigby, 1971.

Anon. (Spillett, P.) *St. Mary's Star of the Sea*. Darwin: Church Centenary edition, 1982.

Ansell, R. and Percy, R. *To Fight the Wild*. Perth: Fremantle Arts Centre Press, 1980.

Apsley, Lord and Lady. *The Amateur Settler*. London: Hodder & Stoughton, n.d. c. 1920s.

Armbrust, B. *The Darwin Bard*. Darwin: published by the author, 1992.

Armour, J. *Burning Air*. London: Hodder & Stoughton, n.d. c. 1920s.

Armour, J. *The Spell of the Inland: A Romance of Central Australia*. Sydney: Angus & Robertson, 1934.

Arrowsmith, H.M. *These Australians*. Sydney: Church Missionary Society, n.d.

Atkinson, H. *The Longest Wire*. Sydney: Angus & Robertson, 1982.

Attenborough, D. *Quest Under Capricorn*. London: Lutterworth Press, 1963.

Baily, E.M. *Pathways of the Sky*. Sydney: Macquarie Head, 1933.

Baker, R. *A Map For Giants: As told to Robert Bateman*. London: Constable Young, 1964.

Barclay, J. *The Bloom is Gone*. Sydney: Australasia, 1977.

Bardon, J. *Revolution by Night or Katjala Wananu (The Son After the Father)*. Double Bay, New South Wales: Local Consumption, 1991.

Barr, D. *Warrigal Joe: A Tale of the Never-Never*. Melbourne: Cassell, 1946.

Barrett, C. *Coast of Adventure: Untamed North Australia*. Melbourne: Robertson & Mullens, 1941.

Barrett, C. *Up North: Australia Above Capricorn*. Melbourne: Robertson & Mullens, 1942.

Barrett, M. *The Gold of Lubra Rock*. London: Robert Hale, 1967.

Barrett, M. *Stranger in Galah*. London: Longman, Green, 1958.

Barrett, M. *Traitor At Twenty Fathoms*. London: Collins, 1963.

Barrie, D.R. *The Heart of Rum Jungle: The History of Rum Jungle and Batchelor in the Northern Territory of Australia*. Batchelor: D.R. Barrie, 1982.

Bartlett, N. *The Pearl Seekers*. Tiptree, Essex: Andrew Melrose, n.d. c. 1953.

Basedow, H. *Knights of the Boomerang*. Sydney: Endeavour Press, 1935.

Baume, F.E. *Tragedy Track*. Sydney: Frank C. Johnson, 1933.

Bayton, J. *Cross over Carpentaria: Being a History of the Church of England in Northern Australia From 1865–1965*. Brisbane: W.R. Smith & Paterson, 1965.

Becke, L. and Jeffery, W. *A First Fleet Family: A Hitherto Unpublished narrative of Certain Remarkable Adventures Compiled From the Papers of Sergeant William Dew of the Marines*. London: Fisher Unwin, 1896.

Bedford, R. *Naught to Thirty-Three*. Melbourne: Melbourne University Press, 1976 (Sydney: Currawong, 1944).

Bell, D. *Daughters of the Dreaming*. Melbourne: McPhee Gribble, 1983.

Bennett, M.M. *The Australian Aboriginal: As a Human Being*. London: Alston Rivers, 1930.

Berndt, R.M. and C.H. *Arnhem Land*. Melbourne: Cheshire, 1954.

Berndt, R.M. and C.H. *The Speaking Land: Myth and Story in Aboriginal Australia*. Ringwood: Penguin, 1988.

Binning, J. *Target Area*. Sydney: Australasian, 1943.

Birtles, D. *The Overlanders*. Sydney: Shakespeare Head, 1946.

Birtles, F.E. *Battle Fronts of Outback*. Sydney: Angus & Robertson, 1935.

Birtles, F.E. *Lonely Lands: Through the Heart of Australia*. Sydney: New South Wales Bookstall, 1909.

Blackwell, D. and Lockwood, D. *Alice on the Line*. Sydney: Weldon, 1989 (1965).

Blakely, F. *Dream Millions: New Light on Lasseter's Lost Reef*. Mansfield, M. ed. Sydney: Angus & Robertson, 1972.

Blakely, F. *Hard Liberty*. Sydney: George G. Harrap, 1938.

Bolton, A.T. ed. *Walkabout's Australia: An Anthology of Articles and Photographs From Walkabout Magazine*. Sydney: Walkabout, 1969 (1964).

Boucher, B. *The Megawind Cancellation*. New York: Atheneum, 1979.

Bowman, A. *The Kangaroo Hunters; or Adventures in the Bush*. Philadelphia: Porter & Coates, 1859.

Bowes, J. *Comrades: A Story of the Australian Bush*. London: Henry Frowde Hodder & Stoughton, 1912.

Boyd, G. *Justice in Jeopardy: Twelve Witnesses Speak Out*. Sandringham, Victoria: Guy Boyd, 1984.

Boyd, M. *Outbreak of Love*. Ringwood: Penguin, 1984 (1957).

Braver, A. *Under the Southern Cross*. Adelaide: Lutheran Publishing House, 1956.

Brewer, A.L. *Leuv-We of Kalmogorr: A Romance of the North Australian Bush*. Glendale, Los Angeles: published by the author, n.d. c. 1946.

Bridges, P. *A Walk-About in Australia*. London: Hodder & Stoughton, 1925.

Brisbane, C. *The Secret of the Desert*. Melbourne: Thomas Nelson, 1943 (1941).

Brissenden, R.F. *Wildcat*. North Sydney: Allen & Unwin, 1991.

Broderick, D. *The Dreaming Dragons: A Time Opera*. Carlton: Norstrilia, 1980.

Brogden, S. *Darwin Holiday: A Guidebook to the Stuart Highway From Alice Springs to Darwin*. Melbourne: Pioneer Tours, 1948.

Bromhead, W.S. *Shall White Australia Fail?*. Sydney: Angus & Robertson, 1939.

Brown, B. *The Flying Doctor: John Flynn and the Flying Doctor Service*. London: Lutterworth, 1967 (1960).

Brown, F.G. *The Lost Mines and Treasure of Northern Australia*. East Malvern, Victoria: Gemcraft, 1988.

Brown, L., De Crespigny, B., Harris, M.P., Thomas, K.K., and Watson, P.N. *A Book of South Australia: Women in the First Hundred Years*. Adelaide: Rigby, 1936.

Brown, R. and Studdy-Clift, P. *Bush Justice*. Carlisle: Hesperian Press, 1990.

Bryson, J. *Evil Angels*. Ringwood: Penguin, 1986 (1985).

Buchanan, G. *Packhorse and Waterhole*. Facsimile edition, Carlisle: Hesperian Press, 1984, (Sydney: Angus & Robertson, 1933).

Bucknall, G. *Flynn's Mantle of Safety: The Story of Adelaide House*. Alice Springs: John Flynn Memorial Book House, 1984.

Buddee, P. *Peter Devlin: Buffalo Hunter*. Adelaide: Rigby, 1973.

Buddee, P. *Peter Devlin: Range Rider*. Adelaide: Rigby, 1973.

Burton, J.W. *The First Century: The Missionary Adventure of Australasian Methodism* 1855–1955. Sydney: Methodist Overseas Mission, 1955.

Caldwell, R. *In Our Great North-West or Incidents and Impressions in Central Australia.* Adelaide: Bonython, 1894.

Campion, E. *Living Here: Short Stories from Australasia 1938–1988.* Sydney: Allen & Unwin, 1988.

Carell, V. *Naked We Are Born.* Sydney: Ure Smith, 1960.

Carell, V. *West Rides the Wind.* Crows Nest, New South Wales: Mount Green, 1971.

Cataldi, L. *The Women Who Live on the Ground: Poems 1978–1988.* Ringwood: Penguin, 1990.

Chamberlain, L. *Through My Eyes.* Port Melbourne: William Heinemann, 1990.

Chaseling, W.S. *Children of Arnhem Land.* Sydney: Department of Overseas Missions Methodist Church of Australasia, 1951.

Chatwin, B. *The Songlines.* New York: Viking, 1987.

Chauvel, C. *Eve in Ebony: … The Story of 'Jedda'.* Sydney: Colombia Pictures, 1954.

Chauvel, C. and E. *Walkabout.* London: W.H. Allen, 1959.

Chester, A. *When the Blood Burns: A Novel of the Flying Doctor Service.* Perth: Patersons, n.d.

Chewings, C. *Back in the Stone Age.* Sydney: Angus & Robertson, 1936.

Clarke, H. *The Long Arm: A Biography of a Northern Territory Policeman.* Canberra: Roebuck Society Publications, 1974.

Clarke, S. *Looking Back.* Darwin: published by the author, 1991.

Clift, C. *The World of Charmian Clift.* Sydney: Collins, 1989 (1970).

Clive, J. *Barossa.* London: Granada, 1982 (1981).

Clune, F. *The Fortune Hunters: An Atomic Odyssey in Australia's Wild West, and Things Seen and Heard by the Way in a Jeep Jaunt.* Sydney: Angus & Robertson, 1957.

Clune, F. *The Forlorn Hope.* Melbourne: Hawthorn Press, 1945.

Clune, F. *The Greatest Liar on Earth.* Melbourne: Hawthorn Press, 1945.

Clune, F. *Overland Telegraph: An Epic Feat of Endurance and Courage*. Sydney: Angus & Robertson, 1984 (1955).

Clune, F. *The Red Heart: Sagas of Centralia*. Melbourne: Hawthorn Press, 1944.

Clune, F. *Try Anything Once: Tlte Autobiography of a Wanderer*. Sydney: Angus & Robertson, 1947.

Cole, K. *Dick Harris: Missionary to the Aborigines A Biography of the Reverend Canon George Richmond Harris M.B.E. Pioneer Missionary to the Aborigines of Arnhem Land*. Bendigo: Keith Cole Publications, 1975.

Cole, K. *Fred Gray of Umbakumba: The Story of Frederick Harold Gray the Founder of the Umbakumba Aboriginal Settlement on Groote Eylandt*. Bendigo: Keith Cole Publications, 1984.

Cole, K. *From Mission to Church: The CMS Mission to the Aborigines of Arnhem Land 1908–1985*. Bendigo: Keith Cole Publications, 1985.

Cole, K. *Groote Eylandt*. Darwin: Nungalinya Publications, 1975.

Cole, K. *Groote Eylandt Mission: A Short History of the CMS Groote Eylandt Mission 1921–1971*. Melbourne: Church Missionary Historical Publications, 1971.

Cole, K. *Groote Eylandt Pioneer: A Biography of the Reverend Hubert Ernest de Mey Warren, Pioneer Missionary and Explorer Among the Aborigines of Arnhem Land*. Melbourne: Church Missionary Historical Publications, 1971.

Cole, K. *Groote Eylandt Stories*. Parkville: Church Missionary Historical Publications, 1972.

Cole, K. *A History of the Church Missionary Society in Australia*. Melbourne: Church Missionary Historical Publications, 1971.

Cole, K. *A History of Oenpelli*. Darwin: Nungalinya Publications, 1975.

Cole, K. *Oenpelli Pioneer: A Biography of the Reverent Alfred John Dyer, Pioneer Missionary Among the Aborigines in Arnhem Land and Founder of the Oenpelli Mission*. Melbourne: Church Missionary Historical Publications, 1972.

Cole, K. *Perriman in Arnhem Land: A Biography of Harry Leslie Perriman, Pioneer Missionary Among the Aborigines at Roper River, Groote Eylandt and Oenpelli in Arnhem Land*. Melbourne: Church Missionary Historical Publications, 1973.

Cole, K. *Roper River 1908–1969*. Melbourne: Church Missionary Historical Trust, 1968.

Cole, T. *Hell West and Crooked*. Sydney: Collins, 1989 (1988).

Conigrave, C.P. *North Australia*. London: Jonathan Cape, 1936.

Conigrave, C.P. *Walk-About*. London: Dent, 1938.

Cooke, K. *The Crocodile Club*. North Sydney: Allen & Unwin, 1992.

Coote, E. *Hell's Airport and Lasseter's Lost Legacy*. Hawthorndene, South Australia: Investigator, 1981 (1934).

Cork, D. *Outback Rainbow*. London: Mills & Boon, 1977.

Cornford, P. *The Outcast*. Sydney: Collins, 1988.

Carris, P. *Beware of the Dog: A Cliff Hardy Novel*. Sydney: Bantam, 1992.

Cossins, G. *The Wings of Silence: An Australian Tale*. London: Gay & Bird, 1899.

Costello, M.M.J. *Life of John Costello*. Sydney: Dymock's Book Arcade, 1930.

Cotterell, G. *Tea At Shadow Creek*. London: Eyre & Spottiswoode, 1958.

Cotton, A.J. *With the Big Herds in Australia*. Brisbane: Watson, Ferguson, 1933.

Cotton, F. (Porkobidni). *Porkobidni's Plan: The Development of the Northern Territory*. Sydney: (no publisher), 1933.

Court, R. *North of Alice*. London: New English Library, 1971.

Courtier, S.H. *The Glass Spear*. Sydney: Invincible, 1950.

Croll, R.H. *I Recall: Collections and Recollections*. Melbourne: Robertson & Mullens, 1939.

Croll, R.H. *Wide Horizons*. Sydney: Angus & Robertson, 1937.

Cronin, B. *The Treasure of the Tropics*. London: Ward Lock, 1928.

Cummings, B. *Take this Child ... From Kahlin Compound to the Retta Dixon Children's Home*. Canberra: Aboriginal Studies Press, 1990.

Dabbs, J. *Top Enders*. Fitzroy, Victoria: McPhee Gribble, 1988.

Dahl, K. *In Savage Australia: An Account of a Hunting and Collecting Expedition in Arnhem Land*. Boston: Houghton Mifflin, 1927 (1926).

Daly, H.W. *Digging, Squatting and Pioneering Life in the Northern Territory of South Australia*. Facsimile edition, Carlisle: Hesperian Press, 1984 (1887).

Danielsson, B. *Terry in Australia*. London: Allen & Unwin, 1961 (1958).

Danvers, J. *The Living Come First*. Melbourne: Heinemann, 1961.

D'Ath, J. *The Initiate*. Sydney: Collins, 1989.

Davenport, L. *Sandshoe Kadaicha*. (no place given): Davells, 1977.

Davidson, R. *Tracks*. London: Granada, 1981.

Davidson, R. *Travelling Light*. Sydney: Collins, 1989.

Davis, S. *Man of All Seasons*. North Ryde, New South Wales: Angus & Robertson, 1989.

Dawe, W.C. *The Golden Lake or The Marvellous History of a Journey Through the Great Lone Land of Australia*. Melbourne: Petherick, 1891.

De Rougemont, L. *The Adventures of Louis de Rougemont: As Told by Himself*. London: George Newnes, 1899.

Dean, B. and Carell, V. *Dust for the Dancers*. Sydney: Ure Smith, 1955.

Department of Territories. *The Australian Aborigines*. Canberra: Department of Territories, 1967.

Devaney, J. *The Vanished Tribes*. Sydney: Cornstalk, 1929.

Dilke, C.W. *Greater Britain: A Record of Travel in English-Speaking Countries During 1866 and 1867*. London: Macmillan, 1869.

Donaldson, R. and Joseph, M. *Wilderness*. Melbourne: Nelson, 1975.

Dorney, M. *An Adventurous Honeymoon: The First Motor Honeymoon Around Australia*. Brisbane: John Dorney, n.d. c. 1927.

Douglas, M. and Oldmeadow, D. *Across the Top and Other Places*. Adelaide: Rigby, 1978 (1972).

Dow, D.M. *Australia Advances*. New York: Funk & Wagnall, 1938.

Downer, S. *Patrol Indefinite: The Northern Territory Police Force*. Adelaide: Rigby, 1963.

Downie, J.C. *Galloping Hoofs: A Story of Australian Men and Horses*. London: Thomas Nelson, 1953 (1936).

Downie, J.M. *The Flying Doctor Mystery*. London: Frederick Warne & Co. Ltd, 1954.

Downie, J.M. *Mutiny in the Air*. London: Blackie, c. 1940.

Downie, J.M. *The Treasure of the Never-Never*. London: Blackie & Son Ltd, n.d. c. 1936.

Downie, J.M. *The Yellow Raiders*. London: The Children's Press, n.d.

Downing, Rev. J. *Ngurra Walytja, Country of my Spirit: A Study of the 'Outstation' or Homelands Movement*. Darwin: The Australian National University, North Australia Research Unit, 1988.

Drake-Brockman, H. *Men Without Wives: And Other Plays*. Sydney: Angus & Robertson, 1955.

Drysdale, I.A. *No More Walkabout: Stories from Arnhem Land and the West Coast of South Australia*. Ilfracombe, Devon: Stockwell, 1967.

Duguid, C. *Doctor and the Aborigines*. Adelaide: Rigby, 1972.

Duke, M. *The Secret People*. Leicester: Brockhampton, 1967.

Durack, M. and E. *Chunuma: Little-Bit-King*. Perth: Sampson, 1941.

Durack, M. and E. *Kookanoo and the Kookaburra*. Minneapolis, Minnesota: Lerner, 1966.

Durack, M. and E. *Piccaninnies*. [Perth, WA?]: (no publisher), n.d.

Durack, M. and E. *Son of Djaro*. Perth: Sampson, 1940.

Dyer, A. *Unarmed Combat*. Sydney: Church Missionary Society, n.d.

Earnshaw, E.H. *Eaglehawk: Chief of the Tribe of the Arunta*. Sydney: William Brooks, 1929.

Earnshaw, E.H. *Yarragongartha*. Sydney: published by the author, 1930.

Easterley, R. and Wilbraham, J. (Potter, Rev. R.) *The Germ Growers: An Australian Story of Adventure and Mystery*. Melbourne: Melville, Mullen & Slade, 1892.

Egan, T. *A Drop of Rough Ted*. Sydney: published by the author, 1979.

Egan, T. *Would I Lie To You: The Goanna Drover and Other Very True Stories*. Ringwood: Viking O'Neil, 1991.

Elkin, A.P. *The Australian Aborigines: How to Understand Them*. Sydney: Angus & Robertson, 1981 (1938).

Ellis, M.H. *The Long Lead*. London: T. Fisher Unwin, 1927.

Epstein, J. *When Tracy Came For Christmas*. Melbourne: Oxford University Press, 1982.

Ericksen, R. *West of Centre: A Journey of Discovery into the Heartland of Australia*. Ringwood: Penguin, 1973 (1972).

Ewers, J.K. *Tales From the Dead Heart*. Sydney: Currawong, 1944.

Favenc, E. *Marooned on Australia: Being the Narration by Diedrich Buys of his Discoveries and Exploits in Terra Australis Incognita*. London: Blackie, 1905 (1896).

Favenc, E. *The Secret of the Australian Desert*. London: Blackie, 1894.

Favenc, E. *Tales of the Austral Tropics*. London: Osgood, McIlvaine, 1894.

Favenc, E. *Voices of the Desert*. London: Elliot Stock, 1905.

Fellowship of Australian Writers. *Scribes in the Centre: A Collection of Writing by Members of the Fellowship of Australian Writers Centralia Branch*. Alice Springs: published by the authors, 1990.

Fenton, C. *Flying Doctor*. Melbourne: Georgian House, 1947.

Fiddian, J.R. *Robert Mitchell of the Inland*. Melbourne: Ramsay, 1931.

Finlay, E. *Journey of Freedom*. Sydney: Publishers Distributing, 1950.

Finlayson, H.H. *The Red Centre: Man and Beast in the Heart of Australia*. Sydney: Angus & Robertson, 1935.

Flinders, M. *A Voyage to Terra Australis,* vol. 2. London: G. & W. Nicol, 1814.

Flynn, F. *Distant Horizons: Mission Impressions*. Kensington: Annals of Our Lady of the Sacred Heart, 1951 (1947).

Flynn, F. *Northern Gateway*. Sydney: Devonshire, 1963.

Flynn, F. and Willey, K. *The Living Heart*. Sydney: F.P. Leonard, 1979 (1964).

Flynn, R.J. *Northern Territory and Central Australia: A Call to the Church*. Sydney: Angus & Robertson, 1912.

Foote, K.S. *Walkabout Down Under*. New York: Scribner, 1944.

Ford, M. *Beyond the Furthest Fences*. Adelaide: Rigby, 1978 (1966).

Foster, D. *Mates of Mars*. Ringwood: Penguin, 1991.

Fowler, D.H. *Guns or God: The Story of Caledon Bay Peace Expedition 1933–34*. Brighton: Lane, 1985.

Fox, A., Davis, S. and Neidjie, B. *Kakadu Man: Bill Neidjie,* New South Wales: Mybrood, 1985.

Fox, M. *Account of an Expedition to the Interior of New Holland*. London: Richard Bentley, 1837.

Frances, C. *The Big One*. New Zealand: Whitcombe & Tombs, 1963.

Francis, D. *In the Frame*. London: Michael Joseph, 1976.

Francis, G. (Browne, L.) *God's Best Country*. Sydney: Currency Press, 1987.

Gardner, M. *Blood Stained Wattle*. Pialba, Qld: published by the author, 1992.

Gee, L.C.E. *Bush Tracks and Gold Fields: Reminiscences of Australia's 'Back of Beyond'*. Adelaide: F.W. Preece & Sons, 1926.

George, E. *Two at Daly Waters*. Melbourne: Georgian House, 1945.

Gibbs, J. *A Bitch Called Tracy is Darwin Cyclone*. Sydney: Surveys and Market Research, 1975.

Glennon, J. *The Heart in the Centre*. Adelaide: Rigby, 1960.

Goldman, P. *To Hell and Gone*. London: Victor Gollancz, 1932.

Goldsworthy, P. *Maestro*. North Ryde, New South Wales: Angus & Robertson, 1989.

Goy, C. *A Man is his Friends*. Mitcham: Graphic Set, 1979.

Grace, H. *Heart of Light*. South Fremantle, Western Australia: Fremantle Arts Centre Press, 1992.

Grant, A. *Camel Train and Aeroplane: The Story of Skipper Partridge*. Dee Why, New South Wales: Frontier Publishing, 1989.

Grant, A. *Palmerston to Darwin: 75 Years Service on the Frontier*. Dee Why, New South Wales: Frontier Publishing, 1990.

Grant, M. *Inherit the Sun*. London: Hodder & Stoughton, 1981.

Graves, R.H. *Spear and Stockwhip: A Tale of the Territory*. Sydney: Dymock's Book Arcade, 1950.

Gray, W. *Days and Nights in the Bush*. Sydney: Robert Dey, 1935.

Green, E. *Alice to Nowhere*. Surrey Hills, New South Wales: James Fraser, 1984.

Green, E. *Journeys with Gelignite Jack*. Adelaide: Rigby, 1970 (1966).

Greenway, J. *Down Among the Wild Men: The Narrative Journal of Fifteen Years Pursuing the Old Stone Age Aborigines of Australia's Western Desert*. Richmond: Hutchinson, 1973.

Gregory, J.W. *The Menace of Colour: A Study of the Difficulties due to the Association of White and Coloured Races, With an Account of Measures Proposed For Their Solution, and Special Reference to White Colonization in the Tropics*. London: Seeley Service, 1925.

Grew, E. and Sharpe, M. *Rambles in Australia*. London: Mills & Boon, 1916.

Grey, Z. *Desert Gold: A Romance of the Border*. New York: Grosset & Dunlap, 1941 (1913).

Gribble, E.R. *Forty Years With the Aborigines*. Sydney: Angus & Robertson, 1930.

Griffiths, H. *An Australian Adventure*. Adelaide: Rigby, 1975.

Griffiths, O. *Dhidgerry Dhoo: A Tale Woven Around Fact*. Sydney: P&S Press, n.d. c. 1940s.

Griffiths, O. *Darwin Drama*. Sydney: Bloxham & Chambers, n.d. c. 1947.

Groom, A. *I Saw a Strange Land*. Sydney: Angus & Robertson, 1950.

Groom, A. *Wealth in the Wilderness*. Sydney: Angus & Robertson, 1955.

Gsell, F.X. *'The Bishop with 150 Wives': Fifty Years as a Missionary*. Sydney: Angus & Robertson, 1956.

Gunn, A. Mrs *The Little Black Princess of the Never-Never*. Sydney: Angus & Robertson, 1963 (1905).

Gunn, A. Mrs *The Little Black Princess of the Never-Never*. Melbourne: Robertson & Mullens, (adapted for use in schools), 1945 (1905).

Gunn, A. Mrs *We of the Never-Never*. Richmond, Victoria: Hutchinson, 1977 (1908).

Guy, R. *What's Rangoon To You is Grafton to Me*. North Ryde, New South Wales: Angus & Robertson, 1991.

Hall, H. *Our Back Yard: How to Make Northern Australia an Asset Instead of a Liability*. Sydney: Angus & Robertson, 1938.

Hall, T. *Darwin 1942: Australia's Darkest Hour.* Sydney: Methuen, 1980.

Hall, V.C. *Bad Medicine: A Tale of the Northern Territory.* Melbourne: Robertson & Mullens, 1947.

Hall, V.C. *Dreamtime Justice.* Adelaide: Rigby, 1962.

Hall, V.C. *Sister Ruth.* London: Neville Spearman, 1968.

Hall, V.C. *Outback Policeman.* Adelaide: Rigby, 1972 (1970).

Hamilton, M.L. *The Hidden Kingdom,* Melbourne: Wentworth-Evans, 1932.

Harcus, W. ed. *South Australia: Its History, Resources, and Productions.* Adelaide: W.C. Cox Govt Printer, 1876.

Hardy, F. *The Great Australia Lover and Other Stories.* Melbourne: Nelson, 1967.

Hardy, F. *The Loser Now Will Be Later To Win.* Carlton, Victoria: Pascoe, 1985.

Hardy, F. *The Unlucky Australians.* Adelaide: Rigby, 1976 (1968).

Harney, W.E. *A Bushman's Life: An Autobiography.* Lockwood, D. and R. eds, Ringwood: Viking O'Neil, 1990.

Harney, W.E. *Brimming Billabongs.* London: Hale, 1964 (1947).

Harney, W.E. *Content to Lie in the Sun.* Adelaide: Rigby, 1971 (1958).

Harney, W.E. *Life Among the Aborigines.* London: Hale, 1959 (1957).

Harney, W.E. *North of 23°: Ramblings in Northern Australia.* Sydney: Australasian, n.d. c. 1943.

Harney, W.E. *The Story of Ayers Rock.* Melbourne: Bread and Cheese Club, 1957.

Harney, W.E. *Taboo.* Sydney: Australasian, 1944 (1943).

Harney, W.E. *Tales from the Aborigines.* London: Hale, 1959.

Harney, W.E. and Elkin, A.P. *Songs of the Songmen.* Adelaide: Rigby, 1969 (1949).

Harney, W.E. and Lockwood, D. *The Shady Tree.* Adelaide: Rigby, 1972 (1963).

Harris, Capt. K. *'Kangaroo-Land': Glimpses of Australia.* Cleveland, Ohio: Kilroy Harris Traveltalks, 1926.

Harris, R. *Rolf Goes Bush.* Sydney: A.H. & A.W. Reed, 1975.

Hasluck, P. *Shades of Darkness: Aboriginal Affairs 1925–1965*. Melbourne: Melbourne University Press, 1988.

Hatfield, W. *Australia Through the Windscreen*. Sydney: Angus & Robertson, 1936.

Hatfield, W. *Black Waterlily*. Sydney: Angus & Robertson, 1935.

Hatfield, W. *Buffalo Jim*. London: Oxford University Press, 1938.

Hatfield, W. *Desert Saga*. Sydney: Angus & Robertson, 1933.

Hatfield, W. *I Find Australia*. London: Oxford University Press, 1939 (1937).

Hatfield, W. *Sheepmates*. Sydney: Angus & Robertson, 1931.

Healy, T.E.A. *And Far From Home*. London: Michael Joseph, 1936.

Henderson, S. *From Strength to Strength: An Autobiography*. Sydney: Pan Macmillan, 1992.

Henry, M. *Unlucky Dip*. London: Cassell, 1960.

Herbert, F.X. *Capricornia*. Sydney: The Publicist, 1938.

Herbert, F.X. *Larger than Life: Twenty Short Stories*. Sydney: Collins, 1981 (1963).

Herbert, F.X. *Poor Fellow My Country*. Sydney: Collins, 1975.

Herbert, F.X. *South of Capricornia: Short Stories 1925–1934 by Xavier Herbert*. McDougall, R. ed., Melbourne: Oxford University Press, 1990.

Herbert, F.X. *Xavier Herbert: Episodes From Capricornia, Poor Fellow My Country and Other Fiction, Nonfiction and Letters*. de Groen, F. & Pierce, P. eds, St Lucia: University of Queensland Press, 1992.

Hercus, L. and Sutton, P. *This is What Happened: Historical Narratives By Aborigines*. Canberra: Australian Institute for Aboriginal Studies, 1986.

Heslop, V. *The Lost Civilisation: A Story of Adventure in Central Australia*. Sydney: St George, 1936.

Hill, E. *About Lasseter*. Elizabeth, South Australia: Scrivener Press, 1968.

Hill, E. *Australia's Frontier*. Doran, New York: Doubleday, 1942 (American version of *The Great Australian Loneliness*).

Hill, E. *Flying Doctor Calling: Tlte Flying Doctor Service of Australia*. Sydney: Angus & Robertson in conjunction with the Flying Doctor Service, 1947.

Hill, E. *The Great Australian Loneliness*. Sydney: Angus & Robertson, 1991 (1937).

Hill, E. *The Territory*. Sydney: Angus & Robertson, 1951.

Hill, J.L. *Christ Church Cathedral*. Darwin: Graphic Systems Print, 1978.

Hodgkinson, F. *Kakadu and the Arnhem Lander*, Willoughby, New South Wales: Kevin Weldon, 1990 (1987).

Hogan, J.F. *The Lost Explorer: An Australian Story*. London: Ward & Downey, 1890.

Holtze, M.W. and Parsons, Hon. J.L. M.L.C. *The Northern Territory of South Australia*. Adelaide: W.K. Thomas, 1901.

Hooker, J. *The Bush Soldiers*. Sydney: Collins, 1984.

Hopkinson, S. *Buffaloes Can't Fly*. Montmorency, Victoria: Yackandandah Playscripts, 1981.

Howchin, W. *The Geography of South Australia Including the Northern Territory*. Melbourne: Whitcombe & Tombs, 1909.

Hunter, R.W. *The Innocent Savage*. Sydney: Horwitz, 1963 (1960).

Huxley, E. *Their Shining Eldorado: A Journey Through Australia*. London: Chatto & Windus, 1967.

Idriess, I.L. *The Cattle King*. Sydney: Angus & Robertson, 1980 (1936).

Idriess, I.L. *Challenge of the North: Wealth From Australia's Northern Shores*. Sydney: Angus & Robertson, 1969.

Idriess, I.L. *Flynn of the Inland*. Sydney: Angus & Robertson, 1990 (1932).

Idriess, I.L. *In Crocodile Land: Wandering in Northern Australia*. Sydney: Angus & Robertson, 1946.

Idriess, I.L. *Lasseter's Last Ride: An Epic in Central Australian Gold Discovery*. Sydney: Angus & Robertson, 1980 (1931).

Idriess, I.L. *Man Tracks*. Sydney: Angus & Robertson, 1935.

Idriess, I.L. *Nemarluk: King of the Wilds*. Sydney: Angus & Robertson, 1958 (1941).

Idriess, I.L. *Our Living Stone Age*. Sydney: Angus & Robertson, 1963.

Idriess, I.L. Our *Stone Age Mystery*. Sydney: Angus & Robertson, 1964.

Idriess, I.L. *Tracks of Destiny*. Sydney: Angus & Robertson, 1961.

Idriess, I.L. *The Vanished People*. Sydney: Angus & Robertson, 1955.

Iggulden, J. *Dark Stranger*. London: Macdonald, 1965.

Ingamells, R. *Aranda Boy: An Aboriginal Story*. Melbourne: Longmans Green, 1952.

James, H.C: *Gold Is Where You Find It*. London: Harrap, 1949.

Johns, Capt. W.E. *Biggles in Australia*. London: Hodder & Stoughton, 1955.

Johns, Capt. W.E. *Biggles Works it Out*. London: Hodder & Stoughton, 1951.

Johnson, D. *The Jewel Box*. Springwood, New South Wales: Butterfly Books, 1990.

Joliffe, E. *Witchetty's Tribe: Aboriginal Cartoon Fun No 35*. Sydney: Pix, n.d. c. 1966.

Joynt, R.D. *Ten Years' Work at the Roper River Mission Station Northern Territory Australia*. Melbourne: Church Missionary Society, Victorian Branch, 1918.

Kelly, J.H. *Struggle for the North*. Sydney: Australasian Book Society, 1966.

Keneally, T. *Flying Hero Class*. London: Hodder & Stoughton, 1991.

Keneally, T. *Outback*. London: Hodder & Stoughton, 1984.

Keneally, T. *Towards Asmara*. London: Hodder & Stoughton, 1989.

Keneally, T., Adam-Smith, P. and Davidson, R. *Australia Beyond the Dreamtime*. Richmond, Victoria: William Heinemann Australia, 1987.

Kettle, E. *Gone Bush*. Sydney: F.P. Leonard, 1967.

King, P.P. *Narrative of a Survey of the Intertropical and Western Coasts of Australia*. vol. 1., London: John Murray, 1827.

Kirmess, C.H. *The Australian Crisis*. London: Walter Scott, 1909.

Knight, J.G. *The Northern Territory of South Australia*. Adelaide: E. Spiller Government Printer, 1880.

Knudsen, P.A. *The Bloodwood Tree*. London: Frederick Muller, 1962.

Kyle-Little, S. *Whispering Wind: Adventures in Arnhem Land*. London: Hutchinson & Co., 1957.

Lamilami, L. *Lamilami Speaks, the Cry Went Up: A Story of the People of Goulburn Islands, North Australia*. Sydney: Ure Smith, 1974.

Langford, R. *Don't Take Your Love to Town*. Ringwood: Penguin, 1988.

Langford Smith, K. *Sky Pilot in Arnhem Land*. Sydney: Angus & Robertson, 1935.

Langford Smith, K. *Sky Pilot's Last Flight*. Sydney: Angus & Robertson, 1936.

Langford Smith, K. *Sky Pilot's Log: Drake's Drum and Other Stories*. Sydney: Christian Press, 1951.

Lee, R. Mrs *Adventures in Australia; or, the Wanderings of Captain Spencer in the Bush and the Wilds*. London: Grant & Griffith, 1851.

Leichhardt, F.W.L. *Journal of an Overland Expedition in Australia from Moreton Bay to Port Essington*. London: T. & W. Boone, 1847.

Leske, E. ed. *Hennannsburg: A Vision and a Mission*. Adelaide: Lutheran Publishing House, 1977.

Lewis, J. *Fought and Won*. Adelaide: W.K. Thomas, 1922.

Lewis, T. *Darwin Sayonara*. Brisbane: Boolarong, 1991.

Leyland, M. and M. *Where Dead Men Lie*. Melbourne: Lansdown, 1968 (1967).

Lindall, E. *Death and the Maiden*. London: Constable, 1973.

Lindall, E. *A Gathering of Eagles*. Sydney: Collins, 1970.

Lindall, E. *The Killers of Karawala*. New York: William Morrow, 1962.

Lindall, E. *The Last Refuge*. Melboume: Gold Star, 1972.

Lindall, E. *A Lively Form of Death*. London: Constable, 1972.

Lindall, E. *Northward the Coast*. London: Heinemann, 1966.

Linklater, H.T. *Echoes of the Elsey Saga: A Research of Pioneer of the Northern Territory in the Epochal Days of the Elsey Station*. Chipping Norton, New South Wales: Surrey Beatty & Sons, 1981 (1980).

Linklater, H.T. and Tapp, L. *Gather No Moss*. South Melbourne: MacMillan, 1968.

Linn, R. *Nature's Pilgrim*. Netly: South Australian Government Printer, 1989.

Litchfield, J. *Far North Memories: Being the Account of Ten Years Spent on the Diamond-Drills, and of Things that Happened in those Days*. Sydney: Angus & Robertson, 1930.

Locke-Elliott, S. *Rusty Bugles*. Sydney: Currency Press, 1980 (University of Queensland Press, 1968).

Lockwood, D. *Australia's Pearl Harbour*. Adelaide: Rigby, 1975.

Lockwood, D. *Crocodiles and Other People*. Adelaide: Rigby, 1966 (1959).

Lockwood, D. *Fair Dinkum*. London: Cassell, 1960.

Lockwood, D. *The Front Door: Darwin 1869–1969*. Adelaide: Rigby, 1968.

Lockwood, D. *I, the Aboriginal*. Adelaide: Rigby, 1962.

Lockwood, D. *The Lizard Eaters*. Melbourne: Cassell, 1964.

Lockwood, D. *Up the Track*. London: Readers Book Club, 1964.

Lockwood, D. *We, the Aborigines*. Melbourne: Cassell, 1963.

Logan, J. *Northmost Australia,* London: Simpken, Marshall, Hamilton, Kent & Co., 1921, vol. 2.

Long, D.F. *Among the Australian Blacks: A Fifteen Year Old Victorian Girl's Stirring Adventures in Arnhem Land, Roper River, Groote Island and Central Australia*. Melbourne: no publishing details, n.d. c. 1935.

Lurie, M. *Inside the Wardrobe*. Fitzroy: Outback Press, 1975.

Macartney, F.T. *Hard Light and Other Verses*. Surrey Hills, Victoria: Galleon, n.d.

Macartney, F.T. *Proof Against Failure*. Sydney: Angus & Robertson, 1967.

Macdonald, A. *The Lost Explorers: A Story of the Trackless Desert*. London: Blackie, n.d. [1906].

Macdonald, A. *The Mystery of Diamond Creek*. London: Blackie, n.d. c. 1930.

MacIntyre, J.N. *White Australia: The Empty North the Reasons and Remedy*. Sydney: Penfold, 1920.

Mackay, H. *Frontiers North by North West*. Sydney: Assembly Communications Uniting Church, 1987.

MacPherson, B. and J. *The Magic Boomerang*. Sydney: Young Australian, 1963.

Madigan, C.T. *Central Australia*. Melbourne: Oxford University Press, 1944 (1936).

Madigan, C.T. *Crossing the Dead Heart*. Adelaide: Rigby, 1974 (1946).

Makin, J. *The Big Run: The Story of Victoria River Downs Station*. Adelaide: Rigby, 1983 (1970).

Malvern, P. *Secret Gold: A Story of Two Boys Who Found Wealth In the Heart of the Australian Desert*. London: Sheldon, n.d.

Marshall, A. *People of the Dreamtime*. Melbourne: Hyland House, 1978 (1952).

Marshall, A. *These Were My Tribesmen*. Adelaide: Rigby, 1976 (orig. *Ourselves Writ Strange,* 1948).

Marshall, A. and Bozic, S. *Aboriginal Myths*. Melbourne: Gold Star, 1972.

Marshall, J.V. *The Children*. London: Michael Joseph, 1959.

Marshall, J.V. *A Walk to the Hills of the Dreamtime*. New York: William Morrow, 1970.

Marshall, V. *We Helped to Blaze the Track*. Townsville: published by the author, 1980.

Marshall-Stoneking, B. *Lasseter: The Making of a Legend*. Sydney: Allen & Unwin, 1985.

Marshall-Stoneking, B. *Singing the Snake: Poems from the Western Desert 1979–1988*. North Ryde, New South Wales: Angus & Robertson, 1990.

Marshall-Stoneking, B. *Sixteen Words For Water*. North Ryde, New South Wales: Angus & Robertson, 1991.

Martin, C.E.M. *The Incredible Journey*. London: Jonathan Cape, 1923.

Masson, E. *An Untamed Territory*. London: Macmillan, 1915.

McDonald, S. *Ungamillia (The Evening Star): A Romance With a Central Australian Background*. Sydney: Deaton & Spencer, 1933.

McGahan, A. *1988*. Sydney: Allen & Unwin, 1995.

McGinness, J. *Son of Alyandabu: My Fight for Aboriginal Rights*. St. Lucia: University of Queensland Press, 1991.

McGuire, P. *Westward the Course: The New World of Oceania*. Melbourne: Oxford University Press, 1946 (1942).

McKenzie, M. *Flynn's Last Camp*. Brisbane: Boolarong, 1985.

McKenzie, M. *Mission to Arnhem Land*. Adelaide: Rigby, 1976.

McLeod, F.J. *Womba: An Aboriginal Stockboy in the Cattle Country in the Heart of Australia*. Melbourne: Georgian House, 1951.

McMillan, A. *Strict Rules*. Sydney: Hodder & Stoughton, 1988.

McNab, C. *Death Down Under*. North Sydney: Allen & Unwin, 1990.

McPheat, W.S. *Flynn: Vision of the Inland*. Sydney: Hodder & Stoughton, 1977 (originally *Flynn: Apostle to the Inland*, Australian Inland Mission, 1963).

Meaney, E. *Esther: The True Story of An Australian Country Girl*. Batchelor, Northern Territory: Esther Meaney, 1988 (1987).

Milford, R.H. *Australia's Backyards*. Sydney: Macquarie Head, 1934.

Miller, J. *The Lost Reef*. London: Oxford University Press, n.d. c. 1930s.

Miller, K. *Call For the Flying Doctor*. Sydney: Horwitz, 1962.

Miller, K. *Flying Doctor Disappears*. Sydney: Horwitz, 1963.

Miller, K. *Flying Doctor Urgent*. Sydney: Horwitz, 1963.

Mirritji, J. *My People's Life: An Aboriginal's Own Story*. Milingimbi: Milingimbi Literature Centre, 1976.

Mitchell, K. *Doctor in Darwin*. Sydney: Horwitz, 1960.

Moffitt, I. *Death Adder Dreaming*. Sydney: Pan, 1988.

Moon, K. *The Fire Serpent Mystery*. London: Ernest Benn, 1963.

Moorehead, A. *Rum Jungle*. London: Hamish Hamilton, 1953.

Morgan, G. *Promise of Rain*. London: Virago, 1985.

Mountford, C.P. *Ayers Rock: Its People, Their Beliefs and Their Art*. Adelaide: Rigby, 1981 (1965).

Mountford, C.P. *Before Time Began*. West Melbourne: Nelson, 1976.

Mountford, C.P. *Brown Men and Red Sand*. Melbourne: Sun Books, 1967 (1948).

Mountford, C.P. *Nomads of the Australian Desert*. Adelaide: Rigby, 1976.

Mudie, I. *The Blue Crane*. Sydney: Angus & Robertson, 1959.

Murray-Smith, S. ed. *An Overland Muster: Selections from Overland, 1954–1964*. Brisbane: Jacaranda, 1965.

Napier, F. *Notes of a Voyage From New South Wales to the North Coast of Australia From the Journal of the Late Francis Napier* [Glasgow, 1876].

Needham, J.S. *White and Black in Australia*. London: Society for Promoting Christian Knowledge, 1935.

Neidjie, B. *Story About Feeling*. Taylor, K. ed., Broome: Magabala, 1989.

Nolan, C. *Outback*. London: Methuen, 1962.

Northern Territory Writers Publishing Group. *Life Beyond the Louvres: A Collection of Contemporary Northern Territory Writing*. Darwin: Northern Territory Writers Publishing Group, 1989.

Nowra, L. *Capricornia*. Sydney: Current Theatre Series, 1988.

Nowra, L. *Capricornia: From the Novel by Xavier Herbert*. Revised edition. Sydney: Currency, 1992.

O'Grady, F. *Francis of Central Australia*. Sydney: Wentworth Books, 1977.

O'Hagan, J. *Against the Grain*. London: Macmillan, 1987.

O'Harris, P. *Goolara*. Sydney: Currawong, n.d. c. 1943.

Owen, Rev. J.E. *A Visitor's Diary Ernabella Patrol 1943*. no place given: Presbyterian Church of Australia, Board of Missions, 1943.

Page, M. *A Nasty Little War*. Adelaide: Rigby, 1979.

Parer, J.J. *The Northern Territory: Its History and Great Possibilities*. Melbourne: J.J. Parer, 1922.

Parsons, H.A. *The Truth About the Northern Territory: An Enquiry*. Adelaide: Hussey & Gillingham, 1907.

Patchett, M.E. *Brit*. London: Hodder & Stoughton, 1961.

Patchett, M.E. *Festival of Jewels*. Leicester: Brockhampton, 1968.

Patchett, M.E. *The Venus Project*. Leicester: Brockhampton, 1963.

Paterson, A.B. *An Outback Marriage*. Sydney: Angus & Robertson, 1906.

Patrick, J. *Inapatua*. Melbourne: Cassell, 1966.

Perkins, C. *A Bastard Like Me*. Sydney: Ure Smith, 1975.

Perry, R. *Blood is a Stranger*. Richmond, Victoria: William Heinemann, 1988.

Petherick, A.W. *Men on the Frontier: A Brief History of the Federal Methodist Inland Mission*. Melbourne: Methodist Publishing House, 1970.

Pike, G. *Darwin Northern Territory: Australia's Northern Gateway*. Darwin: Pike, 1956.

Pike, G. *Early Attempts at Settlement in the Northern Territory*. Brisbane: Royal Historical Society of Queensland, 1960.

Pike, G. *Frontier Territory*. Darwin: Adventure Publishing, 1988.

Pike, G. *Northern Territory Overland Telegraph*. Brisbane: Royal Historical Society of Queensland, 1970.

Pike, G. *An Untamed Land: An Historical Novel Set in the Exciting Pioneering Days of North Australia*. Darwin: Glenville Pike, 1974.

Platt, L.B. *Survival 3*. Brisbane: Unabridged Pilot-Run Platt, 1979 [serialised *Melbourne Herald* 1965).

Plowman, R.B. *Camel Pads*. Sydney: Angus & Robertson, 1935.

Plowman, R.B. *Larapinta*. Sydney: Angus & Robertson, 1939.

Plowman, R.B. *The Man From Oodnadatta*. Sydney: Angus & Robertson, 1933.

Poignant, A. *Piccaninny Walkabout: A Story of Two Aboriginal Children*. Sydney: Angus & Robertson, 1961 (1957).

Polishuk, N. and Lockwood, D. *Life on the Daly River*. London: The Adventurers Club, 1963 (1961).

Porter, J.D. *Our Fertile North: 'Porter's Mob' Through, the N.T.* Melbourne: National, n.d. [1944].

Power, P.M. *Adventure in the Outback*. London: Dent, 1957.

Power, P.M. *Lost in the Outback*. London: Blackie, n.d.

Power, P.M. *Nursing in the Outback*. London: Blackie, 1959.

Power, P.M. *Under Australian Skies*. London: Peal, n.d.

Price, A.G. *The History and Problems of the Northern Territory, Australia*. Adelaide: A.E. Acott, 1930.

Price, A.G. *White Settlers and Native People*. Melbourne: Georgian House, 1950.

Price, A.G. *White Settlers in the Tropics*. New York: American Geographical Society, 1939.

Price, T. *God in the Sand*. Sydney: P.R. Stephenson, 1934.

Pye, Rev. J. *The Daly River Story*. Darwin: Catholic Missions, n.d.

Pye, Bro. J. *The Port Keats Story*. Darwin: n.d.

Pye, Rev. J. *The Tiwi Islands*. Darwin: Catholic Missions, n.d.

Ranken, T. *Fire Over Australia*. Sydney: Angus & Robertson, 1938.

Read, P. ed. *A Social History of the Northern Territory*. a series of nine, Darwin: NT Education Department, 1978.

Read, P. and Read, J. eds. *Long Time, Olden Time: Aboriginal Accounts of Northern Territory History*. Alice Springs: Institute for Aboriginal Development, 1991.

Rees, C. and L. *Australia: The Big Sky Country*. Sydney: Ure Smith, 1971 *(People of the Big Sky Country* 1970).

Rees, C. and L. *Spinifex Walknbout: Hitch-Hiking in Remote North Australia*. Sydney: Australasian, 1953.

Rees, L. *Panic in the Cattle Country*. Adelaide: Rigby, 1974.

Reid, A. *Adventures Around Australia*. Hobart: published by the author, n.d. c. 1958.

Ritchie, P.H. *North of the Never-Never*. Sydney: Angus & Robertson, 1934.

Robinson, R. *Aboriginal Myths and Legends*. Melbourne: Sun Books, 1968 (1966).

Robinson, R. *Deep Well*. Sydney: Edwards & Shaw, 1962.

Robinson, R. *The Drift of Things: An Autobiography 1914–52*. South Melbourne: Macmillan, 1973.

Robinson, R. *The Feathered Serpent: The Mythological Genesis and Recreative Ritual of the Aboriginal Tribes of the Northern Territory of Australia; the Kuppapoingo, Jumbapoingo, Birrikillli, Miarr-Miarr and Leagulawulmirree tribes at Milingimbi; and Murinbata and Djamunjun tribes of Port Keats; and Djauan and Ngalarkan Tribes At Roper River; and the Arranda, Luritja and Pitjantjara Tribes of the Centre; Chanted and Translated By the Old-Men of These Tribes to Roland Robinson*. Sydney: Edwards & Shaw, 1956.

Robinson, R. *Legend and Dreaming: Legends of the Dream-time of the Australian Aborigines as related to Roland Robinson by men of the Djauan, Rimberunga, Mungarai-Ngalarkan and Yungmun tribes of Arnhem Land*. Sydney: Edwards & Shaw, 1967 (1952).

Robinson, R. *Wandjina Children of the Dreamtime: Aboriginal Myths and Legends Selected by Roland Robinson*. Milton: Jacaranda, 1968.

Roland, B. *Beyond Capricorn*. London: Collins, 1976.

Ronan, T. *Deep of the Sky: An Essay in Ancestor Worship*. London: Cassell, 1962.

Ronan, T. *The Mighty Men On Horseback: Sketches and Yarns*. Adelaide: Rigby, 1977.

Ronan, T. *Once There Was a Bagman*. Melbourne: Cassell, 1966.

Ronan, T. *Vision Splendid*. South Yarra: Currey O'Neil, 1981 (Cassell, 1954).

Rose, D.B. *Dingo Makes Us Human: Life and Land in an Aboriginal Australian Culture*. Melbourne: Cambridge University Press, 1991.

Rose, D.B. *Hidden Histories: Black Stories From Victoria River Downs, Humbert River and Wave Hill Stations*. Canberra: Aboriginal Studies Press, 1991.

Rose, L. *Country of the Dead*. Sydney: Angus & Robertson, 1959.

Rossiter, J.L. *Notes on 'We of the Never-Never' and 'The Little Black Princess'*. Sydney: Philip, 1922.

Rowan, C.C. *The Silver Boomerang*. Melbourne: Peter Burchardt, 1978.

Ruhen, O. *Corcoran's the Name*. Sydney: Angus & Robertson, 1967 (1956).

Ruhen, O. *Naked Under Capricorn*. North Ryde, New South Wales: Angus & Robertson, 1989 (1958).

Russell, A. *The Caves of Barakee*. London: The Boy's Own Paper, 1936.

Russell, A. *A Tramp-Royal in Wild Australia: 1928–1929: Being the Record of a 'Walkabout' among the lone Cattlemen and Cameleers of Australia's Vast and Little-Known Central Wonderland, Together With Notes on the Aboriginal, the Physical Features, and the Fauna and Flora of the Desert Home. Done in the Vagabond Spirit Under the Urge to Adventure, and With the Will to See the Country as it is*. London: Jonathan Cape, 1934.

Salter, L. and Wirf, W. with Nichols, S. and Williams, M. *In Silence I Hear: Short Stories About Deafness*. Darwin: Deafness Association of the Northern Territory, 1991.

Sampson, R.S. *Through Central Australia*. Perth: Sampson Brokensha, 1933.

Sayce, C. *Comboman: A Tale of Central Australia*. London: Hutchinson, n.d. c. 1934.

Sayce, C. *Golden Buckles*. Melbourne: McCubbin, 1920.

Sayce, C. *The Golden Valley*. London: Blackie, n.d. c. 1924.

Sayce, C. (Jim Bushman) *In the Musgrave Ranges*. London: Blackie, n.d. c. 1922.

Sayce, C. *The Splendid Savage: A Tale of the North Coast of Australia*. London: Thomas Nelson & Sons, n.d. c.1925.

Sayce, C. (Jim Bushman) *The Valley of a Thousand Deaths*. London: Blackie, n.d. c. 1925.

Sayle, A. *The Last Frontier*. London: Century Hutchinson, 1986.

Scanlon, T. ed. *Arafura: Sixteen of the Best Stories from the Northern Territory Literary Awards*. Darwin: Darwin Institute of Technology Press, 1986.

Scanlon, T. ed. *Rain at Gunn Point: Poems of Tony Scanlon*. Armidale: Kardoorair Press, 1990.

Scherer, P.A. *From Joiner's Bench to Pulpit*. Adelaide: Lutheran Publishing House, 1973.

Scherer, P.A. *Venture of Faith: An Epic in Australian Missionary History*. Adelaide: Lutheran Publishing House, 1975 (1963).

Searcy, A. *In Australian Tropics: Fourteen year Sub-Collector of Customs at Port Darwin. Northern Territory, and now Clerk Assistant of House of Assembly*. London: Kegan Paul, Trench, Trubner, 1907.

Searcy, A. *By Flood and Field: Adventures Ashore and Afloat in North Australia*. London: G. Bell & Sons, 1912.

Sharpe, M. *The Traeger Kid*. Chippendale, New South Wales: Alternative Publishing Cooperative, 1985 (1983).

Shea, H.C. *Notes on Mrs Gunn's We of the Never-Never*. Brisbane: H.C. Shea, n.d.

Shears, R. *Azaria*. Melbourne: Sphere / Thomas Nelson, 1982.

Shepherdson, E. *Half a Century in Arnhem Land*. One Tree Hill, South Australia: E. & H. Shepherdson, 1981.

Shute, N. *In the Wet*. London: The Book Club, 1954.

Shute, N. *A Town Like Alice*. London: Pan, 1961 (1950).

Simpson, C. *Adam in Ochre: Inside Aboriginal Australia*. Sydney: Angus & Robertson, 1956 (1951).

Small, M. *Broome Dog*. Glebe, New South Wales: Walter McVitty, 1989.

Smith, P. McD. *The Strenuous Saint: Being An Account of the Longest Journey of William Magney Wilkinson Mission Priest of the Diocese of Carpentaria 1909–1918*. Adelaide: Diocese of Carpentaria, 1947.

Sowden, W.J. *The Northern Territory As it Is: A Narrative of the South Australian Parliamentary Party's Trip, and Full Descriptions of the Northern Territory; its Settlements and Industries*. Facsimile edition, Darwin: History Unit, University Planning Authority, n.d. (Adelaide: W.K. Thomas & Co, 1882).

Spencer, W.B. and Gillen F.J. *The Native Tribes of Central Australia*. New York: Dover, 1968 (1899).

Spencer, W.B. *Wanderings in Wild Australia*. 2 vols, London: Macmillan, 1928.

Spicer, R. *Catchpole*. Forest Hill, Victoria: Animo, 1989.

Spillett, P. *Christ Church Darwin. Northern Territory*. Darwin: Christ Church Rectory, 1960.

Spillett, P. *The Discovery of the Relics of H.M. Colonial Brig Lady Nelson and the Schooner Stedcombe*. Darwin: Historical Society of the Northern Territory, 1982.

Spillett, P. *Forsaken Settlement: An Illustrated History of the Settlement of Victoria, Port Essington North Australia 1838–1849*. Melbourne: Lansdowne, 1972.

Spunner, S. *Dragged Screaming to Paradise*. Darwin: published by the author, 1990.

Stapleton, A. *Lasseter Did Not Lie*. Hawthorndene, South Australia: Investigator, 1981.

S[tevens], H.W.H. *Reminiscences of a Hard Case*. Singapore: Lithographers, 1937.

Stewart, I. *An H-Bomb for Alice*. Feltham, Middlesex: Hamlyn, 1981.

Stewart, I. *Reunion*. Sydney: Gordian, 1988.

Stokes, J.L. *Discoveries in Australia: With An Account of the Coasts and Rivers Explored and Surveyed During the Voyage of H.M.S. Beagle, In the Years 1837–38–39–40–41–42–43 by Command of the Lord Commissioners of the Admiralty. Also A Narrative of Captain Owen Stanley's Visits to the Islands in the Arafura Sea*. vol. 1. Facsimile edition, Adelaide: Libraries Board of South Australia, 1969 (London: T. & W. Boone, 1846).

Stow, J.P. *The Voyage of the Forlorn Hope From Escape Cliffs to Champion Bay 1865: With the Author's Account of the First Northern Territory Settlement and of the Condition of Western Australia*. Reprinted Adelaide: Sullivan's Cove, 1981.

Strang, H. *The Air Scout: A Story of National Defence*. London: Henry Frowde, Hodder & Stoughton, 1912.

Strehlow, T.G.H. *Journey to Horseshoe Bend*. Sydney: Angus & Robertson, 1969.

Strehlow, T.G.H. *Songs of Central Australia*. Sydney: Angus & Robertson, 1971.

Stretton, A. *The Furious Days: The Relief of Darwin*. Sydney: Collins, 1976.

Stringer, C. *A Gaucho Down Under: The Exciting, True Story of Henry Gayoso, a Real Life 'Buffalo Bill' Who Came From the Wilds of South America's Jungles to Shoot Buffalo, Crocodile, Wild Horses and Donkeys in the Top End of Australia*. Casuarina: Adventure, 1990.

Stringer, C. *High Adventure with Jesus*. Tulsa, Oklahoma: Harrison House, 1980.

Stringer, C. ed. *The Saga of Sweetheart*. Casuarina: Adventure, 1986.

Sunter, G.H. *Adventures of a Trepang Fisher: A Record Without Romance Being a True Account of Trepang Fishing on the Coast of Northern Australia; and Adventures Met in the Course of the Same*. London: Hurst & Blackett, 1937.

Terry, M. *Across Unknown Australia*. London: Herbert Jenkins, 1925.

Terry, M. *Hidden Wealth and Hiding People*. London & New York: Putnam, n.d. c. 1941.

Terry, M. *The Last Explorer: The Autobiography of Michael Terry, FRGS, FRGSA*. Barnyard, C., comp. Canberra: Australian National University Press in association with North Australian Research Unit, 1987.

Terry, M. *Sand and Sun: Two Gold Hunting Expeditions With Camel in the Dry Lands of Central Australia*. London: Michael Joseph, 1937.

Terry, M. *Through a Land of Promise: With Gun, Car and Camera in the Heart of Northern Australia*. London: Herbert Jenkins, 1927.

Terry, M. *Untold Miles: Three Gold-Hunting Expeditions Amongst the Picturesque Border-Land Ranges of Central Aust ralia*. London: Selwyn & Blount, n.d. c. 1932.

Terry, M. *War of the Warra mullas*. Adelaide: Rigby, 1974.

Thiele, C. *Adventure in Australia's Far North Ranger's Territory: The Story of Frank Woerle as Told to Colin Thiele*. Sydney: Angus & Robertson, 1987.

Thiele, C. *Ballander Boy*. Adelaide: Rigby, 1979.

Thomas, N.W. *Natives of Australia*. London: Archibald Constable, 1906.

Thonemann, H.E. *Tell the White Man: The Life Story of an Aboriginal Lubra*. Sydney: Collins, 1949.

Timms, E.V. *The Valley of Adventure: A Story for Boys*. Sydney: Angus & Robertson, 1948 (1926).

Tindale, N.B. and Lindsay, H.A. *The First Walkabout*. Melbourne: Longmans Green, 1954.

Trollope, A. *Australia*. Edwards, P.O. and Joyce, R.B. eds, St Lucia: University of Queensland Press, 1967 (orig. *Australia and New Zealand*. Chapman & Hull, 1873).

Upfield, A. *No Footprints in the Dust*. Harmondsworth, Middlesex: Penguin, 1949 (1940).

Upton, S. *Australia's Empty Spaces*. London: George Allen & Unwin, 1938.

Vodicka, M. *Track to Rum Jungle*. Ilfracombe, Devon: Stockwell, 1970.

Walker, J. *No Sunlight Singing*. London: Hutchinson, 1960.

Walker, L. *The Man from Outback*. London: Collins, 1974 (1964).

Walker, L. *Master of Ransome: A Romance*. London: Collins, 1974 (1958).

Walker, W.S. *The Silver Queen: A Tale of the Northern Territory*. London: Ouseley, 1909.

Wand, J.W.C. *White of Carpentaria*. London: Skiffington & Son, n.d.

Warburton, C. *Buffaloes: Life and Adventure in Arnhem Land*. Sydney: Angus & Robertson, 1934.

Warburton, C. *White Poppies*. Sydney: Angus & Robertson, 1937.

Ward, P. *Azaria! What the Jury Were Not Told*. Epping, New South Wales: P.C.W., 1984.

Watkins, N. *The Kangaroo Connection*. Rabaul, New Guinea: Camwat, 1980.

Watkins, W. *Sun, Sand and Blood*. Melbourne: Gold Star, 1972, (originally published as *Soliloquy in the Simpson*).

Webb, G. *The Numunwari*. Melbourne: Fontana, 1980.

Webb, TT. *Spears to Spades*. Sydney: Department of Overseas Missions, 1938.

Wells, A.E. *Forests are Their Temples*. Hobart: Piglet, 1979.

Wells, A.E. *Men of the Honey Bee*. Adelaide: Rigby, 1971.

Wells, A.E. *Milingimbi: Ten Years in the Crocodile Islands of Arnhem Land*. Sydney: Angus & Robertson, 1963 (also as *Life in the Crocodile Islands*. Adelaide: Rigby, 1976).

Wells, A.E. *Rain in Arnhem Land*. Sydney: Angus & Robertson, 1961.

Wells, A.E. *Skies of Arnhem Land*. Sydney: Angus & Robertson, 1964.

Wells, A.E. *Tales from Arnhem Land*. Sydney: Angus & Robertson, 1959.

Wells, E. *Reward and Punishment in Arnhem Land 1962–1963*. Canberra: Australian Institute of Aboriginal Studies, 1982.

West, M. *The Naked Country*. London: New English Library, 1970 (1960).

White, G. *Round About the Torres Straits*. London: Society for Promoting Christian Knowledge, 1925.

White, G. *Thirty Years in Tropical Australia*. London: Society for Promoting Christian Knowledge, 1924.

White, I., Barwick, D. and Meehan, B. *Fighters and Singers: The Lives of Some Aboriginal Women*. Sydney: George Allen & Unwin, 1985.

Wildey, W.B. *Australasia and the Oceanic Region With Some Notes of New Guinea From Adelaide—Via Torres Straits—to Port Darwin Thence Round West Australia*. Melbourne: George Robertson, 1876.

Wilkins, G.H. *Undiscovered Au tralia: Being an Account of an Expedition to Tropical Australia to Collect Specimens of the Rarer Native Fauna for the British Museum, 1923–1925*. London: Ernest Benn, 1928.

Willey, K. *Boss Drover*. Adelaide: Rigby, 1971.

Willey, K. *Crocodile Hunt*. Adelaide: Rigby, 1977 (1966).

Willey, K. *The Drovers*. Sydney: Macmillan, 1982.

Willey, K. *Ghosts of the Big Country*. Adelaide: Rigby, 1975.

Willey, K. *Joe Brown's Dog, Bluey*. Adelaide: Rigby, 1978.

Willey, K. *Tales of the Big Country*. Adelaide: Rigby, 1972.

Willey, K. and Smith, R. *The Red Centre*. Melbourne: Lansdowne, 1967.

Willmot, E. *Below the Line*. Sydney: Hutchinson, 1991.

Willshire, W.C. *The Land of the Dawning: Being Facts Gleaned from Cannibals in the Australian Stone Age*. Adelaide: W.K. Thomas, 1896.

Willshire, W.C. *A Thrilling Tale of Real Life in the Wilds of Australia*. Adelaide: Freason & Brother, 1895.

Wilson, E. *Churinga Tales: Stories of Alchuringa—the Dream-time of the Australian Aborigines*. Sydney: Australasian, 1950.

Wisberg, A. and Waters, H. *Bushman At Large*. New York: Green Circle, 1937.

Wongar, B. *Bnbaru: Stories by B. Wongar*. Urbana: University of Illinois Press, 1982.

Wongar, B. *Gabo Djara*. South Melbourne: Macmillan, 1988.

Wongar, B. *Karan*. South Melbourne: Macmillan, 1986.

Wongar, B. *The Track to Bralgu*. Boston: Little, Brown, 1978.

Wongar, B. *The Trackers: A Novel by B. Wongar*. Collingwood: Outback Press, 1975.

Wongar, B. *Walg: A Novel of Australia*. New York: Dodd, Mead, 1983.

Wood, C. *Dead Centre*. London: Michael Joseph, 1980.

Woodberry, J. *Come Back Peter*. Adelaide: Rigby, 1969 (1968).

Wrightson, P. *The Book of Wirrun: The Ice is Coming*. Ringwood: Penguin, 1983 (1977).

Yamamoto, M. *Betty-san*. Harcourt, G., trans., New York: Kodansha International, 1983.

Young, D.H. *A White Australia: Is it Possible? The Problem of the Empty North*. Melbourne: Robertson & Mullen, 1922.

Young, M. with Dalton, G. *No Place For a Woman: The Autobiography of Outback Publican, Mayse Young*. Chippendale, New South Wales: Pan Macmillan, 1991.

# Mickey Dewar: Memories, books and museums

David Carment

Mickey Dewar's contributions to the history of her beloved Northern Territory were immense. She was an elegant and original writer, a careful researcher with a knack for discovering elusive sources, the energetic member of numerous heritage and history boards and committees, a mentor for other historians and history students, an interesting and always thoroughly prepared school and tertiary teacher, a much sought after public speaker, the Territory's most innovative history curator and an always helpful librarian. She was also sparkling company and probably the most rapid reader I have ever known. Like many others, I learned a lot from her. I do not in this paper attempt to cover all the numerous aspects of her life as a historian. Instead, I recount some of my own memories of Mickey before discussing examples of her sole-authored books and curatorial work.

## Memories

I first met Mickey in Darwin during 1984. I was on the Northern Territory Literary Awards committee and she was a prize winner in the short story section. Her entry was a beautifully composed and very funny account of schoolteachers in Arnhem Land. She commented to me at the prize-giving ceremony that she was also a historian and was writing a Master's thesis at the University of New England about missionary contact with the Yolngu people of north-east Arnhem Land.[1] A version of it was later

---

1 Dewar, 'Strange Bedfellows'.

published as a book.[2] As she later recounted, her discussions from 1979 onwards with her friends the Northern Territory historians Ann McGrath and Alan Powell and reading Alan's *Far Country: A Short History of the Northern Territory*[3] had already led her to discover that the Territory was 'a very exciting place'. Researching and writing about its past 'really was terrific fun'.[4]

I saw her sporadically over the next several years while she was working with the Territory's Department of Education, looking after two young children and finishing the thesis, which I enjoyed discussing with her. It was during these discussions that she expressed interest in embarking on a PhD thesis dealing with ways in which Australian writers viewed the Northern Territory. In particular she wanted to examine how the Territory was depicted as the region in which the Australian outback tradition was most powerfully idealised. The topic excited me and in due course Alan Powell and I were her joint supervisors at the University College of the Northern Territory and, from 1989, Northern Territory University. I greatly enjoyed reading Mickey's drafts. They were well organised and full of interesting material and perceptive ideas. Little supervision was required but I looked forward to our regular meetings. She was highly efficient, finishing the thesis on time.[5] Not surprisingly, the three examiners, Brian de Garis, Christine Doran and David Walker, commented positively. The thesis later formed the basis of her prize-winning book *In Search of the Never-Never: Looking for Australia in Northern Territory Writing*, which appeared in 1997.[6] She kindly asked me to launch it during a Museums Australia conference in Darwin she had helped organise. During her PhD candidature Mickey also took tutorials in the first-year subject on Australian history that I taught. I received much unsolicited favourable feedback from her students. She worked hard as a member of the organising committee for the 1991 Australian Historical Association conference in Darwin.

---

2   Dewar, *The 'Black War' in Arnhem Land*.
3   Powell, *Far Country*.
4   Dewar, 'Thoughts on Emeritus Professor Alan Powell', 2.
5   Dewar, 'In Search of the "Never-Never"'.
6   Dewar, *In Search of the Never-Never*.

Figure 1: Northern Territory prize winners in the 1984 Northern Territory Literary Awards. Left to right are Mickey Dewar, Graham Calley, Peggie Kerr, David Headon (Chairman of Awards), Connie Gregory, Vivienne Jennings (seated), Kate Veitch and Kathleen Reardon.
Source: Connie Gregory.

Figure 2: Mickey Dewar at the Darwin launch of *In Search of the Never-Never: Looking for Australia in Northern Territory Writing* in 1997.
Source: David Carment.

We remained in frequent contact during the period Mickey was curator and senior curator of Territory History at the Museum and Art Gallery of the Northern Territory (MAGNT, sometimes also officially referred to as Museums and Art Galleries of the Northern Territory) with breaks for a postdoctoral fellowship at Northern Territory University from 1995 to 1996 and to work as adviser and senior adviser to her friend the Territory Chief Minister Clare Martin between 2002 and 2005.[7] We jointly authored a paper on Darwin as an Asian capital for the 1994 Australian Historical Association conference in Perth.[8] It was delightful to have her as a colleague between 1995 and 1996 when she used her postdoctoral fellowship to write a well-received and much referred to book on the social history of Darwin's Fannie Bay Gaol.[9] I took a close interest in her curatorial initiatives, about which I say more later, and a couple of my honours students did internships with her. During 2002, together with Margaret Anderson we debated museum history in *Australian Historical Studies* articles.[10] With Kathy De La Rue and Clayton Fredericksen, I contributed a chapter to the 2005 book Mickey coedited with Julie Wells and Suzanne Parry on the Northern Territory during the 1950s.[11] Mickey's own typically innovative chapter was entitled 'You Are What You Eat: Food and Cultural Identity'.[12] Also in 2005 she and her husband David Ritchie, with whom she shared historical interests, participated in a field trip that my colleague Kate Senior and I organised to the remote Roper River district. Their enthusiasm and knowledge contributed to the trip's success. A site we visited with the traditional owners' permission was a large cave filled with detailed rock art that David previously documented when he worked for the Aboriginal Areas Protection Authority.

---

7   Dewar, Resumé, 3.
8   Carment and Dewar, 'Darwin: Australia's Asian Capital?'.
9   Dewar, *Inside-Out*.
10  Anderson, 'Oh What a Tangled Web…'; Carment, 'Making Museum History in Australia's Northern Territory'; Dewar, 'If I Was Writing My Own History I'd Be a Hero'.
11  Carment, Fredericksen and De La Rue, 'From "Native Relics" to "Flynn's Pillar"'.
12  Dewar, 'You Are What You Eat'.

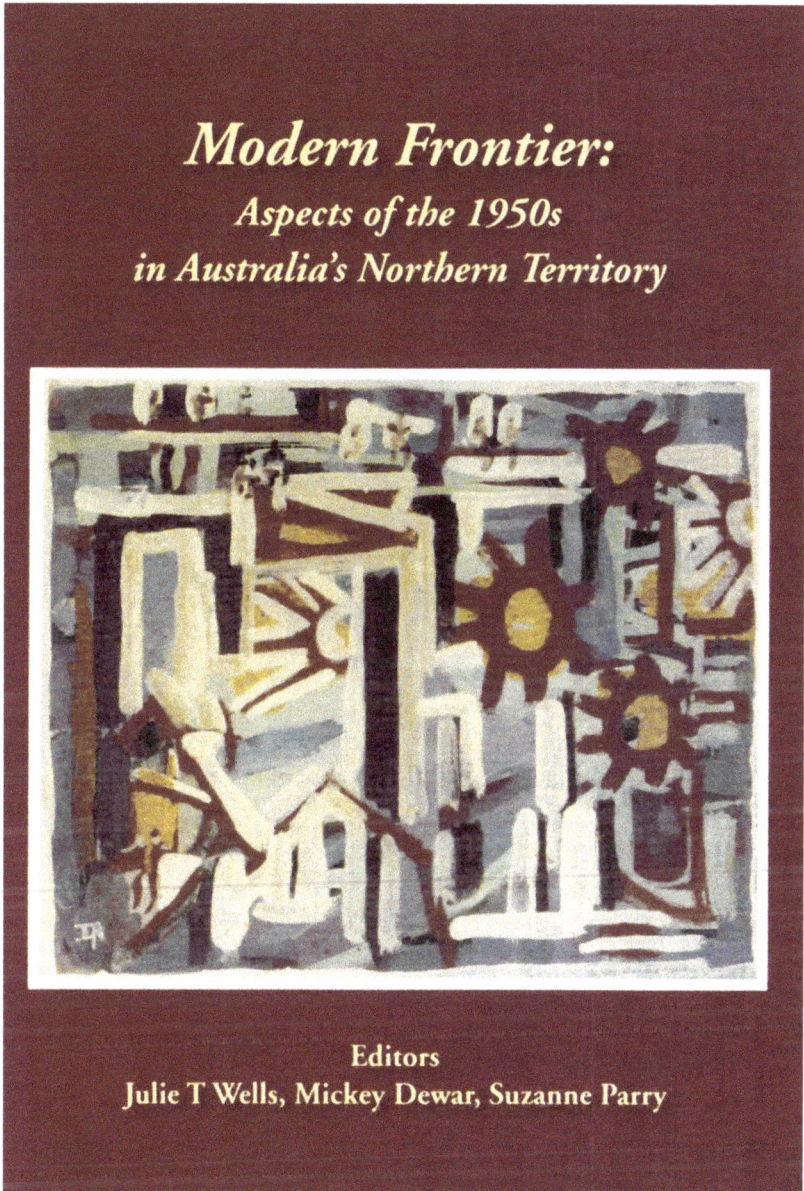

Figure 3: Julie T. Wells, Mickey Dewar and Suzanne Parry (eds), *Modern Frontier: Aspects of the 1950s in Australia's Northern Territory* (Darwin: Charles Darwin University Press, 2005).
Source: Suzanne Parry, David Ritchie, Peter Quinn and © Ian Fairweather/DACS. Copyright Agency.

Figure 4: Mickey Dewar with David Ritchie at the Roper River in 2005.
Source: David Carment.

I saw Mickey a bit less often following my retirement and permanent move to Sydney in 2008, but we kept in contact and quite often caught up for breakfast, sometimes with David joining us, at the Fannie Bay Cool Spot when I visited Darwin. Her productivity and undisguised joy while a researcher, consultant and librarian[13] continued to impress me. At Darwin's annual History Colloquium in 2010, I launched her book on 1950s housing history.[14] Two years later, I enjoyed reading the book she compiled with Clare Martin in which eight Territory chief ministers reflected on self-government.[15] I often called on her for *Northern Territory Historical Studies* (formerly the *Journal of Northern Territory History*) book reviews. She very rarely said no and her polished reviews were always submitted before their deadlines and the correct length.

---

13  Dewar, Resumé, 3.
14  Dewar, *Darwin – No Place Like Home*.
15  Martin and Dewar, *Speak for Yourself*.

Figure 5: Clare Martin and Mickey Dewar (comps), *Speak for Yourself: Eight Chief Ministers Reflect on Northern Territory Self-Government* (Darwin: Charles Darwin University Press, 2012).
Source: Clare Martin, Chips Mackinolty and David Ritchie.

She especially revelled in her final job, which she shared with her close friend Sam Wells, as heritage coordinator at the Northern Territory Library. Among other things, it allowed her to return to curatorship. It also permitted her and David to spend a quite long period each year at their holiday home in Aireys Inlet, Victoria, where they enjoyed the spectacular rugged scenery and the swimming. I spent a memorable day with them there in October 2015. Many of our most recent communications concerned the symposium at the Northern Territory Library in May 2017 to honour Alan Powell that Sam and Mickey organised and I chaired. Mickey had invited me to stay with her and David while I was in Darwin for the event, but I received an email from her in early February advising that:

> I am afraid I am writing as such a fair weather friend. I invited you to stay with us at Alan's symposium in May but the truth is I have to rescind the offer because I won't be there.
>
> This time I was south I was diagnosed with a fairly serious illness. Still having tests etc. but I am afraid it will be serious and I am unlikely to make it back to Darwin any time soon. I'm sorry I can't have you to stay in our lovely new house and I'm disappointed that I am not going back to work as per usual on 1 April. And, well, a whole lot of other things too as you might imagine but not to be boring here.[16]

She added that the illness resulted in her being unable to speak. 'Silence', she wrote, 'is a bit of a change for me as you might imagine!'[17] Shortly afterwards she disclosed that she had motor neurone disease. In spite of all that, before her death on 23 April she wrote a wonderfully warm paper for the symposium that Sam presented for her. 'I wish', she wrote, 'I could be there with you Alan, to celebrate today: an esteemed colleague, a great writer, premier historian, and good friend – make sure you have a drink – or two, for me'.[18] While, as Mickey would have wished, the symposium was mainly about Alan, several speakers also warmly acknowledged her achievements and friendship.

---

16  Dewar, email to David Carment, 10 February 2017.
17  Dewar, email to David Carment, 10 February 2017.
18  Dewar, 'Thoughts on Emeritus Professor Alan Powell'.

Figure 6: David Carment and Mickey Dewar at Aireys Inlet in 2015.
Source: David Ritchie.

## Books

Mickey's many publications and reports, like other aspects of her activities, cover a multifaceted range of historical themes. These include Aborigines, cultural heritage management, crime and punishment, explorers, gender, identity, landscape, library services, literature, living conditions and lifestyles, museums, politics, race relations, sexuality and war.[19] Almost all are also found in the five most substantial of her sole-authored books.

The Australian National University's North Australia Research Unit published Mickey's first major book, *The 'Black War' in Arnhem Land: Missionaries and the Yolngu 1908–1940*, in 1992. Unlike the broader prize-winning Master's thesis from which it is derived, the focus is on the Caledon Bay and Woodah Island incidents of the early 1930s in which Yolngu people killed non-Aborigines. Based on extensive primary sources that include church and government archival records as well as a key participant's private papers and recollections, the book tells an intriguing story.

---

19   Dewar, Resumé, 3–7.

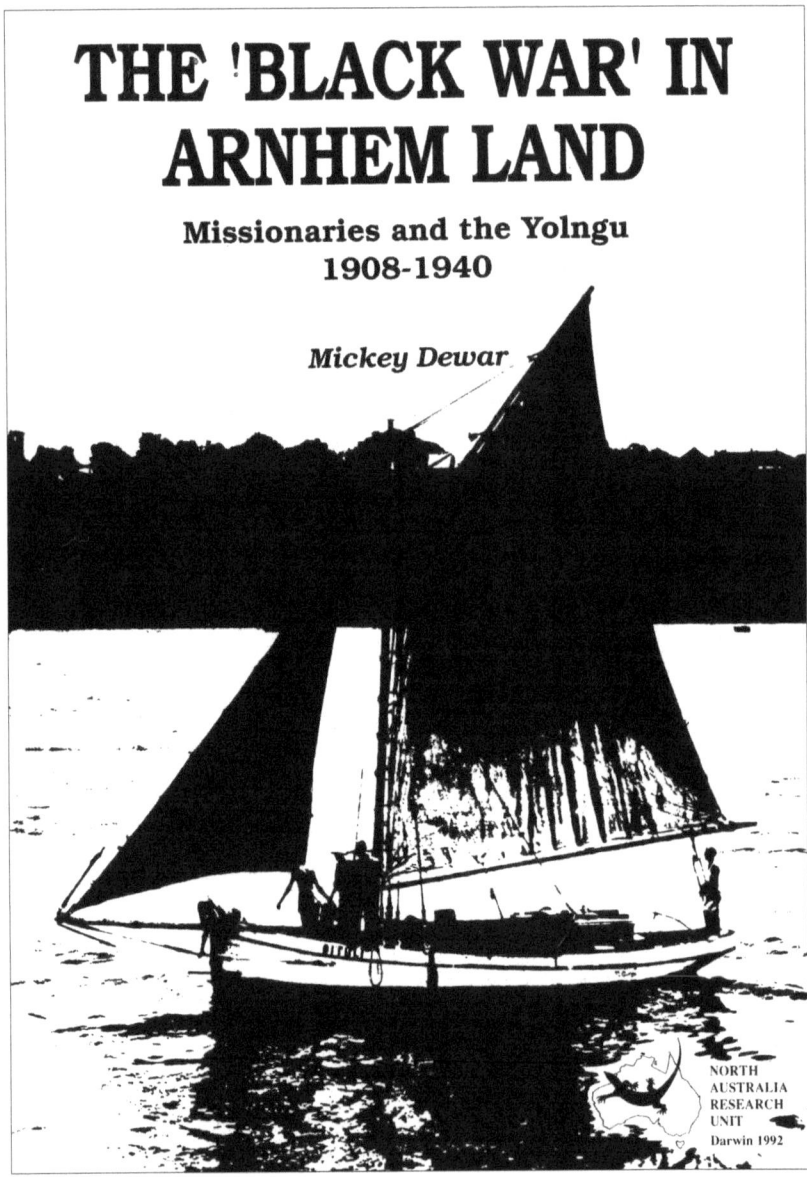

Figure 7: Mickey Dewar, *The 'Black War' in Arnhem Land: Missionaries and the Yolngu 1908–1940* (Darwin: North Australia Research Unit, 1992).
Source: The Australian National University and David Ritchie.

Commonwealth Government policy and missionary activities in Arnhem Land are examined in the wider context of developing Australian racial attitudes. Mickey shows that by the early twentieth century, Anglican and Methodist missionaries in the region had established settlements from which they created an enduring network. The Commonwealth Government was keen for economic reasons to leave Arnhem Land's administration to them. Throughout the 1920s, however, the killings of Japanese trepang crews by Yolngu and allegations of missionary misconduct established Arnhem Land as a wild frontier in the minds of many white Australians. Mickey constructs a detailed and perceptive forensic analysis of how further Yolngu murders of Japanese trepang fishermen at Caledon Bay in 1932 and white men at Woodah Island in 1933, probably as retribution for sexual interference with Yolngu women, resulted in a 'Peace Expedition' led by missionaries that brought the bewildered offenders into Darwin for trials they did not understand. While this was happening, Aboriginal rights to justice and land were increasingly debated.[20] Mickey concludes that the 'dramatic events in Arnhem Land ... which were perceived as the struggle by Aborigines to exercise rights over country, laws and beliefs, became the catalyst for the consciences of white Australians'.[21]

Mickey's next substantial work was *Beginnings: The First Decade of the Northern Territory Women's Advisory Council 1983–1993*, published as a commissioned history in 1994. A significant contribution to regional studies of women's organisations, it makes considerable use of the numerous interviews that she undertook. She was 'totally disarmed by the candid and friendly way that people spoke to me',[22] but perhaps ought not have been given her formidable skills as an oral historian.

*Beginnings* closely examines how the Women's Advisory Council (WAC) influenced Northern Territory Government decision-making. It explains that despite gains made during the 1960s and 1970s Northern Territory women, as in the rest of Australia, had not achieved equality with men in most key areas by the early 1980s. Mickey presents WAC's first 10 years as:

---

20   Dewar, *The 'Black War' in Arnhem Land*.
21   Dewar, *The 'Black War' in Arnhem Land*, 87.
22   Dewar, *Beginnings*, 7.

The transition period from marginalised lobby group to incorporation within the mainstream political process. The ten years of WAC's operation have in large part been taken up with defining roles, establishing parameters of influence and generally working out ways to work effectively for women.[23]

She acknowledges that the council was confronted with a range of obstacles and experienced difficult times, yet also demonstrates that it lobbied successfully for improvements regarding such issues as discrimination against women, the protection of female victims of domestic and sexual violence, and the needs of female child care workers. WAC's advocacy, public education and networking activities are described and critically assessed. Of special interest is her attention to its deliberate consciousness ranging, which often concerned topics that had previously received little or no attention in the Northern Territory.[24]

Northern Territory University Press published Mickey's *In Search of the Never-Never: Looking for Australia in Northern Territory Writing* in 1997. It won the Jessie Litchfield Award for Literature and was shortlisted for the Community and Regional History Prize in the New South Wales Premier's History Awards.[25] Based on her doctoral thesis, it analyses hundreds of fiction and non-fiction books and pamphlets published between 1837 and 1992. 'After reading all I could about the Territory', Mickey writes:

I came to believe that the focus of the region in the writing was an attempt to locate and define the non-Aboriginal occupation of Australia from all aspects: physically, spatially, morally and temporally. Northern Territory writing offers an interpretation of the settlement of Australia which seeks to legitimise European settlement. Representations of the Northern Territory can be seen to have developed and modified in response to changing events in Australian society generally. The Northern Territory as metaphor in Australian writing is the microcosm where the European occupation of the continent is reconciled.[26]

She sees landscape, Aboriginal people and gender as the Territory's principal literary representations. The common theme of the 'conflicting demands of European settlement against the rights of Aboriginal people' is

---

23   Dewar, *Beginnings*, 10.
24   Dewar, *Beginnings*, 9–77.
25   Dewar, Resumé, 2.
26   Dewar, *In Search of the Never-Never*, ix–x.

found, although in varying degrees, in all the publications she examines.[27] The idea of the frontier and the Territory's identity as being in some ways Asian are also of considerable importance.

Each of her eight chapters deals with a historical period but, as chapter titles such as 'Looking for Gold', 'The Atomic Territory' and 'Poor Bugger All of Us' reveal, also focus on particular issues. In 'The Atomic Territory', for instance, Mickey considers the years between the late 1940s and the early 1970s. During this period, the 'mythic theme' that the Territory's landscape contained unlimited wealth was 'buoyed by hopes of the atomic age'.[28] Yet while 'economic optimism and iconic nationalism unite in the same landscape',[29] writers such as Sumner Locke-Elliot and Bill Harney often present a more complicated perspective.[30] Mickey's final chapter concludes that the majority of her authors throughout the 1837–1992 period amalgamated 'the landscape, the politics and the personal' in their attempts to identify the true Australia in their writings about the Territory.[31]

I have a closer personal connection with *In Search of the Never-Never* than any of Mickey's other sole-authored books. Not only is it based on the thesis that Alan Powell and I supervised, but I was also involved with its publication process and it strongly influenced some of my later research and writing. Alan, the examiners and I all considered that the thesis was an innovative and significant contribution to Australian cultural history that ought to be published. My only regret, which Mickey shared, is that following an independent referee's recommendations some of the biographical details in the thesis are omitted from the book. As chair of Northern Territory University Press, I successfully applied for a grant from the Australia Foundation for Culture and the Humanities that funded professional copyediting and indexing, and the inclusion of high-quality colour images. My own 2007 book *Territorianism: Politics & Identity in Australia's Northern Territory 1978–2001* acknowledges *In Search of the Never-Never*'s importance in shaping its arguments, especially those regarding the Northern Territory as an Australian frontier and the relationship between the Territory and Asia.[32]

---

27  Dewar, *In Search of the Never-Never*, xii.
28  Dewar, *In Search of the Never-Never*, 111–12.
29  Dewar, *In Search of the Never-Never*, 112.
30  Dewar, *In Search of the Never-Never*, 95–117.
31  Dewar, *In Search of the Never-Never*, 191.
32  Carment, *Territorianism*, particularly viii, 7, 22–24.

Figure 8: Mickey Dewar, *In Search of the Never-Never: Looking for Australia in Northern Territory Writing* (Darwin: Northern Territory University Press, 1997).
Source: Charles Darwin University and David Ritchie.

*Inside-Out: A Social History of Fannie Bay Gaol*, which Northern Territory University Press published in 1999, differs from most of Mickey's earlier books in not starting as a thesis. It is, instead, an outcome of her MAGNT curatorial activities. Like *In Search of the Never-Never*, it was shortlisted for the Community and Regional History Prize in the New South Wales Premier's History Awards.[33] Most of the research was completed during her Northern Territory University Postdoctoral Fellowship. The gaol was Darwin's prison between 1883 and 1979. Although there were limitations regarding available evidence, especially the loss of all internal gaol documents, Mickey still found much relevant information from interviews, newspapers and government records. She observed that:

> In its time the gaol housed political protesters, criminals, children, illegal aliens and people from all backgrounds and ethnic identities. Fannie Bay gaol was an institution which provided an intersection of race, class and authority. The gaol functioned as the chief place of incarceration for law-breakers in the Northern Territory for ninety six years. As such, it provides a history, not only of the unfortunates who were incarcerated, the staff paid to supervise them, their families and friends and the victims of their crimes, but of the processes of settlement and control of the Northern Territory in the colonial and post-colonial period.[34]

The book's eight chronologically based chapters show how the gaol housed and dealt with people who in very various ways broke the law, as well as those who are often best seen as largely innocent offenders, such as a considerable proportion of the many Aboriginal and Chinese prisoners, children, the mentally ill and the poor. Some died of illness while imprisoned and others were executed. Most chapters give detailed and illuminating attention to the stories of individual prisoners: the Malay fisherman Joseph Abdoolah, who could not or would not settle into prison routines; the trade union leader Harold Nelson, imprisoned for refusing to pay taxes; the Aborigines Nemarluk and Butcher Knight, incarcerated for their involvement in killing non-Aboriginal people; the last prisoners hanged at the gaol, the Czechoslovaks Jerry Koci and John Novotny; the Portuguese seaman Jose Da Costa, whose death sentence was commuted very shortly before he was due to be executed; and the remand prisoner 'L', who was seriously assaulted by other prisoners.[35] Mickey documents the gaol's serious deficiencies yet comments that its closure did not necessarily solve the Northern Territory's imprisonment problems.[36]

---

33  Dewar, Resumé, 2.
34  Dewar, *Inside-Out*, x.
35  Dewar, *Inside-Out*.
36  Dewar, *Inside-Out*, 146.

Figure 9: Mickey Dewar, *Inside-Out: A Social History of Fannie Bay Gaol* (Darwin: Northern Territory University Press, 1999).
Source: Charles Darwin University and David Ritchie.

Mickey's last substantial book is *Darwin – No Place Like Home: Australia's Northern Capital in the 1950s through a Social History of Housing*, which the Historical Society of the Northern Territory published in 2010. She wrote it as a National Archives Frederick Watson Fellow and a Director's Fellow at the National Museum of Australia. It deservedly won the

2011 Northern Territory Chief Minister's History Book Award.[37] Like all Mickey's work, it is impeccably researched. The bibliography includes well over 100 National Archives of Australia and Northern Territory Archives files in addition to many oral history transcripts and other sources. Effective use is made of photographs and plans.

She employs this material to examine the challenges the Commonwealth Government faced during the 1950s as it attempted to rebuild Darwin following the Second World War's devastation and make it a place that its residents could call home. The book comprehensively discusses Darwin immediately after the Second World War, local politics, the Commonwealth's role as Darwin's principal landlord, life in the town's camps, the buildings where people lived, the Northern Territory Housing Commission's establishment and role, and architecture. She explains that, throughout the decade, land and accommodation remained insufficient. In spite of increased Commonwealth funds for housing, many people in Darwin found shelter where they could. In so doing they began to create communities that later emerged as suburbs.[38] She writes that:

> Having a house made the difference between staying and going. Despite (or perhaps because of) the tough conditions, Darwin people had a good time: they partied hard and drank vast quantities of alcohol, the weather was warm and the town was 'free and easy'. The local music scene arguably reached a creative height not matched again with a unique Darwin sound … Along with the lifestyle came identification of a political attitude that was renegade, anti-Canberra, with an aggressive parochialism.[39]

Mickey argues that the demand for housing was the main point of political pressure in Darwin throughout the 1950s. Although the Commonwealth recognised and responded to the problem through increased expenditure and the Housing Commission's creation in 1959, its efforts 'entrenched the divide between public servants … and the rest of the population' and set up a housing system that 'differentiated between Aborigines and other citizens'.[40] More positively, the housing shortage forced a type of democracy on Darwin's citizens that subverted social hierarchies. 'What is really remembered as fundamental to the decade', Mickey notes, 'is the sharing of hardship and the creation of corporate entities of loyalty and political action'.[41]

---

37  Dewar, Resumé, 2.
38  Dewar, *Darwin – No Place Like Home*.
39  Dewar, *Darwin – No Place Like Home*, 5.
40  Dewar, *Darwin – No Place Like Home*, 6.
41  Dewar, *Darwin – No Place Like Home*, 141.

Figure 10: Mickey Dewar, *Darwin – No Place Like Home: Australia's Northern Capital in the 1950s through a Social History of Housing* (Darwin: Historical Society of the Northern Territory, 2010).
Source: Historical Society of the Northern Territory and David Ritchie.

## Museums

Most of Mickey's extensive curatorial work was at the MAGNT, a government organisation responsible for a number of sites. It was often accomplished in the face of difficulties. Until the Country Liberal Party lost office in 2001, the Territory Government sometimes intervened in the museum's operations and reduced its autonomy.[42] Despite this, Mickey remained admirably loyal to the institution and successfully focused on a range of creative initiatives. She wrote conservation and management plans for MAGNT properties in Alice Springs and Darwin and authored scholarly publications dealing with aspects of her museum work. Exhibitions and sites for which she was largely responsible, examples of which are discussed here, were acclaimed for the innovative and thorough ways in which they presented history to diverse audiences. That they were often undertaken with limited resources makes them all the more noteworthy.

Figure 11: Museum and Art Gallery of the Northern Territory, Bullocky Point, Darwin, in 1998.
Source: David Carment.

---

42  Carment, 'Making Museum History in Australia's Northern Territory', 164–65.

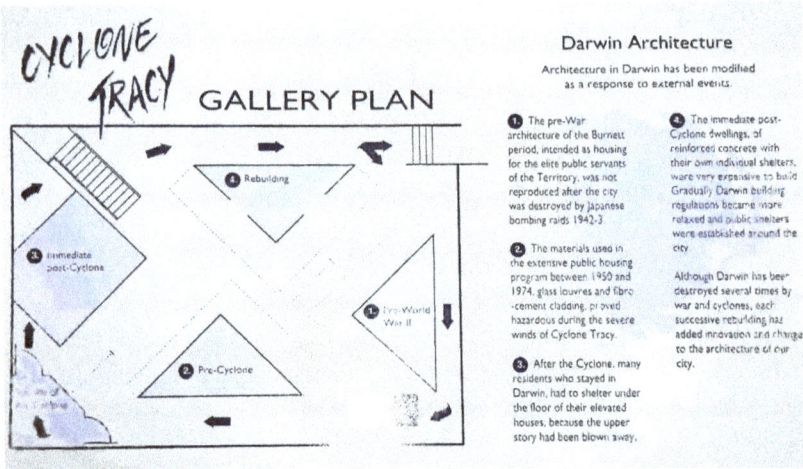

Figure 12: Gallery Plan, 'Cyclone Tracy' exhibition, in 1998.
Source: David Carment, photograph taken with the permission of the Museum and Art Gallery of the Northern Territory.

In the Cyclone Tracy Gallery, as it was officially described, Mickey documented the disaster that destroyed most of Darwin on 24 and 25 December 1974. It opened in 1994. As Peter Read shows in his book *Returning to Nothing: The Meaning of Lost Places*, it was part of controversial twentieth anniversary commemorations that raised the question of whether the cyclone ought to be celebrated or mourned. Read writes that Mickey wanted visitors:

> to understand the different phases of Darwin's history, to make connections between the sites of 1974 and 1994, and to take cyclones seriously. Even the decision to begin was controversial: half the people who contacted her advised *Don't do it: leave the past where it was*. Dewar replied: *These events will always be remembered but it is how we remember them that gives meaning to the present*.[43]

---

43   Read, *Returning to Nothing*, 165–68.

MICKEY DEWAR: MEMORIES, BOOKS AND MUSEUMS

Figure 13: Pre-cyclone house, 'Cyclone Tracy' exhibition, in 1998.
Source: David Carment, photograph taken with the permission of the Museum and Art Gallery of the Northern Territory.

The exhibition, most of which is still in place, was highly effective and extraordinarily popular. In 1996–97, for example, over 168,000 people were estimated to have seen it.[44] Visitors initially encountered Aboriginal artistic responses from Geoffrey Mangalamarra and Rover Thomas. They then inspected photographs of the cyclone's impact and viewed an ABC television report made not long after the disaster. They walked past skilful recreations of houses and rooms that were typical of Darwin in the pre-cyclone period before entering what Read describes as the 'technological masterpiece'. A haunting recording of the cyclone made towards the end of midnight mass in Darwin's Catholic cathedral played continuously in a darkened room. As visitors left the room, they saw the wrecked remains of a high-set house, complete with a fallen Christmas tree. A large, hastily painted sign on a piece of iron warned, 'KEEP OUT WE STILL LIVE HERE'. From there the new post-cyclone Darwin was discovered, perhaps most notably part of the interior of a very solid 'Tracy Trauma' house of the type common in Darwin's northern suburbs. Darwin's people were shown rebuilding their community.[45]

---

44  Museums and Art Galleries Board of the Northern Territory, *Annual Report 1996–97*, 62.
45  Carment, notes and photographs of visit to Museum and Art Gallery of the Northern Territory, Darwin, 1998; Read, *Returning to Nothing*, 168–69.

Figure 14: Cyclone damage, 'Cyclone Tracy' exhibition, in 1998.
Source: David Carment, photograph taken with the permission of the Museum and Art Gallery of the Northern Territory.

Mickey's interpretation strategy for the former Fannie Bay Gaol in Darwin, based on a 1994 draft management plan, was to ensure that all buildings were conserved in accordance with recognised conservation principles and presented to demonstrate the nearly intact features of a medium-security tropical prison.[46] Research for *Inside-Out* provided comprehensive interpretation material that included building histories and biographies of better-known prisoners. Mickey also worked with Clayton Fredericksen from Charles Darwin University on aspects of the gaol's archaeology that illuminated the role of its many Chinese prisoners.[47] The buildings varied greatly: some were constructed in the late nineteenth century, while others were much more recent. Except for the removal of a few portable structures, no attempt was made to alter the gaol as it was in 1979.[48]

---

46  Dewar, 'Fannie Bay Gaol'.
47  Dewar and Fredericksen, 'Prison Heritage, Public History and Archaeology at Fannie Bay Gaol, Northern Australia'.
48  Carment, notes and photographs of visit to Fannie Bay Gaol, Darwin, 1998; [Dewar], *Fannie Bay Gaol*.

Figure 15: Fannie Bay Gaol in 1998.
Source: David Carment, photograph taken with the permission of the Museum and Art Gallery of the Northern Territory.

Figure 16: [Mickey Dewar 1995], *Fannie Bay Gaol*, Museums and Art Galleries of the Northern Territory, Darwin.
Source: Image courtesy Museum and Art Gallery of the Northern Territory.

A guided walk at the gaol presented stories of the places visitors saw: the visitors' building, the guard house, the reception areas, the stores, the remand section, the maximum security cells, the infirmary, a concrete slab, the guard house, the ablution block, the separate confinement area, the covered muster area, the women's section, the kitchen and the mess. Visitors were asked to imagine what it was like to be a prisoner at the gaol over a century before when many inmates were Malay, Chinese or Aboriginal.[49]

Figure 17: Lyons Cottage, Darwin, in 1998.
Source: David Carment.

Another of Mickey's Darwin projects was Lyons Cottage, also known as British Australian Telegraph House. Located on The Esplanade, it was a stone cottage built in 1925 as accommodation for staff maintaining the cable link between Australia and Britain. It was later the home of John Lyons, a prominent lawyer and mayor of Darwin, and his family. Under a draft management plan Mickey developed during the mid-1990s in collaboration with heritage professionals and long-time Darwin residents, the MAGNT restored the building. Its exterior reflected the colour scheme of the period from 1949 until 1970 while the interior reflected the

---

49  [Dewar], *Fannie Bay Gaol*.

period from 1925 until 1942. Housed inside the cottage were displays of telegraphic equipment and photographs depicting local lifestyles. Visitors received a pamphlet outlining the building's history.[50]

Mickey was also responsible for The Residency, a MAGNT property in Alice Springs. The home of the Government Resident of Central Australia between 1927 and 1931, after then it housed senior officials. It was the scene for social gatherings, meetings and vice-regal occasions. Under Mickey's supervision in 1994, the MAGNT formulated a conservation plan and began work on the building to present aspects of its social history. Care was taken not to destroy evidence of any period but to keep examples of all stages of the building's use.[51] As Mickey colourfully recounts in her article 'Attitudes to the Throne: Loyalty and Royalty at The Residency, Alice Springs', following consultation with the Alice Springs community the toilets installed for the visit of Queen Elizabeth II and the Duke of Edinburgh in 1963 were retained as a significant part of the building's history.[52] The colour scheme chosen matched paint scrapings from the original design and the furniture was based on lists in government records. Interpretive texts were minimal, allowing visitors to experience the building's atmosphere.[53]

Figure 18: The Residency, Alice Springs, in 2015.
Source: Wikipedia Commons.

---

50  Carment, notes and photographs of visit to Lyons Cottage, Darwin, 1998; [Dewar], *Lyons Cottage*.
51  Dewar, The Residency Alice Springs Draft Report; [Dewar], *The Residency Alice Springs*.
52  Dewar, 'Attitudes To The Throne'.
53  Carment, notes and photographs of visit to The Residency, Alice Springs, 1998.

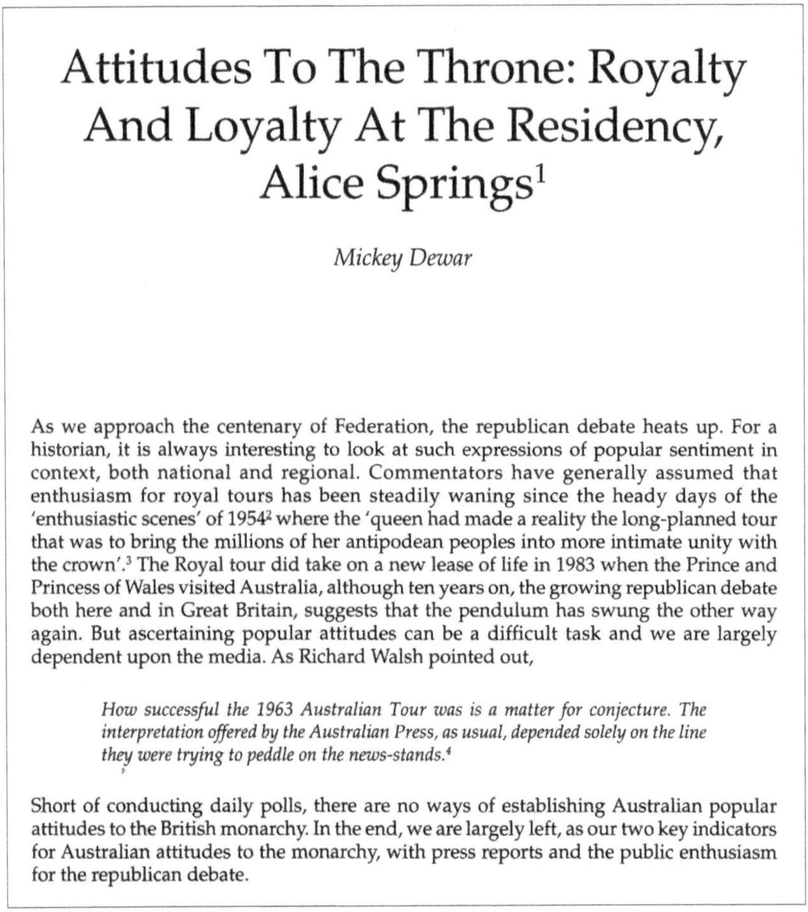

# Attitudes To The Throne: Royalty And Loyalty At The Residency, Alice Springs[1]

*Mickey Dewar*

As we approach the centenary of Federation, the republican debate heats up. For a historian, it is always interesting to look at such expressions of popular sentiment in context, both national and regional. Commentators have generally assumed that enthusiasm for royal tours has been steadily waning since the heady days of the 'enthusiastic scenes' of 1954[2] where the 'queen had made a reality the long-planned tour that was to bring the millions of her antipodean peoples into more intimate unity with the crown'.[3] The Royal tour did take on a new lease of life in 1983 when the Prince and Princess of Wales visited Australia, although ten years on, the growing republican debate both here and in Great Britain, suggests that the pendulum has swung the other way again. But ascertaining popular attitudes can be a difficult task and we are largely dependent upon the media. As Richard Walsh pointed out,

> How successful the 1963 Australian Tour was is a matter for conjecture. The interpretation offered by the Australian Press, as usual, depended solely on the line they were trying to peddle on the news-stands.[4]

Short of conducting daily polls, there are no ways of establishing Australian popular attitudes to the British monarchy. In the end, we are largely left, as our two key indicators for Australian attitudes to the monarchy, with press reports and the public enthusiasm for the republican debate.

Figure 19: Mickey Dewar, 'Attitudes to the Throne: Loyalty and Royalty at The Residency, Alice Springs', *Northern Perspective* 19, no. 1 (1996): 99.
Source: Charles Darwin University and David Ritchie.

Most rooms at The Residency were furnished as they would have been in the early years of its use. The dark wooden furniture in the dining room, for instance, was very typical of the 1930s. The kitchen was fairly primitive. The royal bathrooms were displayed as a 'permanent' record of the Queen's stay. An interpretive text in one of the bathrooms was headed 'The Royal thrones'. Structural changes to the buildings were seen in various places, including a fireplace that was bricked up with only some of the brickwork removed to display what was originally there.[54]

---

54  Carment, notes and photographs of visit to The Residency, Alice Springs, 1998.

Figure 20: Dining room, The Residency, in 1998.
Source: David Carment, photograph taken with the permission of the Museum and Art Gallery of the Northern Territory.

As I mentioned earlier, Mickey returned to curatorship at the Northern Territory Library, where she worked from 2013.[55] Her 2015 exhibition there, 'Borella's War', received an Australian Library and Information Association Northern Territory Recognition Award.[56] The exhibition located the remarkable personal story of the Northern Territory's only First World War Victoria Cross winner, Albert Borella, within the broader context of Territory development.[57] Mickey, though, also warned that while Borella's Territory and wartime experiences were valuable in illuminating the past, they 'were not typical … the inevitable difficulty in any interpretations that focus on the heroic and the parochial is that they can also have the effect of distorting the public perception in a way not reflected in the wider events of the past'.[58]

---

55   Dewar, Resumé, 3.
56   Dewar, Resumé, 2.
57   'Borella's War: The Making of a Legend', 2015, World War One Link, accessed 24 August 2017, worldwaronelink.com.au/projects/borellas-war-making-legend/#WajHkoVRzJx; Dewar, 'Borella's War'.
58   Dewar, 'Borella's War', 57.

Figure 21: Image from 'Borella's War' exhibition, Northern Territory Library, 2015: sailing from Darwin to Townsville to enlist, Albert Borella is standing on the left.

Source: Northern Territory Library.

## 'Still so much to say'

Mickey's resumé lists her passions as 'Northern Territory history, politics, knowledge information and retrieval, collections management, exhibition development, museums, libraries and archives'.[59] She made valued, highly innovative and quite frequently pioneering contributions to all these areas. Ann McGrath wrote in 2004 that Mickey's career 'exemplifies the breadth of roles that a historian might play', referring to her curatorship, advice to the public on historical matters and publications.[60] The Australian Historical Association's President Lynette Russell wrote shortly after Mickey's death that she was, among other things, 'in many ways an environmental historian before the label was used'.[61] As Clare Martin said at a farewell gathering in Darwin, Mickey is perhaps best remembered for being a wonderful storyteller who combined academic perspective and historical research with a 'regular dose of Dewar humour'.[62] Mickey observed in one of her last emails to me that 'Northern Territory history is a subject I still love the best and think there is still so much to say'.[63] Her premature passing means that many stories will never be told.

## Bibliography

Anderson, Margaret. 'Oh What a Tangled Web … Politics, History and Museums'. *Australian Historical Studies* 33, no. 119 (2002): 179–85. doi.org/10.1080/10314610208596209.

Carment, David. 'Making Museum History in Australia's Northern Territory'. *Australian Historical Studies* 33, no. 119 (2002): 161–71. doi.org/10.1080/10314610208596207.

Carment, David. *Territorianism: Politics & Identity in Australia's Northern Territory 1978–2001*. Melbourne: Australian Scholarly Publishing, 2007.

Carment, David, and Mickey Dewar. 'Darwin: Australia's Asian Capital?' Paper presented at Australian Historical Association Conference, Perth, 1994.

---

59  Dewar, Resumé, 2.
60  McGrath, 'The History Phoenix?', 15.
61  Russell, 'From the President', 325.
62  Manicaros, 'Friends and Colleagues Farewell Dr Mickey Dewar'.
63  Dewar, Email to David Carment, 10 February 2017.

Carment, David, Clayton Fredericksen and Kathy De La Rue. 'From "Native Relics" to "Flynn's Pillar": Cultural Heritage Management in the Northern Territory during the 1950s'. In *Modern Frontier: Aspects of the 1950s in Australia's Northern Territory*, edited by Julie T. Wells, Mickey Dewar and Suzanne Parry, 91–102. Darwin: Charles Darwin University Press, 2005.

[Dewar, Mickey]. *Lyons Cottage*. Darwin: Museum and Art Gallery of the Northern Territory, n.d.

[Dewar, Mickey]. *The Residency Alice Springs*. Alice Springs: Museums and Art Galleries of the Northern Territory, n.d.

Dewar, Michelle [Mickey]. 'Strange Bedfellows: Europeans and Aborigines in Arnhem Land before World War II'. MA (Hons) thesis, University of New England, 1989.

Dewar, Mickey. *The 'Black War' in Arnhem Land: Missionaries and the Yolngu 1908–1940*. Darwin: North Australia Research Unit, 1992.

Dewar, Michelle Sue [Mickey]. 'In Search of the "Never-Never": The Northern Territory Metaphor in Australian Writing 1837–1992'. PhD thesis, Northern Territory University, 1993.

Dewar, Mickey. *Beginnings: The First Decade of the Northern Territory Women's Advisory Council 1983–1993*. Women's Advisory Council, Department of the thief Minister, Northern Territory Government, 1994.

Dewar, Mickey. 'Fannie Bay Gaol (Her Majesty's Gaol and Labour Prison, Darwin) Lot 5219'. Draft Heritage and Conservation management plan prepared by the Museum and Art Gallery of the Northern Territory, Darwin, 1994.

Dewar, Mickey. The Residency Alice Springs Draft Report. Museums and Art Galleries of the Northern Territory, Darwin, 1994.

[Dewar, Mickey]. *Fannie Bay Gaol*. Darwin: Museum and Art Galleries of the Northern Territory, 1995.

Dewar, Mickey. 'Attitudes To The Throne: Loyalty And Royalty At The Residency, Alice Springs'. *Northern Perspective* 19, no. 1 (1996): 99–111.

Dewar, Mickey. *In Search of the Never-Never: Looking for Australia in Northern Territory Writing*. Darwin: Northern Territory University Press, 1997.

Dewar, Mickey. *Inside-Out: A Social History of Fannie Bay Gaol*. Darwin: Northern Territory University Press, 1999.

Dewar, Mickey. 'If I Was Writing My Own History I'd Be a Hero … A Response to Professor David Carment on Making Museum History at the Museum and Art Gallery of the Northern Territory'. *Australian Historical Studies* 33, no. 119 (April 2002): 172–78. doi.org/10.1080/10314610208596208.

Dewar, Mickey. 'You Are What You Eat: Food and Cultural Identity'. In *Modern Frontier: Aspects of the 1950s in Australia's Northern Territory*, edited by Julie T. Wells, Mickey Dewar and Suzanne Parry, 71–90. Darwin: Charles Darwin University Press, 2005.

Dewar, Mickey. *Darwin – No Place Like Home: Australia's northern capital in the 1950s through a social history of housing*. Darwin: Historical Society of the Northern Territory, 2010.

Dewar, Mickey. 'Borella's War: The Making of a Legend'. *Northern Territory Historical Studies: A Journal of History Heritage and Archaeology* 27 (2016): 47–64.

Dewar, Mickey. 'Thoughts on Emeritus Professor Alan Powell'. Paper presented at Professor Alan Powell: Beyond the Far Country symposium, Darwin, 31 May 2017.

Dewar, Mickey, and Clayton Fredericksen. 'Prison Heritage, Public History and Archaeology at Fannie Bay Gaol, Northern Australia'. *International Journal of Heritage Studies* 9, no. 1 (2003): 45–63. doi.org/10.1080/1352725022000056622.

McGrath, Ann. 'The History Phoenix? Inventing a History Tradition in the Northern Territory'. In *Northern Encounters: New Directions in North Australian History*, edited by David Carment, 1–24. Darwin: Charles Darwin University Press, 2004.

Manicaros, Ashley. 'Friends and Colleagues Farewell Dr Mickey Dewar After Passing Away with Motor Neurone Disease'. *Northern Territory News*, 9 July 2017. Accessed 25 August 2017. www.ntnews.com.au/news/northern-territory/friends-and-colleagues-farewell-dr-mickey-dewar-after-passing-away-from-motor-neurone-disease/news-story/0998c37e112410f22fba00c55a4d6883.

Martin, Clare, and Mickey Dewar (comps). *Speak for Yourself: Eight Chief Ministers Reflect on Northern Territory Self-Government*. Darwin: Charles Darwin University Press, 2012.

Museums and Art Galleries of the Northern Territory. *Annual Report 1996–97*. Darwin: The Board, 1997.

Powell, Alan. *Far Country: A Short History of the Northern Territory.* Melbourne: Melbourne University Press, 1983.

Read, Peter. *Returning to Nothing: The Meaning of Lost Places.* Melbourne: Cambridge University Press, 1996. doi.org/10.1017/CBO9781139085069.

Russell, Lynette. 'From the President'. *History Australia* 14, no. 3 (2017): 323–25. doi.org/10.1080/14490854.2017.1361785.

# Appendix 1

## Resumé

Mickey Dewar

### Career summary

I came to the Northern Territory in 1979 after gaining my first degree in history and qualified as a teacher and educator working with the Northern Territory Education Department and Charles Darwin University. I finished my doctorate on Northern Territory writing and then was appointed Curator then Senior Curator of History at the Museum and Art Gallery of the Northern Territory. Between 2002 and 2005 I took leave to work for the Chief Minister as Ministerial Advisor for Arts and Museums and was then promoted to Senior Advisor. After leaving the political office I returned briefly to the museum before starting work as a Darwin-based freelance historian. I received national recognition when I was appointed a Frederick Watson Fellow at National Archives of Australia (2007) and then Director's Fellow at the National Museum of Australia (2008). In 2011, I returned to study and began a Masters in Library and Information Management. Since 2013 I have been based at the Northern Territory Library as Northern Territory Heritage Coordinator part-time.

My passions are Northern Territory history, politics, knowledge information and retrieval, collections management, exhibition development, museums, libraries and archives.

## Career highlights

- Winner Chief Minister's History Book Award for the best publication in Northern Territory history: *Darwin – No Place Like Home* (2011)
- Short-listings in NSW Premier's History Award for Community and Regional History Prize *Inside-Out: A Social History of Fannie Bay Gaol* (2000) and *In Search of the 'Never-Never': Looking for Australia in Northern Territory Writing* (1998), which was also joint winner Jessie Litchfield Award for Literature (1997)
- Design and development of the Territory History Gallery and creation of the Cyclone Tracy Gallery Museum and Art Gallery NT (1994–2007)
- ALIA NT Recognition Award for curating the 'Borella's War: The Making of a Legend', exhibition with touring component as part of the NT government's Centenary of Anzac project (2015)

## Qualifications

- Masters of Library and Information Management, 2015, University of South Australia
- Doctor of Philosophy, 1994, Charles Darwin University
- Master of Arts (Hons), 1989, University of New England (Louise T. Daley Prize for Australian History)
- Graduate Diploma of Education, 1981, Darwin Community College (now Charles Darwin University)
- Bachelor of Arts (Hons), 1978, University of Melbourne

## Appointments to boards and statutory authorities

- Chair Northern Territory Place Names Committee 2008–2009
- Northern Territory Government Heritage Advisory Council/Heritage Council 2008–2014; Deputy Chair (2012–2014)
- National Archives of Australia Advisory Council 2008–2014; 2015 – present

APPENDIX 1: RESUMÉ

## Membership of professional organisations

Australia ICOMOS (International Council on Monuments and Sites); Professional Historians Association NT; Australian Library and Information Association (Associate); Australian Historical Association; Historical Society of the Northern Territory; Museums Australia (NT); National Trust of Australia (NT); Life Membership: Fannie Bay History and Heritage Society; Police Historical Society; National Pioneer Women's Hall of Fame

## Employment summary

- July 2013 – present: Northern Territory Heritage Coordinator, Northern Territory Library
- June 2012 – July 2013: Information Services Librarian, Batchelor Institute of Indigenous Education
- February 2007 – present: Principal, Mickey Dewar Historical Research and Consulting
- February 1994 – September 2006: Curator Territory History, Museum and Art Gallery of the Northern Territory
- September 2002 – September 2005: Adviser to the Chief Minister of the Northern Territory, the Hon Clare Martin
- March 1995 – February 1996: Postdoctoral fellow, Department of Arts and Law Charles Darwin University
- 1986–1993: Lecturer/tutor (various contracts), Charles Darwin University
- 1981–1986: Teacher/Editor Northern Territory Education Department (including two years maternity leave)

# Appendix 2

## Selected publications[1]

2016    'Borella's War: The Making of a Legend'. *Northern Territory Historical Studies: A Journal of History, Heritage and Archaeology* 27: 47–64.

2012    'Political Chronicle: Northern Territory, July–December 2011'. *Australian Journal of Politics and History* 58, no. 2: 326–32.

2012    Clare Martin and Mickey Dewar. *Speak for Yourself: Eight Chief Ministers Reflect on Northern Territory Self-Government.* Darwin: CDU Press, ISBN 9781921576751, 231pp.

2011    'Political Chronicle: Northern Territory, January–June 2011'. *Australian Journal of Politics and History* 57, no. 2: 324–29.

2011    *Northern Territory Library Celebrating Thirty Years.* Darwin: Darwin Library, ISBN 9780977563487, no pagination [31pp.].

2010    'Political Chronicle: Northern Territory, January–June 2010'. *Australian Journal of Politics and History* 56, no. 4: 672–78.

2010    'Political Chronicle: Northern Territory, July–December 2009'. *Australian Journal of Politics and History* 56, no. 2: 322–28.

2010    *Darwin – No Place Like Home: A Social History of Australia's Northern Capital in the 1950s through a Study of Housing.* Darwin: Historical Society of the Northern Territory, ISBN 9781921576249, 174pp.

---

1    Excludes shorter pieces such as book reviews, comments, notes, etc.

2010 'Writing a Heritage Assessment for Battery Hill, Tennant Creek'. *Territory in Trust* (National Trust of Australia, Northern Territory) 27, no. 1 (January–June): 8–15.

2010 Sue Dugdale and Mickey Dewar. 'Battery Hill: A Conservation Management Plan'. Report for the Heritage Unit, Northern Territory Government Department of Natural Resources, Environment, the Arts and Sport, October.

2009 'Political Chronicle: Northern Territory, January–June 2009'. *Australian Journal of Politics and History* 55, no. 4: 240–45.

2009 'Political Chronicle: Northern Territory, July–December 2008'. *Australian Journal of Politics and History* 55, no. 2: 236–42.

2009 'Social Climbing or Just Being Cool: The 1950s Ideal of an Elevated House in Darwin'. *Memento* (National Archives of Australia, Canberra) 37 (July): 13–15.

2009 'The Museum and Art Gallery at Bullocky Point: Some Aspects of Its History'. In *Collectors & Museums: Two Centuries of Collecting in the Northern Territory*, edited by Brian Reid, Chapter 1, 1–17. Darwin: Historical Society of the Northern Territory, ISBN 9781921576102.

2009 and Sue Dugdale and Associates. 'Battery Hill Mining Centre: A Heritage Assessment'. Report for the Heritage Unit, Department of Environment, Heritage, Arts and Sport.

2009 'A History of the Old Supreme Court Building, Darwin'. Report for the National Trust of Australia (Northern Territory).

2009 'The Fence at Fannie Bay Gaol: An Opinion of the Heritage Value'. Report for the Heritage Unit, Department of Environment, Heritage, Arts and Sport.

2009 'Michael Terry: The Last Explorer?' *Journal of Northern Territory History* 20: 51–74.

2008 'Political Chronicle: Northern Territory, January–June 2008'. *Australian Journal of Politics and History* 54, no. 4: 651–57.

2008 'Political Chronicle: Northern Territory, July–December 2007'. *Australian Journal of Politics and History* 54, no. 2: 330–36.

APPENDIX 1: SELECTED PUBLICATIONS

2008 'Old Hospital Site Redevelopment Proposal Report of Public Consultation 11 November to 18 December 2008. Volume 1 – Summary of Responses, Public Comment & Brief Site History; and Volume 2 – Submissions & Comments by Community Members; Notes of Meetings'. Report for Department of Planning and Infrastructure, Northern Territory Government, 18 November.

2008 'A Festival Event: Aspects of the Changing Nature and Content of Some Community Celebrations in Darwin in the Twentieth Century'. *Journal of Northern Territory History* 19: 33–49.

2008 Gregory, R., M. Dewar, S. Mitchell, D. Murray and P. Murray. *The Cultural Values of the Central Ranges (including the West MacDonnells): A Preliminary Report.* [Heritage department Alice Springs]: Northern Territory Government.

2007 'It's about Lifestyle: The Territory in the 1950s'. *Territory in Trust* (National Trust of Australia, Northern Territory) 24, no. 1 (January–June): 3–8.

2007 Final Report AusAid Australian Leadership Awards (ALA) Fellowship Museum and Art Gallery of the Northern Territory (MAGNT) Museum Management and Training Program Policy Development Workshops, Darwin, September–November.

2006 *Conservation and Management Plans: Lyons Cottage British Australia Telegraph House, Darwin.* Darwin: Museum and Art Gallery of the Northern Territory.

2005 *Modern Frontier: Aspects of the 1950s in Australia's Northern Territory*, edited by Julie T. Wells, Mickey Dewar and Suzanne Parry. Darwin: Charles Darwin University Press, ISBN 0975761420, 219pp.

2005 'You in Your Small Corner: The Love Song of Alfred J Dyer: Early Days of Church Missionary Society Missions to the Aborigines of Arnhem Land'. *Humanities Research* 12, no. 1: 27–40.

2005 'You Are What You Eat: Food and Cultural Identity'. In *Modern Frontier*, edited by Julie T. Wells, Mickey Dewar and Suzanne Parry, 71–89. Darwin: Charles Darwin University Press.

2003 and Clayton Fredericksen. 'Prison Heritage, Public History and Archaeology at Fannie Bay Gaol, Northern Australia'. *International Journal of Heritage Studies* 9, no. 1: 45–63. doi.org/10.1080/1352725 022000056622.

2002 and Robin Gregory. *Conservation and Management Plans: Connellan Hangar Alice Springs*. Darwin: Museum and Art Gallery of the Northern Territory. April, 47pp.

2002 'If I Was Writing My Own History I'd Be a Hero … A Response to Professor David Carment on Making History at the Museum and Art Gallery of the Northern Territory'. *Australian Historical Studies* 33, no. 119: 172–78. doi.org/10.1080/10314610208596208.

2001 with Robin Gregory. *Conservation and Management Plans: Old Courthouse (and Jury Room) Alice Springs*. Darwin: Museum and Art Gallery of the Northern Territory. July, 53pp.

2001 and Clayton Fredericksen. 'Chinese Labour in Darwin: Fannie Bay Gaol, Northern Territory'. In *1901: Australian Life at Federation: An Illustrated Chronicle*, edited by A. Cremin, 30–31. Sydney: UNSW Press, and Australasian Society for Historical Archaeology, assisted by the National Council for the Centenary of Federation.

2000 'Whose Heritage? A Study of the First Decade of the Alice Springs Cultural Precinct'. *Journal of Northern Territory History* 11: 25–36.

1999 *Inside-Out: A Social History of Fannie Bay Gaol*. Darwin: Northern Territory University Press, ISBN 1876248408, 162pp.

1998 'The Literary Construction of "Half-caste" in the 1930s: Gender, Sexuality and Race in the Northern Territory'. In *Connection and Disconnection: Encounters between Settlers and Indigenous People in the Northern Territory*, edited by Tony Austin and Suzanne Parry, Chapter 7, 177–204. Darwin: Northern Territory University Press, ISBN 1876248262.

1997 *Unlocking Museums: The Proceedings 4th National Conference of Museums Australia Inc* [Darwin, Australia, 6–12 September], edited by Ian Walters, Mickey Dewar, Sue Harlow, Jacky Healy, Daena Murray and Barry Russell. Northern Territory: Museums Australia NT Branch, ISBN 094906923X, 322pp.

1997 *In Search of the Never-Never: Looking for Australia in Northern Territory Writing*. Darwin: Northern Territory University Press, ISBN 1876248068, 234pp.

1997 '"Hard Labour" or "A Salubrious Retreat"?: The Relationship between Gaol and Community in Palmerston 1869–1910'. *Journal of Northern Territory History* 8: 1–12.

1996 'Attitudes Towards the Throne: Royalty and Loyalty at The Residency, Alice Springs'. *Northern Perspective* 19, no. 1: 99–111.

APPENDIX 1: SELECTED PUBLICATIONS

1996  'Frontier Theory and the Development of Meaning in Northern Territory Writing'. *Journal of Northern Territory History* 6: 15–24.

1995  'Blowing Rusty Bugles: Territory Writing and World War II'. *Northern Perspective* 18, no. 2: 65–73.

1994  *Beginnings: The First Decade of the Northern Territory Women's Advisory Council 1983–1993*. Darwin: Women's Advisory Council, Department of the Chief Minister, Northern Territory Government, ISBN 0724528636, 84pp.

1993  'Motives for Massacre: A New Look at the Caledon Bay and Woodah Island Killings'. *Journal of Northern Territory History* 3: 1–14.

1993  *From the Little Black Princess to Biggles: Representations of the Northern Territory in Children's Literature*. Occasional Paper no. 42. Darwin: State Library of the Northern Territory, 15pp.

1992  *The 'Black War' in Arnhem Land: Missionaries and the Yolngu 1908–1940*. Darwin: The Australian National University North Australia Research Unit, ISBN 0731514270, 107pp.

1992  *Snorters, Fools and Little 'uns: Sexual Politics and Territory Writing in the South Australian Period*. Occasional Paper no. 32. Darwin: State Library of the Northern Territory, 10pp.

1989  'The Territorial Imperative: The Hidden Agenda of Missionary Involvement in the "Peace Expedition"'. *Journal of Northern Territory History* 1: 25–33.

# Contributors

**David Carment AM** is Emeritus Professor of History at Charles Darwin University, where he was also Dean of the Faculty of Law, Business and Arts. He is the author of numerous publications on Australian and North Australian history. Active in community and professional history organisations, he is a former President of the Australian Historical Association.

**Chris O'Brien** is an environmental historian with long-standing interests in weather, climate, land, place and culture in northern Australia. Lured to the NT by curiosity, Chris enjoyed several lengthy stints in Darwin between 2003 and 2016: first as a beach bum, then as a PhD student and finally as a postdoctoral researcher. His first sojourn sparked an abiding interest in the region's weather and climate, and how it has come to be understood. This led to a PhD in History at The Australian National University and more stints in the Top End. Today Chris lives on the Hunter coast of NSW.

**Ann McGrath AM** is Distinguished Professor of History and the Kathleen Fitzpatrick ARC Laureate Fellow at The Australian National University. She has published on gender and colonialism in Australia and North America and on deep history, as well as on the writing of history. She has produced and directed films and has worked on public enquiries and museum exhibitions. Her first academic position was at the Darwin Community College, now Charles Darwin University.

www.ingramcontent.com/pod-product-compliance
Lightning Source LLC
Chambersburg PA
CBHW061254230426
43665CB00027B/2935